KINDRED
SPIRITS

CLASS NEW
200 STUDIES
IN
RELIGION

EDITED BY Kathryn Lofton AND John Lardas Modern

Ripples of the Universe: Spirituality in Sedona, Arizona
by Susannah Crockford

*Making a Mantra: Tantric Ritual and Renunciation
on the Jain Path to Liberation*
by Ellen Gough

The Privilege of Being Banal: Art, Secularism, and Catholicism in Paris
by Elayne Oliphant

*Experiments with Power: Obeah and the Remaking
of Religion in Trinidad*
by J. Brent Crosson

*The Lives of Objects: Material Culture, Experience,
and the Real in the History of Early Christianity*
by Maia Kotrosits

*Make Yourselves Gods: Mormons and the
Unfinished Business of American Secularism*
by Peter Coviello

Hunted: Predation and Pentecostalism in Guatemala
by Kevin Lewis O'Neill

The Aliites: Race and Law in the Religions of Noble Drew Ali
by Spencer Dew

KINDRED SPIRITS

Friendship and Resistance
at the Edges of Modern Catholicism

BRENNA MOORE

The University of Chicago Press
Chicago and London

The University of Chicago Press, Chicago 60637

The University of Chicago Press, Ltd., London

Published 2021

Printed in the United States of America

30 29 28 27 26 25 24 23 22 21   1 2 3 4 5

ISBN-13: 978-0-226-78696-4 (cloth)

ISBN-13: 978-0-226-78701-5 (paper)

ISBN-13: 978-0-226-78715-2 (e-book)

DOI: https://doi.org/10.7208/chicago/9780226787152.001.0001

Library of Congress Cataloging-in-Publication Data

Names: Moore, Brenna, author.
Title: Kindred spirits : friendship and resistance at the edges of modern
    Catholicism / Brenna Moore.
Other titles: Friendship and resistance at the edges of modern Catholicism | Class
    200, new studies in religion.
Description: Chicago ; London : The University of Chicago Press, 2021. | Series:
    Class 200: new studies in religion | Includes bibliographical references and
    index.
Identifiers: LCCN 2021000010 | ISBN 9780226786964 (cloth) | ISBN 9780226787015
    (paperback) | ISBN 9780226787152 (ebook)
Subjects: LCSH: Friendship—Religious aspects—Catholic Church. | Catholic
    intellectuals. | Catholics—Intellectual life—20th century.
Classification: LCC BV4647.F7 M657 2021 | DDC 261/.109041—dc23
LC record available at https://lccn.loc.gov/2021000010

♾ This paper meets the requirements of ANSI/NISO Z39.48-1992
(Permanence of Paper).

For John, Tavia, and Jonah

————————

CONTENTS

Introduction: Spiritual Friendship as an Alternative
Catholic Modernity 1

1 Between Latin America and Europe:
Gabriela Mistral and the Maritains 35
2 "Luminous Spiritual Traces" to Islam:
The Passionate Friendships of Louis Massignon 74
3 Marie-Magdeleine Davy and the Hermeneutic
of Friendship in Resistance to Nazism 114
4 The Intimacy and Resilience of Invisible Friendship:
Marie-Magdeleine Davy and Simone Weil 145
5 Friendship and the Black Catholic Internationalism
of Claude McKay 172

Epilogue: Kindred Spirits as Fragments of Modernity 225

Acknowledgments 255   Notes 261   Index 313

INTRODUCTION

Spiritual Friendship as an
Alternative Catholic Modernity

IN *DIVINE PRESENCE in Spain and Western Europe 1500–1960*, anthropologist William Christian invites his readers to imagine a bird's-eye view of a nighttime scene below. Picture it, he writes, as a vast stretch of the modern western European landscape. Now envision seeing mostly miles and miles of darkness but, now and again, catching glimpses of an occasional flicker of lights: "Some brighter, some blinking, some dying out. Some are new, intense and brightly colored, others steady and constant for centuries."[1] These lights on a dark landscape represent flashes of the supernatural realm sensed by people on the ground, Christian suggests, sources of grace beaming with various degrees of intensity, changing over the course of the last four centuries. Some lights go out—"old grace is exhausted, routinized"— and new material replaces it. "In this constellation there is much dark matter that is not, or not yet, powerful, bones unrecognized as relics, relics that do not heal anybody, strangers unrecognized as angels, children who may be saints, images no one cares about."[2] Against this backdrop of darkness, we might see sporadic clusters of radiance in places where someone holy once ambled, for example, someone whose memory still draws the faithful in— places like Assisi, Italy; Lourdes, France; or Covadonga, Spain.

Kindred Spirits considers an often-overlooked global network of Catholic scholars, artists, and activists in 1920–60 for whom the holy lights of previous areas had begun to fade into darkness: not much glowed from Rome nor from even the priesthood and sacramental system. Neither, for this community, did the promise of liberal modernity brighten the future horizon. Their skepticism about modernity prevented them from believing that all the lights of transcendence had gone out, yielding to a monochromatic, immanent frame of secularism. Nor did they envision that the flickers of holiness were now simply within, tucked inside each of their souls. These men and women gravitated toward the old embers whereby people saw in other human beings of flesh and bone flickers of something divine, a holiness that was contagious, spread between people. They were drawn to the lights that were not exactly those canonized saints of the distant past and not quite ordinary people in the present but something in between. It was the realm of extraordinary friendship that offered the most powerful corridor to the sacred, something they called "spiritual friendship." Intimacy among friends was not a trope or a symbol of something else more religiously real: it was a fundamental, experiential way of communing with the world and with God. Religiously meaningful friendships took place not only in face-to-face settings but also with the remembered dead, those held in non-ordinary realms of consciousness—memory and imagination. Peter Brown's description of saint devotion in early Christianity as "invisible friendship" is useful for understanding the spirituality of these twentieth-century Catholics.[3] To explain the sensibilities these men and women felt among friends, living and dead, visible and invisible, they often reached for images of fire: holy friends burn, scorch, ignite, light, or kindle other souls with their inner flame. Even the words for friendship, *amistad* in Spanish and *amitié* in French, with their closeness to the words for both soul (*alma* and *âme*) and love (*amor* and *amour*), convey something of the sensibility that they shared.

Within this community, friendship was not only the context of religious experience but also a political ideal, a worldview and a social practice that members sensed could counter the various modes of belonging offered by the Far Right who were gaining ascendency in the interwar period, including nationalism and the prioritization of the nuclear family. Together, these men and women forged a robust but seldom discussed undercurrent that worked against the prevailing logic of the Far Right in interwar Europe and the United States while also resisting the secularizing tendencies of most leftist movements in the early and mid-twentieth century. Active in the years before the Second Vatican Council, this network included some figures who are well known to readers of religion today, such as Jacques and Raïssa Maritain, the Islamicist Louis Massignon, and the near-Catholic Simone Weil. But other men and women from this community are known mainly in circles of literary studies and rarely included in the history of modern Catholicism, like the Jamaican-born poet of the Harlem Renaissance and convert to Catholicism Claude McKay and his community of

Black Catholic writers and activists, including Paulette Nardal from Martinique and Ellen Tarry from the United States. The Chilean poet, educator, journalist, diplomat, and Nobel laureate Gabriela Mistral is similarly recognized today more for her contributions to literary studies than for her part of the story of twentieth-century Catholicism. Still, other protagonists in the chapters that follow have been almost entirely unknown in the English-speaking world until now, in particular women such as the Syrian-born Egyptian activist and philanthropist Mary Kahil and the French scholar of Cistercian monasticism and Nazi resister Marie-Magdeleine Davy.[4] These men and women were not exactly an isolated group of Catholic friends who were important to one another (though some were), nor can they be divided neatly into dyads and trios. "Spiritual friendship" was a shared worldview and a practice central to a global intellectual community, and attending to it approximates the inner life of an incredibly creative period in Catholicism, pointing to the emotions and perceptions that underlie a unique religious and political moment in modernity. Though they do not appear in this book, many readers will be familiar with friendships such as that between Dorothy Day and Peter Maurin or the literary friendships among Day, Thomas Merton, Flannery O'Connor, and Walker Percy that Paul Elie describes so well in *The Life You Save May Be Your Own*. What Elie coins as the "School of the Holy Ghost," I argue, stretched far beyond these well-known stars of the American Catholic countercultural establishment.[5] It included writers, theologians, artists, and activists from places as distant as Russia, France, Chile, Egypt, and Jamaica, and spiritual friendship was key to its coherence and consolidation.

Jesuit historian Michel de Certeau once aptly described his friend Louis Massignon as "a wanderer, a passionate pilgrim, a loner, a lover of vows, oaths, and holy places, a Don Quixote who practiced a code of honor alone, belonging to another age." While Massignon was odd, a bit of a loner, and controversial both in his own lifetime and today, at the same time, Certeau noted, Massignon also "invented a geography of spiritual, intellectual, and political solidarities" that gave him a vision he constantly worked toward.[6] A map of Massignon's geography of spiritual "solidarities" included friends living and dead, Muslim and Christian. Some Massignon knew through the decades-long study of their ancient texts, like the Persian Sufi mystic of the ninth century Husayn Ibn Mansur al-Hallāj, a spiritual friend who was the subject of Massignon's scholarly life's work. Others were those with whom Massignon carried on face-to-face friendships that lasted decades, leaving "luminous spiritual traces" on his own soul, like Kahil, who he called his "soul-friend" (*âme-amie*). If Massignon's life was guided by extraordinary spiritual friendships, he himself embodied that glimmer of the supernatural for others. "Undoubtedly," the Catholic existentialist Gabriel Marcel wrote to Massignon in a 1951 letter, "you are the only person I have ever known who could transport me directly into the presence of the eternal."[7] This, however, was not unique to Massignon. Many avant-garde Catholics, near-Catholics, and even lapsed Catholic intellectuals in this period endowed friendship with a kind of moral, spiritual, and political power unlike anything else in their lives. Visible and invisible friendship also functioned as a metaphor and an ideal that undergirded utopian projects in this network, like the international commune Davy created in honor of her late friend, the Maison Simone Weil, or the Friendship House, a Catholic interracial apostolate in Harlem and Chicago, where Claude McKay drew close to Catholicism, eventually converting in 1944. This community also reached for the language of friendship to describe their intellectual and scholarly networks, as in the Asociación de Amigos de Léon Bloy that the Uruguayan poet and medical doctor Esther de Cáceres established in Montevideo in 1940.

Yet the binaries that structure modernity—masculine/feminine, public/private, rational/emotional, secular/religious—lead us to interpret something like spiritual friendships as belonging properly to the private realm, the warm sphere of emotion, religion, and women.[8] Spiritual friendships are only relevant to public life by serving as—in Tracy Fessenden's words—its "salvific counterpart," "pious" and "sealed from the energies" of secular modernity.[9] But for these men and women, spiritual friendship was hardly inoculated from the major political crises of the twentieth century. It was at once both a corridor to the sacred and inseparable from their political and humanitarian efforts in the midcentury, including resistance to European xenophobia and nationalism in the 1930s, antiracist activism in the United States in the 1930s and 1940s, the cultivation of *l'internationalisme noir* or Black internationalism in Paris, and solidarity with Muslims during the Algerian War of 1954–62. In particular, spiritual friendship was deliberately cultivated as an alternative to genealogical modes of belonging based on the inherited ties of family, tradition, and nation. This community created for themselves what they called *nouvelles familles spirituelles* based on chosen friends, and these cultivated bonds supplanted the passive models of kinship that stressed blood inheritance and homogeneity. As the Dutch artist Pierre van der Meer de Walcheren described the spiritual family he forged with friends Jacques and Raïssa Maritain and the novelist Léon Bloy, "We were all so different from another, and came from all different horizons. Bloy's wife Danish, my own wife Flemish and French, Raïssa and Vera Russian Jews, Jacques Protestant French, and together we formed *une seule grande famille*."[10] Drawn inexorably toward difference in their friendships, spirituality, activism, and scholarship, the men and women in this community exhibited a commitment to mixed, cosmopolitan solidarities.[11] Unearthing this archive of love among friends opens up possibilities to imagine a different kind of Catholic politics and a counter-history of Catholic love, one meant to oppose—at least quietly—the replicative injunctions to reproduce or the narrower homogeneous bonds based on blood kinship, national identity, or "Judeo-Christian heritage."[12]

These utopian projects or utopian relationships, however, did not always succeed or even come close to the ideals they envisioned for themselves (though sometimes they did). Friendship could also be a retreat into safety, fantasy, and pleasure, away from a realistic assessment of the world and its problems. Friendships were often impossibly caught up in longer, darker histories of colonialism and racism, despite the fervent, emancipatory desires some friends held. Claude McKay, Black writer of the Harlem Renaissance and friend of Dorothy Day's, artfully pointed out the fantasies so many white people had of friendship, particularly between Blacks and whites. His novel *Amiable with Big Teeth* (written in 1941, published posthumously) criticizes the white leftists who used "friendship" to lead Black people to act against their own interests, exemplified in the fictional activist organization he called, satirically, White Friends of Ethiopia.[13] Friends for McKay often meant "friends," as in so-called. McKay entered this Catholic scene later in life. He began to seriously consider Catholicism for himself in 1939, when he was forty years old, and was baptized five years later. But despite his skepticism about certain liberal ideals of friendship, Claude McKay found among the Catholic radicals he met in Paris and, later, in Harlem and Chicago a community that brought together his own eclectic ideals in ways that perhaps no other community in the late 1930s could: at once fervently anti-Protestant, increasingly anticommunist, and rooted in a spirituality centered not on the nuclear family but on friends, a somewhat queer, though muted and largely tacit, sensibility. McKay helps us see that it impossible to separate spiritual friendship from larger dynamics of power and politics, especially race and colonialism. In Harlem in the 1930s and 1940s, to point to just one example, many white Catholics were deeply compelled by the holiness they sensed from the charismatic Russian émigré Catherine de Hueck Doherty, who started the Friendship House in 1938. One longtime volunteer, Ann Harrigan, confessed when describing her experiences with de Hueck,

"This was love." When Harrigan had to leave de Hueck's presence for errands or to go home, it was like "putting out a fire & walking into the cold, away from the glowing one who spoke so strangely, convincingly of Christ—was it Christ that attracted—or was it the lady with the blue eyes?"[14] But for Black Catholic volunteers like Ellen Tarry, de Hueck was yet another domineering white woman, whose main lesson she imparted was "what *not* to do" when it came to Catholic interracial work.[15] The spiritual charisma of holy friends was never an objective, universal fact but an intersubjective experience that took place within broader dynamics of power.

McKay's cautions were a rare voice of skepticism in this circle of Catholics at the time, but his is the one more attuned to present-day academic suspicions. Today, if and when we do probe for a deeper political significance of friendship, the analysis is often troubling: movies like *The Secret Life of Bees* and even *Green Mile* offer a seemingly irresistible narrative that interpersonal friendships between two unequal people are the sole, purest ways to mitigate violence and inequality in our world, a deeply pernicious idea.[16] In some cases, these Catholic experiments flopped, and in the present we can see why and roll our eyes. Yet others, we must admit, had remarkable success. The worldview of "spiritual friendship" contained huge variety that can only be analyzed in concrete instances, so given this range, how is it possible to even describe a single worldview of spiritual friendship among a forgotten network of men and women who hailed from places as distant as France, Russia, Egypt, Chile, New York, and Jamaica?

GLOBAL CATHOLICISM AS COLONIAL CATHOLICISM

Born in countries all over the world, the men and women within this book shared a religious sensorium that traversed the globe. Yet describing the Catholicism here as *global* is too passive as a starting point. Colonial Catholicism is more useful. Though it historically preceded their own lifetimes by centuries, the imperial endeavors of European Catholicism is the first, but not the only, historical thread that ties this community together. Arvind-Pal Mandair helpfully argues for the need to "revive the disavowed memory of contact" between the West and non-West that has existed since their colonial encounters.[17] We could consider just one example: the otherwise unlikely friendship between a French Islamicist in Paris, Louis Massignon, and a Syrian-born, Egyptian feminist activist in Cairo, Mary Kahil, whose story

I take up in chapter 2. Their friendship became the "spiritual center" of a decades-long collaboration in Egypt and France to work toward greater unity between Muslims and Catholics. Kahil was educated in Egypt and Lebanon at elite French Catholic schools, first at Notre Dame de la Mère de Dieu School in Cairo, a missionary school founded by French Franciscan Sisters, and later at Les Dames de Nazareth School in Beirut.[18] Les Dames de Nazareth was founded in 1854 in Palestine by a French order of nuns who eventually set up a school in Beirut to combat the influence of Protestants.[19] Louis Massignon grew up in Paris in a French Catholic family that went back generations. But just as Kahil was trained in the French piety that came to the Arabic world through colonial missions, Massignon's religious imagination was inflected with the sounds, texts, languages, and people of Kahil's Arabic world, all of which was made possible by French colonialism: Massignon began his career as an Islamicist at a French archaeological expedition in Iraq in 1905 and felt his vocation was tethered by a "tiny threadlike web" to the spirit of the late Charles de Foucauld, the wandering French-born Catholic hermit who lived among the Arabic-speaking Muslim nomads in the Algerian desert, a country accessible to the French because of the colonial invasion of Algeria that began in 1830 and lasted until 1962. French colonialism in North Africa and the Middle East laid the groundwork needed for Kahil and Massignon, both fluent in French and Arabic, to meet and feel intense, sudden spiritual kinship that sprang from a shared Arabic-French, Catholic-Islamic religious imagination felt in both Cairo and Paris. It generated a kind of spiritual electricity between them. "Our meeting was a terrible shock," Massignon wrote, and they clicked so immediately and so powerfully that they soon together made a vow to love and serve the Muslim world shortly after their first encounter.[20] This metaphysical connection felt between people from distant countries was made possible, at least in part, by a common training and formation spread around the world from the colonial missionary endeavors.

To draw on another example, in retrospect, it isn't surprising that the poet Gabriela Mistral—born in rural Chile with talents in literature, social activism, and forging connections with the right people—would eventually end up in Paris in the 1930s, meet Jacques and Raïssa Maritain, and feel compelled by their spiritual charisma. The sense of the sacred that elite, literary-minded French Catholics like the Maritains created for Mistral was made possible by many factors, two of which were European imperialism and Catholic colonialism. Chile was a colony of Catholic Spain from 1541 to 1810. Mistral was born in a small Chilean mountain town, Vicuña. From the

Spanish nuns to the later Chilean secular schooling modeled on the French lycée system, European elite education was implemented and remained aspirational throughout Chile, something that began in colonialism but persisted long past the end of colonial rule. The religious orders gave Spanish-speaking children from elite families a shared religious sensorium that could connect Chileans to Catholics as far away as Cairo and France. Mistral came from a Catholic family but was poor, and her formal schooling ended at age eleven, but eventually as a young adult Mistral met with Francophile Spanish speakers, like her good friend Palma Guillén from Mexico, who convinced Mistral that if she was going to make a career as a writer, the best models were French authors. When she left Chile for Mexico as a young adult, Mistral turned her little room into a "Paris in miniature, Rome in eight square meters," as she called it.[21] In part, this compelled Mistral's early decision to accept a job in 1926 with the Paris-based Institute for International Intellectual Cooperation, a think tank within the League of Nations. We see a kind of Francophile sensibility in intellectuals from not only Chile and Mexico like Mistral and Guillén but throughout the Spanish-speaking Americas. In Argentina, "France," wrote Mistral's close friend, the Argentinian writer Victoria Ocampo, "is our second homeland."[22] Like other wealthy Argentines, Victoria Ocampo grew up with French and English governesses. All of this would help wealthy Latin American, Spanish-speaking intellectuals like Ocampo, nourished on European Catholic piety in school and educated in French as well as Spanish culture and aesthetics, make their way to Europe later as adults and sense beauty, spirituality, and depth in the friends they met there. They were trained for it.

Even in countries colonized in part by British Protestants rather than Catholics, like Jamaica, where Claude McKay was raised, children were taught continental European, especially French, culture and aesthetics. European tastes on the ground mixed with strong grassroots cultures from African and local folklore and religion, and this hybrid background was an important foundation of Claude McKay's biography, both inside and outside the formal sphere of education. He was mentored by a white British eccentric living in Jamaica who educated him in radical European philosophy, read him the modernist poets, and taught him French and Latin. Of course, white colonial culture, literature, and aesthetics would eventually become the subject of intense anticolonial critique. Nonetheless, its culture, aesthetics, and spirituality were planted in the inner lives of people around the globe and form the first layer that helped a worldview like "spiritual friendship" become possible on an international scale. This community's religious imagination, the languages they spoke, who and what they saw as holy—these must be situated in the larger stories of Christian missionary zeal and the sense of European civilizational superiority that underwrote it all. This made it possible to connect a network in what anthropologists of religion Samuli Schielke and Liza Debevec have called the space between "ordinary lives and grand schemes."[23]

GLOBAL CATHOLICISM AS EXILIC CATHOLICISM

Indeed, colonial European Christianity existed long before McKay, Massignon, Mistral, and Kahil entered the world, but their eventual friendships became possible because these men and women lived directly through what Carolyn Forché has called "the century of extremity"—warfare, state censorships, genocide, pogroms, dictatorships, and violence, which created mass exiles and refugees around the world.[24] If the longer, older story of European colonialism gave native Arabic, English, Spanish, and French speakers something of a shared religious and cultural imagination, the massive war, racial violence, and pogroms of the twentieth century meant that many left their homelands for safer parts of the globe, where these displaced individuals then came in contact with one another from 1920 to 1960. All the protagonists in this book had direct, personal experience with these traumas, and as exiles, refugees, and activists they also became deeply familiar with anti-imperialist and antiwar movements around the world.

France in particular, and especially Paris, initially had an outsized role in welcoming exiles in the interwar period and bringing different kinds of people together. Immigrants from all over the world came to Paris fleeing violence in the early twentieth century, and every figure in this book had some connection—whether lifelong or brief, thrilling or disappointing—to Paris. By the mid-1920s, France received more immigrants than any other country in the industrialized world. In 1930, three million foreigners resided in France.[25] Interwar Paris, as Langston Hughes put it, was packed with the "seeking wandering ones" from "all over the world."[26] For example, Raïssa Maritain, who appears in chapter 1, immigrated from Russia to Paris with her family when she was a girl, fleeing the Jewish pogroms in 1901. The Jewish population increased throughout the interwar period in Paris, until France, too, proved just as deadly for Jewish men, women, and children when they were deported to Drancy in 1941.[27] In addition to Jews, by the

1930s, émigrés in Paris also included war refugees from Spain, fleeing first Primo de Rivera's right-wing dictatorship, which began in 1923, and then Franco's war in 1936. Very different sorts of Spanish speakers also came to Paris, and wealthy Francophile families from places as far away as Argentina and Uruguay moved to the city and lived in Parisian hotels. From 1926 to 1939, the Chilean Gabriela Mistral (the subject of chapter 1) worked in the Paris-based Institute for International Intellectual Cooperation, where she collaborated with Spanish- and French-speaking activists and intellectuals, both wealthy elite Francophiles and traumatized war refugees. By the mid-1920s, more than fifteen thousand people from Latin America were living in Paris, which transformed the city into a kind of annex capital of the Spanish-speaking global south.[28]

In the interwar period, Muslims from the Arabic world and North Africa also began establishing themselves in Paris. Though Muslims would not immigrate to western Europe on a large scale until the postwar period, seeking political asylum and employment, in the interwar period Muslim life was starting to flourish and become institutionalized in France.[29] The Grande Mosquée de Paris was inaugurated in July 1926.[30] Louis Massignon (the subject of chapter 2), French by birth, began teaching night classes for Muslim immigrants in Paris who worked as day laborers in the 1920s in addition to helping Muslim students who came to study with him. Massignon also worked for long periods in Cairo, and his relationships with the Muslim immigrant community in Paris along with his scholarly connections to the Arabic world would compel Massignon's complex, controversial ideas about Islam to evolve throughout the course of his life.

Likewise, in the United States, African American writers and artists fled Jim Crow America for the relatively more open environment of Paris, first in the 1920s and again after the war. In a 1968 televised discussion on *The Dick Cavett Show*, James Baldwin described the sojourn so many African American artists and writers took in these years: "The years I lived in Paris did one thing for me: they released me from that particular social terror, which was not the paranoia of my own mind, but a real social danger visible in the face of every cop, every boss, everybody."[31] In 1922, Claude McKay arrived in Paris, where he joined other African American intellectuals, along with men and women from other parts of the African diaspora (Senegal, Sudan, and the French Caribbean) who had been, according to historian Jennifer Boittin, conscripted into the French army during World War I and stayed on after the war looking for work.[32] This international network of Black artists, writers, laborers, and soldiers in France also joined an elite cadre of top Black students from Francophone colonies selected to pursue a university education in Paris. This mix made interwar Paris a unique setting for what emerged as *l'internationalisme noir*, a place for new international ties among Black citizens throughout the African diaspora. As Brent Hayes Edwards notes in his work on diasporic Black internationalism, "Paris is crucial because it allowed boundary crossing, conversations, and collaborations that were available nowhere else to the same degree." It "provided a special sort of vibrant, cosmopolitan space for interaction that was neither in the United States nor the colonies."[33]

For those who came to Paris, there was no general experience of exile and displacement.[34] Paris was thrilling for some, while for others it was a disappointing, even terrifying place where they learned the real dangers of racism and authoritarianism, and eventually, the city became no safer than anywhere else. In 1937, Gabriela Mistral said she learned in Europe about fascism, and citizens from Latin American countries needed to make sure what was happening in Europe never came to the global south.[35] Similarly, Claude McKay wrote, "Paris has never stormed my stubborn heart," and he had a much more skeptical read of France's self-proclaimed racial openness compared to the United States.[36] After befriending men and women in Paris who were from the French colonies in Africa, he thought that the notion that France lacked racism was a European, anti-American fantasy. The reservations Mistral and McKay express about Paris took place within a broader context that included, of course, many other people's sense that Jazz Age Paris was the most cosmopolitan place in the world and, by 1934, "the capital of European anti-fascism."[37] This cosmopolitan exhilaration of Paris was a dream that spread across the oceans, and the African American writer Dorothy West would save her money in 1935 to get to Paris like so many other Black artists, "for they say," she wrote to McKay, that Paris "is the nearest to heaven one ever gets on earth."[38]

But in this international community, despite the range of experiences of exile, for every single Catholic in this project, it was friendship, above all, that offered a form of belonging beyond the national and the familial. In the context of massive exile, pogroms, migration, and resistance, friendships sustained in correspondence with individuals scattered elsewhere or forged anew in the international salons anchored their world. Mistral wrote often about her almost spiritual, existential need to hear from her friends in exile: "Always the best thing in my life came from some friends who are dispersed throughout the world."[39] Raïssa Maritain spent the war years in New York exiled from France, and just a few days after her arrival, she wrote to her good friend Abbé (later Cardinal) Charles Journet: "Our soul is there [in France], close to everything we love. . . . Here we're breathing depleted air, insufficient for us to really live. I see myself," she said, "as if in a dream."[40] Raïssa's exilic writings take on a dreamlike, fantasy quality and are centered almost exclusively on memories of her friends. She began her most famous work, the two-volume memoir *Les grandes amitiés*, published in 1941 and 1945, with this: "My friends explain my life, my life explains my friendships."[41]

Crucially, friendships also played a key role in the transatlantic dissemination of ideas concerning the Catholic Left in midcentury. From 1920 to 1950, spiritual friendship was a fuel of pleasure that powered the arduous work of consolidating political ideas, particularly concerning Catholic antifascist, philo-Semitic, and antiracist thoughts that circulated between France, the United States, and Latin America. While religion is often indicted for harboring a deep suspicion of pleasure and desire, in this context, religious desire and pleasure circulated among and between friends, living and dead, working as a kind of scaffolding for their serious, bold political commitments. Friendships sustained a spiritual and sensual undercurrent out of which political action seemed to flow.

FRIENDSHIP AS AN ALTERNATIVE MODE
OF CATHOLIC BELONGING

Catholicism played a major role in helping people make sense of the internationalism of Jazz Age Paris, and the religion was seen as a kind of universal idiom that could contain multitudes, including the artists and avant-garde associated with the *renouveau catholique*.[42] We see this when, for instance, a German Jewish émigré like Joseph Roth observed in his *Report from a Parisian Paradise: Essays from France, 1925–1939*, "Catholicism is a cosmopolitan religion that embraces all religion."[43] At the same time, interwar Catholicism in Paris and throughout Europe was key to swinging the pendulum to the right, fomenting the rise of resentment and nationalism in the form of a "fierce xenophobic backlash" to immigration and internationalism in France.[44] Most of the nativism and xenophobia took the form of a resurgence of anti-Semitism, but other newcomers were targeted too. Catholics from the Far Right in interwar England, Italy, and France like Henri Massis, G. K. Chesterton, and Bernard Wall underwrote an extreme anti-Enlightenment, anti-immigrant, and anti-Semitic agenda. They responded to the increase in immigrants and the economic challenges of the 1930s with a defensive appeal to tradition and Christianity and, almost always, with a return to the culture and ideals of the Middle Ages. The mythic power of medieval Catholicism functioned to imagine a Europe more in touch with tradition, a tradition purged of menacing outsiders and rooted in that which was perceived as homogeneous, stable, and ancient: family, land, and Catholicism.[45] "Fascism," as British Catholic intellectual Bernard Wall put it in 1937, was the "herald of a New Middle Ages."[46] (And he meant that in a good way.) Catholic medieval heritage was seen to counter the decadence of twentieth-century moderns who were rootless and cosmopolitan, immigrants and intellectuals alike, moving country to country untethered from any native roots. In Italy, Germany, and France, the family, the nation, and Catholicism were all evoked in a neo-medieval, mystical key to steer the degeneracy of modernity back on course, to break "the spirit of nomadism," and to move Europe back to an imagined medieval purity.[47] Family, nationalism, and Catholicism went hand in hand.[48] Europe in the 1930s was also the context in which some conservative Catholic intellectuals, activists, and clergy developed what James Chappel calls a "paternal Catholic modernism," which embraced democracy's basic division of the "secular public" and "sacred private sphere."[49] The domain of sexuality and the family, rather than the public domain of state politics, became the key site of proper Catholic regulatory power. Catholic fixation on limiting sexuality toward heterosexual, procreative matrimony complied with the basic design of secular democratic modernity. "Never before in Catholic history," Chappel explains, "had so much emphasis been placed on the multigenerational family unit as the centerpiece of social order."[50]

Today, the historical narrative tends to suggest that the left-wing Catholic response to the resurgence of the Far Right in Europe—whether fascist medievalism, nationalism, or paternalism's fixation on procreative matrimonial sexuality—was to subdue this fanaticism and medieval romanticism with the more sober-minded language of human rights and personalism in the 1930s–50s.[51] Catholic human rights talk stands for scholars as the beginning of a more sane Catholic politics running counter to the right-wing neo-medieval mysticism. Later, the story goes, in the 1960s and 1970s, Catholics would eventually develop a robust theological response in the form of liberation theology and feminist theology. *Kindred Spirits* complicates and enriches this narrative by revealing a group of thinkers who drew on resources typically dismissed as apolitical or private—friendships, spirituality, mysticism—which they channeled toward antifascist, multicultural ends in relationship with one another. Spiritual friendship was key to their efforts. It was a politically attuned Catholicism strikingly different from the way political Catholicism is typically framed around rights, dignity, and law and articulated by prominent male thinkers. With the focus on human rights and the common good, this way of conceptualizing leftist Catholic engagement with politics narrows the frame of religion, and thereby the political itself can only meet religion after it undergoes a process of purification, shedding its mysticism and ritual and aesthetics.

The language of friendship was not only a key to individuals' personal lives but also the central metaphor for Catholic activist organizations of this period. For example, the great historian of Rhineland mysticism and political activist Jeanne Ancelet-Hustache worked with refugee groups in Paris and in 1933 founded two associations, the newspaper *L'ami du peuple* (Friend of the People) and the pro-refugee organization Amis des travailleurs étrangers (Friends of the Foreign Workers).[52] Others, such as Jacques and Raïssa Maritain and Henri de Lubac, SJ, were involved with Amitié chrétienne (Christian Friendship), formed in 1941 in Lyon by the Jesuit Pierre Chaillet and the Ukrainian émigré and Jewish convert Abbé Alexandre Glasberg. Glasberg was also associated with Jules Isaac's similarly named Amitiés judeo-chrétiennes (Jewish-Christian Friendship), formed a few years later.[53] In Paris, interwar associations critical of European colonialism emerged using similar language, such as the association Amitié franco-dahoméenne, founded in 1923 by Kojo Tovalou Houénou, a prominent African critic of the French colonial empire and acquaintance of Claude McKay. Friendship was also a key concept for Catholics working in solidarity with Muslims during the Algerian War. Groups such as the Association de la jeunesse algérienne pour l'action social (Association of Algerian Youth for Social Action)—founded in 1953 and built on student friendships between Algerian Muslims and French Christians—sought to combat Europeans' deeply ingrained prejudices against religious and racial minorities.[54] Friendship also animated Catholic leftist political engagement in the United States, as in the interracial apostolate the Friendship House, founded in Harlem in 1938 and Chicago in 1942.[55] Friendship was a ubiquitous metaphor that drew from a longer history in France, where it signaled the work of political solidarity in networks as far back as the 1788 antislavery group in Paris Amis des noirs (Friends of Blacks).[56]

In the early and mid-twentieth century, Catholics were of course not the only ones drawing from the language and practice of friendship to engage the political world. In 1947, for example, the American Quaker news columnist Drew Pearson created "friendship trains" that traveled from California to New York collecting food donations to send to a Europe still recovering from the war, in an effort to compete with the donations coming from communist countries. It was a huge endeavor, and 270 boxcars worth of food was shipped to Europe, with the sunny confidence of an American flag affixed to each box, announcing that they had come from American "friends" in a "democratic and Christian spirit of goodwill."[57] From 1914 to 1950, Protestant churches created the World Alliance for International Friendship to promote peace, with offices in forty countries. Furthermore, among Protestants in the mid-twentieth century, it was not just the ideal of friendship but the practice of friendship, according to Dana Robert, that was the "key that unlocks the history of the rapid evangelical missionization in the global south."[58] Certainly, in the twentieth century, Catholics had no monopoly on investing friendship with a wide variety of political possibilities. Friendship is a universal idiom, like walking, eating, or child-rearing, capable of becoming imbued with an almost infinite range of meanings. What is central, then, is to mine for the specifically Catholic particularity in this network, attuned to its distinctive nuances.

An in-depth comparison with twentieth-century American Protestants is beyond the scope of this book, but one noteworthy difference is that these Catholics (or would-be Catholic converts) who came from Egypt, Chile, Jamaica, and France had a much darker read of democratic powers, liberalism, and modernity. They criticized the direction that liberal modernity was headed and had an almost apocalyptic sense of doom about the twentieth century. One cannot imagine them cheerfully putting a French or American flag on any of their endeavors, confident about the expressed plans of their democratic governments. These intellectuals found more moral, political, and spiritual sustenance not in liberal modernity but in places that signaled a radical elsewhere, like the medieval period. Spiritual friendship among these Catholics, though attuned to the dramas of the twentieth century, drew from a decidedly medieval kind of intimacy, a neo-monastic sensibility. Several of the men and women in the chapters that follow were oblates of religious orders, tethering their identities to the premodern founders. Gabriela Mistral was a lay member of the Franciscan Third Order and asked in her will for friars to administer the royalties of her estate to the poor children of Montegrande. Jacques and Raïssa Maritain were Benedictine oblates, and Louis Massignon, like Mistral, was a lay Franciscan. Neo-medievalism was so widespread among these Catholic radicals that even Marie-Magdeleine Davy, a scholar of medieval spirituality who never tied herself to an order,

was described by scholars in terms of the medieval communities of untethered religious women as a beguine. For the men and women in this network
of spiritual friends, medieval piety was a potent source of political, ethical, and spiritual renewal. In 1946, Claude McKay published in the *Catholic
Worker* the poem "The Middle Ages," where he characterized the medieval
as a space of heterodoxy and pluralism populated with "Averrhoes, Aquinas, and Maimonides/Mohammedan and Christian and Jew."[59] Medievalism
and monasticism animated this community, including, most of all, a neo-
monastic theology that rejected marriage and centered spiritual friendship,
a practice that traced its origins to the twelfth-century Cistercian text *De
spirituali amicitia* (*Spiritual Friendship*) by Aelred of Rievaulx, where friends
were understood to be essential in the journey to God. Subsequent Christian writers, such as Francis de Sales and Jeanne de Chantal, revitalized and
popularized the notion of medieval holy friendship in the seventeenth century. But for these twentieth-century men and women, medieval monastic
life was appealing not only because of its theology or ideas about friendship but also because monks and nuns lived their actual real lives organized by modes of affiliation outside the nuclear family—these alternative
forms of communal living were inspirations. Yet, though neo-medieval and
anti-family, the men and women in *Kindred Spirits* were for the most part
ordinary laypeople—not monks, nuns, or priests—and lived *in* the world,
immersed in the struggles against fascism, anti-Semitism, white bigotry, and
colonialism. Together with this medievalism, there was a tragic undertow
to their writings, a darkness that puts them at odds with the sunnier con-
fidences of individuals who were involved with projects like the friendship
trains that rolled eastward thanks to the efforts of optimistic Americans.

SPIRITUAL FRIENDSHIP, FAMILY, AND SEXUALITY

When Léon Bloy wrote a letter to his new friends Jacques and Raïssa Maritain in 1905, he announced that he wanted to grab them both with his lion
paws and devour them with his love.[60] The writer Julien Green mourned
after Jacques Maritain died, writing how he would never again see his
beloved friend blow him kisses in the street or hold hands with him and
talk.[61] Mary Kahil and Louis Massignon were never a real couple in public—
he was in fact married to someone else—but they renewed a vow they made
to one another each year in a Franciscan chapel in Cairo. The Iranian po-

litical thinker Ali Shariati, a Muslim who studied with Massignon, wrote of him, "I love him to the point where I sometimes feel that my soul can no longer contain my affection for him." Shariati continued, "My heart hurts, my breathing stops. My throat is tied, my eyes and my whole body starts burning."[62] Gabriela Mistral's letters to Victoria Ocampo swerve between tenderness and obsession, and once she assured Ocampo after a long absence, "I remember you as if remembering you were a sacred tradition, plus a sweet habit."[63] The emotional, even physical sensuality that underlies the spiritual friendships in this community recalls the line from Roland Barthes: friendship, he states, is hard to write about, "the word is too stuffy, too prudish."[64] Indeed, what is *really* going on underneath all this excessive, ardent desire among friends? Isn't it a bit puritanical, or even disingenuous, to say this is all just "friendship," when their attachments come across as so erotic, so obsessive, so passionate? Barthes is right—it's too prudish to call this tangle of desires merely friendship as we typically understand it.

Adding to this skepticism about the word *friendship* as a cover for what was *really* going on, a recent book by the French journalist Frédéric Martel, *In the Closet of the Vatican*, focuses on "spiritual friendship" as a code that signaled the repressed same-sex desire, silence, and shame rampant among Vatican officials in the Catholic Church. In particular, Martel claims that Jacques Maritain's spiritual friendships with men were the key secret code that made it possible for gay Catholic priests from the 1940s to the 1970s to imagine a life for themselves as clergy.[65] Gay priests in these decades vowed to model the implacably charismatic Jacques Maritain, who Martel argues was absolutely gay and closeted but also utterly beloved in the church, sublimating his homoerotic sexual energy into passionate, elaborate spiritual friendships with men. Then, and now, Martel claims, "spiritual friendship" was a code for Catholic homosexual repression and silence. These intense, homoerotic but celibate spiritual friends that Jacques somehow was able to sustain, explains Martel, was impossible for most priests. In Rome, spiritual friendship became an impossible ideal, Martel argues, twisted into closeted sex, lies, and, mostly, widespread self-loathing and homophobia. Jacques Maritain had many gay male friends, and Martel's understanding of his sexuality would also account for the strange vow of celibacy he and Raïssa made twelve years into their marriage. For Martel, spiritual friendship is a scam synonymous with the closet, and it all began in the world I describe here.

On the one hand, Martel has a point. Some of his larger arguments are undeniable, and the scandals in the Catholic Church leave little doubt about the pervasive culture of closeted sex and secrecy that permeates clerical culture. His investigative work has exposed the hypocrisy of a church that denounces homosexuality while simultaneously and secretly practicing it on a frankly colossal scale, particularly at the Vatican. When it comes to sexuality, he notes, "the Vatican is an organization that always obsessively refers to the 'Truth'—and almost never practices it."[66] In that context and outside of it even today in Catholic (and some evangelical) circles, there is a revitalized interest in the term *spiritual friendship* as the right way of living for gay Christians, elevating this old practice of celibate friendships as a mode of intimacy to serve as a directive to live a life of sexless affection among friends. ("Friendship," one of the more popular books suggests dourly, "is a call to suffer.")[67] Spiritual friendship has been, and still is today, weaponized as a cruel mandate for the only way gay Catholics, and now evangelicals, can be intimate. And this advice, according to Martel, is simply never heeded by clergy who offer it.

But when it comes to a historical analysis of the particular network of Catholics who surround the Maritains, Martel misses some of the complexity. Without a doubt, there were queer sensibilities running through this community. When we read about the expressions of friendship that abound in this community of Catholics—begging for photographs of one another, passing them around like relics, blowing kisses, dreaming of one another (not to mention all the other things we can imagine that never make it into the archive)—there is no denying that these friendships were erotically charged. "Spiritual friendship," however, operated on a much wider, *wilder*, and weirder field of desire that resists our simple binaries of gay or straight, sexual repression or fulfillment, erotic or platonic, transgressive or regressive. These spiritual friendships included men and men, which Martel notes, but also, as he and so many other historians of this period miss, men and women as well as women and women. A look at Jacques Maritain's journals and correspondence, for example, shows the spiritual presence of many women in his life, Raïssa above all (unlike the vast majority of his priest friends, who lived in all-male, homoerotic worlds), and they were so bonded by the end of his life that he felt like *she*, not he, inhabited his soul and wrote his last book (even though she had long died).[68] In chapter 1, I explore the spiritual friendship between Jacques Maritain and another woman, Gabriela Mistral. Louis Massignon was also known to be gay, but the friendship of his I treat most at length in this book was with a woman. In this network of spiritual friendship, the desires circulating among both male and female friends were so fluid, moving in so many different directions, that I saw something similar to Amy Hollywood's description of sexuality among medieval Beguine women in her essay "Sexual Desire, Divine Desire; Or, Queering the Beguines": "It is not clear *what* kind of sexuality—within the dichotomy heterosexual and homosexual available to us today—is being deployed." In some senses, the friendships I explore in this book, all animated by a kind of neo-medievalism, seemed likewise to me to "[move] in the direction of greater erotic possibilities," as Hollywood writes, "not entirely containable by our own sexual dichotomies."[69] Anthony Pinn similarly suggests that scholars of Christianity need to rethink the erotic as a kind of unitive force, a love that involves the body and includes but is not limited to physical sex. For Pinn, the erotic encompasses more than sexuality, but when scholars of Christianity focus on love that is not necessarily physically sexual, we tend to focus on agapic or neighborly love, and too often our studies of Christianity are missing "passion and deep enjoyment." He gestures toward a domain that is something beyond both the neighborly love of agape and sex. A focus on these passionate friendship networks gets us somewhere close to filling in the gaps Pinn describes.[70]

Though it is tempting to turn individuals into familiar types—the repressed gay Catholic, the transgressive gay rebel ahead of her time, or even the sweet apolitical group of friends—none feels quite right for the members of these networks. These figures do not conform to the model that outlines extravagant spiritual friendships as closeted, repressed, and self-loathsome, sublimating pent-up sexual desire into weird and exhausting friendships. To insist that sex is the only real truth underneath ardent desire among adult friends is to radically narrow and even secularize this tradition. Overall, there is a persistent overabundance to spiritual friendship that cannot be wholly reduced to genital sexuality, as if sex (and its repression and sublimation) is the only truth these bonds have to tell. It was a different world. Yet, to be sure, there is a risk here in the claim I am making. I do not want to act as if their sexuality is some locked secret garden elsewhere, nor is sex, however, in the binary terms of gay or straight, repressed or fulfilled, the secret truth beneath every one of these extravagant gestures friends made to one another.

Louis Bayard has written a book on Abraham Lincoln that has been helpful for thinking through some of these issues. Bayard found himself caught between newer scholars who insist on evidence for Lincoln's homosexuality and those of an earlier generation who claim his sexuality is of no importance, and I related to his conclusion: "The book I ended up writing," he states, "takes no definitive stand on its subject's sexuality, but neither does it shy away from the question. It lives in the land of the spoken and unspoken, which is the realm where Lincoln himself almost certainly dwelt. When all is said and done, do I need Abraham Lincoln to be gay? No. I just need him to be something more complicated than he's been allowed to be. I would argue we all need that."[71] That said, there is no denying the erotic, sometimes queer energy pulsing through some of these relationships, but I have little interest in unlocking the secret door to their actual sexual practices. For one, these individuals remained quite confidential about their sex lives, even to their close friends (in some letters I found, friends asked questions that were dodged, avoided, ignored). One way to interpret that is the shame of the closet, but that's not the only way. Many of them were simply private, and, when it came to their published writings, the women and people of color especially were reluctant to disclose their intimate practices publicly and especially annoyed when white male reviewers tried to hunt for biographical clues about their sex lives in their works. Claude McKay called Black sexuality a weird obsession for whites. "Maybe they need to see a psychologist about it," he wrote in his 1937 autobiography, *A Long Way from Home*.[72] I think of Saidiya Hartman's line in *Wayward Lives, Beautiful Experiments* about young Black women "in open rebellion" in early twentieth-century Harlem, whose rebellion included "[*claiming*] *the right to opacity*."[73]

Furthermore, many of the women in this book are appearing as thinkers in modern Catholic intellectual life for the first time. From Chile, Egypt, Martinique, and Russia, to probe the sex lives of these non-Western women feels somewhat invasive and predictable. Paulette Nardal claimed people were always bothering her about why she never married and had kids if she wasn't a nun, why only the *amis*, when, she noted, there are so many reasons women end up taking different paths in life. In her case, she explained, it was simple: "I never wanted to bear children because I'm terrified of pain, that's it! I was afraid!"[74]

But I am walking a fine line here. I want to see these protagonists in the book as the intellectuals they were—poets, theologians, writers, artists—but by even asking the question of spiritual friendship, I also want to get underneath the formal polish of their published words and move closer to the nature of their intimate experiences. In the end, I suppose I've settled on approaching their intimate lives while still leaving them some privacy. Moreover, their actual sexual practices—even if I were looking for them—are not discussed in the written material I accessed, either published or archival. I am not saying that these people were not gay or that homosexuality is irrelevant to the story. The desires that flowed among individuals in this network may be more than heterosexual or homosexual, male or female, but they still may be, as Maggie Nelson has put it, "more complete and human." Nelson continues, "It's the binary of normative/transgressive that is unsustainable, along with the demand that anyone live a life that's all one thing."[75] I have come to see that each of these people, men and women, carried enormous complexities within them. And there was also variety around the issue of actual sex in this community. With the exception of the Maritains, most of them, though private and largely not interested in family, did not aim for the resolute renunciation of sex like we find in more well-known countercultural Catholics like Dorothy Day. McKay and Mistral had lovers throughout their lives, Ellen Tarry and Massignon had children, and about the topic, Davy spoke very little.

I admit that I initially saw this network's nonconformist, nonfamilial forms of love as emancipatory and exciting, but they became more complex and sobering the deeper I dug. For instance, when I first came to know this community of Catholics, I was compelled by the seeming commitment in their lives to a kind of love so much wider than the replicative, the heteronormative, the narrow. The women especially had lives and loves so far beyond what official Catholicism could ever account for, with its confining "genius of women" sloganeering. It was refreshing to immerse myself in the pleasures of their friendships, their expansive loves that we rarely hear about, which reached across the walls that separate women from women, men from women, men from men, native-born from newcomer, descendants of white settlers from the descendants of Black and Brown enslaved people, Christian from non-Christian, elite from working class, medieval from modern, even life from death. In so many ways, I loved these people and their bold and deeply spiritual loves.

But this idealized love grew increasingly strange, even disturbing. I realized, for example, that while the "anti-family" thrust of their lives sounds radical and emancipatory in the abstract, the rejection of family was not purely a slogan. There were actual children, siblings, and parents in these networks whose lives I learned about with some horror. It might have been truly amazing to befriend the people I studied, but it would be much less desirable to have been their child. While most individuals were not married, some were, and spouses and children were seen universally as a kind of threat or rot encroaching from the outside to ruin the spiritual fervor that circulated among *amis*. Massignon confessed to a friend that being with his wife and three children felt like he was undergoing Chinese torture, his face getting eaten by a rat.[76] Gabriela Mistral raised a child whom she claimed to be the son of a widowed half-brother who could not care for him. With her

exile and moves around the world, Mistral was sustained by a global network of spiritual friendship, but her child was isolated, depressed, and lonely
and died by suicide as a teenager. Claude McKay had a daughter but never
met her in person; he had nothing to do with his wife after she became pregnant in the United States and returned to Jamaica without him. McKay and
his daughter carried on an awkward, halting brief correspondence late in his
life. Kate Hennessy, Dorothy Day's granddaughter, wrote an unforgettable
memoir, *Dorothy Day: The World Will Be Saved by Beauty*, which provides a
revealing and often heartbreaking glimpse at what it would have been like to
be a child in a family where the most ardent love is directed toward friends.[77]

The elderly parents of these adults also suffered from their children's
choices. These parents for the most part watched in horror as their smart,
educated, famous children got caught up with the strange faith of Catholicism. One of Massignon's spiritual friends was a young Moroccan Muslim
named Jean Mohammed Abd-el-Jalil who had come to Paris to study, but
under the spell of Massignon and Jacques Maritain he converted from Islam
to Catholicism. He was the star of his hometown, and his devastated Muslim
parents begged him to change his mind and come home. When he wouldn't
relent, they held a funeral for him, as if he had died. Raïssa Maritain's Jewish
parents, émigrés from Russia who struggled with French, were bewildered
by their daughter's conversion to Catholicism under the guidance of the
truly bizarre Léon Bloy in 1905. But she pressured them to convert too, and
in their frailty and with her father nearly on his deathbed, they capitulated.
Simone Weil's parents provided absolutely everything for her and supported
her crazy ideas. Nevertheless, she kept refusing health, sanity, and normalcy,
and they buried their only daughter when she was thirty-four. She died after
refusing to eat more than the poor were rationed during the war.

Yet there were other cases in which I cheered individuals on as they
ditched their families for friends, one after another. Marie-Magdeleine Davy
never conformed to the expectations of a French Catholic girl, and her parents treated her horribly. She rarely went into details in her own memoirs
and interviews, but her mother never liked how she dressed or behaved and
always asked what they did to deserve a child like her. When her older sister
was killed in a car accident, she couldn't stand it any longer and left home
at the age of fifteen. Her parents refused to pay for her education, but Davy
made it on her own from age fifteen on, earning a PhD and becoming a
preeminent scholar. "When it comes to family," she wrote, "I chose friends."[78]
And who could blame her? Ann Harrigan, an Irish Catholic young woman
who volunteered with the Friendship House in Harlem, recalled that her
white Irish mother was racist and a "huge" stumbling block to her interracial

work.[79] She insisted that her daughter was wasting her life in Harlem and would make her listen to salacious stories of rapes and murders in the city to dissuade her from going. These families' understanding of love was meager and joyless and closed, and it is natural to root for their children when they find something better.

Spiritual friendships offered a way out of repressive familial ties, in a distinctively Catholic key. But the conformist impulses they resisted came from Catholicism too: the predictable gender norms for men and women; the expectation that lay women are meant, for the most part, to suffer, placate, procreate; the insular Irish Catholic racism; the assumption that children are not fully persons (although many of our subjects did not unlearn this value). Catholic spiritual friendship was an escape valve from Catholic family values and a politics that relied on ever narrower forms of homogeneous identity. While there was much to admire in this community of more expansive spiritual kin, there is no way to disentangle one purely emancipatory thread out of the complex tangle of their lives. It was compassionate, courageous, pluralistic, rebellious, and creative, but sometimes it held within it too much fantasy about the possible, caused pain for families and created an erotic and sensual world in which actual sex was still, for the most part, an unspoken taboo. This is especially true for the many in this network who did not conform to heterosexual notions of desire. I wonder, therefore, if it is not fully separable from what Mark Jordan calls the scandal of silence around sexuality in Catholicism, about which telling truths would "begin as a whimper, then rise through fevered moans, racing syllabus, hoarse shouts to end in a high scream—unbearable, unmeasured, unrelieved, the centuries of believers deceived, abused, tortured, executed by the church in defense of its 'purity,' that is, its power."[80] It is impossible to separate these darker silences from the silences in Catholic spiritual friendship, even when it contains something of the radical, transgressive, and avant-garde.

THE FEEL OF THE ARCHIVE
AND THE PRESENCE OF DIFFERENCE

Accessing the story of these relationships entails the immersion into a complex and strange underworld of twentieth-century religion. To use the word *underworld* in relation to Catholicism, I admit, furthers the sense that we're diving into a subterranean realm of neo-Gothic sexual secrecy. But I have in mind here Hannah Arendt's vision of the scholar as a pearl diver who "descends to the bottom of the sea" to "pry loose the rich and the strange, the pearls and the coral in the depths and to carry them to the surface."[81] Arendt's image of thinking as an effort to rescue the lost treasures of human experience and reflection—especially those that, when surfaced, appear strange in our world—is a useful one for this story. Much of what appears in the chapters that follow has been "pried loose" either from private archives or from long-out-of-print Catholic periodicals that were part of the feverish creativity among lay Catholics in the years leading up to the Second Vatican Council, buried in the now-defunct artistic, philosophical, and political journals that thrived on the utopian margins of the mid-twentieth-century religious Left.[82] Even with the many out-of-print published sources, the realm of spiritual friendship is still obfuscated beneath the smooth surface of the history of ideas. Traces of this port of experience must be sought at the edges of formal academic prose—tucked into handwritten notes, reminisced on in memoirs, announced at eulogies. In addition to their published scholarship, it was published and unpublished correspondence, memoirs, and diaries that enabled me to move past the formal ideas of these scholars into the emotional and even physical realms that animated their work. Friends sustained their love and communicated its spiritual worth through photos mailed to one another and little sacred objects tucked in the letters they exchanged. But I was able to see these materials, and *see* friendship, only because I was originally researching women's intellectual contributions, which required archival work. Jeanne Ancelet-Hustache, a friend of Marie-Magdeleine Davy's and the Maritains', for instance, put tiny crosses made out of dried leaves, like small palm fronds, inside the correspondence she mailed to friends. But this knowledge only surfaced after I visited her and others' archives and held, touched, and opened envelopes and folders, where photos and religious treasures, tucked inside, fell out. At the home of Jacques and Raïssa Maritain, framed photos of their friends joined those of recognizable holy figures, which I was able to see because the Maritain archives have recreated Raïssa's private study, a visual boon to scholars.[83] To study spiritual friendship, one must be able to look underneath the even polish of these writers' voluminous scholarship and acknowledge the candid materiality that grounded and made palpable these highly charged affective relationships.[84] Although it was Catholic women's archival materials that first made the power of friendship apparent to me, the more evidence I found, the more I discovered that they pointed to a vast network of intensive, affective bonds between women and men, men and men, women and women.

The story of these men and women and their relational religious lives are also somewhat buried, in Arendt's sense, for reasons less obvious than the practical matters of translation, access, and the personal nature of the topic. There are other reasons many of the names are not yet familiar to most English-speaking students of Catholicism, particularly the women, like Davy and Kahil, and the people of color, like McKay and Mistral. While they were all prominent thinkers and creators, when it comes to Catholic intellectual history, women and people of color are too often treated as suffering, silent, or asleep until the rise of feminist, Black, and Latinx theology in the years following Vatican II, when they awoke at last. For the most part, the women and people of color in these pages were extraordinarily prolific scholars as early as the 1920s, though none were offered top academic posts or tenured professorship: most were independent writers and scholars, affiliated with research institutes rather than the seminaries or universities, or were self-proclaimed "vagabond" artists and writers.

Indeed, when it comes to pre–Vatican II Catholicism, we have histories on mothers who passed on their faith to their children, nuns who staffed orphanages, grandmothers who filled the pews, but very little on modern religious women who were *intellectuals*, the critical thinkers of their time, engaging with the cutting-edge social and political issues of their day. This omission persists not only in the fields of theology and Catholic history but also in comparative religion. With some recent exceptions, women are largely absent from nearly all the genealogies of the study of religion, including influential texts such as Tomoko Masuzawa's *The Invention of World Religions*.[85] This neglect continues even as women were earning doctorates in religious history and theology by the 1930s, in both universities and Catholic seminaries, and trained less formally in previous decades. Further complicating our understanding of their lives is the secular cast of most feminist historiography, which has made it hard to think about religious women in the past as critical thinkers. There was no blind adherence to inherited communities or traditions among these women, and they all lived lives against or outside the norms of the mainstream, but none wrote anything today we would consider feminist theology. Many modern Catholic women's writing still remains unpublished, cataloged confusedly, if at all, and untranslated.

Another factor is that scholars of Catholic intellectual history are all in broad agreement that Paris from the 1930s to the 1950s was a key site that fomented the most theological creativity that helped lay the foundations for the changes later inaugurated at the Second Vatican Council. The story tends to veer almost invariably toward a handful of prominent French-born, clerical male theologians—figures like the Jesuits Henri de Lubac and Jean Daniélou or the Dominican Yves Congar—who played key roles in the incredibly theologically creative moment known as *ressourcement* (or turn to the sources) and eventually served as theological advisors at Vatican II.[86] But the full story has truly not yet been told, both about the presence of *difference* in this theological community and about the role of friendship in the theological creativity of this world. Nonclerical intellectuals, women like Kahil, Davy, and Jeanne Ancelet-Hustache, and a diverse range of male and female editors, writers, archivists, poets, and theologians worked alongside these well-known theologians, or in distinctive spheres that overlapped and even anticipated the theological work that followed. I uncover how these lesser-known men and women weave their spiritual friendships more prominently into the story of twentieth-century Catholic thought, and in doing so I follow the paths laid out by religious historians Ann Braude, Mia Bay, Farah Griffin, Martha Jones, Natalie Zemon Davis, and others, who have shown how women cannot simply be tacked on to existing religious histories. Attention to the presence of women in religious history forces scholars to examine what is considered the domestic or private sphere and to reassess what is normally considered political.[87] The story thus shifts from seminaries, parishes, and institutions connected to juridical politics and turns instead to places such as salons in the Maritain household, gatherings on mysticism hosted by Davy at the Château de la Fortelle in Paris, the secret meetings around the underground journal *Témoignage chrétien* (Christian witness), or the Dar-el-Salam center founded in 1941 in Cairo by Kahil. At the same time, the Catholic Worker Movement's Houses of Hospitality were sprouting in the United States, and by the 1960s, base communities appeared in Latin America, Italy, and France as well. Catholic women intellectuals played key roles in these off-center places. Nor were these locales wholly separate from clerical spheres: Jesuits like Jean Daniélou were often guests at Fortelle, the salon Davy ran outside of Paris, which, because she was neither male nor a priest, brought Jesuits in contact with a much wider range of intellectuals than they would ever encounter in their more insular seminaries. Likewise, Jacques Maritain's philosophy of Christian humanism, social Catholicism, and democracy is widely accepted as fundamentally turning Catholic intellectual history from the Far Right, not only in Europe but around the world. It is never acknowledged, however, that the Chilean poet Gabriela Mistral, whose biographer calls Maritain her "spiritual brother," was key to the dissemination of Maritain's ideas in Latin America from 1937 on.[88] Yet in Catholic intellectual history, their efforts are scarcely recognized.[89] Instead, the Catholic intellectual history centered in

France before the 1960s remains incredibly white, male, clerical, and loveless because we still see European Catholicism in those terms.

Likewise, people of color cannot be assimilated neatly into this old story starring the white male clergy, nor can they be added at the end, the narrative unchanged. For instance, in studies of the early stirrings of progressive Catholicism, many intellectual historians point to the Dominican priests in Paris—Yves Congar and Marie-Dominique Chenu—whose progressive ideas emerged from new readings of Thomas Aquinas and the Saulchoir seminary's openness toward historical methodology. But what would happen if we took seriously the fact that Paulette Nardal and her cousin Louis Thomas Achille, Black Catholic intellectuals from the Caribbean who were in Paris in the interwar period, held an important inter- and intraracial salon grounded in friendship, where they hosted Claude McKay and Marcus Garvey, along with a cadre of progressive Dominican priests, whom they considered their "Catholic family" while abroad in France? That has yet to be incorporated into the largely white and European story of Catholic modernity before the Second Vatican Council, and this book aims to begin to fill in that gap. In thinking about the presence of men and women from the African diaspora in France and Spain, such as Nardal and McKay, we join the works of scholars like Kennetta Hammond Perry, Kira Thurman, Allison Blakely, and Tyler Stovall who explore how the presence of people of African descent has shaped European history, thought, and culture. This gives us a notion of Black Europe, which, as Perry and Thurman note, "complicates, unsettles, and disrupts imaginaries of Blackness and Europeanness. It deconstructs the foundations of the Black/White binary that underwrites both of these categories." Thus, by examining Black lives and experiences in Europe's past, we help "unsettle what it means to be European, and they unsettle what it means to be Black."[90] We can think analogously about Spanish-speaking intellectuals from the global south who were in France between the wars too, like Gabriela Mistral.

These white, Brown, and Black avant-garde Catholics in the 1920s–50s, male and female, who all spent time in Paris, had a shared cultural imaginary across racial and gender divides, but their experiences of the world were very different from the more well-known white male philosophers and theologians. Thus, when we include them, the story of Catholic intellectual history in this period expands, but it shifts too. Take, for instance, figures like Jacques Maritain (chapter 1) and Claude McKay (chapter 5). We do not have evidence that McKay and Maritain ever met in person, but in McKay's final decade, 1938–49, he and Jacques Maritain moved in similar circles in

New York and Chicago, both non-US citizens and émigré intellectuals who occupied the world of the Catholic Left. Both Maritain and McKay visited the Catholic Worker and the Friendship House in New York in the late 1930s and early 1940s, both knew Dorothy Day and had known Paulette Nardal in Paris, and in Chicago, both were linked to Bishop Bernard Sheil's Catholic Youth Organization (CYO). They also shared a poetic and mystical sensibility and had politics that elude easy classification—anticommunist while somewhat illiberal, but resolutely attentive to those on the margins of power. By the time McKay converted to Catholicism in 1944, there was so much that tied his worldview to a figure like Jacques Maritain. But their differences are also stark: Jacques Maritain, a well-connected and beloved white European Catholic, arrived in the United States in 1939 with an academic visa secured for him at various institutions where he served as affiliate faculty, first at the New School, then Princeton, then the University of Chicago, with visiting appointments at Notre Dame. Houses were set up for him each stop of the way, and audiences filled the room every time he approached the lecture podium. But when Claude McKay first arrived in the United States in 1912 as a Black man from Jamaica, he was allowed entry only if he agreed he would never apply for public assistance. And unlike Maritain, in the late 1930s, McKay really needed it. Though McKay had been a best-selling author and internationally renowned poet in the 1920s, when he returned to the United States from his travels in Europe in 1933, he was poor with few opportunities as a Black writer.[91] The Great Depression hit him in a way it never did Maritain. McKay couldn't find work, his connections had dried up, and in 1934, he was desperate. He ended up moving to the Greycourt work camp in upstate New York, a labor camp for the unhoused and addicts, and there was nothing romantic about this "proletariat" experience. It was depressing, awful, like a prison, a place where he felt like a "caged wild animal." McKay once said that he could have written a story about the work camp, but he didn't like to write about suffering or revel in it. In the United States, McKay noted, "now I can understand why people commit suicide rather than become paupers."[92] He was able to leave three months later, but his health never recovered, and he struggled with illness off and on for the rest of his life, dying young in Chicago in 1948. Yet McKay's story belongs with Maritain's in our understanding of mid-twentieth-century Catholicism—while they inhabited such similar worlds, the story of this moment in Catholic modernity looks so different when we include McKay into the more familiar narrative starring Jacques Maritain. We begin to see, for example, why McKay was so skeptical in the 1940s of Catholics who were eager to fight against fascism abroad but refused to take racism seriously at home. In the 1940s, fascism was *the* political emergency for most progressive Catholics, particularly for exiled Europeans in the United States, like the Maritains. In 1943, McKay wrote a poem while staying at the cottage of a white Catholic woman he met at the Friendship House, Mary Jerdo Keating:

> Lord, let me not be silent while we fight
> In Europe Germans, Asia Japanese
> For setting up a Fascist way of might
> While fifteen million Negroes on their knees
> Pray for salvation from the Fascist yoke
> Of these United States. Remove the beam
> (Nearly two thousand years since Jesus spoke)
> From your own eyes before the mote you deem
> It proper from your neighbor's to extract!
> We bathe our lies in vapors of sweet myrrh,
> And close our eyes not to perceive the fact!
> But Jesus said: You whited sepulchre,
> Pretending to be uncorrupt of sin,
> While worm-infested, rotten from within![93]

Incorporating the story of Claude McKay gives us an enlarged, more capacious sense of truth, reality, the twentieth century, and the limits of Catholic notions of empathy. Catholic antifascism of the sort we see in Jacques Maritain is admirable, but the story of McKay points out its blind spots. At the same time, examining McKay in the context of other subaltern voices who appear in this book—Jewish and female—helps us resist the notion that our empathy depletes as it extends, so it can only be directed at either Jewish or Black victims, not both and no more. We read of McKay's "fifteen million Negroes" alongside the poetry of others in this network, like Raïssa Maritain, a Russian Jewish émigré convert who begged Americans to take the treatment of Jews seriously as soon as she arrived in 1939. One of her poems, also published in 1943 (the same year as McKay's above poem), describes how "4 million Jews—and more—have suffered death without consolation / Those who are left are promised to the slaughter."[94] Who cannot be moved by both these poets to think larger about the events of the twentieth century and where Catholic empathy was placed? By lifting up the stories of Black and Jewish writers, as well as writers from the global south, like Mistral, together with white European writers, like Jacques Maritain, I draw inspiration from

Michael Rothberg's *Multidirectional Memory*. Rothberg draws connections among different legacies of violence, trauma, and loss in modernity, arguing against a competitive notion of memory, one that would claim our empathy can only be directed at one history at the expense of another.[95]

We do more than just rectify previous scholarly omissions when we incorporate the intellectual contributions of men and women who found themselves on the margins: we attend to the site where the most creative thinking often took place. Scholars such as John Connelly have shown that in early twentieth-century eastern Europe, it was those on the margins of official Catholicism and national centers of power—the converts, émigrés, and "border transgressors"—who brought a more empathetic perspective of Jews and Judaism to the table, the willingness to identify with the dispossessed.[96] Connelly focuses on émigré Catholics from eastern Europe, but Catholic émigrés fleeing violence from elsewhere in the world wrote movingly about the plight of refugees in the century of war, using their own experiences as starting points of compassion. Take, for instance, Gabriela Mistral's poem "La Hella" ("Footprint"), published in *Lagar* (Winepress), her last book of poems in 1954, a vivid, dreamlike depiction of a nameless refugee fleeing on foot:

> Of the fleeing man I have
> only the footprint,
> the weight of his body
> and the wind that blows him.
> No signs, no name,
> No country or town
> only the damp
> shell of his footprint
> only this syllable
> absorbed by the sand
> and the earth, Veronica
> who murmured it to me.
>
> Only the anguish
> that hurries his flight:
> hammering pulse,
> gasping breath,
> glistening sweat,
> teeth on edge,

And the thorn he leaps,
the marsh he crosses
the bush that hides him
and the sun that reveals him,
the hill that helps him,
and the one that betrays him,
the root that trips him
and God who gets him to his feet.

. . .

Holy sands,
eat up his sign
Dogs of mist,
cover his track.
Falling night,
swallow in one gulp
the great, sweet
mark of a man . . .
I see, I count
the two thousand footprints.
I go running, running
across old Earth,
mixing up his
poor tracks with mine,
or I stop and erase them
with my wild hair,
or facedown I lick
away the footprints.

But the white Earth
turns eternal,
stretches endless
as a chain, lengthens out into a snake,
and the Lord God does not break its back.
And the footprints go on
to the end of the world.[97]

By examining carefully chosen viewpoints along its edge, we engage in a fuller, more complete reckoning with the twentieth century, its traumas, violence, and its instances of creativity and courage, especially when we bring to the surface a wider cast of characters who were not at the centers of ecclesial or academic institutions of power. Including these writers thus begins the work of breaking open the insular nature of Catholic intellectual history. Maureen O'Connell has an image I find useful: she compares white Catholics to disciples "locked away in the upper room" after the crucifixion ("the doors being shut where the disciples were," an image from John 20:19), safeguarded in the whiteness of so many Catholic institutions: parishes, presses, academic departments, and scholarship that excluded people of color.[98] Part of this projects aims to unlock that upper room, open up that closed space, and listen to other stories.

To be sure, a deep dive into the lives and loves of these subaltern voices, like Claude McKay, Mary Kahil, Marie-Magdeleine Davy, and Gabriela Mistral, gives us a more honest assessment of the century of extremity and violence. But at the same time, we see that their suffering is far from the only lesson of their lives. Too often, women or people of color appear in white Catholic intellectual history as victims. Hilton Als describes this white desire to constantly ponder Black agony: "Tell me about yourself," he writes, "meaning, Tell me how you've suffered. Isn't that what you people do? Suffer nobly, even poetically sometimes? Doesn't suffering define you?"[99] Along these lines, Amy Hollywood has also raised the question why it is that modern critique so often fixates on trauma as the site of realness and truth but seems "unable," she writes, "to hear joy."[100] Along with the bouts of poverty and illness, time in Claude McKay's archive shows how so many of his friends loved his boyish face and his poems about love, shyness, pleasure, and beauty that have little to do with pain. One of his fellow Black Catholic writer friends, Paulette Nardal, was wealthy, genteel, and fluent in English and French. She played piano. Her world was an elite, comfortable one. Mary Kahil, from Cairo, may have had to navigate a patriarchal culture, but in so many other ways she hit the jackpot of life. She dedicated herself to Muslim-Christian friendship and carried on a passionate, decades-long spiritual friendship with Louis Massignon because she could afford to remain unmarried. Kahil inherited a massive fortune from a family lumber business and was gorgeous, spoke three languages, and used her wealth to advance feminist and interreligious causes in Egypt. I lift them up not only as people who endured the violence of the twentieth century but also as friends, agents, creators, dreamers, artists, men and women who experienced joy. Taken together, these voices stretch our notions of Europe, Catholicism, and theology as well as Blackness, women, and Latin America.[101]

Yet despite this range, today friendship, much like human relationality more generally, has, as Constance Furey writes, "the whiff of something apolitical—appealing or irrelevant, depending on your perspective because it denotes the realm of the personal and intimate, untainted by social calculations, questions of identity, and instrumental needs."[102] This way of thinking about friendship has had epistemological consequences, steering serious attention away from unconventional religious moderns for whom the realm of relations was the loci of their most serious spiritual and political work. This is true not only for the study of modern Catholics. For example, in her book *Affective Communities: Anticolonial Thought, Fin-de-Siècle Radicalism, and the Politics of Friendship*, Leela Gandhi describes a powerful but overlooked network of anticolonial thinkers in nineteenth-century England, who, much like the men and women I explore here, also advanced a politics that placed an emphasis on friendship, religious experience, and affection as bridges to other cultures. It was a "hybrid style of politics," as Gandhi calls it. Derided as unserious and sentimental by the secular political philosophers of the nineteenth century, they were denounced as immature advocates of "mishmash" who spoke of friendship and spirituality with the "the babble of children." This politics and experiential religion of relationality in the world eventually faded from the scene.[103]

CONCLUSION

This community of men and women and the affective bonds that sustained them imparted a radically distinct religious, intellectual, and political energy into their fields. To a large degree these writers, artists, and activists pushed against the way in which Christianity has, throughout history, divided some human beings against others and arranged them hierarchically.[104] Their activism and friendships stretch outside the confines of narrow tribalism, across the fence. They reached for the sacred beyond the mundane, for other traditions beyond the one they inherited, for people from other countries beyond those where they were born. Most rejected the identities set out before them and yearned for the other-oriented relational ties that spiritual friendship could enable.

Today we are witnessing a powerful, global resurgence of Christianity that furthers rather than breaks down discourses of division, xenophobia, and violence. Catholics in the United States, as well as eastern and western Europe, are playing prominent roles in the widespread global scapegoating of immigrants and religious minorities, projecting ideology about others—immigrants, Jews, Muslims—that never encounter the reality of their lives. We see this in the dangerous, fanciful calls for Europe and America to return to our "Judeo-Christian roots," all associated with a mythically pure past that is recoverable only by silencing, blocking, deporting, imprisoning, or killing those who cannot trace their lineage to this heritage of racial and religious purity. This cruelty has a long and robust history, from the Catholic animus against non-Christians in the fifteenth and sixteenth centuries to Catholic policies of *limpieza de sangre*, or the purity of blood, to justify discrimination. Throughout the modern period, Christianity has long provided the discourse to cast some as "others" against which an "us" could be consolidated.[105] The individuals in the network described in the pages that follow dedicated their lives to pushing *against* the weight of this long, violent, and ongoing tradition.

It was not the faceless immensities of "modernity" or "religious difference" that compelled this community forward but their friendships, in practice and memory or as political ideals.[106] As historian Marci Shore explains, "Ideas do not move around independently of people. There is always involvement; 'life' intrudes." She continues: "There are no pure ideas uncontaminated by human encounter. If ideas come into being though dialogue, then friendship is historically significant. Friendship is a site of disclosure, a reminder that intellectual production is by nature dialogical, and an illumination of the interplay between emotions and intellect. Friendship offers a window into the infinite complexity of human relations and into the infinite mysteries of the minds producing the ideas that interest intellectual historians."[107] Recovering these scholars from historical obscurity offers new insights into crucial threads of twentieth-century intellectual history in the West: the censure of mysticism and poetry as insufficiently political and realist; the profound skepticism about the Western ability to know the other without violent appropriation; the predominance of historicism in the humanities rather than the imaginative, affective, or aesthetic approach; the sentimentality and inadequacy of friendship for the task of politics. All these forces ushered in the eventual demise of the men and women I describe in this volume. But by prying them loose from the archives and bringing them to the surface, we conjure new images for thinking about Catholic modernity and about other ways of imagining modes of belonging and connection.

BETWEEN LATIN AMERICA AND EUROPE

Gabriela Mistral and the Maritains

INTRODUCTION

AFTER THE CHILEAN POET Gabriela Mistral died on January 10, 1957, in New York, a requiem mass was held in her honor at St. Patrick's Cathedral. Just a few weeks before, the French Catholic philosopher Jacques Maritain, a fellow émigré in the United States, had sat at Mistral's bedside as she fought pancreatic cancer. There Mistral and Maritain spoke "like two Christian poets," over a period of several days, "about God, life, and death, all the religious questions that were so close to their heart."[1] Mistral went into a coma two weeks later, just after Christmas. Maritain telegrammed her caretaker and partner, Doris Dana, "Our hearts are with you in your profound grief. We pray with you. God bless you for having been her sister and her angel."[2] Dana responded to Maritain, recalling his visit, "After you left, Gabriela fell asleep and did not return to this world until the next morning. When I reminded her of your visit, and showed her your flowers, the tears flowed and she just said, 'He's a saint.'"[3] After New Yorkers paid their respects, Mistral's body was airlifted to Lima and met by a Chilean military transport back to Chile, where the nation's president declared three days of mourning. "Crowds of people took to the streets consecutive days and nights to see her coffin," and thousands poured into the center of Santiago for her funeral procession.[4] In Chile, Gabriela Mistral was larger than life: a celebrated poet, teacher, journalist, and diplomat anointed as the "spiritual queen of Latin America" when she won the Nobel Prize in Literature in 1945. She was also a humanitarian who fought for the rights of children and mothers and deeply identified with the causes of indigenous peoples, land reform, and education.[5] In the late 1950s, Jacques Maritain, too, was a luminary, the best-known Catholic philosopher in the world.

Gabriela Mistral and Jacques Maritain's friendship offers a window into the internationalization of newly emerging ideas about Catholicism and politics in the 1930s and 1940s, which focused initially on antifascism. Mistral and the Maritains did not merely share thoughts about faith and politics and collaborate toward those ends as friends, but their practice of spiritual friendship provided the energy that animated this work, as a poetic undercurrent of creativity that moved between the Spanish- and French-speaking Catholic intellectuals, artists, and activists in the years surrounding World War II. But friendship is also slippery, elusive—it spirals out and multiplies, nearly impossible to pin down. A look at Jacques Maritain's and Mistral's relationship quickly becomes populated with more and more people, until the network's scope is almost overwhelming. In this chapter, I focus on their meeting and their bond, as well as its evolution and significance, but along the way this relationship expands, forming more and more links between Latin American and French intellectuals and artists, first in Paris, then in New York. Mistral eventually developed a close friendship with Jacques's wife too, the fellow poet Raïssa Maritain. Thanks to Mistral's introductions, the Maritains welcomed several Spanish-speaking intellectuals into their interwar salon on the outskirts of Paris, people who eventually helped disseminate Jacques's ideas about democracy in Argentina, Uruguay, and Chile, where Maritainism remains influential today.[6] Many of these thinkers were women, as María Laura Picón notes: in addition to Gabriela Mistral, her friends Esther de Cáceres from Uruguay and Victoria Ocampo from Argentina also shared a close relationship with the Maritains and collaborated with them on issues of art, politics, and Catholicism. And for their part, Jacques and Raïssa Maritain took the Spanish-language writings of these women more seriously than most other French speakers at the time, especially that of Gabriela Mistral.[7]

I begin this chapter with a brief introduction to the life and works of Gabriela Mistral, a figure who remains far less well known for scholars of twentieth-century Catholicism than Jacques Maritain.[8] The early stirrings of progressive Catholicism before Vatican II were not only in Europe, and Mistral was a key player in global antifascist and philo-Semitic movements from as early as 1919 while living in Chile and Mexico.[9] Mistral lectured on social Catholicism in Chile in 1925 and lived in Europe from 1926 until 1940, where she soon saw the dangers of fascism first in Europe and then in South America. A wanderer and cosmopolitan writer of poetry and prose who "changed addresses as often as other people change clothes," Mistral was also a trailblazer in the transatlantic exchange of ideas, immersed in key international, intellectual networks in France and Latin America and, eventually, the United States.[10] But although she is often described more as a general "humanitarian and mystic," known today in the English-speaking world primarily in the circles of literary studies and poetry, Mistral was indeed Catholic, though an eccentric one, pulled toward the poetic undertow of the tradition, its saints and poets and rural poor, far from the institutional structures of the clergy or the Catholic university system.[11] Neither a nun nor a devout married woman nor a secular feminist, Mistral is hard to fit into the silos we often use to understand women in the twentieth century.

After tracing the story of Gabriela Mistral from Chile, Mexico, Spain, and Italy, the chapter settles in Paris. When Mistral met the Maritains in the mid-1930s, the Maritains offered stature and structure around friendship, spirituality, and experimental thinking about Catholic internationalism and antifascism at their home, where people from across the world gathered. Here friendship was visibly, explicitly rendered holy. For reasons I describe in this chapter, the Maritains embodied an alternative to the procreative, matrimonial ideal in a quiet way, lavishing love on their friends and organizing their lives around them. A queer scene also surrounded the married couple, and Mistral, too, had unusual, but understated, domestic arrangements. When she met the Maritains, she lived with a female friend from Mexico, probably her lover, with whom she was raising an adopted young boy. She, too, lived her life for friends. The Maritains' salon was deeply appealing to unusual, spiritually inclined artists and thinkers like Mistral, and in this chapter I also offer something of a genealogy of the Maritains' commitment to spiritual friendship while paying close attention to the Spanish-speaking community that gathered around them. I then follow these friendships after the war, which dispersed so many individuals out of Europe and into various places in the Americas: Canada, New York, Brazil, Uruguay. In the end, I show that the appeal that deeply charismatic Catholics like Jacques Maritain and Gabriela Mistral held for one another, and for others, lied most of all in the fact that they appeared to friends as representatives of something beyond the ordinary, the mundane, whose lives were extreme in their commitments and unusual in their habits, demeanor, and sensibilities. These figures were endowed with a kind of spiritual charisma shared among friends, which fueled this period of intellectual and artistic creativity for Catholicism on a transnational scale.

Before moving on to Mistral's biography, let me add one final note: several years ago, when I was at the Maritain archives in Kolbsheim, France, René Mougel, the archivist, told me that the most common visitors these days to the archives are Chilean Catholics. I was curious about this—people from Chile traveling all the way to a tiny village in France to learn more about a long-dead Catholic philosopher, Jacques Maritain, even today? It was only later that I would discover the story behind this, a story that begins with spiritual friendship and Gabriela Mistral.

GABRIELA MISTRAL: THE EARLY YEARS AND THE (RE)TURN TO CATHOLICISM

Mistral was born in 1889 as Lucila Godoy Alcayaga in the valley of Elqui, a rural, remote area in Chile's Norte Chico region, located between the Central Valley and the vast Atacama Desert. Her father, a former Catholic seminarian, left the family before she turned three years old, but growing up, Mistral was regaled with romantic stories about her father's talents as a poet and a musician. She was raised by her mother, a seamstress, and her older sister. Mistral was particularly close with her paternal grandmother, who lived in a nearby convent in a room the nuns had given her after she left her unfaithful husband. Both of her daughters had joined the order.[12] Mistral's grandmother loved the Bible and poetry and taught young Gabriela to memorize the Psalms. For her official schooling, Mistral went to a local public school, where she was unjustly accused of stealing and eventually dropped out.[13]

For the people in this rural valley, Mistral recalled, it was "starve or work, everyone," so when she was fifteen, Mistral began work as a teacher's aide in a poor schoolhouse whose students during the day were the children of local workers, and then, at night, their parents.[14] Mistral had loved writing poetry as a child. She won a poetry contest in a regional Chilean newspaper when she was a teenager. In 1908, at the age of nineteen she began publishing under the pen name Gabriela Mistral, which she later claimed she chose for its evocation of a fierce, strong mountain wind, the world of the spirit, and the French poet Frédéric Mistral. Various awards followed, and by 1915, she was contributing to prestigious literary magazines and accepted in serious artistic circles. Mistral had also developed a correspondence with Rubén Darío, who had been living in exile in Paris running the magazine *Elegancias*, and he began publishing Mistral's poems there in 1913, giving a French audience for Mistral's work. Thanks in part to her far-flung friendships, developed through correspondence, Mistral quickly became a sought-after writer while she still earned a living by teaching. Though her upbringing did not seem particularly pious, according to Elizabeth Horan her early poetry had several Catholic hagiographical tropes, including redemptive suffering, renunciation, imitatio Christi, and the subversive power of weakness.[15]

By 1917, she was fascinated by Tagore and Russian literature, identifying with their concern for and spiritual connection to the land. In 1921, she met and began mentoring the young Pablo Neruda. Neruda later recalled, "Gabriela introduced me to the dark and terrifying vision of the Russian novelists, and that Tolstoy, Dostoyevsky, and Chekov soon occupied a special place deep within me. They are with me still."[16] But far from a life sealed off among elite writers, Mistral earned her living as a rural public school teacher throughout her early years as a writer, and this kept her connected to the poor and their real, actual lives, a tie she never severed that provided the sources for her later reflections on poverty, indigenous communities, women, and children. Reflecting on their lives, Mistral developed a political consciousness about the purpose of education among the poor and the structural causes of poverty. During her years in her home province, Mistral became acquainted with a network of politically conscious writers associated with Chile's Radical Party, which was resolutely anticlerical. But Mistral had been nourished by the European roots of Latin American modernismo and Russian realism, admiring both Walt Whitman and John Ruskin, and discovered forms of experimentation with religion that departed from the inherited wisdom of the Radicals and the anticlerical Left. These writers rejected religions' traditional conservatism: "The old gods had deserted them," as Pericles Lewis explains, but they were not exactly secular. They sought "new gods in unorthodox places, and sometimes even orthodox ones."[17] In this spirit, Mistral befriended Chilean realist novelist Eduardo Barrios, who moved in similar circles and was, like herself, an outsider looking to gain entrance to a literary world populated mainly by writers from the nation's elite, compelled by the idea of Catholicism containing sources of literary truth: they were very close friends from 1915 onward, and half-jokingly, she addressed him as "hermanito" as a sign of their friendship. She was drawn especially to his 1922 supernatural realist novel about the life of Saint Francis, *El hermano asno* (Brother brute). "Your book," she wrote Barrios, "stoked the mystical fire in me."[18] As Mistral made her way into these intellectual and activist networks, she primarily did so not as a politician and organizer but as a teacher, journalist, and poet.[19] As a busy teacher whose publications were her only credential, she directed her energies toward the literary side of leftist politics.

In 1922, Mistral moved to Mexico to assist with education reform, and according to Elizabeth Horan, there she became fascinated with the entirety of Mexico's mixed indigenous and colonial heritage, especially the life of Sor Juana Inés de la Cruz, writer, mystic, and nun. She had already encountered Sor Juana through the modernist poet Amado Nervo's book *Juana de Asbaje* (1910), which inspired Mistral's short essay "Silueta de Sor Juana Inés."[20] Early twentieth-century modernists in the Spanish- and French-speaking worlds were both similarly drawn to saints, piety, and the underworld and read them as a rebellious, elite refusal of the mainstream. Sor Juana, in Mistral's story, leaves the noisy masses of the crowd in Mexico and enters the convent to find solitude at last, where she puts her bare feet on the clean cement of the convent floor, walks in silence to the library, and begins a transcendent search for knowledge and truth.[21]

For Mistral, the modernists' evocation of the religious imagination did not only offer poetics but actually hewed more closely to the worldviews of the rural campesinos in her classrooms than to the philosophers of the atheistic Radical Party. By traversing these distinctive worlds, Mistral developed a unique mystical perspective in her poetry and prose, alongside her activist commitments. Mistral's poetry grew to become bold and fresh, the stuff of both earth (salt, the feet of babies, hunger, pine) and spirit (God, mourning, loss, lovesickness, the Psalms, the cross). By the early 1920s, Mistral was a rising star in the intellectual and artistic circles of South America, and her poems were read in Europe and even the United States. In Mexico, she worked closely with Palma Guillén (who became her closest companion and possible lover for many years), who was "a devout Catholic with commitments to the poor."[22] During Christmastime of 1922, Mistral and Guillén worked as organizers in Michoacán, a village in southern Mexico populated with devout peasants who later engaged in an armed uprising against the state's attempt to suppress the Catholic Church in their region. Mistral denounced "the stupid and empty persecution going on in Mexico," which she saw as the "reverse of medieval fanaticism. . . . Catholicism, the religion of 12 million inhabitants, is being persecuted in acts of violence that aim at tearing a huge Indian and Spanish population from their faith."[23]

This setting of face-to-face contact with the lived piety of the Mexican indigenous and Spanish-descended campesinos led Mistral to start writing her own poetic hagiographies of saints committed to the sick and the poor, like Saint Francis and Vasco de Quiroga, a sixteenth-century Franciscan whose story was loved by the indigenous peasant communities she lived among in Mexico. She and Guillén recognized the power of popular devotion and worked with the community on education reform through oral storytelling and religious narrative.[24] Sometime in this period, Mistral began identifying herself as a Catholic, returning to the faith in which she was born, though always with caveats ("I'm Catholic but without hatred or narrowness,"[25] or, "I have a very personal conception when it comes to religion. That is to say that I'm not dogmatic and I speak to God *muy a mi manera*"[26]). At the time in Latin America, the Catholic Church was a force of conformism and conservatism; faith and justice were worlds apart. "But I believe," she wrote, "that Christianity, but with a profound social sensibility, can save the people."[27]

In 1925, she began theorizing new ways to think about the relationship between religion and social change. "Those interested in social justice," she argued, "have not understood religion. . . . A faith which has nourished so many generations cannot be so be easily uprooted." She claimed it was time for a new "sharp analysis" of the role religion played in how society is structured economically and politically. She explained,

> Our form of Christianity has divorced itself from the social question, indeed has even disdained it, and has held a paralyzed or dead sense of justice, until this sense has risen up in others and has taken the Church's following way. Catholicism must regain what, either by neglect or selfishness, she has lost, and this will be possible if Catholics show that they are capable of the very essence of her teaching. The hunger for justice awakened in the people cannot be satisfied by a few meager concessions. . . . If we are to be whole-hearted Christians, we will go to the people. Our religion must not restrict itself to mere worship.[28]

Mistral's 1925 plea in South America was for Catholics to take up the social question on behalf of those struggling, not merely through charity but through agrarian and educational reform. She called for a church pressed in closer to the actual lives of the campesinos, ideas that anticipate the concerns later raised by progressive Catholic theologians and philosophers in Europe in the 1930s–50s (those Gerd-Rainer Horn called the "First Wave" of the Catholic Left) and liberation theologies in Latin America in the late

1960s–80s.[29] But in 1925, when Mistral penned these words, Jacques Maritain, widely considered a forerunner of the Catholic Left, was still a member of the Far-Right organization Action française, Gustavo Gutiérrez, the Peruvian priest called the father of liberation theology, was not yet born, and the Second Vatican Council was forty years away.

In 1925, Mistral retired from her teaching post in Chile. In the following year, she moved to France for a position with a League of Nations subcommittee, the Paris-based Institute for International Intellectual Cooperation, and she would stay in Europe until World War II, first in Paris, then Madrid, Italy, and then back again to France. Mistral's work constantly pushed against nationalistic and isolationist trends: in the context of her work at the Institute for International Intellectual Cooperation, she oversaw the translation and publication of Latin American authors into French and French writers into Spanish. Her own prose, including more than eight hundred articles and speeches, consistently promoted Spanish-, French-, and English-speaking writers for international readership.

In Europe, Mistral's Catholicism drew closer to the mystical and poetic dimension of faith. Mistral discovered in Spain in particular those she called the "wild ones" of the Catholic tradition. One of these was Teresa of Ávila, with whom she became fascinated with on a brief visit to Spain in 1924: "I have once again embraced the living flame of the Catholic faith. I have come to warm myself in the hearth of my Spanish mystics."[30] She wrote a long dreamscape essay in which she imagines Teresa leading her by the hand, both of them barefoot, through the rocky landscape of Castile, in north-central Spain. Likewise in the 1920s, Mistral visited Italy, the land of Saint Francis, and in Assisi she decided to become a Franciscan oblate, announcing shortly after her retirement from teaching in Chile in the following year: "I'm Catholic and belong to the Third Order of St Francis, but I'm free. It's an order for free Catholics. I have, of course, duties. For example, I should give at least ten percent of all I earn, and other things."[31] As a Franciscan oblate, Mistral wrote to a friend that she found herself moving away from her older sense of family and thinking instead about friendship. Perhaps she was inspired by hagiographies of Saint Francis, who famously rejected his biological family and created a spiritual one in which kin included Clare of Assisi and even "Brother Sun," "Sister Bodily Death."[32] Mistral wrote the year she became Franciscan:

> Human beings came into this world only to learn everything and to improve by way of love, friendship, and pity. All else is extra: culture,

social life, ingenuity, good taste, a comfortable house, cities. The meaning of friendship is much more difficult than love or charity, more prodigious for me every day. . . . To defend the ones whom one loves, to ameliorate their lives, to communicate to them the news of the soul, so that they can have as much as they can of an inner life, to consolidate each one in another and to give sustenance in turn. The old sense of the family has moved away from me: instead it is intimate friendship.[33]

Mistral's sense here is not that faith is merely shared among friends but that spiritual life itself is enacted intersubjectively: communion among friends ensures that *each can have as much as they can of an inner life.* Friendship became increasingly important as an anchor in Mistral's life of exile and constant transition. Mistral changed homes sometimes as often as every few weeks, depending on her writing projects, her sense of safety, and, eventually in the 1930s, the war zone delineations in Europe. Later in life, Mistral reflected to Doris Dana that amid so much exile and uprootedness, "One can't live without friends."[34]

Throughout this period, her friendship networks included other mystically inclined artists and diasporic intellectuals, Catholic antifascists, fellow exiles, travelers, and international émigrés with whom she maintained a steady correspondence. She began several collaborations with left-leaning activists who were open to religion, including Henri Bergson, with whom she worked closely in Paris. In interwar Paris, Mistral found many other artists and writers like her who lived their lives in disjunction from the mainstream norms available for women at the time.

Because of her far-flung network of correspondents and her extensive contacts with diplomats, journalists, and other writers, Mistral was keenly aware that within all the mystical beauty of the Spanish and Italian countryside, Far-Right ideologies of xenophobia and authoritarianism were gaining ascendency. In 1924, she arrived in Italy shortly after Mussolini's Brownshirts assassinated a young senator, the leader of the opposition. She was horrified, writing that fascism pervaded the cultural and journalistic institutions throughout Europe. Mistral wrote her friend Victoria Ocampo in the early 1930s, "Fascism will befall South America if it wins in Spain. And it looks like it's winning, Vic. So it's a matter of beginning, right now, to stave off the white plague (fascism) invented by the whites, who are making a disgrace of their famous Europe."[35] These factors together—antifascism, internationalism, a mystically attuned faith, and a focus on friendships—would all combine to make Jacques Maritain a bracing, ideal match for Mistral.

SPIRITUAL FRIENDSHIP AT MEUDON

While we do not know for certain how Maritain and Mistral met, it was likely in May of 1935 in Portugal, where they were both invited by the Salazar government. Mistral's friend Esther de Cáceres once described the scene of this meeting: in Portugal, Jacques approached Mistral, who was sitting alone at a government party for writers, and said to her, "I think neither you nor I know what we are doing here."[36] A momentous friendship then began for each of them, a typical story for Maritain: he was incredibly talented at finding all sorts of elite but somewhat misfit writers and artists with anti-bourgeois sensibilities, gathering them together, developing with them a shared political, spiritual, and intellectual purpose, and pulling them into his vortex. When Mistral traveled to Paris in 1937 for several large conferences, she sought out Jacques, and they started to collaborate on their common antifascist commitments.[37]

It makes sense that they would click. While they were from different parts of the world, as young adults, Mistral and both Jacques and his wife Raïssa Maritain had all encountered similar cultural material and come to similar conclusions. All three warmed to religion after passing through a phase of disillusionment with the atheism of leftist political activism. Through a kind of bohemian, anti-bourgeois, mystical modernism—with inspiration from Tolstoy and Dostoyevsky, Bloy, the modernist takes on medieval saints and mystics, and serious engagement with Bergson—they all turned officially to Catholicism as adults.[38] Neither the Maritains nor Mistral became typical Catholic parishioners when they converted, each instead expressing their piety more radically, with more intense and fervent commitment that remained somewhat off-center from the institutional powers of Rome. Gabriela Mistral was a third-order Franciscan oblate, and the Maritains had become lay Benedictines in 1911. They were also all attuned to the lived piety and spirituality of those on the margins. For the Maritains, attention to the lives of the poor was owed mostly to the witness and writings of their beloved godfather, Léon Bloy.[39] All three were aware of the dangers of fascism and anti-Semitism long before most Catholics in Europe would acknowledge the rise of the Far Right's xenophobia. Raïssa was a Jewish convert to Catholicism, and Mistral in later life also claimed some Jewish ancestry on her paternal grandfather's side. Both sought in their own writings to advance a kind of Catholicism attuned to its Jewish roots.[40] The three friends were interested as well in a Catholicism that directly engaged Latin

Christianity's rich artistic and aesthetic traditions. Jacques's 1920 *Art and Scholasticism* was a revival of Thomist aesthetics, exploring the fundamental link between faith and art for a new generation. Raïssa, like Gabriela, wrote as a Catholic poet, and the two women shared a similar style, their poems focusing on vivid, concrete detail, a kind of aesthetic realism. They were Catholics, but remained apart from the mainstream institutional faith at the time: this marginality additionally contextualized their antifascist commitments and condemnations of Franco, who was supported by the vast majority of Spanish bishops.

In the summer of 1937, shortly before leaving for an extended tour of South America designed to promote sympathy for the situations of Republican Spain and refugee children, Gabriela Mistral went to the Maritains' famous salon in their home in Meudon. One of Mistral's letters to the Maritains ended with "save me a room at Meudon," and she was almost certainly among the few close friends who stayed after the larger crowds left for more intimate discussion and overnight respite.[41] "This was where my soul was most full, in your house that is now empty," she reminisced to Jacques in 1947.[42] Right away, Mistral seems to have understood their friendship and her connection to their salon in religious terms. Mistral called their salon at Meudon that "supernatural group," which was the most "saving, redeeming" of everything among her activism and writing in the interwar period.[43] Early on in their friendship, both the Maritains and Mistral spoke about and to one another, and of their bond, in religious terms. In 1939, Jacques wrote, "May God bless you dear Gabriela! Believe in our great friendship!"[44] That phrase—*grande amitié*—would become central to the life of the couple, words that Raïssa chose as the title of her memoirs published three years later.

We can imagine the scene Mistral encountered going to the Maritains' salon: when guests would take the train to this small village on the outskirts of Paris, they were greeted by a married couple, Jacques and Raïssa. But part of the Maritains' allure was that they did not represent a bourgeois or conservative Catholic notion of reproductive matrimony—there was something unusual about their domestic arrangements. The Maritains were married in 1904; however, in 1912, after they became Benedictine oblates, they took a vow of celibacy they held for the remaining forty-eight years of their marriage, a loving relationship that ended only after Raïssa's death. They never had children. The notion of forgoing sex in a marriage for higher ideals such as the love of God was at the time called a *mariage blanc*. Most of the intellectuals in this network were highly skeptical of both Protestantism and the secular state, as they saw in Protestantism a compulsion toward marriage and reproductive sexuality that was in direct opposition to the Catholic monastic and clerical ideal. Martin Luther's theology of sexuality and marriage was a main target of Jacques Maritain's passionate critiques in *Three Reformers: Luther, Descartes, Rousseau*, written in 1928, sixteen years into his and Raïssa's vow of celibacy.[45] For Luther, "be fruitful and multiply" was more than a command from God; it was a divine ordinance built into our very selves, as impossible to overcome as the need for sleep, and the celibacy of monks and nuns was "wretched by its very nature."[46]

To understand how the Maritains would have been viewed as counter-cultural, even in a Catholic country like France, it is worth noting that in the 1930s, the primacy of the reproductive, nuclear family in western Europe was moving away from a largely Protestant ideal and closer to the center of Catholic identity, particularly among conservative Catholics. James Chappel's work has shown that in this context most Catholic intellectuals and activists had finally accepted that a fully Catholic state in Europe was no longer an option; there was no going back to a state under the control of religion. The church had to acquiesce to secular rule of law, but they accepted that secular law could be respected so long as it promoted the rights of the Catholic "private sphere." States could have their own autonomy, provided that the Catholic family and Catholic teachings about the family were secured into law.[47] The church, according to this logic, should focus on the primacy and protection of the heteronormative family by banning abortion, contraception, divorce, and homosexuality. For Chappel, this was a way for Catholics to carve out a particularly Catholic way of being modern—which by this time was more and more centered on the promotion of the procreative marital unit.

The Maritains offered a stark and explicit alternative to these fixations.[48] In contrast to the sexually reproductive matrimonial ideal, the Maritains instead formed what they called *le petit troupeau* (a little flock) of three, made up of Raïssa, her sister Vera, and Jacques. Though Raïssa and Jacques were married, their household preserved something of an ideal of revolt—a kind of monastic community in the middle of the twentieth century set in the world, not in the cloister. Gabriela Mistral was one of the many people who came to Meudon with similarly unusual domestic arrangements. Mistral was still living with Palma Guillén and in 1929 had accepted responsibility for a toddler whom she affectionately nicknamed Yin-Yin, claiming that he was the child of her half-brother and raising him with Guillén. Elizabeth Horan describes Yin-Yin as a "shadowy figure in his short lifetime," noting that Mistral and Guillén "maintained his existence as something of a secret, mentioning him only to closest friends."[49] The scene was cultivated and cultured, and kids were absent or in the shadows like Yin-Yin. Many other guests at Meudon also led lives in explicit contrast to the ideals of heterosexual reproductive matrimony.

There was a quiet queer vibe at Meudon. But in their memories of the salon they hosted in Meudon, friends commented on the Maritains' relationship as a sort of holy contagion to guests. As Jean Cocteau described in his memoir, "So shy when he was 'officiating alone,' Jacques Maritain acquired next to Raïssa and Vera a surprising magnetism, as if the ardor of his wife and sister-in-law had the power to inflame his gentle, vibrant soul."[50] Ignited by one another, the Maritains somehow kindled the religious lives of countless men and women who came to their home. While some were inspired more by one partner in particular, and others by the couple together, people's attachment to them was the indisputable fuel for countless people's faith. The Maritains kept up elaborate correspondences, lavishing attention on their friends, especially religious seekers, and innumerable people converted or returned to Catholicism through friendship with the Maritains. It must have been intense. Jacques and Raïssa were the godparents to seventy-eight individuals, most of which were adult baptisms.[51] The French writer Julien Green explained to Jacques: "For me as for so many others, you have been God's friend and witness. You have helped souls, whom perhaps you don't even know. . . . It is in great measure due to you that I have kept the Faith."[52] Later in his life, after decades of friendship with Maritain, Green confessed, "It is God Who has placed us on one another's path, so that you might speak to me, and speak to me in His place. Of that I am very sure."[53] For people like Green, communication with Jacques Maritain was not about religious experience. Instead their correspondence *enacted* it. For the Maritains too, this feeling was mutual. Their lives as Christians cannot be understood, Raïssa once wrote, apart from the "precious spiritual help" they received from "those who have been intimately associated with us by friendship."[54] When the young Maurice Sachs described his attraction to the church in 1925, it was his friendship with Raïssa above all that generated a real inner experience of something transcendent. As he got to know Raïssa, Sachs admitted to her, "I felt an electricity go through my body and redirect my life." He continued: "May God let me always be among you! Perpetually surround me, my soon to be godmother! When I think of you I am filled with joy, and I came to God because I was at a dead end—but I pushed myself forward. I think the goodness of our Lord wanted me to LOVE, even in all my unworthiness, and I did this through you, through Jean [Cocteau], through the calm of your house."[55]

At Meudon, something transcendent was sensed by seekers to come *directly* from the Maritains "through [the] body" and transformed their friends. These inner experiences (feeling electrified, filled with joy, or capable of love) were made possible only through sustained, intersubjective encounters. The Maritains did not point to holy power; they were carriers of it.

But they were also subtle communicators of a message about friendship. When guests came to their salon, the material setting of their home directly communicated the religious power of friendship: framed photos of friends were grouped with frames of recognizable holy figures—Thomas Aquinas, Teresa of Ávila, the pope.[56] Jacques and Raïssa had special permission to have a chapel in their house as well, where friends gathered to pray. In Raïssa's devotional study, she had books by and about her friends, paintings of friends, even a religious medallion she had made out of the face of her friend and beloved godfather, Léon Bloy, all carefully set among traditional devotional objects: saints' cards, a missal, a Bible, and a crucifix.[57] Raïssa clarifies in her memoir, "Our friendships were part of our life, our life explains our friendships." This included both face-to-face friends as well as the medieval saints, like Thomas Aquinas, to whom the Maritains "became attached, as a real friend."[58]

When reading Gabriela Mistral's correspondence and memoirs of her collaboration with the Maritains, it is clear that Jacques was a person to whom she was deeply bonded, rather than someone whose ideas simply influenced her as a philosopher.[59] In the context of their relationship, Mistral felt and remained "Catholic," though she sensed herself to be utterly on the margins of the institutional church. Jacques, who was much closer to the church hierarchy than Mistral, perhaps helped incarnate the poetic, visionary faith that Mistral envisioned in her dreamlike prose and poetry. In a 1938 letter to Maritain, she described her friend Palma to him in a way that would have been an apt description for herself: "I feel that she remains distant from official and clerical Catholicism, but that she doesn't abandon her faith. She reads you with discipline and venerates you."[60]

After winning the Nobel Prize in Literature in 1945, Mistral stated in an interview that "Jacques Maritain was the one who exerted an especially great influence on me, for the meaning that he gives to Christianity. . . . I returned to Catholicism because of Bergson and above all, Maritain."[61] Years later, Mistral wrote to her friend Victoria Ocampo, the Argentinian writer, "Jacques Maritain seems almost a saint, to me, and at any rate, a soul capable of saving and an extraordinary guide. . . . What a relief and a pleasure to know that, ceaselessly, humanity produced these beings, and they are within our reach during great crises."[62] Mistral confessed to Ocampo that

she thought of Maritain every day, ever since they met. Ocampo wrote similarly of Jacques several years later, in 1952:

> Gabriela asks me how I feel about religion. I answer:
>
> When I see a man like Maritain, or rather when I am around him,
> in the atmosphere of his royal presence (not when I read him, his books
> appeal to my intellect in a way that doesn't change my spiritual tempera-
> ture and thus doesn't lend itself to germination), I say to myself the words
> of Pascal, "Joie, pleurs de joie," Joy, tears of joy. How could this way of
> living his life, his habit of demanding everything of himself and nothing
> of his neighbor be the fruit of a misguided idea? Or a false conception of
> what the Eternal One (this is how I most like to refer to God) is? Is it pos-
> sible that an exemplary human being as admirable as Maritain can build
> his beliefs on foundations that are totally or partially false, feeble? How
> could his interpretation of mystery produce such results?[63]

Ocampo and Mistral clearly drew from traditions of sainthood to interpret Maritain as a carrier of the holy, but there was a long genealogy of Catholic spiritual friendship that was slightly distinct from which this community drew and amplified. *Amitié spirituelle* was a medieval Christian ideal,
drawing from scriptures on the example of Matthew's and Mark's Jesus,
who "demanded a readiness to forsake marriage and family" (Mt. 10:37),
and given articulation by the twelfth-century Cistercian Aelred of Rievaulx
in *Spiritual Friendship*, which defined human friendship as sacramental.[64]
Throughout the medieval and early modern periods in Christian history,
friendship in particular provided a rich alternative for spiritually significant
intimacy outside of the nuclear family for monks and nuns.[65] Alan Bray's
book *The Friend* presents the most graphic image of spiritual friendship's
persistence from medieval Catholicism to early modernity: priests who had
been close friends in life wanted to lie together in death and share a grave,
like John Henry Newman and his friend Ambrose St. John.[66] The Maritains'
Catholicism was thoroughly neo-medieval, even as it was immersed with
concerns of the twentieth century, and they lived out these monastic ideals
not in the monastery but in the world.

But it was the Maritains' godfather, the writer Léon Bloy, who laid the
groundwork for the ideological edifice within which friendship itself would
be enshrined as holy among laypeople in the twentieth century, away from a
monastic context. He gave the boldest articulation and most fervent encouragement of this sensibility. This was due in part to the powerful affective

responses his own writings evoked, but his deliberate fostering of networks of friendship and spiritual kinship when the Maritains were younger held an even greater influence. These groups included a close circle of godchildren and friends and, even more importantly, a huge international community of readers who *imagined* themselves inhabiting Bloy's personal orbit of intimacy, even long after he died. All of this was despite the fact that Bloy himself—as a person and in his writings—could come across as harsh and disparaging. As the novelist Georges Bernanos once described Bloy, "For thousands of men the world over, this old man is a friend. No one, it would seem, has sought out friendship less than he; rather, he essentially discouraged it, stumped it, he often challenged it, provoked it with a sort of righteous anger, the way a believer blasphemes the God he adores."[67]

Included among Léon Bloy's close circle of *amis* were the Maritains and the Dutch artist Pierre van der Meer de Walcheren, who in 1920 published his memoir, a vivid pilgrimage to meet Bloy, whose novels he had long admired. When Walcheren confessed to Bloy his own spiritual dissatisfaction and inquietude, Bloy advised Walcheren that the first step for the religious seeker was to leave one's blood family to forge a *nouvelle famille spirituelle* based on friendship. Bloy volunteered to be Walcheren's godfather and "give him a brother and sister also," referring to Jacques and Raïssa Maritain, who were by that time within Bloy's intimate circle. They, too, were his godchildren and had converted under Bloy's influence in 1905.[68] Walcheren accepted, and he remembered these years of "strong spiritual kinship" as a period of "spiritual initiation" into Christianity. Bloy was a recluse and a writer on the fringe of society, but he abhorred the violence of the state, war, and nationalistic forms of identity. The spiritual families Bloy cultivated were deliberately international to counter notions of identity based on homogeneous bonds of blood or nation. Walcheren was from the Netherlands, his wife was Dutch, Raïssa was Russian, and he and Jacques were French. As Bloy attested, "From the point of view of friendship these years were like the Acts of the Apostles."[69] This language of a "core spiritual family" was one whose purpose was "initiation into the profound gifts of Christianity" and enabled, at least for Walcheren, the "discovery of new and luminous treasures."[70] The internationalism of spiritual families would be developed much further by Mistral and the Maritains.

Bloy rendered Christianity for his friends as something "real, living, not a jumble of misleading words, not just a dream, or a rule of conduct." Through sustained, intimate friendship with Bloy, "apparently life was as it was before," Walcheren recalled, "but everything was transformed. It was extraordinary! Every idea, every attitude, inner or outer, every action, even the most common and daily activity, was totally different. All things now had meaning, and operated in a climate far more exhilarating and more real."[71] Bloy's friends did not simply learn *about* Christianity from their mentor; by interiorizing the dispositions of their new friend in a deliberate and deeply desired way, they could better apprehend and materialize the religion.

Beyond the publication of Walcheren's memoir, the rest of the world witnessed the affective intensities that circulated among the Bloys, the Maritains, and the Walcherens in 1926, when Bloy's widow Jeanne published the intimate correspondence within this spiritual family in a collection entitled *Lettres à ses filleuls* (Letters to his godchildren). Jacques Maritain described the publication of this correspondence as "painful," something he "never would have dreamed of publishing." It was to "surrender to the public the secrets of a friendship that one thought was reserved for the sight of God alone."[72] But Bloy's widow asked them to do so, and both Maritain and Walcheren reluctantly agreed. These letters laid bare for readers an affectively, even erotically charged community that inculcated religious sensibilities: in the pages of *Lettres à ses filleuls*, Bloy exclaims to Raïssa only three months after meeting her, "Oh Raïssa! Do you know what a friend you are to me? I want to die while thinking of it!"[73] The Maritains and Walcherens fawned over their godfather with almost as much intensity, thanking him for "awakening the evangelical spirit," "representing the doctrine of God," and teaching them to "love Love." (This notion of friends teaching the Maritains' to "love Love" [*aimer l'Amour*] appears throughout their correspondence.)[74] Readers found something oddly universal and appealing about these highly personal accounts of lavish affection. When reading these letters, Thomas Merton recalled being moved to tears, feeling that "I too am somehow of the family of Bloy."[75] Julien Green had met Jacques in 1925, and the letters published in *Lettres à ses filleuls* a year later deepened Green's own growing affective attachment to him: "The letters that Léon Bloy wrote to you and your wife have made it possible for me to know you better and love you all the more. I want you to know that I think of you often, every day and several times a day, and what you say to me always has a great importance in my eyes."[76] Georges Bernanos, who never met Bloy personally, experienced something similar when he discovered Bloy's writings years after Bloy died yet considered himself among Bloy's "friends, if not his disciples, in the very least one of his godchildren in the same sense as Maritain or Van Der Meer." At the close of World War II, while exiled in Brazil, Bernanos wrote the essay "L'amitié Léon Bloy" (Friendship with Léon Bloy), dedicated to "friends of

Bloy, I write this only for them. Friends of Bloy the world over."[77] Raïssa also reprinted some of Bloy's letters to them in her memoir, which make it clear that the spiritual friendships were just as transformative to him as to his new spiritual kin: "I have never seen anything more astonishing than your dear friendships, Jacques and Raïssa, you who give us your heart, as one gives blood to Our Lord Jesus Christ."[78]

For many others in the world of the *renouveau catholique*, Bloy's charismatic power for friendship transferred to his godchildren, Jacques and Raïssa Maritain. The Maritains' gift in shaping the religious sensorium of their friends certainly stems from their early formation in Bloy's *famille spirituelle*, but Jacques and Raïssa each had their own unique gifts in the arts of emotional intimacy. Their encouragement and willingness to take on their friends' sorrow and pain in addition to, crucially, their antifascist and international solidarities enabled the Maritains to bring Bloy's model of spiritual friendship into new, more eclectic and global directions. They took this neo-medieval notion of spiritual friendship and tethered it to an emerging engagement with the project of antifascism, which connected them to a much wider range of exiles, resisters, writers, and political activists on the left, a world that differed greatly from that of their godfather.

MEUDON AND LATIN AMERICANS IN PARIS

Between 1920 and 1955, Paris "became," according to Denis Pelletier and Jean-Louis Schlegel, "a laboratory of choice for an innovative Catholicism at all levels: intellectual, theological, and apostolic."[79] Yet I have come to see that it was the *internationalism* in Paris at the time that was so important to this moment of Catholic creativity.[80] This helps explain the context of the Maritains' friendship with Gabriela Mistral. As a Chilean consul and major figure within the Latin American diaspora, Gabriela Mistral was close to many Spanish-speaking intellectuals who came to Paris in the 1930s, and she introduced many of them to the Maritains.[81] Latin American intellectuals with whom Mistral collaborated had fled violence and authoritarian regimes in their homelands. "Only in France could these friends speak so freely," Elizabeth Horan explains. "The rise of military and other dictatorships made Paris into an epicenter of a transnational, Spanish-speaking republic of letters."[82] It was in France where many Spanish speakers from very different countries—Spain, Argentina, Uruguay, Chile—found one another and connected around the salon and work of the Maritains, including Victoria Ocampo, Esther de Cáceres, and Eduardo Frei, along with Mistral.

The town of Meudon itself was actually a center of Russian immigration: Raïssa and Vera spoke Russian at home, and their house was a welcome salon for émigrés from eastern Europe and Russia. This transcontinental atmosphere must have made it an inviting place for Spanish speakers who found themselves in Paris, fellow outsiders like their hostess Raïssa. The widespread orientalist exoticism in interwar Paris also made Meudon's internationalism more alluring, endowing foreigners like Mistral and Raïssa with an exotic, primitivist gravitas in the bohemian circuit. Waldo Frank recalled Mistral as "a great dark woman wandering through Europe and always bearing Chile, a mysterious treasure in her fragile hand."[83] People spoke of Raïssa, a Russian-born Jew who spoke French as a second language, in similarly exotic terms.

The Maritains were especially eager to connect Catholics from Spain and the Spanish colonies, who had a greater inside perspective on Franco's impact in the Spanish-speaking world. By the 1930s, the Spanish Civil War was at the center of urgent concerns for Jacques. Spain's war seemed to him a "prophetic dream" of what would happen in the rest of Europe and, eventually, Latin America.[84] Mistral was of a similar mind: the Spanish war was an ominous catastrophe. Because this war was cast as the anticlerical communists on the left against the Catholic Franco on the right, most Catholics supported Franco, despite his alliance with Hitler and his regime's fascism, anti-Semitism, and authoritarianism, not to mention the incredible violence Franco had unleashed on his own citizens. In the spring of 1934, Jacques Maritain prepared lectures that might enable Catholics to imagine resisting Franco's fascism, even though he was allegedly Catholic and on the side of the priests. Maritain's lectures focused on new Christian humanism, and he delivered them in Spain at the University of Salamanca. There he conceptualized an implicitly Christian order of politics that takes the side of the poor, fights economic injustice, and protects the rights of minorities in a pluralistic society. These speeches were all published as articles and included in Jacques's *Integral Humanism*, which became known as a pro-democratic, Catholic manifesto against fascism and authoritarianism.

Jacques's ideas about a Christian philosophy that could ward off fascism compelled Spanish speakers from Latin America like Mistral, Ocampo, and Frei. Stemming the tide of European fascism was increasingly *the* urgent issue, and by 1935, Mistral was (rightly) worried that fascism in Spain would next set its sights on the Spanish-speaking world of Latin America. Mistral

used her considerable network with the Institute for International Intellectual Cooperation to disseminate Jacques Maritain's conception of a Catholic
democracy in Spanish-speaking regions in the global south. Mistral's friend
Victoria Ocampo was an ideal person to oversee the publication of Jacques's
thoughts in Latin America, since she was a highly educated Argentinian,
fluent in French, at ease with the Maritains, and leaned politically left. She
was also a wealthy philanthropist who had founded the cosmopolitan, Francophile, leftist literary journal *Sur* in Buenos Aires.[85] Mistral introduced the
Maritains to Ocampo in Paris, who arranged the Maritains' first visit to Latin
America, where they both lectured widely, Raïssa on aesthetics and Jacques
on his "Carta sobre la independencia." In 1937, *Sur* published two key essays
of Jacques's from his new 1936 book *Integral Humanism*—"Sobre la guerra
santa" and "Con el pueblo: Nuevo humanism."[86] In "Con el pueblo," which
talked about how war impacts the poor, Maritain insisted that to win over
the working classes from Marxism, Catholics needed real relationships with
them: "Before 'doing good' *to* them, and working *for* their benefit, we must
for choose to exist *with* them and to suffer with them, to make their pain and
their destiny our own." Echoing the ideas on social Christianity that Mistral
had described in the 1920s, Maritain insisted that most Catholics are far
from this kind of solidarity. Those "to which we give the name Christian,"
he continued, "fail to exist in this way *with* the people. The strength of the
socialists and the communists comes less from their ideology than from
the fact that they exist with the people, they bind themselves to them. But
whoever wants to replace in real life the errors of their ideology with a true
vision of things must first exist with the people."[87]

  This realism as a way into the "people" resonated with Mistral most of all.
"We believe," Mistral wrote to a mutual friend in 1937, as her bond with the
Maritains deepened, "with St Thomas, in what is seen and touched. . . . We
have faith in what we make, in what we do, enjoy, suffer, faith in *reality*."[88]
The following year, Mistral's second book of poetry, *Tala* (Harvesting), was
published, and she donated all proceeds to the children orphaned in the
Spanish Civil War.

  Together, Mistral, Jacques Maritain, and Ocampo gradually steered the
journal *Sur*, which had been primarily literary in focus and had an editorial
board evenly balanced between left- and right-wing writers, toward taking on unequivocal antifascist and philo-Semitic stances, commitments it
would hold until its last regular issue in 1970.[89] The evolution of this position
merits note: In the early era of the journal, the key transatlantic issue was
warding *off* European xenophobia and Far-Right ideology from the shores

of the global south and advancing the ideals of a democratic, social alternative. By publishing Jacques Maritain in particular, according to historian
John King, *Sur* became linked to a "radical Catholic tradition, an anathema
to many members of what in Argentina at the time was a very traditional,
Spanish Catholic Church."[90] *Sur* thus established itself as the Catholic progressive alternative to more traditional Catholic Argentine journals like *Cri-
terio*. Thanks to their efforts, *Sur* also became the most important site for the
Spanish translation of key French Catholic intellectuals, including Jacques
Maritain, Emmanuel Mounier, Marie-Magdeleine Davy, and later Michel
de Certeau, disseminating their thinking throughout South America. The
motive for this distribution, however, was less focused on importing the
French Left into the global south and more on summoning an unambiguously international counter-narrative to the Far Right's narrow nationalism,
which was ecumenical and broadly humanistic in scope and included theologians, critics, poets, philosophers, and novelists from countries throughout the Americas and Europe. Spanish speakers from South America and
Spain published French Catholics' essays side by side, and English speakers were also included. *Sur* printed work from writers as diverse as Jack
Kerouac, Jean-Paul Sartre, Octavio Paz, Mistral herself, Jorge Luis Borges,
and Miguel de Unamuno.

As Mistral and Ocampo helped promote and distribute Jacques's ideas
in Argentina and Chile, Mistral also introduced another intellectual who
would become important for French–Latin American collaborations among
the Catholic Left: the Uruguayan poet and medical doctor Esther de Cáceres, who Mistral brought to Meudon in the late 1930s. The spiritual charisma
of the Maritains drew Cáceres in just as it had effected Mistral. She later
recalled, "The order, the lucidity, and the depth shone in the majestic and
simple presence of Raïssa. This is how I remember her in that house in
Meudon, open to all the pilgrims; the house in whose serene scene, presided
over by the images of Saint Thomas and Charles de Foucauld, silenced all
anguish and distracting noise from the outside."[91] When Cáceres returned to
Uruguay from Paris, she established the Centro Jacques Maritain in Montevideo in 1937, and in August 1938, she lectured in Montevideo on the topic
of the value of Jacques' Maritain's philosophy and published extensively on
Maritain. Friendship was key to these actions. Cáceres created the Asociación de Amigos de Léon Bloy in 1940, and she hosted a salon at her home
in Montevideo, where they talked about "psychoanalysis, religion, Maritain,
and Bauhaus."[92] The Argentinian scholar María Laura Picón describes the
world that the Maritains, Mistral, Ocampo, and Cáceres shared: "They wove

a complex network in which the threads of world politics, friendship and social commitment intermingled."[93]

It wasn't only that Jacques Maritain had spiritual charisma, but in this atmosphere, spiritual friendship was sensed as shared and spread among many others. Gabriela Mistral wrote the preface to one of Cáceres's books of poetry in 1941, three years after they met in Paris and developed their own spiritual friendship, beyond the Maritains. "Although for years I knew nothing about Esther de Cáceres," Mistral states, "it was some force, some nourishing element of her being, came to me from her. I know that, quiet or epistolary, close or distant, I am within her prayer when my pain arrives."[94] Mistral did not only sense that her spiritual friend prayed for her, but rather she saw herself *within* Cáceres's prayer. Like so many in this network, when describing the religious nature of their *amistad*, Mistral drew from metaphors of fire. Cáceres has "half a forest" capable of supplying "the embers of affection for our own souls."[95] Indeed, the Maritains created an atmosphere that resonated deeply with Mistral and their other visitors, who soaked it in, taking it with them throughout their travels and sharing it with others. The Maritains helped set in motion a worldview and sensibility that eventually extended beyond themselves, the bonds spreading out and entangling with many others.

In addition to Ocampo and Cáceres, Mistral's introduction of the Chilean lawyer and eventual president of Chile Eduardo Frei to Jacques Maritain was also significant. Mistral met Frei in Madrid sometime in 1934, and they became friends. By 1938, they engaged in constant communication about the Maritains and what Mistral called *maritenisme* as a resource for resisting the Catholic alliance with the politics of the Far Right. The collaboration between Frei and Jacques Maritain is fairly well known to scholars of modern Catholicism, but less well known is the fact that their friendship was formed entirely by Gabriela Mistral. As Frei's granddaughter notes, "Art, philosophy, and politics, intertwine in a unique, mysterious way in the spiritual communion that bound these three [Frei, Jacques Maritain, and Mistral]."[96] Frei, too, had traveled to Paris, where he took classes under Jacques at the Institut Catholique in 1933. The teacher and student did not initially develop any particularly close bond, but after Frei learned that his friend Mistral knew Jacques, he felt bold enough to ask her, "If you could get a portrait with his signature for me. Don't think I have a habit of collecting autographs, but he has had so much influence on my thought and life." She ignored him; he asked again. "If you see Maritain, Get me his picture with his signature! I don't collect autographs, but I need to have the image of a man who I love so much, and who has exerted so much influence among us."[97] Mistral eventually agreed and introduced Jacques Maritain to Frei, the beginning of an important, decades-long sensual, platonic, spiritual friendship. Frei counted Jacques among the most significant influences on his political thought. In Frei's private study, he had two framed photos, one of Jacques and one of Gabriela, mounted on his wall and separated by a large, bronze crucifix. Many people in this community shared and circulated photos of Jacques. The friendship bonds were remarkably intense, sensual, and erotic. In his memoir, Frei describes an evening in 1950 in New York outside the embassy in Chile, when he and Maritain were saying goodbyes and talking about their gratitude for their bond, even their love, and Maritain took Frei's face in his hands and kissed him.[98]

The dissemination of Jacques's ideas throughout Latin America was fueled by spiritual friendship. It is impossible to understand the staggering internationalization of Jacques Maritain's influence in this period without acknowledging the emotional undercurrent of friendship that powered it. The women, too, sustained and supported one another intellectually and spiritually, outside of Jacques's aura. Gabriela Mistral was always urging Victoria Ocampo to make time for her books. In 1940, Mistral wrote to Ocampo, "May they give you—may you give yourself some long stretches of peace in order to write. Don't let your life be infested by what they call *the social scene*—ladies who serve tea with almond dainties. Preserve your precious soul for your writing. Protect yourself with the force of courage. Don't delay very much because a book, like an angel, passes from your hands if you don't hold onto it."[99] Later in her life, Raïssa Maritain was thrilled to hear from Esther de Cáceres, who was planning to offer a course in Montevideo on Raïssa's poetry and essays. "Your letter has moved me deeply," Raïssa replied, "and I want to thank you with all my heart. It is a great honor that you're offering a course on my work. I'm a little confused and very excited, and want to express my appreciation. I never believed that I have achieved a 'work,' but voila! My friendships make me a 'work,' and I am so happy you like what I have written."[100]

WARTIME AND POSTWAR FRIENDSHIPS

The fears of the Spanish speakers at Meudon turned out to be prescient. Fascism in Spain was only a test run before it spread throughout western

Europe and launched World War II. When it was clear by 1939 that their communities of resistance would not keep them safe, many of the exiles in Paris fled Europe, and the Maritains left for Canada, as Raïssa was still considered Jewish under Nazi law. Together with Palma Guillén and her thirteen-year-old nephew Yin-Yin, Mistral was evacuated from Nice to Brazil by way of Bordeaux and Lisbon on March 22, 1940. Georges Bernanos had already relocated to Brazil, influencing Mistral's decision to move there.[101] Mistral and the Maritains, along with many of their friends, were spread out around the world.

Mistral called herself disparagingly *la descastada* (the wanderer and outcast) or *patiloca* (crazy wanderer) from all her moves, exiles, relocations, and temporary homes.[102] But she was able to take her experiences of exile and displacement and identify with the millions who found themselves fleeing from pogroms, persecutions, and war in the violent twentieth century. In her 1939 poem "Emigrada judía" (The immigrant Jew), Mistral writes:

> I am two. One looks back, the other turns to the sea.
> The nape of my neck seethe with goodbyes and my breast with yearning.
> The stream that flows through my village no longer speaks my name:
> I am erased from my own land and air like a footprint on the sand.[103]

Mistral's "Emigrada judía" is similar to a poem Raïssa Maritain published five years earlier entitled "Chagall," about his painting *White Crucifixion*. Raïssa and Marc Chagall were friends, both Russian Jews who had been exiles in Paris. Raïssa describes the colors and vivid scenes in Chagall's painting of the destruction of Jewry in Russia and Europe, which ends:

> Fire and flame
> Poor Jews everywhere go their way
> No one asks them to stay
> They have no place left on earth
> Not a stone to rest on
> Hence they must lodge at least in heaven
> The wandering Jews
> Whether alive or dead.
> Misery without remedy.[104]

In the poems of both writers, a recurrent theme is human life thrown off course by disaster, a fact that is never abstract but experienced in the lives of particular mothers, fathers, and children. The tensions between systems of violence and the people intractably caught within them are some of Mistral's and Raïssa Maritain's most abiding poetic subjects. The first time Mistral went to their home, she was given the gift of Raïssa Maritain's first book of poetry, and Mistral later called Raïssa her "Señora y hermana en la poesía" (lady and sister in poetry).[105]

As for Raïssa Maritain in the United States, she never learned English and, unlike Jacques, was never was able to replicate the networks she had in Paris. Her wartime writings take on a dreamlike, fantasy quality and are centered almost exclusively on memories of her friends. She began her memoir *Les grandes amitiés* by admitting, "In the present I do not feel that I am present. . . . I turn my thoughts towards my future, towards the future hidden in God and our past life with our friends."[106]

The Maritains carried on a vast correspondence with people who stayed in Europe during the war, especially with the future Cardinal Charles Journet, who remained in Switzerland. Memories of spiritual friendship sustained them in exile. Journet wrote to them in 1940, "Mass at Chartres, St. Anne, St. Pierre together, all of these memories of us, they are like stars in the dark night. Your love has always been that you saw me as God wants me to be. . . . Your kindness is a sweet gift from heaven and I want to become every day less unworthy." In response, Jacques wondered how he and Raïssa could ever explain the joy they received from Journet's letters, letters "that are graces from God, God, who has given us your marvelous friendship." Later, he professed, "You are our consolation, you are Friendship itself, and for us even Love itself." Here the beloved (Journet) is the embodiment of these religiously significant ideals and enables Jacques, through memories and letters, to experience them. For Journet, the feeling was mutual: "I thank you Jacques," he wrote, because through their friendship, Journet could "love Love! I embrace you in this Love!" Not only did religious ideals (Love) circulate within this relationship, but even Jesus became present in these intimate exchanges. Journet, Jacques, and Raïssa regularly signed off their letters with "I embrace you in Jesus Christ" or "Sweet friendship in Jesus."[107] In this tumultuous context, friendships among Catholics, sustained in correspondence, anchored their world and evoked a transcendence that was absent amid Europe's ruins.

Mistral lived in Brazil and confessed how "orphaned" she felt there politically among Catholics. "Help me with about 3 or 4 publication names," she asked Raïssa in a letter, looking for reading that would help offer guidance during the war, since most of South America practiced a "type of Spanish

Catholicism which seems to me the worst sort of Catholicism that I know of." She also asked for Raïssa's prayers and assured her, "I have prayed for you several times, and today especially."[108] From abroad, the relationship turned into something more mutual. "We think of you and we pray for you with deep affection," Jacques wrote Mistral, "and we thank God for the union that has established between us. Pray for us and believe in our faithful and devoted friendship. With all our hearts."[109] Mistral assured them, "Whenever I speak to someone of my poor soul, I tell them about the good I received from Jacques and continue receiving. I keep you [Jacques and Raïssa] a veneration full of tenderness."[110] She closed her letter confessing, "My poor soul is in your hands and hangs on your prayers. Don't forget me." During the war, Mistral would often check libraries of universities and seminaries to see if Jacques's books were there and when needed coordinated with Jacques to physically get his books delivered.[111] Mistral conveyed to him the fact that in Chile there were circles of "maritenistas" and "más o menos maritenistas" that had formed in response to his lectures and articles, young Catholic lawyers and philosophers open to his ideas about democracy and justice.[112] Mistral corresponded regularly with Jacques on the status in Chile of what she called the "vieja Catholicism" of the conservatives and the *maritenistas* of the future.[113] It was also Mistral who kept tabs on the resistance to Jacques's ideas by Far-Right Catholics in Chile, who always painted him as a heretic.[114] In the 1940s, Mistral warned him that Luis Arturo Pérez was Jacques's most vocal attacker, claiming Maritain was not "orthodox" and "filling theaters in Chile" denouncing him.[115]

In Brazil, Mistral's home and garden came to be known as a place frequented by "people from all corners of the world who had fled persecution and chaos," who could "sip tea, listen to their hostess's long, seductive monologues, and forget the atrocities that were devouring the earth."[116] Among Mistral's neighbors in Petrópolis, Brazil, was Stefan Zweig, the famous Austrian Jewish writer who had fled fascism and Nazism first in London and then in South America. By the early 1940s, Zweig grew despondent over the infiltration of violent anti-Semitism and fascism even in Brazil. In 1942, while living in Brazil, Zweig and his young wife died by suicide in despair. At the time, Zweig was the most translated writer in Europe, and their deaths were featured on the front page of the *New York Times*.[117] The day their bodies were discovered, Mistral was among the first to learn of it. She was heartbroken by what these deaths portended for the unknown future of Europe, and she wrote a public letter published in the Argentine newspaper *La Nación* to her friend Eduardo Mallea. "A saner writer," Mistral wrote of Zweig, one more a master of his soul, less insane (although he has described insanity as no one else could, is perhaps not to be found in our generation). I think without claiming to have solved the riddle, that the recent war distressed him greatly, especially the beginning of the war in the Caribbean. He had seen the war come to so many shores! One should add the last news he heard, the events in Uruguay. That too had a terrible similarity to what he had experienced in Europe, painful as it may be to confess it. He had had enough of horrors. He could not stand it anymore. . . . His repugnance to violence was not only sincere, it was absolute. . . . We could do nothing for him but love him. The three us of in this house loved him because it was the most natural thing in the world.

Speaking to Christians who might condemn his act of suicide, she wrote, "Ah! Let not the believers disturb these bones of one doubly fugitive, and let them desist from the easy exercise of pointing a moral about a death which leaves humanity impoverished, at least the best of humanity. In him was the honey of Isaiah, the flame of Paul, the ambrosia of Ruth."[118] Mistral's writing here shares something with many in her community—often their richest, most probing writings were about friends, written in personal genres, like memoirs, eulogies, and letters.

The following year, this tragedy would be compounded, as Yin-Yin, Mistral's nephew whom she raised as a son, also took his own life, a suicide that Mistral would never understand and from which she would never fully recover. Mistral's friends from around the world sent condolences and helped ensure that the boy would be given a Catholic burial despite the suicide. Mistral's health declined. Her letters to the Maritains always asked them to pray for Yin-Yin, and her late poems evoke the pain of his absence. The details of this teenager's tragic life are obscure, a boy just outside the radiance of spiritual friends.

POSTWAR WRITINGS

In the 1950s, the final decade of Mistral's life, though she had suffered devastating personal losses and was in steeply declining health, she continued to write prolifically and, with the near-constant aid of her secretaries and friends, to take an active role in postwar peace initiatives around the world. She continued to move as well, traveling from Brazil to California and New

York. Her prose and poetry tended to frame politics within the poetics of the religious and even mystical imagination, often with her spiritual friends in mind. In 1950, for example, Mistral had written to Jacques assuring him that the *maritenistas* they had nourished in Chile and Argentina were still active—she had connections in these countries who gave her the on-the-ground scene—though under the dictatorships of Perón and Pétain, they had gone deeper underground.[119] In 1951, Mistral published the poem "Lámpara de catedral" (Light in the cathedral), dedicated to Jacques and Raïssa Maritain.[120] "Lámpara de catedral" is both an intimate communication to the couple as well as a deeply public demonstration of a conscious commonality, engaging with a world of readers. It appeared in the English-language volume *Religious Faith and World Culture*, edited by the World Alliance for International Friendship through the Churches, which had been founded in Germany in 1914. The World Alliance for International Friendship was part of a broader, global network of international Christian activist organizations that evoked the language of friendship to describe political efforts for peace, solidarity, and combating fascism. These included the Sembradores de Amistad (Sowers of Friendship), founded in Monterrey, Mexico, in 1936;[121] the pro-refugee newspaper *L'ami du peuple* (Friend of the People) and Amis des travailleurs étrangers (Friends of the Foreign Workers), founded in France in 1933; and the Catholic interracial apostolate the Friendship House, founded in the United States.[122]

The World Alliance for International Friendship through the Churches gathered essays and speeches by the ecumenical Left around the world, including the American Protestant theologian Harry Fosdick, the German Jewish philosopher Martin Buber, and the Indian poet Amiya Chakravarty. When the editors invited Mistral to contribute the volume's opening poem, they explained, "You speak for Latin America. More important, however, is our conviction that, even while you speak for Latin America, the spirit you embody in your rich poetry is universal."[123] Yet "Lámpara de catedral" is strikingly different from the other contributions to the volume, which centered more explicitly on peace, democracy, technology, anti-nuclearism, and ecumenism. "Lámpara de catedral" appears less as homage to world peace than as a textual parallel to Salvador Dalí's surrealist 1957 painting "Explosion of Mystical Faith in the Midst of a Cathedral." The poem describes a mystical vision that takes place in the "heart of a dark Cathedral," where there is "no day, no night," near a small lantern illuminated by fire. The poem shifts from the perspective of the flame to that of the author herself, who hears "hisses, tears, a call from above." She becomes "*loca*" and "hovers near the flame of the lamp, suckled and anointed with oil and blood." She then imagines herself with "clothing afire, feet sliced in pieces, staggering in her dense smoke, drunk with sorrow and love." She hears "Christ, the prisoner whisper to the flame, 'rest, endure.'" But neither "she nor He have rest, or death, or paradise."[124]

It is difficult to understand how visionary, mystical experiences like the one Mistral describes in this poem relate to serious plans of ecumenism and peace, the purpose of the volume. But the poem took the form of an epistle dedicated to her friends Jacques and Raïssa, and the Maritains and Mistral all shared the belief that mysticism could sustain a vision of reality beyond political arrangements or institutional plans, both church and state. Mistral evoked a mystical language that doubts, hesitates, and detaches in a space of prophetic distance from the norm, "drunk with sorrow and love" in the face of the sobriety of politics, *loca* in the face of certainty. It refuses to settle for the compromised realm of politics, and although politics can make do without the transgressive language of mysticism, without it, the vision is always in danger of stagnation, compromise, ossification. Mistral's mystical poetry keeps alive a restless creativity and imagination, which reenvisions new possibilities and refuses to settle for an untransfigured world. Gabriela Mistral's and Raïssa Maritain's writings, and sometimes even Jacques's, offer more than didactic lessons. They engage the political sphere in a similarly mystical way. Without smoothing over tensions, Mistral's mystical poems and spiritual friendships enrich her political reflections, endowing them with a sense of the unruly and the transcendent.

We see something similar in one of Jacques's postwar pieces, an unambiguous commitment to peace and justice with a mystical, indirect approach. In a 1947 essay published in *The Nation*, Jacques wonders what kind of faith is even possible in the aftermath of the Shoah. Raïssa, though a convert from Judaism, maintained contact with her Jewish roots after she converted to Catholicism. The Maritains had reckoned with the reality of the Holocaust much earlier than most, especially before other Catholics. Jacques begins with a note of realism:

> Yes we see we should have faith in man. But we cannot. Our experience keeps reason in check. The present world of man has been for us a revelation of evil; it has shattered our confidence. We have seen too many crimes for which no just revenge can compensate, too many deaths in desperation, too sordid a debasement of human nature. Our vision of man has been covered over by the unforgettable image of the bloody

ghosts in extermination camps. . . . Sadism has let devils loose everywhere. Everything we loved seems to have been poisoned; everything in
which we trusted seems to have failed. Science and progress are turned to
our own destruction. . . . Our very language has been perverted, all our
words have become ambiguous and seem only able to convey deception.
We live in Kafka's world. Where is our faith to live by?[125]

Jacques continues, claiming that faith is hope not in humanity but in something "superhuman, an entrance into the realm of invisible and divine things."
Though we are living in what appears as an "apocalypse, the liquidation of
several centuries of history . . . we are picking the grapes of wrath," which are
necessary, he writes, to "stir up, from the depths of human bewilderment,
the moral and spiritual revolution that is incomparably more needed than
any other revolution." He called it the

terrestrial triumph of gospel inspiration in the social behavior of man-
kind. We do not lose hope in the advent of fraternal communion and true
human emancipation. . . . Every effort made in this direction will finally
bear fruit. I refer not only to the spiritual struggle of those who have
heard, as Henri Bergson put it, the call of the hero, and who awaken men
to evangelic love, but also to the temporal struggle of all those—scientists
like Washington Carver, poets like Walt Whitman or Peguy, pioneers of
social justice like the "radicals" called up by Saul Alinsky—who give
themselves to the improvement and illumination of their brothers' lives,
and who can know no rest as long as their brothers are in enslavement
and misery.[126]

Those Maritain mentions here—Carver, Whitman, and Alinsky—were not
even Catholic, but for him they embodied that selfless spirit, immersed
completely in a world outside of oneself, the world of "enslavement and
misery," to bring "improvement and illumination." This so radically tran-
scends natural human instincts that it more properly evokes the world of
the *supernatural*: "the entrance into invisible and divine things." Jacques
Maritain writes that in lives like those we can witness not merely a faith
to live "by" but a faith to live "for" and even "die for." By invoking the lives
of these people and framing them in the context of holiness, he presents a
spiritual and relational way into politics, with human stories and realism at
the center. In this sense, we can understand why Mistral called the Maritains' salon at Meudon a "supernatural group," one that centered on spiritual

friendship and kept their politics open to the transcendent and the mystical. The spiritual charisma that came from these networks spread far beyond the relationship between Mistral and the Maritains; they each took these sensibilities all over the world, gathering people into their orbits.

For instance, in the postwar period until his last book published in 1968, Jacques Maritain held up the life and work of his friend Saul Alinsky, the Jewish community organizer, countless times as a way forward. When Jacques was living in America, the two men developed a close bond, and Jacques described Alinsky as "one of my closest friends who was an indomitable and dreaded organizer of 'People's Organizations' and an anti-racist leader whose methods are as efficacious as they are unorthodox."[127] Through Alinsky, Jacques saw in these community organizations seeds of renewal: the grassroots efforts to put pressure on governments to protect the vulnerable—immigrants, the poor, mothers who cannot afford childcare, and low-wage earners. One of Alinsky's great contributions to politics was helping organizers understand the world as it *is*—he shared Jacques's realism—instead of the world they *wished it to be*, while recognizing how power hinges on personal relationships built in one-on-one meetings. The realism and relationality of Alinsky cohered deeply with Jacques Maritain's worldview. But again, Jacques did not only appreciate Alinsky's ideas and even his life; their collaboration had all the markings of another intense spiritual friendship. Consider, for instance, the condolence letter Jacques wrote to Alinsky in 1947, after hearing about the death of Alinsky's wife in a tragic drowning accident. When Jacques learned of this "monstrous event," he expressed to Alinsky, "Our hearts are full of your distress and agony, and what is our love capable of, unless suffering with you? Everything human is powerless in the face of such a tragedy, there is no help on earth. . . . You cannot be consoled, every fiber of happiness in your body has been struck by lightning."[128] For Alinsky, the letter itself became a treasured object, sacred: "Jacques dear. I wept over your letter. It has been placed in a special folder where I can always look at it. I want my children to know it so that in later years they will understand how their parents lived and died." Alinsky was not a religious person, but he dedicated one of his books to Jacques: "To Jacques Maritain: that rare person who not only professes Christianity but whose heart is filled with it and who lives a Christian way of life. . . . To know Jacques Maritain is to know a richness and spiritual experience that makes life even more glorious."[129]

To be sure, like Jacques, Gabriela Mistral's prose often focused on the transgressive power of religious language to summon new realities, again with the language of friendship at the center. For example, in 1951, Mistral published the article "La palabra maldita" (The damned word) in response to Chilean anticommunist persecution and hysteria. She wrote to those who had been persecuted by anticommunist governments for signing the famous Stockholm Appeal declaration of peace:

> There are some words that, when smothered, speak all the more, precisely because of suffocation and exile; and the word "peace" is surging even from people who have been deaf or indifferent. Because, after all, Christians distributed throughout all branches of Christianity, from Catholic through Quaker, must remember all of a sudden, like an ecstatic, that the most insistent word in the Gospels is precisely this word: this word excised from the newspapers, this word hidden in a corner, this monosyllable forbidden to us as if it were a dirty curse. It is the word par excellence that is present and repeated throughout Holy Scripture, as an obsession. We must keep calling it out every day, so that something from the holy obligation may float up, even if it only be like a meager cork on the stream of the prevailing paganism. Have courage my friends. Pacifism isn't the sweet confection that some may think it to be; vital conviction impresses a courage on us, so that we can't stay still. Let us say it wherever we are, wherever we go, until it generates a body and creates a "militancy for peace," to fill the filthy, crowded air and starts to purify it. Keep saying it out loud, against the wind and the tide, even if you go friendless for three years. Rejection is difficult; loneliness often produced something like the buzz in your ears when you descend into a cave . . . or a catacomb. It doesn't matter, my friends: we must go on![130]

This essay was published in 1951 in a newspaper in Costa Rica, then reprinted in Chile in 1957. Mistral claimed that within the Christian imagination lay dormant seeds of renewal and change: like the kiss Saint Francis planted on the leper's mouth, which Mistral once wrote about, or the fire that Teresa of Ávila touched, the word *peace*—a weak, condemned little word, *la palabra maldita*—uttered into the void of "suffocation and exile" can surge, gathering momentum and strength. Mistral urges readers to inject this radical word into the present, even if in doing so they find themselves totally alone, "friendless," as if descending "into a cave . . . or a catacomb." But Mistral never truly experienced the world as a friendless tomb, and in the same breath, even as she speaks of the loneliness and rejection that come from prophetic language, she communicates in the first person plural: "Have courage, my friends. . . . It doesn't matter, my friends: we must go on!" The essay is both a request for moral courage and a negation of isolation: to read this work is to establish a community though the medium of reading. She summons her readers as friends, a transnational community of Christians (Quakers, Catholics, even those just "casi Católicas," as she once called Victoria Ocampo) committed to shared ideals in a violent world.

At the end of her life, when living in New York with her caretaker and lover Doris Dana, Mistral published in 1954 a poem for her old friend Roger Caillois, the French sociologist and antifascist activist whom she had met through Victoria Ocampo. "The Fall of Europe" appeared in her final volume of poetry, *Lagar* (Winepress). Mistral echoes her beloved Saint Francis, who rejected the nuclear family to create a larger, holy spiritual family, with brothers and sisters including the poor, (for Saint Francis) animals, the sun and moon, even "O Sister Bodily Death." Here Caillois is reimagined as a brother, invited to pray with Mistral his sister and mourn for Europe, the aging mother who had sheltered them all, now old, blind, mad, choked, and burned:

> Come brother, come tonight
> to pray with your sister who has
> no child or mother or people here.
> It's bitter to pray and hear the echo
> sent back by wall and empty air.
> Come, brother or sister,
> through the cornfield paths, before day ends
> in blindness, madness, not knowing
> what pain she suffers who never suffered,
> and riddled with fires, choked with smoke she burns,
> the Old Mother who sheltered us
> in her olive orchard and her vineyard.[131]

Summoning and speaking to a spiritual family, Mistral's poem is a stroke against isolation in the context of mourning, both personalizing and concretizing the vast, impersonal violence of state warfare.

By the time Mistral was penning these final poems in the 1950s, she had not only risen to the height of the literary firmament (winning the Nobel Prize in Literature and receiving honorary doctorates from universities around the world) but also, owing in part to her collaborations with Jacques Maritain, become celebrated by the global Catholic establishment too. In

1950, she was awarded the Serra Award by the Academy of American Franciscan History for her "lifelong service to the highest ideals of Brotherhood among Men and of her achievement in expressing with singular beauty the deepest Emotions of the Human Spirit."[132] In 1946, Mistral even had a private audience with Pope Pius XII in Rome. Mistral reported that she told the pope about the plight of indigenous communities in South America. "He had never even heard of those human beings," she later mused. "He only knew of the gigantic and European cathedrals in Buenos Aires. No one had ever spoken to him of those melancholy street corners."[133]

When she spoke to the pope of the indigenous *campesinos* she had come to know first in Chile, then in Mexico and Argentina, Mistral was by that point one of the most celebrated, socially minded cosmopolitan Catholics of the century. Yet she was not an overtly political or party-identified writer. Nevertheless, her emotional involvement with the class from which she came, that of the *campesino* schoolchildren and teachers and farmers, ran deep. While Europe offered her a clear chance to escape her social origins, to join the cosmopolitan intelligentsia, she refused that offer, and she never lost sight of the reality of the people who have little control of their lives. This, too, is what Maritain had in mind in as early as the 1930s when he was writing about the lives of the poor who suffered from the war in Spain—the reality of people's lives that could only be discovered in real relationship.

After Gabriela Mistral published *Lagar*, her final book of poetry in 1954, she lived only three more years. She and the Maritains both found themselves living near New York City toward the end of their lives, they in Princeton, she in Long Island, where she had moved in March of 1953. Jacques and Raïssa sent Mistral a postcard in 1953 wishing her a merry Christmas and telling her how often they thought of her, how happy they were to finally have her address again, how eager they were to see her.[134] In May of 1954, Raïssa assured Mistral that they thought of "their vagabond Chilean poet" often.[135] In one of Mistral's last letters to Jacques, she wondered what would happen to their projects for a social Catholic Left. She sensed she was reaching the end of her life, noting how the young look at her, she confessed to Jacques, "like an old lady." But "you," she wrote, "God has blessed you with good health."[136] Since Jacques was teaching at Princeton, she told him that in North America he must rebuild what they had made in Europe and in Chile and Argentina, on "the old bones and ashes" of their network before the war.[137] She could sense Jacques was moving in that direction.

Until the very end of her life, her spiritual friendships, even with those who were absent, dead, exiled, or imprisoned, seemed to have been Mistral's center of gravity. Waldo Frank wrote of Mistral,

Wherever she was, she was ready to talk till dawn with her friends, over a cigarette and a cup of coffee. Each night, she prayed on her knees beside her bed. . . . She loved above all to talk with her friends about her friends. Three years ago for instance, when Peron put our friend Victoria Ocampo into jail, Gabriela (already a sick woman) made the hard trip to Cape Cod to talk with me for three solid days about Victoria. Victoria, scrubbing filthy floors in the Argentine prison, became, it seemed to Gabriela, present: breathed the good air we were breathing.[138]

As the years wore on, Mistral wrote about her ability to make the absent beloved present: "Ever since I became a vagabond, in voluntary exile, I seem to write only amid phantoms. . . . My people, alive or dead, come back to me in a wistful but loyal procession, which rather than surrounding me, contains and presses in on me."[139]

Mistral died in 1957 and was buried, as she had arranged, with a white Franciscan cord tied around her waist, and she left the profits from her literary estate to the Franciscan friars to administer on behalf of the poor rural children of the remote village where she spent her childhood.[140] After her death, Mistral's partner Doris Dana aimed to complete some of the projects that had been closest to Mistral's heart. Chief among them were the ongoing efforts to promote Latin American and European collaboration around the ideals of the Catholic Left, the work Mistral had begun over thirty years earlier when she left for Spain in 1925. Even after Mistral's death, Jacques Maritain was at the center of these efforts. Dana kept in close touch with Jacques after Mistral's passing and even attended one of his seminars in Princeton as an auditor. Eventually, she was baptized as a Catholic, and Maritain was her godfather—the spiritual contagion crossed the Atlantic. In 1966, Jacques was planning to republish a new French and English edition of *Integral Humanism*, and he wanted an appendix added to the book describing the history of the Christian Democratic Party in Chile, where *Integral Humanism* had been so influential. Mistral had passed away, however, and Jacques's beloved friend Eduardo Frei was serving as the president of Chile, so he had his hands full. Jacques asked if Dana knew of anyone else who could help with the appendix, and on November 3, 1966, Dana wrote to an old friend of Mistral's, the Chilean diplomat Radomiro Tomic, who had been in the Christian Democratic Party in Chile and was serving at the Chilean consulate in New York. He was part of the group of original *maritenistas* decades before, along with Frei. Mistral had been close with both men and was the godmother of one of Tomic's children. At the end of her letter, Dana mentioned to Tomic that she knew someone—John Howard Griffin—who had three photographic portraits of Jacques Maritain in his possession. Griffin had promised to give them to her, and Jacques had promised to sign them. Dana vowed to gather them up—just like the relics that the most ardent of the faithful Christian disciples have always gathered, bits of holy cloth, tooth, and bone—and redistribute them: "One for you, one for Frei, one for myself."[141]

Jacques himself lived his last thirteen years as a widow after the death of Raïssa in 1960. The prayers surrounding Raïssa's death occasioned opportunities for Jacques to deepen bonds with other friends. For example, although he hadn't spoken to the Maritains in many years after a public falling out, the playwright and artist Jean Cocteau came to their Paris apartment the day Raïssa died. Cocteau prayed "like a child," Jacques said, over Raïssa's body. Here prayer over the body smoothed over a broken friendship among the living ("I will always love Cocteau," Jacques later wrote), and just before Cocteau died three years later, Cocteau said to the executor of his own will, "When I'm dead, who will pray for me?"[142]

Similarly, Jacques wrote to Julien Green in 1963, explaining that he had penned *The Peasant of the Garonne* while praying to Raïssa the whole time and developed a sense (confirmed by Jesus at mass) that Raïssa, not him, had authored the book and written it for friends. Jacques Maritain stated, "In fact, during the whole time I was working on the book, it was only of our friends that I was thinking and to whom I was speaking. The idea of a general public never crossed my mind."[143] Still he wondered if his friends love it, love her? To which Julien assured him he *does* love the book.[144] This "consoles me more anything else I could receive," Jacques replied, "since I love you most of all." Jacques had been the object of Green's devotion for decades, but late in his life Jacques began confessing to friends how much he needed them too: "There is that marvel of friendship that God has put in your soul for the poor man that I am, and to think of such a mystery is overwhelming." At the end of his life, Jacques admitted to Green a sentiment that many people had conveyed to him over the years: "You would never believe how much I need that encouragement, which seems to come to me from Heaven, like many things that come to me through you."[145]

Buoyed by Green's encouragement, *The Peasant of the Garonne* was published in 1966, and that year, Jacques began corresponding again with old his friend Esther de Cáceres, the poet from Uruguay whom Mistral had introduced him to many years earlier in Paris. In 1963, Cáceres had convened a conference about Raïssa Maritain in Montevideo, which touched Jacques deeply. He had just finished publishing Raïssa's spiritual journal. Jacques spent his final years in Toulouse, where he had joined the religious order of Charles de Foucauld, and he wrote to Cáceres at the end of her own life, when she was living in the Benedictine abbey of Santa Escolástica in Buenos Aires, after losing her husband Alfredo. Through their correspondence, a Spanish-speaking widow and a French-speaking widower who both joined monastic orders in their old age, with oceans between them, distributed "food for their souls" in the letters they sent in the mail. In 1968, Cáceres translated Jacques's last book into Spanish as *El campesino del Garona*. He signed his last letter to Cáceres just two months before he died, "I am with You. With all my heart. A kiss, Jacques."[146]

CONCLUSION

This kiss Jacques tucked into a letter and mailed from France to Uruguay in 1968 is just a small window into the affective power that animated the collaborations among Catholic artists, writers, and activists between France and Latin America in the middle of the twentieth century. Spiritual friendships internationalized progressive Catholicism in this period. Mistral's sense of the spiritual power of Meudon compelled her to help promote Jacques's work in Argentina and in Chile among politicians like Frei, where his ideas took root more deeply than anywhere else in the world. In her poetry and her speeches, Mistral had enunciated a socially progressive, antifascist Catholicism well before Jacques, but he had the ear of the Thomists, lawyers, priests, and politicians, the people in power in Europe. Like Raïssa, Gabriela inhabited the realm of art, a different sphere. But spiritual friendship powered the collaborations in both realms: We see it in Eduardo Frei, future president of Chile, begging Mistral for a photo of Jacques when he was a very young man and displaying it along with a portrait of Mistral in his study years later. We glimpse it in Jacques sitting at Mistral's bedside at the end of her life, and in organizations like Amigos de Léon Bloy popping up in Uruguay.

For all the spiritual intimacy among friends in the Maritains' circle, furtive pressures to convert to Catholicism darkened the skies of some friendships, particularly in the earlier years. Jacques was, in the words of Cocteau, "a born activist, always trying to straighten out his friends' lives and dreaming of making them less accustomed to pleasure."[147] As for Gabriela Mistral, a shadow hovered around the edges of her love too, and especially late in life her attachment to friends verged on obsessive. She was desperate to hear from friends, who could never write enough. In the Mistral archive, there are telegraphs and notes to friends she hadn't heard from in some time—some who were in jail, others ill or recovering from surgery—panicked, angry, possessive, lonely.[148] The Maritains were also worried about Mistral, sending her a telegram when she was ill: "WE EXPECTED YOU TODAY ARE REALLY ANXIOUS PLEASE TELEPHONE."[149] "Spiritual groups were as passionately linked as lovers," wrote Maurice Sachs. "After the embrace, they withdraw exhausted."[150]

Other factors disclose that these bonds did not share the sunnier, simpler associations we might have with the word *friendship*. In old age especially or after friends passed away, stories circulated, reputations set. But the stories from people who loved the figures in this network were unusual, emphasizing the strangeness and otherworldliness of these men and women. Eduardo Frei Montalva gave a speech in Chile on the anniversary of Mistral's death, describing her "strange countenance and attitude of the ancient priestesses."[151] Waldo Frank, a close friend of Mistral's, said she "walked more like a man than a woman, more like an Indian than a European, more like a great rhythmic animal than like a groping human being. Her dress, always black, grey, and loose; always ungainly, announced her complete obliviousness to style. Her verse issued from this paradox of her nature. Superbly sculptured, it was warm, spontaneous, and the loom of the mountains, the dark of death was miraculously in it."[152] Another friend remembered walking Mistral to a prominent lecture she was giving and noticing she was wearing unmatched shoes.[153] Of Jacques Maritain, the writer John Howard Griffin wrote that he wore a scarf, day or night, rain or shine, and even when Griffin visited him at 10:00 a.m., the "philosopher lay fully clothed, with a scarf around his neck, under the covers."[154] Jean Cocteau wondered if Jacques's "body might be a kind of clothing thrown haphazardly on the exceptional soul: the Thomist seemed to belong so little to current life, to have so little need to eat!"[155] This emphasis appears to insist that, yes, these were friends, but not in the ordinary sense. What made these individuals so beloved was the feeling that they came from elsewhere, that they inhabited, on some fundamental level, a world not our own. This gave them a holiness that operated on a realm not quite social, emotional, or ethical but something else akin to sainthood, the closest tradition to describe these friends. Like the fools for Christ, David Tracy explains, "all powerful saints come from somewhere else, beyond the usual human measure."[156] They are liminal figures, to borrow a category of Victor Turner, in the sense that they do not wholly belong to ordinary reality. We see this among many Catholics in this international culture, as, for instance, when Dorothy Day spoke of Peter Maurin, it was not his ethics or politics she stressed but how truly out of sync he was with his own norms ("dirty, ill-clothed, unwashed, in our day when we put such an emphasis on showers, daily baths, and the toilet in general").[157] The stories that spiritual friends circulated about one another tried to rescue them from the grasp of readers, as if we would dust them off and put them to work in our narrative of ethics, morality, and politics.

In *The Mystic Fable*, Michel de Certeau claims that the grammar of mysticism speaks of a presence that cannot be fully grasped or contained in any particular language: it "overpowers the inquiry," he states, "with something resembling a laugh."[158] Such a laugh is a natural response when reading about the lives and habits of some of these truly unusual men and women, a laugh that gestures toward a presence beyond the ordinary and mundane. They operated on a plane in excess of the social, the instrumental, the moral. As Waldo Frank put it, within Mistral he felt there is something more, something funny, like her clothes and mismatched shoes, but it's a laugh that points to something deeper: "the loom of the mountains, the dark of death" that enchants. Jane Bennett's *The Enchantment of Modern Life* argues that enchantment is a sense of openness to the unusual, the captivating, the disturbing in everyday life, the "extraordinary that lives around the familiar."[159] Bennett advocates for the ways in which enchantment can be cultivated to build an ethics of generosity, for moments of wonder that can help gather the positive energy that can transpire into such an ethics.

There was something about the Maritains, Mistral, and their vast network of friends that I believe evoked some of that enchantment. When we consider what they went through—from fleeing the Jewish pogroms in Russia, as Raïssa's family did, to escaping Europe again in 1939 because of the same hatred, then seeing anti-Semitic authoritarianism gain ground in Latin America—in the face of a current of hate that ran through the twentieth century and touched each of their lives, it is easy to imagine just how different friendships, and all their wonder, must have felt.

"LUMINOUS SPIRITUAL TRACES" TO ISLAM

The Passionate Friendships of Louis Massignon

Louis Massignon was very religious. But he was religious in a strange way.

JEAN JACQUES WAARDENBURG, *Muslims as Actors*

INTRODUCTION

IN CONVERSATIONS ABOUT Catholicism and Islam in modernity, the late scholar Louis Massignon invariably holds the center of gravity. "Massignon," notes Anthony O'Mahony, "is the most influential figure in the Christian encounter with Islam in the modern world."[1] Even studies of other Catholic thinkers who worked to advance Muslim-Christian relations, such as Dominique Avon's magisterial analysis of twentieth-century Dominicans working in the Middle East, steer irresistibly back to him. "It was above all one man," Avon describes, "Louis Massignon, who provoked a reversal in Church teaching on Islam."[2] Massignon played a prominent role in the major European academic and religious institutions of his day—he held the chair of Islamic studies at the Collège de France from 1926 through 1954, was friends with Pope Pius XII, and had a voice at the Second Vatican Council—but at the same time there was something remarkably singular about him.[3]

Seemingly unattached from broader intellectual and cultural trends, he was a master philologist and expert on premodern Islamic sources, yet his methodology was, as Agnes Wilkins puts it, "almost the opposite of a historical approach" and more like the mystical, meditative approach to texts in the monastic tradition of *lectio divina*.[4] Massignon entered into the spiritual, lived reality of the Islamic sources he studied not as artifacts of the past but as testimonies of the living God in the present. Nevertheless, he remained a devout Catholic and called himself simply a "Catholic friend of Islam."[5] He was anti-historicist but would surely bristle at being called a theologian: "Jacques Maritain is the only theologian whose writing doesn't make me sick to read," he once confessed to a friend.[6] And while was trained as an orientalist, even Edward Said found Massignon to be an "individual genius" who was oddly freed, at least in some ways, "from the old ideological straightjacket" of orientalism.[7] The spiritual power Massignon exerted on others seems unusual as well. "Like a fire that lights up aflame," wrote his friend Marie-Magdeleine Davy, "it was possible to see Massignon gradually become like the burning bush alluded to in the book of Exodus."[8] Jacques Maritain saw in Massignon a "man of singular grandeur and extraordinary genius."[9] From almost every perspective, Massignon appeared sui generis.

But when it came to his inner life, Massignon was never alone. Massignon was fueled almost entirely by the oxygen of his spiritual friends, living and dead, Muslim and Christian. Both his vocation as an Islamicist and his spirituality were guided entirely by a handful of extraordinary men and women who left "luminous spiritual traces," as he called it, on his own soul.[10] Massignon believed passionately in God's presence in specific, special people who passed on a palpable sense of the divine to others. These companions kept alive in Massignon a deeply spiritual vision toward which he constantly worked. He occasionally called these special men and women links in a chain that connected others with the presence of God, person by person. Elsewhere he imagined that each one held a small, brightly lit torch of holiness that illuminated those around them. According to Massignon's English-language biographer Mary Louise Gude, "It was as if all who touched his life, be they living or dead, formed a kind of spiritual constellation with which Massignon stayed in contact. He visited the graves of the dead. The living received letters to mark occasions important to them and to him."[11]

The late Jean Jacques Waardenburg once described his former teacher Massignon's ideas as rooted in a "kind of experiential reality difficult to assess in rational terms."[12] The challenge in assessing his experiential reality stems in part from the interiority of this realm, which was fully relational and mostly private, available to readers only in glimpses through bits of correspondence, interviews that veered toward the personal, and a handful of autobiographical essays. These sources offer just a peek at Massignon's complex relational terrain of spiritual intimacies, all of which he invested with powerful religious meanings. While each of Massignon's *amitiés spiri- tuelles* had dimensions that will never be fully transparent to scholars, Mas- signon wrote openly about some of them, like his bond with Charles de Foucauld and the one he sensed with the long-dead Islamic mystic from Persia, Husayn Ibn Mansur al-Hallāj. Others, like his relationship with the Egyptian activist and philanthropist Mary Kahil, were more controversial, even risqué, the source of confusion and pain for his own family, and rarely discussed directly by Massignon (after his death, his family also forbade any mention, and it is said that Massignon's own wife never allowed the name of Mary Kahil to be uttered in her presence).[13]

While there are considerable obstacles to surmount, nonetheless, in this chapter, I try to get as close as possible to this complicated, obscure experi- ential domain and offer a map and an analysis of the "spiritual solidarities" (as Certeau described Massignon's bonds) that fueled Massignon.[14] Under- standing these solidarities helps us move beyond the formal content of his ideas into the personal and embodied realm that stimulated his influential work. I begin with Massignon's earliest friendships, starting with his spiri- tual connections to al-Hallāj and Foucauld, and then explore his relation- ship with his godson, Jean Mohammed Abd-el-Jalil, a Moroccan convert from Islam to Catholicism. The chapter then focuses on Massignon and Kahil, the most dramatic love story there is to tell in this community. It was Kahil who, in 1934, rekindled Massignon's spiritual bonds with his first loves, reigniting in him a more radical vision as an Islamicist.

Studying Massignon in terms of his personal relationships admittedly risks producing a picture of his life that is *too* private, stifled, and personal. However, through combinatory work, we can see the way in which these extraordinary spiritual ties were woven into a life that went well beyond them. Massignon's spiritual solidarities with Sufis like al-Hallāj, for example, stimulated his scholarship, which, though not without biases and limita- tions of its own, pushed against generations of anti-Islamic scholarly preju- dice in the West. He proved that Sufism derived from neither the Chris- tians nor the Greeks but was itself a thing of beauty, and a *Muslim* thing of beauty, rooted deeply in the Qur'an. Although many in the later generations of Islamicists would find problematic aspects in Massignon's approach, in the 1920s when he began publishing, it was a formidable rejoinder to prevailing anti-Islamic sentiment in both orientalism and Catholic theology. Later, Massignon's spiritual friendship with Mary Kahil, a seasoned activist in Egypt, rather than the quiet muse that historians have often viewed her as, stirred Massignon toward more overtly political work of solidarity with Muslim communities in Algeria and the Middle East living under French colonial rule. Only by attending to both of these levels—the public and the interpersonal—can we approximate the dynamism, complexity, and richness that animated Massignon's vision of a world. For all of its strangeness, some aspects of Massignon's worldview were almost eerily prescient. His concern for refugees, his solidarity with Muslim victims of colonial violence, his trenchant critiques of simplistically carving up the world into the "Christian West" and the "Islamic Middle East," his attention to Christian minorities in countries ruled by rising Islamic fundamentalism—these are only some of the issues that focused his life's work and speak to our own time. The story of Massignon's spiritual friendships as the invigorating force for his scholarship and politics draws from and extends recent scholars who expand on Edward Said's notion of European scholarship of Islam. Said established the idea that Western scholarship served the hegemonic powers of domination and subjugation of the non-European Muslim world. Suzanne Marchand, Susannah Heschel, Umar Ryad, and Mehdi Sajid have complicated this narrative, showing that modern study of Islam in Europe took place within diffuse networks of intellectual exchange that included Christians, Jews, and Muslims themselves, who produced knowledge that functioned for a wide variety of religious and political interests in the world that, as Heschel and Ryad put it, "were both colonial and anticolonial, pious and heretical, enlightened and reactionary, scholarly and popular," a tool for both hegemonic power and creativity and resistance of colonial power.[15] Louis Massignon and his network of spiritual friends in the realms of imagination (al-Hallāj), memory (Charles de Foucauld), and in ordinary time, face-to-face (Jean Mohammed Abd-el-Jalil from Morocco and Mary Kahil from Egypt) amplify Heschel and Ryad's point.

THE EARLY MASSIGNON:
INTIMACY WITH AL-HALLĀJ AND FOUCAULD

Louis Massignon was born in 1883 in France, where he and his childhood friend Henri Maspero became fascinated with the languages and cultures of *l'Orient* as teenagers.[16] Both boys grew up to become celebrated scholars of Eastern religions and held endowed chairs at the Collège de France, Maspero in Chinese religions, Massignon in Islam. When Massignon was fifteen years old and just beginning to explore the field of orientalism, he assisted on an archaeological expedition in Morocco. There he learned about the contemplative Catholic hermit Charles de Foucauld, who was still alive at the time, living in poverty and imitation of Christ alongside the communities of Muslim nomadic people moving through northern Africa. Massignon and Foucauld began a correspondence and eventually met in 1909. Foucauld represented for Massignon an engagement with the Islamic world that differed radically from the professional text- and archaeology-based approaches of the orientalists he knew in Paris.[17] Foucauld inspired Massignon "by communicat[ing] to me," he wrote, "through spiritual contact, in very simple words," a way into the Islamic world that gravitated toward the margins of the mainstream and analysis that came from both linguistic knowledge and firsthand contact with Muslim people.[18] Through Foucauld, Massignon also learned of what he called the "experiential discovery of the sacred *in others*," other people, living and dead.[19] These teachings offered more than ideas about a method to study Islam but something much more personal: "I cannot speak to you," Massignon recalled of their early meetings, "of the outward, physical contour of Foucauld's and my relationship . . . but only of the luminous spiritual traces . . . that my memory preserves . . . a constellation of tiny weblike threads between our two vocations and our two destinies." This guiding sense through the Muslim world by a radical hermit in the desert lasted long after Foucauld's death in 1914. "How many times," Massignon wrote in 1959, almost five decades after his passing, "have I been taken again beyond the realm of the dead by the angelic contact of the soul of Foucauld, in a state of muffled shock, blinded by compassion."[20]

With Foucauld as an inner mentor, Massignon began his scholarly career as an Islamicist by seeking texts and traditions of Islam that were obscure, overlooked, or fringe, and he always insisted that the best way into such study was to literally be with Muslims, spend time in their countries, and learn their language fluently. Massignon focused his graduate work on the Arabic texts of al-Hallāj, an obscure Sufi mystic who had been martyred in the ninth century and whose writings were at the time virtually unknown. Massignon discovered these texts in 1907, and his eventual translations and analyses of al-Hallāj's poetry and sermons solidified his career as a renowned Arabic philologist and scholar of Sufi mysticism. In the works Massignon translated, al-Hallāj testified to the soul's potential ability to become fully united with the divine. Al-Ḥallāj claimed that these teachings were meant for all, not just secret elect Sufi masters, and he wandered and preached unity with the divine to the masses throughout Baghdad. For his controversial teachings (he infamously stated, "I am Truth"), al-Ḥallāj was imprisoned and eventually killed. Intimacy and friendship governed Massignon's approach to his scholarship: "Ḥallāj's thought reached me personally," Massignon wrote. He felt with him a "friendship of the spirit."[21] Massignon increasingly committed to a scholarly method that relied on the science of religion (language, philology) but directly countered scientism: "Many Europeans," Massignon argued in 1940, "have studied Muslim thinkers only 'from outside,' without entering into the heart of Islam itself."[22] Massignon explained that his method was gleaned from Islamic thinkers themselves: "Al-Ḥallâj said that to comprehend something" means to "be transferred, through a decentralization of ourselves, into the very center of the other thing in question. . . . We help ourselves understand only by entering into the system of the other thing."[23]

Massignon's sense of his personal connection with Muslim thinkers, especially al-Ḥallāj, would radically intensify in subsequent years, starting with a near-death experience in 1908, one year after discovering al-Ḥallāj's texts. Traveling in Iraq, Massignon was mistakenly apprehended as a spy, beaten, and imprisoned, and when in his desperation he considered suicide, he suddenly sensed the presence of a purifying "inner fire." Massignon felt saved ("resurrected") by what he understood to be the intervention of special intercessors, in particular al-Ḥallāj, whom he saw in a vision engulfed in flames. The name and face of Foucauld also came to him.[24] Massignon had the distinct sense that these spiritual mediators had arrived to take on his suffering. Touched and saved by their presence, Massignon experienced a flash of mystical insight, which revealed that the "secret of history" is to understand that the world is held together by the "heroes of compassion" who willingly take on the sufferings of all.[25] From that point, Massignon's career as an Islamicist was guided by this sense of the hidden power of compassion, sacrifice, and mystical substitution (the willing substitution of oneself for another who is suffering). Thereafter, Massignon did not just learn about al-Ḥallāj in his studies and teach others what he knew through his scholarship. Nor did he merely love the Sufi mystic as a friend. Massignon felt touched by, even loved *by*, this Sufi teacher, whom he sensed had reached to him from beyond the grave. Massignon explained to a friend years later, in 1938, that he felt connected to al-Ḥallāj through an "exquisite chain of grace" that "snatched [him] away" from his ordinary life as a young scholar in 1908.[26] In 1922, Massignon confessed, "Not that the study of his life, which was full and strong, upright and whole, rising and given, yielded to me the secret of his heart. Rather it is he who fathomed mine and probes it still. . . . A simple sentence by him in Arabic . . . and the meaning of sin was returned to me, then the heart-rending desire for purity."[27] Massignon's scholarship on Islam over the next fifty-four years rested on the foundation of the bond he felt with the wandering ninth-century Persian teacher of mysticism.[28] He published his first work on al-Hallāj in 1922 and continued to write about him his entire life. In the bonds Massignon imagined with both Foucauld and al-Hallāj, spiritual friendship appears as something slightly different from the threads that wove together the Maritains and Gabriela Mistral. Massignon in his personal life was more of a solitary eccentric, and he didn't cultivate the abundant atmosphere of intellectual, social, and spiritual networks of face-to-face friends we saw in the world of the Maritains and Mistral. Instead, for Massignon, spiritual friendship more greatly resembled an erotics of spiritual intimacy, a feeling of inner attachment that compelled his entire approach to Islam forward.

Some have criticized Massignon's eccentric and intimate way into Islam through al-Hallāj and Foucauld for privileging marginal figures in Islamic studies rather than more mainstream figures like Muhammad or the Muslim philosopher and scientist Avicenna. It is true that if one imagined Massignon traveling to the foreign country of Islam on a journey that started with al-Hallāj, you would find him on the back roads and in small villages, insisting that more interesting materials, with greater intimacy and beauty, were to be found there. But Massignon approached Catholicism in a similar way, preferring obscure pilgrimage sites and saints and the lesser-known feast days to the more conventional material of the tradition. Nor were his back roads entirely "other" and marginal: one of Massignon's greatest intellectual achievements was showing that the early Persian teachers of Sufism were deeply rooted in traditional Islam. The most interesting way into Islam may have been the roads less traveled, but Massignon demonstrated that they were *Muslim* paths, paved with the sacred Arabic language of the Qur'an and the witness of the prophet Muhammad.

Massignon's first major piece of scholarship appeared in 1922, entitled *Essai sur les origines du lexique technique de la mystique musulmane* (*Essay on the Origins of the Technical Language of Islamic Mysticism*).[29] This was also the same year Massignon's major work on al-Hallāj first appeared in French. These two volumes resulted in Massignon's appointment to the chair in Muslim sociology at the Collège de France and established his international reputation as a groundbreaking Islamicist. His major claim in both texts was that Islamic mysticism is rooted in the Qur'an and inherent to Islam, rather than a derivative from Christian or Greek sources, and that al-Hallāj is a culmination of this Islamic tradition, instead of, as others had claimed, a heretical split from it. Massignon counteracted those "theorists who deny the authenticity of Islamic mysticism."[30] The essay contained a detailed lexicon of Arabic mystical terms that appear regularly in premodern Sufi texts, and the "lexicon's principal source, the one to be consulted first," Massignon noted, "is the Qur'an."[31]

Although these two theses—Islamic mysticism is in fact Islamic; al-Hallāj was in fact Muslim—seem like relatively simple points, they were incendiary for their time and still relevant today.[32] With this idea, Massignon pushed against generations of European orientalist scholars who had reformulated the mystical dimension of Islam into a category separate from Islam called Sufism.[33] Nineteenth-century orientalism included some Catholic scholars, such as the Spanish diocesan priest and Islamicist Miguel Asín Palacios, who discovered the richness and depth of Sufi mystical texts, but they insisted that the spiritual depth and beauty of these works were due to influences from outside Islam: Hinduism, Christian mysticism, or Greek philosophy. No one denied that Sufism was beautiful, but it was a beautiful Christian, Hindu, or Greek pearl hiding in a dry, legalistic Muslim shell.[34] As Omid Safi explains, "Even though they admired the poetry of mystics like Sa'di, Hafez and Rumi, they could not admit that Muslims could come up with such beauty, mysticism and poetry. Therefore, the Orientalists decreed that Sufism must be 'un-Islamic' and due to Christian, Persian, Hindu or Neoplatonic 'influences'—anything but Islam, anything but the experience of Prophet Muhammad in encountering God, which is what the Sufis have always claimed as the primary source of their inspiration."[35] When Massignon claimed Sufism as Islamic—through detailed, technical philological work tracing Sufi language to its Qur'anic, Arabic roots—he cracked the edifice of this widespread and fundamentally anti-Islamic assumption.[36] Massignon's great initial contribution to the European study of Islam was to reattach Sufism to the religious tradition from which it had been severed and thus to endow Islamic religion with the beauty and poetry that was rightfully its own.

Massignon stated that he pushed against popular opinion only because of his spiritual kinship with al-Hallāj: a claim that Sufism is fundamentally un-Islamic, Massignon argued, will "not convince anyone, who has lived with intimacy with the works of these great men [early Sufi mystics]." By "knowing" not only the Sufi mystics but also the inner workings of the Arabic language they spoke—as well as knowing each thinker intimately, even "loving" them—then it would be clear that all the early Islamic mystical writers "knew the entire Qur'an by heart" and could only be seen as Muslim.[37] From this, he argued that it was neither Greek philosophy nor Christian asceticism but the Qur'an that was the primary source of al-Hallāj's mysticism. Massignon often wrote about al-Hallāj as a spiritual presence who invited *him*, the scholar, into al-Hallāj's religious world and probed *his* heart rather than the other way around: "He [al-Hallāj] had come to seek me, and I could not refuse his love."[38] This language of love, intimacy, friendship, and even passivity before al-Hallāj is at the foundation of all Massignon's groundbreaking, ethically and politically relevant early scholarship on mysticism.

These early works also aimed to situate al-Hallāj in a living community, instead of as a lonely mystic who enjoyed the sweetness of the divine alone. Al-Hallāj was marginal, he was executed, he wandered the periphery of mainstream tradition singing of his unity with Allah, but he was not solitary. Intimacy and friendship were not only a hermeneutic but a theme that featured prominently in Massignon's 1922 analysis, which insists on the importance of al-Hallāj's Muslim companions, like Ibn 'Ata, whose correspondences with al-Hallāj "bear witness to the level to which their friendship soared: 'God bless me,' wrote al-Hallāj, 'in the lengthening of your life and spare me from seeing your death!'"[39] The spiritual friendships surrounding al-Hallāj offered another way to insert the Sufi writer back into the Islamic community from which he came.[40]

But Massignon also delved into more controversial terrain as he started to explore what this Islamic beauty might mean for Christianity and for a Christian understanding of God. Are these Muslim texts divinely inspired? What do they mean for the exclusive claims of Christian salvation? Citing the beauty of the mysticism, the lyricism of the poetry, the piety of the prayers, and the heroism of its saints, Massignon wrote in 1922 that "*within Islam itself*, eminent graces, planted by the Holy Spirit, have come to germinate."[41] Throughout his career, Massignon articulated the spiritual connections between Islam and Christianity in a range of ways, often eschewing systematic reflection in favor of poetic bursts of vision, but his initial 1922 claim that the Holy Spirit is somehow present *in* Islam, that Islam is more than a heretical sect *outside* the circle of Christian salvation, was a major intervention in the twentieth-century European milieu. The erotics of friendship animated Massignon's approach. He continued as a prolific scholar, contributing essays to the *Revue du monde Musulman* and serving as the director of the Institut d'études Iranienne at the University of Paris.[42] Accolades, awards, and international prestige followed Massignon both in Europe and in the Middle East.

To get a sense of the scale of Massignon's early scholarly intervention, consider the anti-Islamic edifice Massignon aimed, if imperfectly, to crack.[43] In the interwar period in France, the old orientalists' biases against the "Orient" and Islam were starting to transform into something more pernicious, an active, xenophobic political loathing and resentment.[44] In the 1920s, new immigrants began moving to France, England, and Germany, organizing themselves, and making their presence known. Though most immigrants came from eastern Europe and Russia, some came from the Arabic world. The Grande Mosquée de Paris was built in July 1926. In 1928, the first mosque opened in Berlin-Wilmersdorf.[45] Many prominent Catholics throughout Europe from the Far Right responded defensively to the presence of new immigrants from Russia, eastern Europe, and the Middle East, who practiced Judaism, Russian Orthodoxy, and Islam, with an appeal to the "Christian roots" of European identity, hoping to steer things back on course. In 1927, Catholic writer Henri Massis published the essay *Defense of the West*, which blamed immigrants for Europe's many woes. Infatuated with the purity of Western Christendom, Massis resented the influence of what he called *l'Orient*, "Orient," "the East," and "Asiatics" interchangeably, as they were empty symbols his readers easily and variously filled themselves. Tony Judt describes fascist thinking in Europe of this period as "much clearer in style and enemies than in content," and Massis's text fits the bill.[46] For Massis, the mixing of Eastern cultures with "the Western soul" presented one of the most "monstrous unions" in human history. Only a return to "Latin civilization and Catholicism" could turn everything back around.[47]

This attitude was not limited to France. In England, the Catholic writer G. K. Chesterton's 1914 dystopian novel *The Flying Inn*, on the Islamicization of England, gained a wide readership in the interwar period (with a chilling resurgence after the publication of new 2017 edition).[48] Future elites in Chesterton's novel have lost contact with their medieval Christian roots and become enamored with exotic Middle Eastern Muslims. Aiming for a "for a full unity between Christianity and Islam," they then create a legalistic England ruled by an authoritarian militarized Islamic state. It would be a mistake to dismiss the xenophobia of these Catholic writers because of their context. As Adam Gopnik argues in an essay on Chesterton, "The context *is* the issue."[49] This was their response to the heterogeneity of the world they lived in. They wanted to create a firmer sense of "us" and "them," with

Christianity and its imagined homogeneity, spirituality, and values inside, and everything else—Muslims, Jews, immigrants—outside.

For Massignon to enter into this discourse and publish on the beauty, even *holiness*, of Islam itself redirected the conversation. This set in motion the very first generation of Catholic intellectuals interested in studying Islam as a religion appreciatively—with feeling and emotion—humanistically, and, at the same time, scientifically. The Belgian Jesuit Joseph Maréchal drew on Massignon's work for his groundbreaking 1926 account of comparative mysticism, *Studies in the Psychology of the Mystics*, which included Islamic texts as authentic sources testifying to genuine mystical experience that could be studied alongside classic authors of Christian mysticism, such as John of the Cross and Teresa of Ávila.[50] Massignon's approach in 1922 demonstrated that Islam possesses its own religious *sources*, which segued into the Jesuits' and Dominicans' establishment of the *ressourcement* (or "turn to the sources") movement in precisely this period, where they engaged the work of translating and analyzing ancient Christian sources to breathe new life into modern theology.[51] For example, inspired by Massignon, in 1939 Marie-Dominique Chenu, a Dominican theologian and one of the leading figures of *ressourcement*, suggested Islamic studies as a new direction for the *ressourcement* work of the Dominicans: "It is necessary to engage in a preliminary and in-depth task—to *know* Islam, its history, its doctrine, its civilization, its resources, to know it through serious, and extensive studies to which true apostles consecrate their lives."[52] Chenu sought young Dominicans who could pick up Massignon's mantle in their order, someone with technical Arabic skills as well as an interest in and sensibility for texts that were theological and mystical rather than archaeological or historical.[53] In 1939, Chenu found a promising young Dominican, Georges Anawati, who was born in Syria but grew up mainly in Egypt, a Muslim-majority country. Anawati was a rare Catholic priest who knew Arabic but was also a Francophile, having chosen the Dominican religious order after discovering Thomas Aquinas through reading Jacques Maritain.[54] Anawati was eventually mentored by Massignon and wrote in his journal in 1934 after meeting him, "What seems to me to be my path ... is *Islam*."[55] This path of Islam for the sole purpose of learning was unheard of for a scholarly priest at the time. Launching his program of studying Islam in the method of *ressourcement*, Anawati claimed, "We want to study Islam according to the sources. We want to study the matter according to its *own* foundations, as it is known, not otherwise. In the same way, when people study Christianity, we would give them sources. I won't be speaking, the sources will speak for themselves."[56] Anawati heeded Massignon's advice to "follow Muslims literally" and moved to Algeria, which allowed him to meet more Muslims personally while he studied.[57] Eventually, Anawati published *Introduction to Muslim Theology* in 1948 and went on in 1953 to serve as the director of the Institut dominicain d'études orientales (Dominican Institute of Oriental Studies) in Cairo, which he founded as an "apostolate of friendship" with Muslims and which still exists today.[58] Anawati became, along with Massignon, one of the most preeminent Islamicists in the world. He joined Massignon in helping dismantle European biases that depicted Islam as dry, legalistic, and lacking spiritual depth and beauty.

Though Massignon's approach and influence on other scholars did crack the edifice of anti-Islamic sentiment among Catholics, one can also see how it subtly contributed to larger currents in interwar France that depicted Muslims as eternally and inherently religious (even if, according to Massignon, they were beautifully so) and thus outside the confines of French secularism, France's internal and eternal "other." The work of Naomi Davidson studies the collaborations between North African Muslim émigré leaders and state officials in interwar Paris to create the Mosquée de Paris and the Franco-Muslim hospital, for example, arguing that the particular kind of "French Islam" they set up, with its aesthetics, architecture, and opening ceremonies, established the Muslim community in France as thoroughly religious and especially recalcitrant to the assimilation of secularism. Even the most sympathetic representations of Muslims in terms of Islamic religion as spiritual and as countercultural played into this logic of Muslims as the inassimilable religious others within a secular state.[59] As Mayanthi Fernando notes, the history of secularism in France has always been a process of state management that relies on an array of disciplinary techniques aimed at cultivating secular religious subjects. When it comes to Muslims, the sense that they are inherently religious and hence unsecular and un-French remained the essential basis for the political and legal claim that Algerian Muslims were not French.[60]

Louis Massignon's work spiritualizing Islam is entangled in these larger dynamics of power, but his expansive networks of relationships with living Muslim communities (rather than textual analysis of "spiritual Islam" alone) complicated matters. In 1922, he was invited by King Farouk to teach Arabic at the new Egyptian University and eventually was appointed to the Egyptian Arabic Language Academy, and Massignon's connections with Muslims communities would continue to deepen, pushing him toward perspectives of increasing solidarity. This combination of erudition and intimacy with texts and people that worked against the logic of xenophobia seemed to endow Massignon with an incredible charismatic, religious power. There was some remnant of the orientalist fantasy of the "mystic East" that made people see *in* Massignon all those Sufi mystics in whom he was absorbed, giving him a spiritual charisma that was unmatched in this context by anyone except perhaps Jacques Maritain. The medievalist Marie-Magdeleine Davy once described Massignon as "the man in whom God comes alive." She wrote, "I know no other way to say it. I felt next to Massignon the presence of the mystery of God." She continued, saying that as their friendship strengthened, "the more I came to see Massignon as living proof of the reality of God. Not a simulation, but proof." When he spoke it was as if the "eternal flowed through him and he was only the instrument." "Watching him," she wrote, "one had to think of one of the visions of the prophet Daniel when he sees a river of fire flow."[61] In an obituary for Massignon, Jean Lacouture described how those around him wondered if "this man of fire was not inhabited by a singular presence, and if that feverish, precipitous, hissing voice was not that of a prophet."[62] Stirred by his own inner guides, for some, Massignon embodied something of that transforming, contagious power of the supernatural that Victor and Edith Turner made famous.[63] With this unusual religious charisma, he not only moved his readers and listeners toward different and new conclusions about Islam but also stirred in people—fascinated with Islam—something of the transcendent other, Catholic France's exotic outsider.

These feelings elicited among those who knew him certainly flowed, at least in part, from wider currents of exoticism and orientalism in interwar Paris, especially for the many in interwar Europe who had grown disillusioned with Christianity.[64] But Massignon himself was more rooted in firsthand knowledge of the living Islamic world, rather than merely an exotic fantasy. Eventually in commitment to the political struggles of Muslims in the context of colonialism, Massignon's approach both drew from and went beyond the old orientalist assumptions and its exoticizing tendencies to see the Islamic world as Europe's shadow.

JEAN MOHAMMED ABD-EL-JALIL AND A NEW SPIRITUAL FAMILY FOR MASSIGNON

Despite his public accolades, Massignon's private life was complicated. He had always felt pulled toward something more dramatic than the life of a comfortable, prestigious scholar, a family man enjoying the fruits of a university position. He had long desired to live as his spiritual companions Foucauld and al-Hallāj had: unconcerned with rank, acclaim, or family, someone who pitched his tent alongside the poorest Muslims, outside the seductive safety of the university or the mainstream institutions of religion.[65] A life that rejected the comforts of marriage and children was also surely tempting for Massignon because of his sexuality. As a young adult, Massignon was openly gay and had at least one serious lover, about whom he often spoke.[66]

After his 1908 conversion to Catholicism, in an era when any form of sexuality was shrouded in silence and homosexuality an unspoken taboo, Massignon decided as much as possible to deny his sexuality and live the life of a celibate. After this decision, he was sustained by dreams of living a life of radical asceticism and detachment in the desert, like Foucauld or even al-Hallāj, immersed somewhere in the Muslim world. But in 1912, Massignon's spiritual director urged him to relinquish his radical dreams of solitude in the desert and instead "have a Christian family" by getting married, having children, and pursuing the life of a scholar in Paris. Massignon found out late in life that his own mother had secretly gone to his spiritual advisor and begged him to advise her adult son to marry and have children.[67] Massignon obeyed and, in 1913, married and went on to have three children. Little is known about Massignon's wife, whose life bore immense strains. She was a young woman married to a gay man who was passionate about a religious world that was totally foreign to her. But she and Massignon had a marriage that lasted almost fifty years. They were together as he rose to the heights of the academic firmament, though Massignon's life was stirred by others outside it.

While Foucauld and al-Hallāj were his first spiritual friends, other significant *amis* followed. A decade into his marriage, Massignon met a new spiritual friend in Paris, a young Moroccan man named Jean Mohammed Abd-el-Jalil. Abd-el-Jalil became an honorary member of Massignon's family, one of Massignon's academic protégés, and an outlet for Massignon's frustrations with domestic life.[68] Massignon and Abd-el-Jalil exchanged letters over a period of thirty-five years, a correspondence unmatched in length for Massignon. Most of the letters by Louis Massignon (277 in total) have been preserved, but only 84 by Abd-el-Jalil remain. Until the mid-1920s, Massignon's spiritual companions were men from the past, who kept the door to the sacred ajar through memory, relics, translations, visits to graves, and prayers. But his relationship with Abd-el-Jalil was different.

In 1925, Jean Mohammed Abd-el-Jalil was a talented Muslim student who had graduated from a Franciscan missionary high school in Fes, Morocco. After finishing at the top of his class, he was selected to pursue higher studies in Paris, and his Franciscan friends from Morocco arranged for him to stay at a room in a Franciscan convent in the city.[69] He left to complete a degree in Arabic language and literature at the Sorbonne. He also secured permission to take courses at the Institut Catholique to gain a better understanding of his new host country's Catholicism and was the institute's first Muslim student.[70] Events during his first two years in Paris, however, would conspire to warm him to the Catholic faith in ways he had never planned. In retrospect, we can see that these are linked to his formation at a Catholic colonial missionary school as a Muslim child: his connections set him up with devout Catholic French right away, and in Paris, he lived with a Catholic host family with whom he became close, then met Jacques Maritain, most likely at the Institut Catholique where Maritain was teaching. Abd-el-Jalil also befriended Father Paul Mulla Zade, a Turkish priest who had converted from Islam to Catholicism. Unlike many students and exiles from the international community, Abd-el-Jalil was not drawn into the artistic scene but fascinated by what he perceived as the old Catholicism of France, the piety of the Franciscan monks and nuns in the convent in which he stayed. In the late 1920s, Abd-el-Jalil became close with Massignon, who had knowledge of both Catholic and Islamic cultures, and although he claimed Massignon tried to actually dissuade him from doing so, on Holy Saturday of 1928, Abd-el-Jalil was baptized into Catholicism. Massignon and Paul Mulla Zade were his godfathers.

After Abd-el-Jalil's conversion, a telegram was sent to the minister of foreign affairs in Morocco: "Abd-el-Jalil, Moroccan student sent to Paris for schooling has just converted to Catholicism. His conversion was particularly notable as he was baptized by the Archbishop of Paris and he received for his First Communion a missal and rosary from the Pope himself. This conversion is quite significant for a Moroccan and is a result of a long moral and intellectual evolution, and was not purely spontaneous."[71] Regardless of the prestige of his conversion, Abd-el-Jalil's Muslim family was devastated. For his father, it was as though his son had died. He had a funeral rite in Morocco celebrated for Abd-el-Jalil.[72] His parents join the ranks of those like Mistral's son, the Maritains' elderly parents, and Massignon's wife, family members left confused and heartbroken by these new spiritual friendships.

But Massignon stepped in, referring to Abd-el-Jalil as his "infinitely cherished son," and together they had the common goal of "reconciling Muslims and Christians." The two sustained a spiritually passionate correspondence—over three hundred letters spanning thirty-five years have been preserved—and they alternated between Arabic and French in their exchanges.[73] Abd-el-Jalil and Massignon also developed a deep spiritual bond with Saint Francis, the medieval saint who, according to Christian hagiographic legend, traveled extensively in the Arabic world after the pope sent him to convert Muslims, which he did through service and love rather than violence. Abd-el-Jalil became a Franciscan in 1929, and Massignon became a tertiary Franciscan in 1933, taking on the name Ibrahim, Arabic for Abraham: "I believe in the God of Abraham; real, close at hand, personal. . . . This is the first link which links me to my Muslim friends," Massignon explained.[74]

After they became Franciscans, the friendship between Massignon and Abd-el-Jalil became more erotically charged, secret, and intense. "It is unnecessary to tell you," Abd-el-Jalil wrote his godfather in 1929, "that I think of you constantly, since now more than ever we find ourselves together in the Divine Heart."[75] Abd-el-Jalil later described how, "God has imposed in our souls a secret, deep tie," and Massignon assured his godson, "Our souls are linked together beyond death."[76] Massignon reflected over twenty years later that Abd-el-Jalil's "friendship was able to break the wall" of his own heart so that he might be able to "know more the chain of Love that the divine grace has passed down through all the turns of my life, with such heart-rending beauty."[77] Al-Hallāj and Foucauld were Massignon's first links in the chain of grace. By the late 1920s, there was a spiritual constellation consisting of al-Hallāj, Foucauld, Saint Francis, and Abd-el-Jalil lighting up Massignon's religious imagination. Abd-el-Jalil, however, was invited into Massignon's own nuclear family in a way that no one else ever was. Abd-el-Jalil attended the First Communion of Massignon's daughter, prayed for the health of each of Massignon's children, had weekly lunches at their home, took vacations with them, and looked after Massignon's children when both he and his wife were away. When Massignon's son Yves died tragically after a long illness, Abd-el-Jalil was the celebrant at the first anniversary of his death.

As their relationship strengthened, Massignon also began to confide in his godson his longings to escape the confines of family life and his regrets at having succumbed to it. He confessed in 1930 that he yearned for the hermitage where he could have lived, waiting for martyrdom, in simple service to Muslims in North Africa. He told Abd-el-Jalil that he married only in obedience to his confessor, who was "weak enough" to obey the tearful pleadings of his mother behind his back. He admitted to Abd-el-Jalil, "I can only think

of that corner in the desert where I could have prayed, out of this world. . . .
It is a sort of slow death I endure, nibbled by family concerns, like the figure
of the Chinese man, condemned under the mask in which rats swarm."[78] In
a 1935 letter, Massignon described to Abd-el-Jalil his disappointment in the
lukewarm faith of his family, how even Yves, his dying son, did not place
God "in the center of his heart." Most of all, his family took time from his
mission: "It is remarkable," he wrote to Abd-el-Jalil, "that with each step I
take towards God, God responds by hitting me in the heart. . . . My work is
paralyzed and stopped abruptly with each instant of unpredictable worry
or difficulty."[79] For his part, Abd-el-Jalil surprisingly often defended Massignon's wife, even urging Massignon to be more understanding and kind.
But "friendship," Massignon wrote to another friend late in his life, "is the
cornerstone of human spiritual life, not family."[80] There is a troubling undertow to the Massignon and Abd-el-Jalil friendship that Massignon saw at the
foundation of his spiritual life. It is impossible to untangle the intensity of his
bond outside the logic of colonial power and desire—Massignon an older,
established French male scholar, Abd-el-Jalil a younger Moroccan student.

Within this set of complicated feelings that inhabited broader social and
political structures, sanctified as godfather and godson, Massignon and
Abd-el-Jalil forged a kind of Islamic-infused Christian spirituality. Massignon advised Abd-el-Jalil not to take a Christian name at baptism but to
keep Mohammed Abd-el-Jalil.[81] Together they read bits of the Qur'an each
day, along with the Arabic translation of the New Testament. They engaged
in practices like praying for Muslims on Friday, their holy day, and fasting
during Ramadan so that they might obtain, according to Massignon, what
they imagined as a peace between Muslims and Christians. In 1932, on the
1300th anniversary of the Prophet Mohammad, Abd-el-Jalil organized a
nine-day novena in the Franciscan chapel in La Verna, Italy, where Saint
Francis received the stigmata. Abd-el-Jalil ended up becoming a Franciscan
priest and a specialist in Islam, teaching and writing on his native religion at
the Institut Catholique, as well as publishing with some success works such
as *L'Islam et nous* (1938) and *Aspects intérieurs de l'Islam* (1949). These works,
along with Massignon's, can be counted among the early works of Catholic
scholars studying Islam sympathetically and descriptively. More than mere
friends, now Abd-el-Jalil was another portal to the sacred. "You," Massignon
wrote to Abd-el-Jalil, "who are in front of God together with al-Hallâj, my
Arabic consolation."[82]

Yet despite the desire for Muslim-Christian harmony that guided their
efforts, and their own work in objective scholarship on the sources of Islam,
according to Dominique Avon, the early emphasis on conversion (embod-

ied by Abd-el-Jalil) "clouded and darkened" these initial efforts at Catholic-Islamic understanding.[83] Late in life, Abd-el-Jalil began to denounce what he called the "pseudo-amitié" of many Christian and Muslim friendships. Abd-el-Jalil wrote to Massignon that Frenchmen espouse "flattery [to Muslims] but it's hypocritical. There's an atmosphere in Paris that envelops French-Muslim, Christianity-Islam relationships that I sometimes find stifling."[84] It is difficult not to imagine the intense bond with Massignon as part of this atmosphere. He claimed that he felt "more free" when he traveled to Cairo and Tehran than he did in Paris, despite the risks of being a convert and the relatively more sparse intellectual resources. He confessed to Massignon that in Paris, it was only in the quiet serenity of the convent, alone, that he felt comfortable.[85] For one year, in 1936, Abd-el-Jalil was admitted to a sanatorium for mental health issues. He spent his final years in France, for the most part cloistered, venerating the cross and the stigmatized Saint Francis. The split from his own family was a terrible ordeal. He tried to reconcile with them to no avail. The story of Abd-el-Jalil strikes me as a tragic one. The atmosphere around Massignon was one in which a spiritual, volitional family replaced a biological one, but Abd-el-Jalil's separation from his own family was terrible for him. His conversion caused massive controversy and concern among many Muslim families in Morocco and even beyond about sending their children to study in France.[86] Would this also happen to their Muslim children? To be sure, Abd-el-Jalil's works on Islam were well received as scholarly accomplishments, and he also produced general scientific works on textual studies in Islam aimed at Catholic audiences that made an impact. These works, though significant, emerged from an intense friendship and its swirls of desire and power between mentor and young scholar, France and North Africa, and were clouded, too, by family loss.

Although Massignon stayed in close contact with Abd-el-Jalil all his life, the vision of Christian and Muslim solidarity that their bond represented—a totally male, prayerful approach to textual study that blended traditions with the aim of serenity, even through conversion (without overt proselytizing)—would be increasingly unsatisfying for both Massignon and Abd-el-Jalil. By 1929, Massignon yearned for something else, something closer to the vision of his first companions al-Hallāj and Foucauld, so he began teaching night classes that year to low-income North African Muslims working in Paris through the group Équipes sociales nord-africaines, something he would continue to do until he died. Five years after he began this work, Massignon met another friend, the Egyptian feminist and activist Mary Kahil, whom he called his *âme-amie* (soul-friend) and who would reignite Massignon's earlier, more radical commitments and change the course of his life.

MARY KAHIL AND MASSIGNON

———————

Massignon first met Mary Kahil in Cairo, where she lived, in 1912, the year before he married. Their first encounter was brief, but they became reacquainted more than twenty years later, when Massignon returned to Cairo in 1934. It is safe to say that Massignon had never known anyone quite like Kahil. Kahil was beautiful and wealthy, having inherited a considerable fortune, but never married. She deliberately created a life for herself that was, as she put it, immersed in the world unlike a nun but independent unlike a mother, just as Massignon had long dreamed to do.[87] There was much about Kahil that would have drawn Massignon to her: she was Catholic, but an Eastern Catholic of the Melkite tradition indigenous to the Middle East, which uses Arabic as its liturgical language. As an adult, she chose to dedicate her considerable resources and talents to the well-being of Christians and Muslims in the Arab world through philanthropy in general and Egyptian feminist causes in particular. (Kahil told Massignon at their first meeting, "I'm not involved in Christian organizations. I'm involved in Muslim good works.")[88] Educated in Cairo by French nuns, with a Syrian father and German mother, she became well connected to Muslim intellectuals and activists in that country. In 1923, when Kahil was thirty-five, she cofounded the Egyptian Feminist Union (EFU), along with other Egyptian women (some Muslim, some Eastern Christian), including Huda Sha'arawi, Ihsan al-Quisi, Gamila Abou Shanab, Ceza Nabarawi, and Asis Fawsi.[89] Kahil and these women benefited from the (at the time) relatively liberal inheritance laws for Muslim and Christian women, and these Egyptian women of means funded their own feminist movement. The EFU had a building in Cairo, where they hosted elaborate celebrations and political events to advance the position of women in society, which even once featured a performance by the famous Egyptian singer Umm Kulthum.[90] Fluent in French, German, and Arabic and with a vast network of connections to Muslim and Christian politicians and activists throughout Egypt and Europe, Kahil played a key role in the EFU's work. In 1940, she joined the Egyptian Jesuit priest Henry Habib Ayrout to help found the Association for Christian Schools in Upper Egypt, which provided free education for thousands of Egyptian children of all faiths and still exists today. She also served as a codirector with Hidaya Afifi Barakat, who was Muslim, of Mabarrat Muhammad 'Ali, an Egyptian women's philanthropic organization dedicated to creating health clinics in poor sections of Cairo for women, mostly Muslim mothers. The work of

Mabarrat Muhammad 'Ali remained for Kahil a "central lifelong mission."[91] She and Barakat expanded the organization to include alleviating malaria and cholera, in addition to providing outpatient health clinics. Kahil helped pay for teams of doctors to go into poor communities and combat the spread of cholera.[92] According to one Egyptian friend who knew Kahil for over forty years, "She was frank and direct, never afraid to speak her mind and challenge people's views. She was also extremely generous with her personal wealth, which was quite considerable. Although she was from an upper-class family and wealthy background, she lived her own live in austerity and gave out quite a lot of money to various charitable organizations, both Christian and Muslim."[93]

Kahil thus represented a very different model of Christian engagement with the Muslim world from Massignon: on the ground, face-to-face, part-nering with Muslim activists and intellectuals, responding to social issues by meeting practical needs, and using her own privilege to improve the flourish-ing of Muslims and Christians together. She was Catholic but Arabic in her language, culture, and friendships. With the exception of the night classes he taught with the Équipes sociales nord-africaines, Massignon's work for Christian and Muslim unity resided more in the realm of prayer and schol-arship, though his scholarship undeniably made significant inroads in the Christian perception of Islam. Massignon also represented something new to Kahil: he gave to Kahil a powerful religious, spiritual, even mystical way of understanding her work; he sanctified it, intensified it. "It seemed to me that he had confirmed in me what I was already doing, when he said I had a vocation to live among Muslims and devote myself totally to them. And thus I became attached to Massignon, not as a man, but as my spiritual master. It was a silent call in the depths of my being, quite unexpected."[94] Massignon had a way of igniting those sentiments.

The day they were reacquainted in February 1934, Kahil and Massignon seem to have connected right away. They took a train together to Damietta, on the outskirts of Cairo, most likely Massignon's idea: an old Franciscan chapel sat there, made famous by Saint Francis of Assisi. It was the chapel where Saint Francis purportedly made an offering of himself to be burned "by fire" as a test, in 1219, "if it would touch the heart of a single Muslim."[95] At this Franciscan chapel in Egypt, Kahil recalled "sitting in this church with three large windows overlooking the Nile, and palm trees swayed behind the windows. I then prayed in an intense devotion, in a way that was frightening, difficult to explain. I was praying about the disappearance of Syrian Chris-tians, but Louis told me to keep 'praying for them, for Muslims. Give your life to them. Make a vow.' 'What vow?' 'A vow to love them.'" She did it. She and Massignon made a vow to live their lives on behalf of Muslims, "not so that they would be converted, so that the will of God might be accomplished in them, through them." The vow purportedly transported Kahil from the mundane to "an exalted state, impossible to explain." Massignon joined her, and he, too, vowed to live his life for Muslims, to pray for them, to love them, and to stand in their place when they suffer (their understanding of what this would mean would evolve over the course of their lives). As they walked out of the church, Kahil recollected, "I found a carpenter's nail on the floor and gave it to Massignon. 'Why the nail?' he asked. 'To pierce your heart,' and he put it in his pocket." They left, exhausted. "We made this vow with great fervor," she explained, "in a state of illumination that I have never known since. On coming out of church, I felt transformed, no longer my former self." Kahil and Massignon took the train back to Cairo directly to the Jesuit residence where her spiritual director lived, a priest whom she loved. She told him what happened, then "we threw ourselves into his arms, we were so happy and everything in my life changed." Massignon's life changed too. "My heart," he wrote that day, "burns anew. Our meeting was a terrible shock that made me become holy (a saint)."[96] Massignon had contacts in high places, and Pope Pius XII approved their vow that summer. For the rest of their lives, they would experiment and wrestle with the meaning of this new vow and its implications for their lives.

A few days after they professed their vow, Massignon had to leave Cairo and return home to Paris, at least physically, and to his normal life as esteemed professor at the Collège de France, husband, and father. But every-thing had changed. For the rest of 1934 and the following year, Massignon and Kahil exchanged letters at a feverish pace, almost every couple of days. Each year, Massignon would travel to Cairo to visit Kahil, and they would renew their vow at the Franciscan chapel in Damietta. Kahil also regularly came to Europe. Their friendship lasted until Massignon's death in 1962, and their correspondence from 1934 to 1962 makes up a massive collection of 1,488 letters. We only have access to some of them; Kahil destroyed many of hers, and others are today held in a secret case in the Vatican to which no one has access, not even Massignon's children.[97] Most of what is available comes from the result of a meeting Kahil had with the young scholar Jacques Keryell in Egypt in 1972, when she was eighty-three years old, ten years after Massignon died. Kahil allowed Keryell to view much of what remained of her correspondence with Massignon, along with parts of her diary of the time. In 1987, Keryell transcribed several of the letters she showed him and published them in French, along with a detailed introduction and short biography of her life, in *L'hospitalité sacrée*.[98] Keryell's transcriptions offer us a glimpse—even if an undeniably partial one—into a truly extraordinary archive of spiritual friendship, one that provides occasion for thinking through the complex issues of spiritual experience and politics, relationality, sexuality, and celibacy. It helps us see how Massignon's renewed commitment to a life radically dedicated to the service of Muslims—a seed planted in him by al-Hallāj and Foucauld—grew and flourished through his *amitié spirituelle* with the Arab feminist Kahil. Their spiritual friendship intensified, radicalized, and transformed their lives and commitments.

Most scholars of Massignon acknowledge a more radical turn in his work toward more overt political activism on behalf of Muslims in the Middle East and Algeria in the late 1940s that lasted until his death, but they tend to see it as a result of Massignon's deepened understanding of Gandhian nonviolence.[99] While Gandhi did play an important role in the politicizing of Massignon's religious worldview, it was the intensity of his spiritual bond with Kahil, the seasoned activist, that provided Massignon the most fertile soil for the flourishing of his considerable public commitments. Massignon's early letters to Kahil signal that, above all, their reconnection had reawakened his devotion to a life that was sparse and intense, with a God-given purpose he could move toward. It stirred a desire that had lain dormant for twenty-five years to leave behind the complications of Paris—his professional prestige, obligations, and family—and fulfill his vocation to love and serve the Muslim world. Massignon explained to Kahil in a 1934 letter, "Our meeting pierced my heart, and revived within me, in a wrenching manner, my promises to belong to God alone, in all holiness, forever."[100] It overturned what he called "the normal framework of my life, which I never believed in, but which, for the past two years, I had consented to, in lukewarm and cowardly abandon." He continued:

> Your spiritual presence, so direct, so fraternal, is a piercing reminder to me, like some sudden-felt anxiety: it made me realize that God did not resurrect me, praying in Arabic in 1908, so that I could just fall asleep in France, surrounded by general regard, scorning the example of the mystics who guided me and whose study earned me my name and my position. What shamefulness! They *themselves* chose exile, the desert, deprivation, persecution, and torture. I, the friend of al-Hallāj and Foucauld, I was thinking of staying alive by comfortably exploiting their works until death. May you be blessed for having called me back to the desire for

martyrdom. My heart is once more enkindled, and I have promised God
to tear myself away from everything, gradually, gently, but firmly, so as
to be judged worthy of martyrdom in a Muslim land if God permits.[101]

If al-Hallāj and Foucauld had set his heart aflame for God and Islam when
he was a young scholar, something about Kahil—her "spiritual presence"—
reignited it all over again. He had been on a different path in the 1920s
and early 1930s, godfather to a Muslim convert to Catholicism, engaged
in prayerful scholarship, and enjoying incredible distinction as an international scholar. But Kahil enabled Massignon to reach into the other world
again, just as he had done decades earlier, delivering him from a life of ordi-
nariness.

Massignon's sense of God's presence in his reawakened vocation gradually gave way to an abiding divine feeling in his and Kahil's spiritual friendship *itself* and in the ever-deepening love they shared. He wrote to her in
1935: "I ardently pray in thanksgiving for the year 1934, the year when God
clearly told us that He loved you and I for the common work we share and
which will survive us. This intoxicating certitude bathed my Heart after Holy
Communion this morning. This great fire of Love between friends, which
can no longer be denied, nor can it be overcome, and this flame rises more
and more, nourished by all our desires for perfection, which we conceived
of in the past but which we have now transfigured."[102] Massignon's increasing belief that God was present in the intimacy of their bond had a way of
letting this love off its leash, as they experienced a madder and deeper passion. Massignon remained married and lived primarily in Paris, while Kahil
stayed in Cairo, but their contact was nearly constant. Blessed by God, all
uncertainty was removed from their affections. Sanctioned and sanctified,
the love Massignon described was something much more overwhelming
and intense than what one might normally understand as friendship. He
depicted the "great fire of Love between friends" as something "inebriat-
ing and intoxicating," transformative for both of them, and enflamed with
transcendence ("the flame rises more and more"). In the presence of the
heavenly, their love became Love, elevated to the status of holy: "I continue
with you, this fraternal dialogue in the presence of God, which eternity will
not even interrupt, since there is no question, only the Love." Massignon's
conviction of the sacred presence sustaining their love helped him disregard
the gossip directed their way, as she was single and he married: "What does
this [other people's] incomprehension matter. . . . The more we are friends,
the less we will be understood, but He [God] will be our enclosure."[103] Other

times Massignon seemed more concerned and nervous: "Let's keep our fervor underground," he once wrote to Kahil.[104]

At least in the 1940s, early in the friendship, Massignon seems to have been the more theologically passionate of the pair, and he thought Kahil needed reminding on this score: "You do not insist enough," he once cautioned, "on the supernatural character of our fraternal bond that God has placed between us. I love you (and wanted you), my friend." He added, "God's heart is placed between you and I." Massignon needed God in the friendship, but just as importantly, he needed Kahil for God. Not only did she reconnect him to what he sensed was his God-given purpose in life, but he wrote to her in 1934 of his sense that his experience of God had come to him *through* her. He viewed her as quite literally the vehicle for God's grace and referred to her as Maryam, her name in Arabic:

> From time to time when I find something that astonishes me, that expands and unfetters me, I think it is our Angels who are communicating. How silent it is, the wonderful perfume of incense, the mute prayer of my Arab sister, Maryam, which rises toward God and reaches me hereby the supernatural delicacy of grace. . . . This grace I had never known in such a direct way, constituted by the spiritual presence of a soul-friend [*âme-amie*] who understands and who shares. It is such a direct sign to my heart of my membership in the community of the Church that I praise God for it with all my soul.[105]

One might assume that Massignon's experience of God from Kahil, his "soul-friend," would be a *less* direct way to experience the sacred and that the most direct path to God must be one that is unencumbered by others. (We might think of the words of another Christian Islamicist, Wilfred Cantwell Smith, who stated that faith is an "act I make, alone, naked before God.")[106] But here it is the opposite. God is more immediately apprehended because of her. Massignon writes of his bond with Kahil as "this grace, I *had never known it, in such a direct way*."[107] Likewise, Kahil wrote in 1950, "I do not know how to meditate alone, it is only in writing you, and in my journal, that I put myself in His [God's] presence."[108] God was made real for Massignon and Kahil through one another, and they were each a vehicle of supernatural presence. This was how spiritual friendship worked.

Massignon and Kahil's intimate, religious world was fueled by the language and materiality of both Islam and Christianity. Not only did they often refer to one another by their Arabic names, Ibrahim and Maryam, but

their use of Islamic idioms stretched the French and Christian descriptions
of spiritual friendship. When writing Kahil, Massignon often quoted love
poems from Sufi mystical writings, textual traditions that offer a vividly
sensual spirituality in the form of erotic love poetry, which was addressed,
at the same time, to God or Allah *and* an earthly beloved.[109] The Sufi poets,
like the eighth-century Sufi mystic el-Isha, supplied Massignon with passionate language that could describe the holy love of their friendship, which
he quoted to Kahil in 1949: "God is the Lover, the Love and the Beloved and
it must be said that God is essentially desire (el Isha). . . . Let us eternally
live from this desire that created us."[110] Here Massignon's sense that their
Love is blessed by God deepens into something more: Love *is actually God*.
Massignon also wrote to her the words of the Persian poet Abu Sa'id: "Night
comes, according to the beautiful thought of the Persian Abu Sa'id. 'Rise
up at night: it is at night when the lovers converse . . . seeking the Beloved,
everywhere at night, the doors are closed, except for the door of love.'"[111] The
language of Abu Sa'id and el-Isha intensified Massignon's earlier descriptions of their bond as a "communion of friendship," which he drew from the
Christian gospels in 1935: "We are here," he wrote her, "at the very roots of
the evangelical and Pauline teaching of solidarity in Jesus Christ, who was
the firstborn in a multitude of brothers."[112] Platonic and erotic, the friends of
the Gospel and the passionate erotics of the Sufi masters were seen to flow
together in the Christian-Muslim, French-Arabic religious imagination that
invested their bond with meaning and fervor.

Each year in February—with the exception of 1940–44 when Massignon
waited out World War II in Paris, in painful exile from the Middle East—
they celebrated the anniversary of their vow. Kahil wrote Massignon on the
anniversary in 1950:

> Oh my friend. It is the evening of our vows . . . this mad, holy hour of our
> fraternal union, this "bond of perfection," as Saint Francis de Sales says,
> that nothing can slice apart, not even death. Nothing can extinguish the
> love we have sworn to the Father. Kneeling at the feet of the Father, lying
> down and bowing low in front of the divine majesty of our Father from
> whom all tenderness and mercy flows. This marvelous tenderness that
> covers me with a river of love and joy. Let's reject all thoughts of society
> so that we can welcome the King of Glory. The King of Glory, covered
> with a divine humility, that he lowers down to our levels, lowers down to
> where we are, in this shabby bedroom, to this worn-out, frayed bedroom

where so many times we talked about thousands and thousands of ordinary issues, by this window, where I kept watching out for nosy people.[113]

Kahil's letter depicts the realm of non-ordinary reality, a religious vision or
a memory, and the sensuality of her words is palpable, just as it is in Massignon's correspondences. In some phrases, Kahil seems to imagine herself
alone, where God "covers me with a river of love and joy." Other phrases
envision her and Massignon together, as when God lowers himself "to where
we are," and the location is a shabby, worn-out bedroom. (Whose bedroom?
Hers? Is that really where they so often talked?) Linking their bond with the
seventeenth-century mystic Saint Francis de Sales, who famously carried on
an important spiritual friendship with Jeanne de Chantal, Kahil describes
the two of them together: "*we* welcome the King," "*we* bow low" in a bedroom, *together* offering and receiving God's love, so long as they "reject all
thoughts of society." It is a love she receives from the "King of Glory" with
Massignon, and with her body, which she prepares and positions, "kneeling,
laying down, bowing low."

We have no evidence that Kahil and Massignon's spiritual friendship was
ever physically sexual, but it was undeniably and overtly sexually charged,
and it is unlikely that we will ever know how physical their relationship
was. Massignon's bond with his earlier *amis* was also erotic, and it is tempting to offer this rich, complex archive of Kahil and Massignon's passions as
a straightforward counter to Jeffrey Kripal's claim that Massignon is best
understood as a "morally tortured homosexual."[114] Kripal argues that Massignon's sexual desire for men was repressed after his 1908 conversion. It
never went away but moved underground, only to later "escape" into the
liminal, Catholic-sanctioned realm of mystical experience. This explanation
of sublimation, Kripal contends, explains Massignon's subsequent homoerotic passion for al-Hallāj and Foucauld. Though Massignon's relationship with Kahil does complicate an understanding of Massignon's sexuality
as either heterosexual or homosexual, interpretations focused mainly on
sexual repression and sublimation operate within a binary framework that
narrows, rather than enlarges, our consideration of Massignon and spiritual
friendship. Was he gay or straight? Did they have sex or not? Did they *wish*
they did? Was all this spirituality just a flourish, an elaborate but potentially
unnecessary cover of the real, grittier, but in many ways simpler, physical
passion, which today we may be less likely to condemn?

On one level, there has to be some affirmative answer to the last question especially. Yet these questions prevent us from exploring the richest and most complicated aspects of spiritual friendship. How can we advance a conversation about spiritual friendship and sexuality that probes complexity and mystery rather than stopping just short of it? Overall, there is an over-abundance to the spiritual friendship of Kahil and Massignon that cannot be entirely reduced to genital sexuality, as if sex (and its repression) is the only truth the bonds can reveal. Given the "unnecessarily elaborate panoply," to borrow a phrase from Dipesh Chakrabarty, of religious symbols they used to describe their bond—the great fire of love, the river of joy, angels' commu-nications, the carpenter's nail Kahil gave Massignon as a reminder of their pierced heart—the question whether they just wanted to have sex does not strike me as the only one worth asking.[115] Constance Furey frames this well when she cautions against reading erotically charged religious writings as "hard shells we can crack open to find sexual experience inside."[116]

In an attempt to do justice to the fullness of their experiences of God and of one another, and of one another *with* God and *through* God, I draw on Maggie Nelson's suggestion to "let an individual experience of desire take precedence over a categorical one."[117] We might consider the bond between Kahil and Massignon as neither sacred *nor* profane, neither repressed *nor* expressed; we might think of Massignon's sexuality as neither heterosexual *nor* homosexual. But this relationship may yet be "more complex, more human, more mysterious."[118] Maggie Nelson describes a kind of "contami-nation" in desire that "*makes deep* rather than disqualifies" human experi-ence.[119] For example, one could view Kahil's erotic passion for Massignon as contaminating her love of God or her love of God as mere cover for her real love of Massignon, just as one might interpret Massignon's earlier homosexual relationships as contaminating his heterosexual passion for Kahil (even if potentially celibate). In this framework, the intellectual work would center on merely exposing these contaminations and examining what is *really* underneath all that talk of God if you take away the contamination and the distraction.

In order to remain open to the range and complexity of their experiences, we have to resist the binary logic of God *or* sex, sacred *or* sexual, heterosexual *or* homosexual, platonic love *or* erotic love and situate their relationship in a rich matrix of desires that swirled among Massignon, his spiritual friends, and God. All are on what Elliot Wolfson calls "equal phenomenal footing."[120] Furthermore, if we insist that the friendship was at the same time both celi-bate and erotic, we should resist assuming that the only feelings accompa-nying this were frustration and repression. As Anthony Petro notes in his analysis of a different set of sources in twentieth-century Christianity, "We often think of celibacy as the repression of sexual desire, but what if we ask instead: what kinds of desires could celibacy itself create? Can we imagine a sexually productive celibacy? What might celibate sexuality look like? What might celibate pleasure be?"[121]

When asking these kinds of questions, it is helpful to see the correspondence between Massignon and Kahil as a mystical text, a source about the direct experience of God aimed to describe these experiences and inculcate them for one another while reading. Mystical experience, sexual experience, and intense spiritual friendships share in their efforts, as Constance Furey states, to "imagine the isolated, ordinary self in new, transformed ways," which is *the* predominant theme of the Massignon-Kahil correspondence.[122] When Massignon and Kahil are at their most sensual *and* their most religious, for example, their language centers on the dissolution and transformation of the self before God *and* before one another: Massignon was "transformed, no longer my former self," in a way Kahil found "frightening, difficult to explain"; she herself was in a "state of illumination that I have never known since," "shocked" hearts "burning," "enkindled" *away* from the seductions of the ordinary and mundane and *into* something that "expands and unfetters me." Mysticism and sexuality both have deep reservoirs of words and symbols that signal this process of self-transformation, and Massignon and Kahil drew on these symbols to invest their friendship with meaning, passion, and holiness.

Both the Islamic and Christian mystical traditions have long histories of using relational, embodied, and erotic language to describe human love of the divine. Much like spiritual friendships that are sensual, if not explicitly sexual, mystical texts often evoke a love and longing that is passionate but never fulfilled, since God is understood to be in excess of, or to transcend, what we can experience on earth. Massignon employed Sufi mystical writers to make this claim, but these are prominent themes in Christian mysticism as well. This language of unfulfilled passionate longing has a long history in the Christian tradition that in modernity becomes, according to Bernard McGinn, "a kind of embarrassment to 'decent' Christians."[123] A spiritual friendship could be, for Christians like Kahil and Massignon, the earthly relationship that most closely mimics the affective range of the longing for a transcendent God who is always just out of reach.

Mystical traditions often also express the dark anguish that becomes part of these experiences of love.[124] Likewise, for all the pleasure in Massignon and Kahil's spiritual friendship, the relationship was also incredibly painful, and this seems to be connected to the fact that it could never be consummated. Massignon was married, and for a brief period in the 1950s, he suggested they limit their contact (seemingly a mandate from his spiritual director), and they began to communicate much less frequently. It was devastating to Kahil. Sometime in the early 1950s, Kahil wrote a note in a private journal in the form of a prayer to God: "I would like to tell you about my love," she said, describing her relationship with Massignon. She went on,

> My sick love, imprisoned, enslaved, enclosed in the family, in the dust, this chain around my neck, this millstone around my neck that I drag on the gravel, on the dusty roads where I drag myself on the gravel, on the dusty roads of life, with pain, with anguish, with so much powerless love, useless distress, praying for them, suffering for them, loving them all so much. I want Your Grace, I want to reach You directly, into the storm of Your presence in me. And it is evening of my life, it is evening. Let's go with a new heart, let us go to You.[125]

As much as her spiritual friendship with Massignon brought Kahil in contact with God, late in life, she wanted to "reach You [God] directly," presumably without the messy, painful mediation of Massignon and all the complications it entailed. She switches to the third person plural ("useless distress, praying for them, suffering for them") in a way that suggests "they" may refer to the Muslim community at the center of their shared religious and erotic imagination. To insist on the fullness, complexity, and humanity of Massignon and Kahil's bond—erotic and spiritual, possibly celibate though sexually charged, constrained and fulfilling—and of Massignon's sexuality as heterosexual and homosexual, we must also admit that this bond, which lasted nearly thirty years, was one they experienced as both exhilarating and heartbreaking, life-giving and incredibly painful: a "chain around my neck . . . that I drag on the gravel."

Within this wide range, one of the most remarkable aspects of Massignon and Kahil's story is how the erotic mysticism of their spiritual friendship—in all its fervor, pleasure, and heartbreak—became the vitality for an entirely new kind of activism for both. Very little is written on Massignon and Kahil's spiritual friendship and subsequent public projects, and what has been published tends to interpret their bond as one in which Massignon had ideas about Muslim-Christian relations that Kahil, much more the activist and organizer, then carried out. Keryell argues that Kahil "incarnated" Massignon's vision. Others refer to Kahil as Massignon's "muse."[126]

This predictable reading of the pair greatly follows binary gender stereo-
types (she has the body to do; he has the brains to think, or she is the silent
muse; he is the creative genius). But they were on more equal footing than
that. The pair *together* constituted a complex bundle of cognitive, emotional,
spiritual, and physical attributes. They moved through the world *together*
with their bodies, their imaginations, their language, and the stuff of the
material world: the nail she handed him after the vow; the physical letters
themselves; the "shabby" bedroom where they talked; his tiny, inscrutable
handwriting transcribing Sufi mystics; and on and on. This total package
was transformative for both of them, altering their thinking, their lives, and
their politics in Cairo and in Paris and leavening activist work that was, at
least for a time, global in scope.

THE ACTIVISM OF MASSIGNON AND KAHIL

Both Massignon and Kahil seem to have been constantly reworking what
it meant to live their lives for Muslims and to step into the world on their
behalf. They used the language of poetics and the religious imagination,
rather than formulating a clear political mandate or program. It was an
ongoing, spiritual experiment. But gradually, in the 1940s, their vow evolved
into a commitment rooted in prayer that expressed itself in terms of justice for vulnerable Muslim communities living under colonialism. Kahil
had been working alongside Muslim Egyptian activists in different philanthropic and feminist communities since the mid-1920s in Cairo, but by
1945, Massignon began to frame his understanding of their vow, and indeed
his spiritual friendship with Kahil, in terms of prayer united with justice.
Massignon wrote to her in July of that year describing how justice, God,
and the presence of Kahil would come to him all at once: "I think of you
before God, in these solemn hours or in a single flash. Our prayer must,
more than ever insist on a renewal of the world through justice."[127] Two years
later, in 1947, Massignon and Kahil made their private vow into a public
association, forming a small organization they named Al-Badaliya. The stat-
utes received official recognition by the Greek Catholic patriarch in 1947
and were blessed by Pope Pius XII in a private audience with Massignon in
1949.[128] *Al-Badaliya* is Arabic and means "to take the place of," or substitute
for another, as in "step in on another's behalf."[129] Members were mainly Arabic Christians in Egypt and Roman Catholics in Paris. Kahil gathered the

group weekly in Cairo, and Massignon wrote the newsletter and held meetings in Paris monthly.[130] On one level, the work of their fledgling association drew from the Franciscan approach Massignon had practiced years earlier with his Franciscan godson, Abd-el-Jalil. Members were meant to connect to Muslims through prayer three times daily, and the prayers were modeled on the Franciscan liturgical cycle.[131] The plan was also for them to fast with Muslims during Ramadan and on Fridays. It was a Franciscan model of engagement with Islam, not based on coercion, debate, or even dialogue but imagined through the frameworks of prayer, sacrifice, and love.

But gradually their efforts went beyond the realm of prayer into the explicitly social, political, and cultural spheres. In 1941, Kahil had purchased an abandoned Anglican church in Cairo and paid to have it refurbished and consecrated in the Melkite rite of the Greek Catholic Church under the name Sainte Marie de la Pax. In the building next to the church, she founded what became known as the Dar-el-Salam center, which was dedicated to Muslim-Christian encounters and support for the cultural and intellectual heritage of Arabic Christianity. Since this work was attached to a Greek Catholic church, it was a kind of outgrowth of Eastern Catholicism in Cairo, where she aimed to "create a community of Arab Christians sensitive to the spiritual reality of Islam."[132] The Eastern Catholic community in Cairo of the 1940s was, according to Dominique Avon, "of all Christian communities in the Middle East at the time, the most open to encounters with Muslims and to a spiritual *repprochment* [sic] with Islam."[133] Dar-el-Salam held conferences and led discussions throughout the 1940s and 1950s, which were attended by both Muslims and Christians, mainly Egypt's intellectual and cultural elite. Just as Kahil had done with her activism associated with the EFU, she paid for many of the events out of her own personal funds. Ibrahim Madkour, president of the Arabic Academy of Cairo, described Kahil's rare ability to enter the Islamic and Christian communities equally in her efforts: "Mary spoke the same language to Christians and to Muslims. For her there were no differences. Her action was founded in universal principles and we absolutely can all respect [that]."[134]

Massignon returned to Cairo regularly in support of Kahil's work. He wrote the text for a plaque Kahil ordered for the entrance to the Dar-el-Salam, which declared it a center that "works in the Mediterranean crossroads in order to keep itself in the heart of the renewal of thought in Arab countries. The axial perspective is engaged year to year with its Christian and Muslim participants."[135] Massignon also regularly served as a speaker for the gatherings and, according to Avon, "gave an aura to Dar-el-Salam that nobody else could claim." But because Massignon was in Paris during the war, and they had a break in contact and on the ground in Cairo, Kahil's main partner for greater Christian and Muslim unity was the Dominican priest Georges Anawati. Anawati was an ideal partner for Kahil at Dar-el-Salam. Like Kahil, he was a French- and Arabic-speaking Catholic with Syrian family roots living in Egypt, as well as an active intellectual who aimed for closer Christian-Muslim unity and had also been influenced by Massignon.

Conference themes at Dar-el-Salam rotated among philosophical and theological studies in the Islamic and Christian traditions, Arabic cultural studies, social and legal study, and historical and literary programs. Massignon, Anawati, and Kahil collaborated to set up the roster of speakers, and participants included "professors from universities in Egypt, Europe, and America, directors of institutes and cultural centers, writers and journalists, diplomats, and specialists of all kinds including exegetes, archeologists, patrologists."[136] In addition to conferences, scholars also gave courses to the public, and the center became known as a place where Egyptian intellectuals could publicly experiment with their thinking. Course topics included Christianity in Iran and the mystical teachings of Abdullah Ansari. The Christian Egyptian Naguib Baladi, a professor of philosophy at the University of Alexandria, gave one course on Sartre and another on religious experience in Graham Greene. Muslim professor Ibrahim Madkour gave a course in 1954–55 on readings of Avicenna in Tehran.[137] Another joint collaboration between Kahil and Anawati was a more personal group called Frères sincères (Ikhwan al-safâ'), where Muslim and Christian professors and clergy shared their religion through personal experiences and prayer. Taken together, these efforts at Dar-el-Salam worked to dismantle the simple, dramatic, and binary worldview of a Muslim Middle East on the one hand and a Christian West on the other. Christians praying for love of Muslims during Islamic holy hours, scholars highlighting the intellectual heritage of Christianity indigenous to the Middle East, and Egyptian intellectuals teaching on western European and Muslim writers alike: all of these were ways to perforate an imagined but seemingly impenetrable wall between Christian Europeans and Muslim Arabs, which compelled people to see them as so fundamentally different, so naturally antagonistic, that violence was natural and inevitable.[138] They pushed against an ideology stemming from this dramatic belief that envisioned peace only in xenophobic isolation.

The leaven for all of Kahil's work, as she put it, was the vow she and Massignon made together and the Al-Badaliya community they established. Al-Badaliya was the sole "critical point in her life," the "spiritual source" of the center.[139] For his part, Massignon's annual newsletters from Paris to the Al-Badaliya community, written from 1947 until his death in 1962, increasingly reflected on the vow to "stand in" for Muslims in terms of the darkening political situation for Muslims living under colonialism.[140] The deepened attention to colonial politics was due to many factors that changed the landscape of Muslim and Christian relations in the postwar period, including the 1948 creation of the State of Israel and the cause of the Palestinians, the rise of pan-Arabism and Islamic nationalism, and violent clashes between colonial powers and movements for independence in the Arabic world.[141] In May 1946, France bombed Damascus in response to Syrian and Lebanese calls for independence. Estimates range from hundreds of thousands to one million Algerian Muslims who were killed in the battle for Algerian independence from France, a war that lasted throughout the 1950s and ended in 1962.[142] After World War II, France was still an imperial power, and it became increasingly clear to many, including Massignon, that its model of secularism was deeply hostile to devout Muslim communities in France and its colonies.

In response to these changing realities, Massignon gradually came to see the intercessory work of Al-Badaliya as one that included not only praying for Muslims or working to create closer connections between religions and cultures but also physically stepping into Muslims' situation of political vulnerability and even violence. On January 16, 1955, he wrote to Kahil, "They say that the Badaliya is an illusion because we cannot put ourselves in the place of another, and that it is a lover's dream. It is necessary to respond that this is not a dream." But he admitted, "It certainly appears powerless, yet it requires everything. . . . It is suffering the pains of humanity together with those who have no other pitiful companion than us."[143] For Massignon, the "suffering humanity" came to signal the experience of Muslims living in Algeria protesting the French colonial presence. As the violence of French colonial politics and use of torture were made known, Massignon's writings on Islam and Catholicism no longer gestured toward the "serene peace" that he and his godson Abd-el-Jalil once envisioned so intimately and instead grew darker. By the mid-1950s, the situation in Algeria became, in Massignon's words, "terrible, all poor people, plundered, hunted, tortured to death, smoked in napalm, in caves (like Auschwitz)."[144] Massignon witnessed the cruelty of imperialism and French violence with shock and horror, and the experience gave him an almost apocalyptic sense of injustice that was reflected in the dire eschatological language of the journal he coedited from 1945 to 1957, *Dieu vivant*. The opening pages of the journal notes to readers that it is published during a time that "reminds one of the darkest shadows of the Apocalypse."[145] In response, Massignon began to live out his vocation less exclusively in the lecture halls of the Collège de France and instead took to marching and protesting French policies and the use of torture in the streets (Massignon was arrested for these efforts in 1957), visiting in prison those who had been arrested, helping sort out bodies of victims at morgues, organizing in committee meetings, serving as president of the Comité pour l'amnistie aux condemnés politiques d'outre-mer (Committee for Amnesty for Political Prisoners Overseas) to secure amnesty of political prisoners in Morocco, and writing newsletters extolling nonviolent action to members of the Amis de Gandhi.[146] Even as their public activism was centered in different parts of the world, working at different levels of culture, Massignon and Kahil were with one another in spirit. Kahil wrote to Massignon from Cairo in 1960, "This morning, we protest for Algeria! I share your pains and fears and everyone here is saddened and concerned for this world, where justice no longer prevails."[147] Massignon knew Kahil understood more than anyone his desire for political action that put him in contact with what he called in a letter to Kahil "danger, contempt, calumny, sequestration," just as Massignon imagined that his beloved Foucauld and al-Hallāj did in their own lives.[148]

In Cairo, Kahil's focus remained largely in the cultural and intellectual realm, while Massignon became more radical, but by training or personal disposition, Massignon was never a politician. "It is in fact a mystical position," he explained, "that I have transposed in the field of political phenomena."[149] In other words, his approach to politics drew from the underworld of the religious imagination and evinced something more personal and attentive to the ritual and symbolism of the inner life than the juridical realm of state politics. For example, in 1961, the French newspaper Le Monde ran a story on Massignon's condemnation of what he described as "Muslims killed in secret, in the name of order and nation. We demand they must be stopped."[150] After one particularly violent clash between Algerian activists and the French police, Massignon worked with a student from his evening classes and paid the morgue in Paris to release the body of one of the Muslims who had been killed. He also demanded publicly that the "dead receive from the nation a descent Islamic burial, in the cemetery of Bobigny." He suggested appointing a point person at the mosque who could connect the dead properly with the Muslim community. Massignon's approach engaged the political realm indirectly: What would proper Islamic burial have to do with resisting state-sanctioned killing of Muslims? Why focus the attention on the dead rather than the living? But the state-sanctioned killing of Muslims "in secret," as he called it, "in the name of order and nation," resulted in deaths that happened continually behind the scenes, in undisclosed prisons, and were rarely publicized. This secrecy and silence—no names, funerals, mourning—is a profound act of dehumanization key to the perpetuation of violence. Is not the act of recovering anonymous, inert bodies and returning to them their names, reimmersing the dead in their communities, and giving them a proper, public burial in their own religious tradition a great act of rehumanization? Without stating it directly, the use of ritual expressed the conviction that the lives of Muslims should be mourned, each body and soul prayed for and grieved. Moreover, to ensure proper Islamic funerals was a way for this grief to be a *Muslim* expression of grief. This then brought together universal experiences—grief, resistance to violence—with something specific to Islam, acknowledging that there is a specifically Islamic way for Muslim Algerians to mourn their dead. This is just one example of Massignon's "mystical position" woven into the sphere of politics.

The vow and bond gave both Massignon and Kahil a sense of duty, conviction, and decisive action before God in their work. "For we do not accept apathy," Kahil reminded Massignon in a 1950 letter, "nor mediocrity, nor the spiritual sleep of the age. We will go to Him in the fire of the love that He lights in our heart."[151] As his activist commitments started to deepen, Massignon wrote her, "my thoughts are with you in Damiette, in that ruined church," the place where he recalled "the strong love, which you have revived in my heart, since I found you."[152]

As Massignon and Kahil saw it, French colonial violence against Muslims was stoked by the flames of what he referred to as the rivalry between cultures. If Muslims were so fundamentally unlike European Christians in their religion and culture and were destined for conflict, then eradication, violence, and dehumanization were inevitable.[153] For Massignon, as he wrote to the Al-Badaliya community in 1958, "Are we going to put them [Muslims] in cages like wild beasts under the pretense that their race and their religion are inciting them against our race and religion[?]"[154] In different ways, after their vow, both Kahil and Massignon worked to dismantle the worldview pitting Muslims and Christians against one another. By 1958, Massignon framed this theologically to the Al-Badaliya community:

> There are no chosen people, the grace of Christ circulates everywhere. Christ is present in every living soul. There is no danger in seeing the rising up of grace in Islam, it is the fruit of redemption. . . . The canonical questions intervene from outside and are not the heart of the ques-

tion. Rivalry isn't between religions, it also exists between Rites and Sects and is found everywhere as part of being human. . . . The essence of the Badaliya is to lift the screen by our presence, delivering us from this kind of scandalous rivalry. . . . It is necessary to maintain the presence of Jesus living in us.[155]

To combat the "scandalous rivalry" keeping Christians and Muslims apart, Massignon also insisted on what he learned from Kahil and Anawati about the historical and actual presence of Christians in the Middle East and Muslims in Europe. Even a recognition of this fact worked to perforate a simple mapping of the world of the Muslims in the Middle East and an antagonistic Christianity in the West. Massignon noted in a 1959 report to Al-Badaliya, "It's not too late in Egypt and Syria to convince our Muslim brothers that Christianity is also indigenous to the Middle East, that Arab Christians and Jews can and must support and root for the Arab renaissance. It is the essential foundation of *al Badaliya*."[156] Kahil and Anawati themselves were embodiments of this blending of cultures. The same went for Europe. "The Muslims are inside," Massignon reminded members of Al-Badaliya, "not outside."[157] Massignon knew many Muslims living in Paris, all of whom subverted the idea of a neat division, with Muslims "out there" in the Arab world and Christians "in here" in Europe. He worked closely with many young Muslims in Paris, not only the Muslim immigrant students of his night classes but also young intellectuals who came to Paris to study with him and learn about their own religious tradition. The Arab fiction writer Mahmud al-Mas'adi studied with Massignon, who "revealed to me," described al-Mas'adi, "the horizons of al-Hallāj's experience and the greatest source of meaning, which is Sufism. Sufism is the summary of human adventure."[158] Al-Mas'adi went on to write *Mawlid al-nisyan* (The genesis of oblivion), one of the major novels of the twentieth century that dealt with Sufi themes, published in 1944–45. Massignon also took the Egyptian Muslim scholar 'Abd al-Halim "under his wing."[159] Other students included Mohamed Talbi from Tunisia and Osman Yahya from Cairo. The Iranian political thinker Ali Shariati remembered studying with Massignon in Paris:

The most remarkable course of Professor Massignon is not at the Sorbonne or at the Collège de France, but at the foot of the columns of the mosque of the Muslims in Paris, he sat there with a few vegetable traders and some unfortunate Algerian Arab workers who, in colonial France, had forgotten their religion and their language and taught them

the Qur'an. . . . I love him to the point where I sometimes feel that my
soul can no longer contain my affection for him. . . . My heart hurts, my
breathing stops, my throat is tied, my eyes and my whole body starts
burning. That torments me a lot; I would like to be able to cry a little, to
weep with tears, to relieve myself, but I am ashamed to be told: "Look at
this respectable man, crying for his teacher! A kindergartener, or a little
elementary school pupil, who is this Massignon?"[160]

Though Shariati's memories are effusive, they are not unusual when it comes
to recollections of Massignon, whether from a Muslim or a Christian. But
not all of Massignon's efforts with Muslim students were well received. Some
former students saw his work in mysticism as a "mask" that covered up the
age-old, colonial ambitions that had long been part of orientalist scholarship in Europe.[161] Others accused him of tricking Muslims into having too
much faith in a Europe that never made good on its promises, while some
Catholics labeled him as self-hating for abandoning his European roots in
light of his stances during the Algerian War.

As his thinking on Al-Badaliya evolved, Massignon's own perspective
grew more self-critical, and he began to see the organization no longer primarily as an expression of Christian love extended outward for the benefit
of Muslims (a notion that still relies on colonial logic) but as something that
required the transformation of Christians themselves. It is Christians who
often stand in the way, he wrote, of breaking down barriers between "us" and
"them." "The greatest obstacles," he explained to his Al-Badaliya community
in 1959, "come from *ourselves*. It is we who need to be purified, *our* thoughts,
our vision."[162] Massignon wrote to Kahil, "Not through seeing but through
feeling in my heart" that even "you and I should not delude ourselves. It's
not because we would have envisioned an ideal that we would then believe
to have fulfilled it. It's not because we would have tried to describe the ideal
life of a Christian today within the Church and its conflict with the Islamic
world, that we fully partake in it."[163] He had more fully extracted himself
from subtler colonial mentalities late in life, arguing in 1962 that racism was
the obstacle preventing European Catholics from standing in real solidarity
with Muslims.[164] Massignon was also disappointed in the church's failure to
speak about the cause of oppressed Muslims in the world and the violent
legacy of colonialism. Although the Second Vatican Council did, eventually,
include one line about Islam, it originally had no plans to do so. In August
1958, he wrote about Algeria, "My dear country is getting possessed by evil

spirits, and the cowardice of our Cardinals and Bishops keeps me awfully in AWE."[165]

Massignon remained a professor at the Collège de France, but as the 1950s progressed, his domain became the night schools, the streets where marches took place, the tiny chapels where immigrants worshipped, and the obscure caves that drew, at least as he imagined it, Muslim and Christian pilgrims. In the late 1950s, Massignon reflected on his work in an unpublished paper, as he grew more and more distant from the elite centers of academic and religious power: "I have become a prison-visitor and I must say that I have found the experience of God more in these prisons than among free people, among people in power."[166] He confessed to Kahil that he began to locate God not in "pious materials" but evermore often in tiny places where he went "alone, as you [Kahil]" say, "into the most abandoned places."[167] In the end, Kahil, too, framed her understanding of their vow, their experiment, in precisely this shared sense of a holy weakness. Despite her accolades, wealth, and the thriving center, it was Al-Badaliya she sensed at the center of the work, which she described in a 1962 letter to Anawati: "This is my hope, my prayer for the Badaliya, this little thing, sick and dying, that it be like a lamp of sanctuary that never extinguishes."[168] Though both Massignon and Kahil evoked images of emptiness, weakness, abandonment, and solitude late in life, it was the fullness of an intense and unusual decades-long spiritual friendship that fueled the descent.

CONCLUSION

In 1962, while she was in Cairo, Mary Kahil learned of the death of her soul-friend Louis Massignon in Paris. She wrote:

> How can his death be real, possible, acceptable? He brought life. He died in the hospital at 11:30 on the 31st of October, the eve of All Saints. He will not be mentioned with all the other saints. He will be a saint on his own. . . . I went back to the small Franciscan chapel that he loved so much. In front of the crèche there were roses in front of the infant Jesus. Oh! Infant Jesus, I told you how much I loved him and my heart is burning like a furnace. I'm burning like a blaze. And you, Jesus, you allowed me to love him, you planted this love in my heart like a cross. Like a cross,

and it is my cross, this burning love I have for Louis Massignon. You Jesus
Christ compelled me to love him. Louis also told me that Jesus compelled
him to love me, otherwise it is inexplicable. It is a divine decree, God's
command. . . . Louis Massignon is my cross to bear and I bear it lovingly on my shoulders, this bright cross. . . . Louis wrote to me always
of resurrection. He *knew* he was going to die, but I didn't. I keep Jesus,
lovingly, dead, but living by his Presence, in this Heart-Tomb [*Coeur-
tombeau*], lovingly guarded by me, in my heart, whose Massignon's love
has given me.[169]

Here, Kahil draws on a long devotional tradition that uses the image of
Christ's grave as carved out of the devotee's own heart, but she adds a third
person. Massignon's love was the vehicle that gave her Jesus, "dead, but living." To describe her love, like all the protagonists in this book, she draws
on symbols of fire: "burning," "bright," a heart "like a furnace." But uniquely,
Kahil also pulls from classic theological images of the cross she bears to
make sense of a bond that has been "otherwise inexplicable" without God,
so difficult and full of sorrow, "like a stone around her neck"; so full of heartbreak even with all the accomplishments; so crowded with the many "nosy
people" hovering nearby. But understood religiously, the cross of their *amitié*
fits within Kahil's sense of salvation in her religious imagination. The year
Massignon died, Kahil wrote in her journal of a vision she had in church,
in which Abd-el-Jalil appeared to her, telling her that Massignon sacrificed
and suffered too in their love, a vision that brought Kahil great peace. This
painful, unusual love bore fruit in vivid experiences of God for both, experiences that reawakened their commitments to the world and generated
Dar-el-Salam, Al-Badaliya, and activism for Egypt, Algeria, Morocco, and
beyond. Though Massignon is remembered as the most influential Christian
Islamicist in the modern world, it was Kahil who reawakened his most fervent commitments. While Kahil's efforts are largely unknown in the West,
she was awarded the Egyptian national humanitarian award for her work
in 1972.[170] Seven years later, in 1979, Mary Kahil died, and Georges Anawati
celebrated a home mass in her honor.[171]

Massignon's biographers and friends are right when they describe him
as strange, unique, and a loner, a wandering Don Quixote and something of
a charismatic, unusual genius. We tend to imagine intellects like Massignon
as the brave ones who take on the faceless immensity of the world, society,
or modernity—or, in the case of Massignon, Islam or Catholicism—alone.
I have tried to adjust this perspective and focus the lens to get closer to

the nature and sensations of Massignon's experiences. These inner, spiritual experiences were intersubjective through and through, notably in the bonds he felt with al-Hallāj, Foucauld, Abd-el-Jalil, and most of all Kahil, who reignited his early passions and changed the direction of his life. It was a vow, a "great fire of Love between friends," as Massignon described the bond in a letter, a fire of Love for Kahil that was at once a way to God and to unimagined pleasures, a fuel for their politics, and a stone around her neck. When we take a longer view of Massignon's extensive friendships, the paradoxical threads woven into the fabric of his deeply relational life are more difficult to disentangle. There was an undeniable erotics to his bonds—both male and female, living and dead, Muslim and Catholic. His relationships with his living friends, those who were pulled into the vortex of Massignon's spiritual charisma like Abd-el-Jalil and Mary Kahil, were utterly transformative both for them and for Massignon. These friendships opened up new vistas and sent their lives into unimaginable directions, helping to evolve Massignon's more anticolonial perspectives, forging a more expansive and open Catholicism, and even making God real. But there is a tragedy to these friendships too. They had a silent, darker side, filled with heartbreak and confusion. After Massignon died, Jacques Maritain wrote that "ecumenism" and "dialogue" alone do not quite get at the heart of Louis Massignon. Instead one must probe the *splendides amitiés* that were at "the bottom of the soul" of his late friend. Maritain, too, knew something about this.[172]

0

3

MARIE-MAGDELEINE DAVY AND THE HERMENEUTIC OF FRIENDSHIP IN RESISTANCE TO NAZISM

> And might it not be, continued Austerlitz, that we also have
> appointments to keep in the past, in what has gone before and
> is for the most part extinguished, and we must go there in
> search of places and people who have some connection with
> us on the far side of time, so to speak?
>
> W. G. SEBALD, *Austerlitz*

INTRODUCTION

IN 1942, MARIE-MAGDELEINE Davy was riding a train from Switzerland
back to her home in occupied France. Davy, in her late thirties, was by then
a fairly well-known scholar of medieval Christian mysticism.[1] Davy had
been the first female student to enroll at the Institut Catholique, the Catholic seminary in Paris, and during the war she was a lecturer on religion at
the École pratique des hautes études. On this particular afternoon, as she
settled in for the long train ride, Davy dug up some work from her suitcase
to review in her seat, two photocopied documents excerpted from a Latin
medieval commentary on the *Song of Songs* at the Bibliothèque nationale
archives, and began reading. She noticed two Swiss officers staring at her
and looking at one another, while she squinted at the documents. When

Davy got off at a station to change trains, the officers, assuming the Latin was some clandestine code language, accused her of being a spy, demanded the texts she had been reading, and arrested her. Davy insisted they were harmless ancient Christian sermons that "had absolutely no subversive character," but the police, poorly educated, "were intrigued by a language that they did not know." Davy asserted that a priest who knew Latin could vouch for her, but none were around. She was still closer to the Switzerland border than France, so they drove her back to Berne. En route, she thought of the Swiss priest, Catholic theologian, and future cardinal the Abbé Charles Journet. She had just seen Journet the day before. She called and happened to reach him, and he drove to the border. Journet verified Davy's explanation, and the officers released her.[2]

Marie-Magdeleine Davy recounts this story in her memoir, and it contains several wonderful surprises. First, Davy actually *was* an active member of the underground resistance in Paris combating the Nazi occupation of France.[3] She had been traveling under a pseudonym with a falsified passport. Journet knew this and covered for her. Though Davy spoke and wrote very little about this time in her life, she played a significant role in two networks in Paris, which operated under the names "Comète" and "Felix le Chat."[4] After the war, Davy won a national medal for heroism and received letters from both Charles de Gaulle and Dwight Eisenhower for her service.[5] Second, in Davy's story about her encounter with the Swiss officers, she rightly assures them that the text they confiscated was an innocuous, theological Latin sermon, however, perhaps counterintuitively, this text actually did play a prominent role in her political efforts. The officers were correct. It *was* politically subversive material. Throughout the wartime and postwar periods, Davy worked feverishly as an academic who specialized in the mystical writings of the twelfth-century Carthusian and Cistercian monks. Publishing widely on this topic, she earned academic prizes in the field of medieval studies while also holding a salon at Fortelle (the famous "rencontres de la Fortelle") where medieval mysticism was often the topic of discussion.

Some have seen Davy's and others' work on mystical texts during the war as a cover for their impressive humanitarian work, but this is not how Davy herself understood it. For Davy, these Christian works were more than historical documents from premodernity. They were galvanizing sources of personal transformation and focus and harbingers of ethical, theological, and political renewal. She was not alone in this: Davy was a friend of Journet's because she had begun her career in modern Catholic theology's "turn to the sources" (*ressourcement*) movement, which emphasized the translation and analysis of premodern theological and mystical texts in western Europe from the 1930s to the 1950s and laid the foundations for the changes later inaugurated at the Second Vatican Council.[6] Davy was one of the very few women to be trained by, and eventually work alongside, these prominent Catholic theologians and historians, such as Étienne Gilson, who introduced her to medieval studies when she was a student at the Sorbonne. For Davy and her Jesuit and Dominican colleagues, the medieval monks, like her beloved Cistercian monks Guillaume of Saint-Thierry and Bernard of Clairvaux, were not merely the authors of texts that were accessed cognitively. They were instead imagined as flesh-and-blood people, writers with whom Davy felt intimately bonded. Much like Massignon's method for reading al-Hallāj, in her approach to the premodern Christian mystics, Davy did not only seek to understand these sources in their original context but aimed to summon them back to life. The medieval monks were more like friends (Bernard of Clairvaux was her "best friend," she wrote in 1943).[7] Spiritual friendship was a hermeneutic, a way into the texts and a method of reading she learned from the medieval monks themselves.

This *amitié* with her monks compelled Davy to eschew the simplistic, binary, and adversarial tradition of interpreting medieval writings by the Right. She saw her medieval authors as real people, far more complicated than mere representatives of French or Christian purity. In the context of fascism, xenophobia, and Nazism, Davy offered an interpretation of medieval Christendom that stressed the religiously plural roots of Latin, Western Christianity, emphasized its historical connections with other Eastern traditions, and forged thematic links between Christian mystical texts and those from the Islamic, Jewish, and Hindu traditions. Her efforts explicitly aimed to counter fantasies of medieval Christian purity. While Catholics like Henri Massis and G. K. Chesterton imagined medieval Christendom as a solid, pure foundation on which Europe could stand to create more purity in the present, the medieval authors appeared to Davy as full of heterogeneous influences. Davy also never succumbed to their view that the world was in decline. Rather than painting a picture of a golden era sullied by modernity, she sought to highlight overlaps between the themes in medieval sources and developments in modern philosophy, such as existentialism and psychoanalysis.

Davy's alternative reading of medieval Christianity also certainly stemmed in part from her experiences laboring at what John Connelly calls the "borderlands" of mainstream Catholicism.[8] A woman in a man's world, she found limits to her inclusion in the community of Catholic priests associated with *la nouvelle théologie*. Davy was by all accounts brilliant. She won academic prizes all her life, and by the start of the war, she had published several important translations and commentaries and would go on to publish forty books and over a hundred articles. She spoke in a deep, husky voice, was a chain-smoker, lived alone among piles of papers and manuscripts, and hosted an influential salon. But she never sustained significant relationships in the Catholic theological circles, certainly nothing that matched the intensity the *ressourcement* priests had with one another. Davy could only ever be at the edges of the clerical theological community that formed her. During the war, she therefore reached out and forged connections with different kinds of people, collaborating with scholars working on sources outside of medieval Christianity in fields such as Russian philosophy, Islamic mysticism, Jewish Hasidism, and existentialism. Friendships with non-Catholics, like her good friend the Russian philosopher Nicholas Berdyaev; near-Catholics, like Simone Weil, who refused baptism in an institution she felt was too exclusionary; or unusual Catholics, like her friend Massignon, all helped introduce difference into Davy's intellectual, political, and religious approach to medieval Christendom. They even shaped her own spiritual life in ways that were much more powerful than what we typically understand by modern platonic friendship. Friendship was key to her approach to medieval Christianity *and* to her experiences outside of it. Attending to all these realms—friendship, mysticism, scholarship, and politics—helps us access the depth, complexity, and humanity of Marie-Magdeleine Davy and her small community of resisters who pushed back against the ascendency of midcentury xenophobia at great risk to their own lives.

"WITH PASSION, I DISCOVERED MYSTICAL THEOLOGIANS WHO BECAME MY FRIENDS": DAVY'S EARLY INTELLECTUAL FORMATION

Marie-Magdeleine Davy was born in 1903 in Paris, but even as a young child, she never embraced the ideals of the young French Catholic mademoiselle. She preferred pants to dresses, used the masculine pronoun for herself as a young girl, and had a difficult relationship with her family. ("I'll never know what I did to God for such a child," Davy remembered hearing often from her mother.) "My family," Davy eventually wrote, "became strangers to me."[9] However strained this upbringing was, she claimed that her childhood ended in 1918 at the age of fifteen, when her older sister, the one family member with whom she had been close, died in a tragic accident. Davy finally left home three years later, enrolling at the Sorbonne and moving into her own studio on the Boulevard Saint-Michel.[10] At the time, very few women lived alone during their studies, which only made matters worse with her family, and they refused to pay for her education. To support herself, Davy taught classes for children and became the secretary for the philosopher Julien Benda. The secretarial work was bizarre, but it paid the bills and secured for Davy the freedom she sought from her family's middle-class expectations. From then on, she never came close to fulfilling any of the circumscribed roles allotted to young Catholic women, as neither the good daughter, wife, mother, or nun. Like her acquaintance Simone de Beauvoir, she associated this kind of life and freedom with masculinity: "If I was given the choice," Davy wrote, "I might have opted for being male. I'm not sure I accommodate myself well to my femininity. The bottom line for me was to be able to live my life in a way men did—that is to say independent and free—at a time when women were mostly under the authority of men."[11]

Shortly after beginning her studies while still a teenager in Paris, Davy met the Maritains at their house and was "seduced" by Jacques and Raïssa as people, as many others were, although she noted she was not "seduced" at all by Jacques's Thomism. (Davy constantly uses *me séduisait* [seduced me] to describe her intellectual journey.) Ideas were then understood to be spread through affectively charged bonds with those who persuasively, even occasionally beautifully, embodied them. While Davy was never as compelled as Jacques and Raïssa were by medieval writers like Aquinas, still other medieval texts enticed her. During her studies at the Sorbonne, she took a number of courses with philosophers Émile Bréhier, Jean Baruzi, and Henri Gouhier, but it was her history courses with Étienne Gilson, the Catholic historian of the twelfth century, that captivated her most of all, changing the direction of her life. She remembered Gilson as "an extraordinary, wonderful interpreter of the Middle Ages," whose ideas "*me séduisait*."[12] Gilson taught at the Sorbonne between 1921 and 1933, and by the time Davy took courses with him, the Sorbonne was no longer the bastion of secular positivism it had been a generation prior. Gilson was a practicing Catholic who had been influenced by a diverse set of teachers (Lucien Lévy-Bruhl, Henri Bergson, and his own colleague Jean Baruzi). Unlike previous Catholic scholars who had been stimulated by the 1879 church document *Aeterni Patris*, which presented the "medieval mind" as one single, undifferentiated set of beliefs,

Gilson's great contribution to Catholics was to expose this as an ahistorical myth and emphasize the complexity within twelfth-century Christian thought. Gilson, according to Florian Michel, modeled a kind of *catholicisme d'ouverture* (Catholicism of openness) in his own approach to the medieval period, and in his own life.[13] As for the secular scholarly community, Gilson brought into the Sorbonne's history department the notion that medieval Christian sources not only could be taken seriously as objects of scholarly inquiry but also offered windows into a compelling, cosmopolitan world that should be studied with emotion, heart, and soul. Gilson's method rebelled against the approach to history modeled in Germany, which had defined the historical discipline through training more aligned with science than with philosophy and literature.[14] When Gilson described his work with medieval sources, it was not with scientific language but with metaphors of life and death. He urged his students to have the prophet Ezekiel in their mind's eye as they pored over their ancient manuscripts: "Prophesy! Make these dry bones live!"[15] Émile Poulat describes the Sorbonne's notions toward medieval studies in the years 1920–40 as focused principally on mystical sources that offered a new alternative to the reigning atmosphere of positivism, and even non-Catholics in this period approached medieval mystical materials with the hopes of "un monde mort reprend vie" (bringing a dead world back to life).[16]

Gilson's influence worked. For Davy, the discovery of these texts was thrilling. She began with a major intellectual advantage over many other students, having earned prizes in Greek and Latin as a high school student, which allowed her to delve into these primary sources immediately, without language hurdles to surmount. As Gilson guided her through the twelfth century, he described it as an area that shared her ideals. The monks and scholars dedicated their lives to study and travel without attachment to home and family. They were also, as she put it, "geniuses of the inner life."[17] Bernard of Clairvaux's famous set of sermons on the *Song of Songs* was her favorite of his writings, which evokes the category of religious experience. Bernard was her first Christian source, her inspiration and guide for the theme that would dominate her scholarly career for the next sixty years. As she would later explain,

> The God to whom Saint Bernard is turned is not the God of the philosophers of whom they speak with the confused tongue of Babel. Like Pascal, Bernard's God is the God of Abraham, the God of Israel and of Job. . . . He is not a theologian of the faith, not interested in proving whether or not God exists. His is an interior God, a living God that cannot be proven

without experience—God who can be seen, touched, contemplated, a God so intimate that he can be felt without any need for elaboration, as palpable as a piece of bread. Mysticism does not demonstrate God. It perceives, experiences, penetrates into God.[18]

For Davy, Bernard's vivid language not only described religious experience but generated it for her. Her discovery of the medieval Christian monks' sermons as a student "was food for me," she wrote. The texts "gave me joy." These mystical writings enabled her to, as she understood it, "internalize" the freedom and joy she read about and helped her feel "gradually released from my prison" of middle-class family expectations.[19] Among these new texts and experiences, Davy thrived. In 1932, she finished her thesis (for which she won the top prize from the Académie française). Under Gilson's advice, she focused on lesser-known twelfth-century figures for her next academic projects, such as Guillaume of Saint-Thierry and Pierre de Blois, as her beloved Bernard was already well-trod territory among medievalists.

When Davy was a graduate student, friendship emerged as the way she began to frame her budding relationships with the medieval monastic authors themselves: "With passion, I discovered mystical theologians who became my friends. Sort of companions," Davy explained in 1935, "so close to me, they were part of my daily life, lived with me."[20] Likewise in 1935, in the first of many projects on the twelfth-century Cistercian monk Guillaume of Saint-Thierry, a close friend of Bernard of Clairvaux's, she wrote, "But what we can assure is that we have worked with love. For eight years, no days have passed without reading a few lines of Guillaume's words. And it is because Guillaume is a friend to us that we regret that we cannot make his language heard even better. Those who understand the Latin text will do well to use it, constantly: for even in Guillaume's thought, there is movement, rhythm, cadence, the turns of phrase, even a refined musicality."[21] Davy's scholarship was governed by a sense that immersion into the original language of the author was key to the intimacy she felt with monastic writers like Guillaume, something she shared with Louis Massignon (like Massignon, Davy had a remarkable brilliance when it came to languages and worked with Hebrew, Latin, Sanskrit, Greek, French, and German texts). Here Davy laid the foundations for her interpersonal, relational approach to her sources, insisting that she should be understood not as a scholar of "la pensée médiévale" (medieval thought) but as a scholar of "plus exactement à des auteurs du XIIe siècle" (more precisely the authors of the twelfth century).[22] Her reading strategy, which brought together interpersonal affection with exacting

technical precision and original languages, likely drew from Cistercian traditional understandings of scriptural reading, which were articulated most
extensively by Guillaume of Saint-Thierry himself. According to Rachel
Smith, Cistercian views of scriptural reading expect the reader to undergo
affective transformation by the text, "inhabiting and being inhabited by" the
words and world of the author. The ideal spiritual reader does not merely
learn about something from writing on the page but makes present the text,
cultivates a bond with it, and interiorizes both the words and the writers,
bringing them to life in the present.[23] When we see Davy refer to the monks
she studied as friends, close friends, best friends, undoubtedly Davy's hermeneutic was shaped by the Cistercians themselves.

Friendship also governed one of Davy's first major topics of research.
In 1932, she published a translation and annotation of *Un traité de l'amour
du XIIe siècle: De amicitia christiana de Pierre de Blois* (A treatise of love in
the twelfth century: On Christian friendship by Pierre de Blois). De Blois
was a clerical theologian whose work on Christian friendship drew deeply
from the twelfth-century Cistercian abbot Aelred of Rievaulx's classic *Spiritual Friendship*, but he reflected on friendship in the wider Christian milieu
outside of the monastic setting.[24] Davy's analysis of spiritual friendship grew
increasingly sophisticated, highlighting tensions and irreconcilable paradoxes and probing both the attraction and the resistance to having a "soul
mate" on the pathway to God. In her 1936 book on Guillaume of Saint-
Thierry, for instance, Davy shows that Guillaume had suffered from being
understood by scholars only "in the shadow of his illustrious friend St. Bernard of Clairvaux." She tried to correct the then-widespread view that Guillaume was merely a promoter of his famous friend and demonstrate that
their bond was mutually influential and, as she put it, "of a friendship that
never ceased to grow and that lasted all their lives" (she notes that one only
has to look at their correspondence to see this).[25] Although Jean Leclercq
would make this claim famous years later, Davy's early scholarship argues
for the epistolary genre as an important source of theological writing.[26] Davy
focused with delight on the humanity of Bernard and Guillaume's bond:
Bernard, according to Davy, "pleasantly teased Guillaume for thinking that
he loved Bernard much more than Bernard loved him."[27] But Davy was just
as interested in Guillaume's writing, which argued for the irreducibility of a
personal experience with God, an experience between one's soul and God
alone. She chose to translate one of Guillaume's texts that exhibited precisely
this tension: a treatise on solitude in the form of letters to others, written
at the request of Bernard: *Un traité de la vie solitaire: Epistola ad fratres de*

Monte-Dei. Davy's work centered on what Amy Hollywood calls the "dia-
lectical interplay" between solitude and community—what she describes
as a constant source of tension and debate within the Western Christian
mystical traditions.[28] Davy concentrated on the power of friends to enable
an apprehension of the sacred as well as, when it comes to the soul and
God, friendship's inadequacy and the irreducibly personal nature of mystical experience. Despite the power of friendship in Davy's intellectual, social,
political, and spiritual life, she also noted, "There is no path to the Absolute
without loneliness."[29]

Friendship was also an aspect of Davy's involvement in 1933 with the
Catholic student group Amis du Spirituel (Friends of Spirituality) in Paris,
where members would give mini lectures for one another on classic spiritual
texts and themes according to a rotation of responsibilities. As a university student, Davy also started a group called Bibliothèque des étudiants
catholiques (BEC), where students worked closely with Dominican clergy
and attended a reading group she hosted at her apartment on the Boulevard
Saint-Michel.[30] During this period, many religious orders in Europe became
interested in the founding spirit and history of their communities, and in
1934, Davy published *Les dominicaines*, a history of the Dominican order,
in a series on the great monastic orders of Europe.[31] Dominican theologian
Marie-Dominique Chenu reviewed it favorably, appreciating her emphasis
on the order's commitment to contemplation and action.[32] Chenu would go
on to review Davy's later works as well, including writing a lengthy piece on
one about the theme of love in Guillaume of Saint-Thierry, which praised
her technical philological and theological skills. Chenu noted that Davy's
translations and commentaries were incredibly expansive and remarked on
her hundreds of notes with biblical references from the Old and New Testament, clarification of doctrinal and theological terms, references to patristic
authors, and more.[33] Outside of the Dominicans, the Jesuit theologian Henri
de Lubac cited Davy's early translations frequently in his own theological
scholarship, including his important works on medieval exegesis and the
history of the Eucharist.[34]

These early projects of translation and commentary were part of a scholarly genre shared by many Catholic clerical scholars working within the
ressourcement movement. Far from mere translations, these works offered
massive, detailed introductions to the thought-world of newly discovered,
premodern monastic materials. Scholars typically added hundreds of footnotes to their translations to establish the text's atmosphere, situating the
source within its historical milieu and identifying the voluminous scriptural

references. Several of Davy's early translations contain over nine hundred notes, and her introductions to her translations were often over one hundred pages long. Davy's texts from the 1930s and early 1940s were all published by the Catholic publishing houses of particular religious orders.[35] In the early twentieth century, several new religious publishing houses popped up in the effort to sustain the widespread interest in premodern religious sources that scholars like Gilson, Baruzi, Davy, and many others were working on. Davy's early works were published by the Benedictine journal from Leuven *Recherches de théologie ancienne et médiéval*, the Jesuit *Recherches de science religieuse*, and the Dominican publishing house Éditions du Cerf. Although Davy would eventually expand her scholarly reach to include a staggeringly wide range of sources, Christian and non-Christian, Davy turned over this same corpus of writings from the twelfth-century Carthusian and Cistercian monks throughout her life with unremitting regularity.

It is within this broader theological milieu that the *Revue d'histoire de l'Église de France* declared Davy a "serious scholar of theologies and philosophies of the Middle Ages" when she was just starting out in 1936.[36] Indeed, Davy was a rising star in Catholic theological circles. It made sense, therefore, that in the late 1930s, Étienne Gilson encouraged Davy to supplement her secular training at the Sorbonne with theological graduate study in a Catholic setting. Davy enrolled at the Institut Catholique, the Catholic seminary in Paris, in 1936.

PAINFUL VENTURES INTO CATHOLIC THEOLOGY

Davy was the first woman to enroll in the Institut Catholique and, at the time, the only one. In her memoirs, she wondered how differently her life might have turned out had some of the best *ressourcement* theologians taught at the Institut Catholique when she was a student there. "I would have probably been spared many disappointments," she surmised. Her friend Jean Daniélou, for example, began his professorship there in 1944, just after Davy left. Her time at the Institut Catholique was "the most painful period of my youth, without a doubt." The professors, mostly Jesuits, she wrote, "were excellent, but the teaching given seemed to me sad, pathetic, and in any case of little interest."[37] She describes having to sit in the far back of the auditorium during lectures, "the place furthest from the professorial chair near the door. Apart from those who shared my bench, nobody saw me. Apart from two or three students, I was ignored."[38] Men were not allowed to *look* at her. Although bold theologians were pioneering new work of Catholic theology, the overall culture of the seminaries was unchanged in the 1930s. Davy's problem was not only her isolation as a woman. Even more, there was no humanity, no real men and women behind the early Christian sources they studied. Whereas with Gilson she had seen the monks as people and as friends, who themselves had lives and friendships, in the seminary the atmosphere was stifling and lifeless: "[At the Institut Catholique] the Fathers of the Church were no longer people with flesh and bone, with intelligence, sensitivity, faith, doubts, problems," she lamented, adding, "They were reduced to an inhuman dimension, a kind of algebraic equation. I had the impression I was assisting at the autopsy of a cadaver."[39] Instead of poking at a lifeless body, she wanted to summon the ancients back to life, as she and Gilson had done at the Sorbonne. By this time, she had felt the medieval mystics and monks were "friends," "companions so close to me," who introduced her to a God "so intimate" that He could be "felt without any need for elaboration." But here the medieval monks were transformed into dead, cognitive abstractions.

Davy enrolled at the Institut Catholique on a trial basis, but in 1941, after five years of successfully completing courses, she made an appointment with the institute's director, a bishop, to inquire about earning credit toward a degree for her work done so far. She recalled the meeting: "'No. There's no question,' he said. 'You are a woman!'" Davy added that he "pronounced the word 'woman' as if it was 'plague' or 'cholera.'"[40] She left the meeting without saying goodbye. Later she would earn her PhD in philosophy from the Sorbonne, but she never obtained the *agrégation de philosophie*, the golden key to France's top teaching positions.[41]

In the late 1930s, it was extremely rare—almost unheard of—for a woman to gain theological training like Davy did.[42] But it makes sense that she would try it. A kind of new spring was just beginning to be felt in Catholic theology with *ressourcement. Ressourcement* theologians and Davy shared a theological worldview, but the world that was fomenting around these creative scholars had not yet penetrated traditional establishments like the Catholic seminary in Paris. For example, Davy's friend the Jesuit Jean Daniélou noted in 1946 that not only are the ancient Christian writers "the veritable witnesses of a bygone state of affairs," but they also "provide the most enduring and 'contemporary' nourishment for men of our own day."[43] The Dominican Marie-Dominique Chenu described how the "pathetic, dry" teaching of the Catholic seminaries at the time could only be renewed by a "return to the sources" to offer readers "spiritual power," "rejuvenation," and "fertility."[44] For the priests associated with *ressourcement*, the main site for the sap, the lifeblood of religious life, *la sève*, was found in the sources from the past: patristic and medieval texts had an "inexhaustible richness that truly enables the name *sources*," and they could be awakened as "living nourishment for souls."[45] Nourishment, explosive vitality, rejuvenation, fertility—the hopes of the *ressourcement* theologians described Davy's intellectual yearnings exactly in 1936, when she enrolled at the Institut Catholique.

But people like Chenu, Daniélou, and Davy were pioneers far ahead of most Catholic seminaries. At the Institut Catholique, Davy didn't find passion, excitement, or spirituality in the context of her theological training—she found boredom and cruelty. In addition to her own experiences, Davy watched in horror throughout the 1940s and 1950s as the *ressourcement* theologians were silenced and excommunicated (later to be rehabilitated at Vatican II). "The Church," Davy concluded, "seeks out theologians to punish as if they were rabbits during hunting season."[46] "And so I asked myself," Davy reflected upon leaving the seminary, "not without anxiety, if the Holy Spirit had not deserted the Institut Catholique, the seminaries and the homilies of the preachers." Her strong reaction ("violent") was a stimulus for her thinking, and she determined that the juridical aspect of Catholicism was a "false religion" and misguided. Not only was it punitive and authoritarian, but it "had allowed itself to become bourgeois . . . adapted itself to human interests, thus enslaving the holy, prostituting it, and in a sense becoming the gravedigger of the holy within itself."[47]

Furthermore, for someone who wrote intensely on friendship, Davy had very few friends in the world of Catholic theology. The clerical world of *ressourcement* did not lack intimacy, however, because it was populated with celibate priests. Many of the priests working in *ressourcement* were otherwise intimately bonded with one another. For instance, Yves Congar and Marie-Dominique Chenu, both lauded as pioneers in the *nouvelle théologie* movement, had a close relationship they endowed with religious meaning. In a tribute he wrote to his friend after Chenu's death, Congar recalled the early days of their friendship in the 1930s. He and Chenu "found ourselves in profound accord. . . . It was an intense and total spiritual union." He continued, "The fraternal friendship of Father Chenu formed in me, little by little and in depth, the tissue of a theological life. . . . It was there that we encountered one another and were joined to one another, that we communed intensely in the same service to the truth, as if it were to a woman to whom we had consecrated our love and our life."[48] Chenu and Congar's bond with each other and with their work ("as if it were a woman") was the setting of "intense and total spiritual union," "forming the tissue" of the theological ideals of service and truth. Into this world Davy could only peer from the outside.

After she left the Institut Catholique in 1941, Davy claimed she simply tried to "forget about theology, and only focused on the painful occupation and resistance."[49] But soon her training in theology, particularly medieval mysticism, would turn out to be a critical piece of her clandestine work in the resistance. This work grew out of Davy's firsthand awareness of the escalations of anti-Semitic violence and fascism. Although her friend Jeanne Ancelet-Hustache, the scholar of Rhineland mysticism, had advocated for the rights of Jewish refugees in France since 1933, Davy gained firsthand knowledge when she lived in Berlin in the 1930s, having taken time off to teach medieval studies at the French Institute of Berlin.[50]

DAVY'S MEDIEVALISM AND ACTIVISM
IN THE RESISTANCE

Although Davy had little preparation as an academic and mystically in-clined medievalist, beginning in 1940, she joined the underground resis-tance movements in Paris that defied the collaborationist Vichy regime from 1940 to 1944. The historian Timothy Snyder's conclusions about Nazi resist-ers similarly ring true for Davy: "People who bragged about rescuing Jews had generally not done so; they were, in fact, more likely to be anti-Semites and racists. Rescuers almost never boast."[51] Davy never boasted and wrote very little about the time in her life after she left the Catholic seminary and joined the resistance. But thanks to the work of Jean-Dominique Durand, Margaret L. Rossiter, Régis Ladous, and Anne Thoraval, we know that with her friend Marianne Coltel, in 1943, Davy played an important role in two resistance networks in Paris, "Comète" and "Felix le Chat." One aspect of her efforts was to ensure the safe evacuation of British and American soldiers who had escaped Germany. Coltel and Davy helped obtain false paperwork for soldiers and hid the documents under the carpet of a step in the stair-case in Davy's apartment (Davy was known among the Allied airmen as "Mademoiselle Bourgeois").[52] She was also in charge of finding underground accommodation for the soldiers, and she helped lease several rooms to them under false names. The soldiers were instructed to remain in these apartments until the paperwork for their safe evacuations was in place, when they would then depart by train through the southern zone to Spain and on to England. Davy also convinced the wealthy Parisian d'Eichthal family to let her use their vacant Fortelle chateau, which was located just outside of Paris in Rozay-en-Brie. Davy headquartered much of her resistance activity at Fortelle, turning the chateau into a kind of training camp to prepare those in hiding to make the trek on foot to Spain. In 1943, there were at least ten Allied resistance fighters hiding at Fortelle. Davy organized with her students from the École pratique des hautes études a system for rotating the preparation and cooking of meals for those in hiding.

Davy was also still involved as a leader of the Catholic student group Bibliothèque des étudiants catholiques during the war, and she had keys to its chapel at 135 boulevard Saint-Michel. Davy was responsible for hiding suitcases that contained the official stamps for false paperwork under the unassuming altar of the chapel.[53] While it is unclear what kind of false paperwork Davy primarily hid, these could have included false passports or false baptismal records for Jewish men, women, and children, members of the resistance, and Allied soldiers who escaped Germany. Another young Catholic female resister recalled that many young resisters in France, young women in particular, often met in churches and chapels, grasping early on that "the Germans took some time to realise that you could do other things there apart from say your prayers."[54] For this work, Davy was almost arrested several times. In December 1943, the Gestapo raided the Rue Racine, near the BEC's chapel. Davy narrowly escaped by taking shelter for twenty-four hours in the cellar of a bakery at the corner. The shopkeepers eventually alerted Davy's comrades, who helped safely evacuate her by hiding her in an ambulance.[55]

Alongside her work in the resistance, Davy continued to labor in the field of medieval Christianity, toiling over the monks with whom she "worked with love" and on whom she published widely. No longer at the Institut Catholique, Davy lectured in religion at the École pratique des hautes études and eventually completed a PhD at the Sorbonne. She also joined journal editorial boards, directed an academic center, and convened conferences, all drawing on her training in twelfth-century mystical theology. But during the war, Davy began to situate these texts in new conversations.[56] Medievalism was already a potent political force. The Far Right nursed fantasies of Europe's need to restore contact with its allegedly uncorrupted (purely Christian and white) "Latin" medieval roots. This dream of a past medieval purity became a powerful marker of identity and a way to shore up authoritarian discourses to purge Europe of difference in the present. (Jews, immigrants from the East, and Muslims were not present in the glorious, earlier era of medieval Christendom, they seemed to suggest, thus only with their removal will we be glorious again.) A particular kind of medievalism underwrote an extreme, anti-Enlightenment, anti-immigrant, and anti-Semitic agenda whose aim was to homogenize western Europe.[57] In the United States, we still hear chilling echoes of this tradition in today's Identity Evropa leaders who voice fantasies of a return to the "rich heritage" of European uniformity. Scholars used to claim that the interwar xenophobia and nativism *lacked* culture and aesthetic and that the allure of the Far Right was primarily economic in nature. To understand this resurgence of xenophobia, they argued, one need only look at unemployment, not culture, art, or religion. But scholars such as Mark Antliff, Sandrine Sanos, and others have compellingly mined a robust aesthetic cultural and religious dimension to the rise of nativism, authoritarianism, and xenophobia in the late interwar period.[58] According to their work, this right-wing movement responded to a widespread search for values that were perceived as older and organic to Europe, values that had been lost in the decline of modernity but, if reawakened, could be solid enough to counteract the perceived terrible decline that liberal modernity set in motion. Catholic medievalism was a crucial piece of this imaginary.

The Catholic Henri Massis's writings, for instance, valorize all the canonical figures of medieval Latin Catholicism: scholasticism, Thomas Aquinas, Joan of Arc.[59] In England, Massis's counterparts were Catholics like Hilaire Belloc and Bernard Wall, who both came to believe that fascist movements in Italy and Germany were the only honest movements bold enough to react forcefully against the perceived excesses of liberal modernity, the failures of war and capitalism, and the influx of immigrants. They advocated for a "revival of traditionalism."[60]

These ideas were not buried down in the gutters but were found in the respectable mainstream. In 1929, Massis won the Grand prix de littérature de l'Académie française. To package his violent rhetoric, Massis had a warm, charismatic personality and was a kind of "spiritual father" to a younger generation of Catholic thinkers nourished on the idea of Christian values under attack. Massis mentored the new young right-wing intellectuals associated with Paris in the late 1930s. Many were students at the École normale supérieure and affiliated with the conservative journal *Revue universelle*, where, under the guidance of Massis, they experienced, according to Sandrine Sanos, the warm "ties of friendship, forged in a shared love of literature, affection for rebellious acts, and desire for revolutionary politics."[61] Indeed, thanks to Massis, the École normale supérieure harbored a strong right-wing culture where Catholic medievalism, mysticism, friendship, and xenophobia merged. The notion of medieval Christian glory, on the one hand, and a degenerate modernity that had mingled with "the Orient," on the other, was a trope central to many European Catholic writers, even those beloved still today. Take, for instance, G. K. Chesterton, who stoked the fears of both Muslims (see chap. 2) and Jews: "The 'Jewish Spirit' is a spirit foreign to Western countries," he wrote in 1932.[62] He picked up these themes again in his 1933 *Saint Thomas Aquinas* (republished in 1955), which valorized Aquinas as the saint embodying religious ideals explicitly *against* those of Islam, Buddhism, and Judaism. When it comes to Aquinas, Chesterton views only contrasts: "As compared with a Jew, a Buddhist, a Moslem, a Deist, or any other alternative, a Christian means a man who believes that deity or sanctity has attached to matter and entered the world of senses."[63] Only with a return to Saint Thomas Aquinas can we recover a sensibility that is at once spiritual *and* modern. Of this book, Étienne Gilson wrote, "I consider it as being, without possible comparison, the best book ever written on Saint Thomas."[64]

The imagined purity and perfection of the Middle Ages was central to this work. Even the fairly liberal Catholic journal *Esprit*, founded by Emmanuel Mounier, exhibits some of this xenophobic sentiment. *Esprit* suggested the possibility that a "Hitlerless Nazi party" could lead to a positive spiritual revival in Germany, one emblematic of Joan of Arc's political mysticism.[65] Furthermore, while this discourse of medievalism, mysticism, and anxiety about *l'Orient* initially only took place within the realm of the religious imagination, by 1940–44, its impact reached well beyond it. "It was tempting," historian Claude Bourdet states of France in 1940, "for people in whom political illiteracy and a certain mysticism were closely associated, to retreat to 'sacred France' and to imagine . . . a sort of social brotherhood turning its back both on the French Revolution and on capitalism, like a mythic Middle Ages, revisited and idealized." Without it, he continues, "recruitment for the Resistance would have immediately been easier and more widespread."[66]

Davy's approach to medieval mysticism was deeply at odds with the currents of thought coming from all sides: the Far Right, with their dream of medieval purity; the center, with their emerging human rights activism and philosophy; and the secular Left, exhibited by someone like Jean-Paul Sartre, who insisted that religion only served as an archaic obstruction to the ethical and political promise of secularism. Davy situated medieval mysticism within a more diverse, ecumenical academic conversation that advanced international and interreligious solidarities. Her interpersonal, affective, humanizing way into the Christian monastic authors (and bonding to them as friends) was central to her method. For example, while she was active in the resistance, Davy held a teaching post in religion at the École pratique des hautes études and taught courses like "Love of God and the Cistercians of the Twelfth Century" and "Mystical Knowledge in the Twelfth Century." In her memoirs, Davy recalls a remarkable afternoon in Paris in December 1943. She was lecturing on the likeness between the soul and God in twelfth-century mystical theology. About ten minutes into her presentation, three German officers walked into the auditorium, stood by the door, and stared at her. "I went pale. My jaw tightened. All my efforts were required to concentrate on keeping my voice steady." "In those moments of fear," she wrote, "one's imagination takes over. I instantly saw myself shot."[67] Convinced that she would never again have an opportunity to speak, Davy abandoned her planned lecture topic and shifted to her most beloved: the idea of love in Bernard of Clairvaux. Davy plunged without introduction into "the sweetness of love described by the Cistercian Abbot." She claimed to have experienced Bernard's words in that moment as a sudden but welcome encroaching presence, a force before which she willingly surrendered: "The tenderness of his words," she wrote, "invade me, and I forget, momentarily, the unusual presence [of the soldiers]." Bernard's words realigned her imagination from a panicked visualization to something that engendered sudden happiness as she quoted "by memory texts that delight me."[68] Davy finished the lecture, after which the students and, shockingly, the officers left the lecture hall. She arrived at her studio, breathless, with the texts of Bernard "still floating in me."[69] After another brush with danger in 1943, Davy turned to Meister Eckhart's treatise on divine consolation as soon as she was safe at home: "Do I need to be consoled? No. But I feel the need to focus my thoughts on the essential."[70] For Davy, Eckhart's and Bernard's words were powerful enough to act as animating, directive forces in her own life. They were interventionist, able to fortify one's attention and keep up the courage needed. This sense that one's psyche demanded constant vigilance was shared among other Catholics involved in this antifascist work. They thought that the mind, soul, and psyche required persistent attention in the context of fascism, xenophobia, and authoritarianism. Medieval mystical texts were powerful tools that aided this deliberately self-disciplinary work.[71] The resistance was both spiritual and political, and medieval texts played a key role. The Jesuit Gaston Fessard was a friend of Davy's who came to her salon at Fortelle and was also active in the resistance. Fessard authored the first issue of *Témoignage chrétien*, which appeared in 1941, the clandestine journal articulating "armes de l'esprit" (weapons of spirit) for resisters. The rallying cry of the journal was "France, prend garde de perdre ton âme!" (France, take care not to lose your soul!). This journal often referred to Nazism as its own kind of mysticism and spirituality, a worldview, practice, and inner life that could only be combated at that level. Mysticism was not a distraction from the real work of politics but the domain of the political, and the medieval texts that Davy and the *ressourcement* theologians were excavating, translating, publishing, and teaching were central.

This practice of both resistance and commitment to premodern Christian sources was important to the Jesuits as well, especially those working further afield in Lyon. Recalling the war years in Lyon, for example, Henri de Lubac wrote, "The tension was constant. We lived in a fever increased by hunger, by the daily horror of the news, by the next day's uncertainty. And yet," he added, "work was carried on, became even more intense. It was at this time that the series *Sources chrétiennes* began, that the *Revue du moyen âge latin* was founded."[72] De Lubac described the "whole task of theology" in that time as the "rediscovering" of Christianity by "going back to its sources, trying to recapture it in its periods of explosive vitality."[73] These sources included not only medieval texts (Davy) and patristic Church Fathers (Jesuits) but also, crucially—and less well known—the Hebrew Bible. According to de Lubac, *l'Ancien Testament* had become for Christians an "embarrassment rather than a support in their faith. . . . It was a cumbersome treasure which people no longer knew how to use."[74] De Lubac spoke those words in a 1941 lecture under the benign topic "Un Nouveau 'Front' Religieux," in which he waged war on the Nazi program to purge Christianity of Judaism and restore it to a purer "Aryan mysticism." The lecture was published in Switzerland in 1942 and circulated clandestinely in France.[75] When de Lubac first gave this lecture, he had been involved for more than a year with a group of underground communities focused on Jewish-Christian friendship in Lyon, started by the Jesuit Pierre Chaillet and the Ukrainian émigré and Jewish convert Abbé Alexandre Glasberg.[76] In Lyon, with the support of Chaillet, Abbé Glasberg formed an "organization of solidarity" that would be of "an interconfessional character" and became known as Amitié chrétienne (Christian Friendship).[77] De Lubac called the meetings between Jews and Christians "a small oasis of peace in the center of hatred."[78]

Davy shared in this two-tiered approach: summoning friendship as the metaphor to arouse Christian solidarity with Jews and, at the same time, looking at Jewish influences on Christian sources and mining the spiritual power of the Jewish texts themselves. During the war, for example, Davy began research that materialized in a postwar course she taught at the École pratique des hautes études, "L'influence de la pensée juive sur la théorie de la creation dans la philosophie et la théologie du XII siècle" (The influence of Jewish thought on the theory of creation in twelfth-century philosophy and theology). Jewish and Christian interaction in the medieval period became such a prominent part of her scholarship in the 1940s that some works refer to Davy as a scholar of Jewish and Christian philosophy in the Middle Ages. Davy was active in her teacher Étienne Gilson's series Études de philosophie médiévale, which published her first books. This series published not only texts on medieval Christianity but also the prominent Jewish scholar Georges Vajda, who, after the German occupation, went into hiding at Le Chambon sur Lignon, where many Jewish refugees fled.[79] There he wrote *La pensée juive du Moyen Age* and *L'amour de Dieu dans la théologie juive du Moyen Age*, both published after the war. The influence of Judaism on Christian medieval thought and the theological richness of Jewish sources were direct counters to Far-Right propaganda that Judaism corrupts, constrains, and pollutes Christian purity.

This scholarship was critical because both Catholic and Protestant anti-Semitic clerics and theologians were advocating a purge of Judaism from Christian history, such as Georges Bernanos with his rabidly anti-Semitic *La grande peur des bien-pensants* (1931), Christian writers in Germany like Arthur de Gobineau and Houston Stewart Chamberlain, and Hitler's own racial "expert" Alfred Rosenberg.[80] Davy's research and teaching on Judaism helped summon a countertradition and paved the way for her 1946 participation in the international Emergency Conference on Anti-Semitism at the Swiss village of Seelisberg. Davy was the only woman on the committee to work specifically with Christian churches on anti-Semitism at the Seelisberg convention. Out of the efforts of this conference, Jewish scholar Jules Isaac founded Amitiés judeo-chrétiennes (Jewish-Christian Friendship) and helped draft the *Ten Points of Seelisberg*, an interfaith statement that reminded the world of Christianity's Jewish origins and called for curbing anti-Judaic rhetoric, exegesis, and catechesis. Its goal was fighting the roots of anti-Semitism still rampant in many parts of Europe after the war. Davy also began major translation projects on Jewish mysticism, completing first Gershom Scholem's *Die jüdische Mystik in ihren Hauptströmungen* as *Les grands courants de la mystique juive* (1950), which became a classic in the field, and another by Ernst Müller in 1950.

Davy's work in the resistance and her scholarly interest in Judaism also began to steer her research on Bernard of Clairvaux in new ways. During the war, she wrote a new biography of him that appeared in 1945. In the introduction, she assures readers that she knows there are already many books on Bernard, but she promises her portrait of the monk would be more than those found in "pious and romanticized biographies." The Bernard that Davy penned was not just an object of critical longing. She was unusual among the *ressourcement* theologians in admitting that Bernard's sermons helped intensify anti-Jewish sentiment in the Crusades, although she also claimed Bernard tried to end the pogroms. "Sometimes Bernard surprises us, sometimes he misguides us: we question him with a certain concern, even anxiety. . . . He is uncompromising, passionate, violent . . . and though he denies it, unites himself with the age. He is sectarian. Sometimes we see," Davy concludes, "that the sweetest mystical theologians have the soul of an Inquisitor. Oh terrible and cruel paradox!"[81] Bernard's dazzling mystical texts, according to Davy, are part of a mixed package, and Davy refuses to see him as emblematic of an "unsoiled medieval" Christianity. It was her earlier approach—interpersonal, affective—that compelled her to view Bernard as more mortal and down to earth: "We wish to present," Davy states in the introduction, "a human person, not a stylized doctrine, but a living one." She adds one caveat: "Our only regret is not having been able to speak better of a person who has been, for a long time, our best friend."[82] This effort at humanizing and relating with the sources of medieval knowledge ran counter to the nationalists in Europe who were nostalgic for medieval purity, totality, and unity, in which, according to Françoise Meltzer, "any kind of real knowledge of medieval people is sacrificed on the altar of this belief in totality."[83] This early work that recognized the humanity, the beauty, *and* the darkness in Christian medieval thinkers was rare in scholarly practice at the time (even the most sophisticated *ressourcement* theologians veer, as if irresistibly, toward uniformly positive assessments of the sources they studied). It laid the foundations for one of Davy's most widely read articles that she wrote late in life on the role of vengeance in Christian medieval thinking, "Le thème de la vengeance au Moyen Âge." Even today, it is rare to see a scholar exhibit this realism about medieval anti-Semitism and violence and, at the same time, delve so deeply into the beauty of its mystical theology. Seeing these monks as men, as humans—more than that, as friends—helped Davy refuse to settle for simplicity or co-optation.

Davy also began to situate her beloved medieval monks within a new conversation, in varied journals and alongside differing voices, which summoned a countertradition to an imagined monolithic Christian past. Against a racialized, homogeneous, geographically bound medieval Christianity, she showed its overlaps with not only Judaism but also *l'Orient*, highlighting the presence of Eastern traditions *within* Occidental (Western) Christianity. If *l'Orient* for the Right was consolidated as non-Christian—pagan, Jewish, Muslim, Buddhist—and the West as homogeneously Christian, then the whole notion of the Eastern Christian churches, indigenous to the Middle East and Russia, complicated this settled binary. She spearheaded scholarly attention to Eastern Christian churches in Russia and the Middle East. In 1941, Davy served as the director of the Centre de recherches philosophiques et spirituelles in Paris, and she organized conferences that brought together the Russian émigré community and French philosophers for colloquiums on Eastern and Western Christianity. Under her directorship, she oversaw the publication of texts that later became classic introductions to Eastern Orthodox Christian theology in the West, including the 1944 publication of Vladimir Lossky's *Essai sur la théologie mystique de l'Église d'Orient*. If Massis wanted Asiaticism, Bolshevism, and *l'Orient* purged from the purity of Europe's Western Christian soil, Davy worked hard to keep them there, woven into the story of both Europe's present and past. We see this deliberate blending of East and West in Davy's work on the editorial board of *Cahiers de la nouvelle époque* in Paris, which she joined with her friend Nicholas Berdyaev. They "published for a new époque: spiritual, universalist, and social," with a special emphasis on bringing the discussion of spirituality out of the France- and Catholic-only focus.[84] Editors ensured that each issue deliberately contained a mixed authorship, Jewish and Christian, Eastern and Western, Russian and French, émigré and native, all representing a range of perspectives on shared themes. The inaugural 1945 issue featured Berdyaev on personalism in the Russian tradition, and Davy contributed an essay entitled "La révolution et l'église." The same issue included a French translation of the Russian Jewish philosopher Lev Shestov's essay on Luther and the Catholic Church, an intentional mix of national and religious filiation. Similarly, when in 1941, Davy joined the board of the new literary journal *L'âge nouveau*, she guided it down the precarious path of engaging increasingly religious themes while avoiding confessionalism or narrow French Catholic parochialism ("We will always be *l'avant garde*," they assured readers in their masthead, "we serve one faith: our art and peace, we ask nothing from our audience except intellectualism.")[85] In *L'âge nouveau*, Davy published on medieval Christian pilgrimage and sanctity, but her articles were set within the same issue as Emmanuel Levinas's earliest works on Judaism.

A Christian medievalist, Davy hosted a conference on Massignon's work on Islam in 1944 and published an essay on Massignon's reconversion to the Catholicism of his childhood in *L'âge nouveau*. Massignon's conversion was a strange story of a decidedly religiously *mixed* spiritual experience (described in chap. 2): it was a vivid mystical experience where he felt the presence of both Islamic and Christian saints in Iraq. Similarly, in 1944, Davy hosted a session at the Centre de recherches philosophiques et spiritu-elles on "the mystical life of ancient Taoism" that featured the extraordinary Jewish scholar of Chinese religions Henri Maspero.[86] A conference on Taoist mysticism hosted by Davy, an expert on Christian mysticism, led by a Jewish scholar in Paris in 1944 might seem conflicting, apolitical, or a distraction from the "real" political work at hand. But these were conscious efforts to put forward a more heterogeneous, cosmopolitan vision of mystical religion in history, advanced by a more diverse scholarly community in the present. Many of these scholars' very selves embodied that mixed identity targeted by nativists and xenophobes. Maspero, a Jewish scholar of Asian religion, was arrested in France later that year in July 1944, along with his wife, and sent to the Buchenwald concentration camp. He endured brutal conditions for six months and tragically died there in March 1945, three weeks before the camp's liberation.[87] De Lubac's speeches written in clandestine language, Vajda's research while in hiding with other Jewish refugees, and Davy's work were all done under constant risk of arrest. Without some understanding of the wartime context for these conferences, books, and salons dedicated to medieval Christianity and comparative mysticism that were so prominent at this time, the gravity, violence, and trauma are hidden from view. While they might seem too spiritual for a context with such political demands, I have found that it is impossible to isolate the spiritual and political actions of this community in the early 1940s. The work on medieval mysticism and comparative religion aimed to intervene at the cultural level and introduce an alternative to the theological and mystical ideologies of Nazi xenophobia. The realism, attention to violence and war, and their willingness to put their own lives at risk differentiates their work on religion from earlier oriental-ist fascinations with mysticism and East Asian religions and from the late Victorian interest in the magical and the numinous, which had always been part of European Christian and secular modernity.[88]

In addition, though she never published in it, Davy also worked closely with the establishment and running of the journal *Dieu vivant* (The living God), which Jesuit theologian Jean Daniélou and Massignon started in 1943, after the idea for the journal was launched at her salon (it was originally

suggested that Berdyaev direct it, but he was getting too old). Davy worked
behind the scenes and helped published essays by orientalists, comparativists, and theologians on topics ranging from the Syriac church fathers to
the Qur'anic roots of Sufi mysticism to Hasidism. *Dieu vivant* took its name
from Psalm 42, which was printed on the masthead: "My soul is athirst for
the living God."[89] In all this work, Davy and her colleagues operated in the
realms of the intellect, imagination, and culture—journals, colloquiums,
essays—to trouble the settled boundaries that the Right was consolidating:
us and them, medieval and modern, East and West. They possessed an abiding optimism in the power of study and imagination to reach what they
often called *la sève* (the sap) behind diverse religious texts. The "sap" was
a kind of spiritual lifeblood; once it was discovered in these texts, it could
be translated and analyzed, which would ideally bring new life into modernity and modern Christianity, Hinduism, Judaism, and Islam alike—all of
which, in these scholars' minds, had lost contact with their own sources of
vitality. This notion of *la sève* was pivotal in enabling them to break through
the predominantly binary way most Catholics and European orientalists
viewed religious others as fundamentally *unlike* Christians (either spiritually vibrant exotics or menacing outsiders in need of expulsion). Some
rendering of *la sève* cut through that dualistic approach to religious difference: all religions have life buried under the rubble, even Christianity, as
well as Islam, Judaism, and Hinduism. It was this concept that helped mark
their break from both exoticizing orientalists and rightist imperialists, and
it seemed to offer another path.[90]

Texts that gave glimpses of a kind of "inner" religion kept Davy tethered
to Bernard, Eckhart, and Guillaume of Saint-Thierry, her early Christian
mystics. Davy saw in these sources a religiosity that emphasized personal
experience, secrecy, mystery, and the inability of language to fully encap-
sulate the experience of God. This seemed far removed from the prevailing
orthodoxies and authoritarian violence around them. Despite their fascination with poetics and spirituality, Davy and her communities that gathered
at Fortelle and at the Centre de recherches philosophiques et spirituelles,
as well as around the journals *Dieu vivant, L'âge nouveau,* and *Cahiers de la
nouvelle époque,* were also realist, often fairly attuned to the dark undertow
of religion and its propensity toward violence. In the context of 1940–44 and
its aftermath, Davy claimed that the role of mystical texts was to keep alive
the reality of the "inner voice that can guide and support" people, without
which they become constantly susceptible to the "audible outside voices of
influence and authority." The only "real revolution," she wrote, "is spiritual," a

claim that might sound suspect had it not come from someone who engaged in real political action (operating clandestinely, risking arrest, forging alternative communities) alongside her scholarship with spiritual materials. "The prophets, mystics, seers, sages, poets"—the ones who have "experienced God's way of divine union"—were also the least likely to speak with clarity about God and God's plans for the world. "Authoritarianism," Davy wrote, "is both political and religious," in that they both speak with too much certainty of God, whereas "mystics have an experience of God but are discreet when it comes to talking."[91] The antifascist intellectuals like Davy and the *ressourcement* theologians knew that mysticism, particularly in its apophatic mode, was an important language in modernity that could challenge claims to religious and political certainties. Perhaps for these reasons, Davy seems most herself, her voice most unencumbered, when she is writing on the ravishing language of the mystics, the power of their experience, and the uncertainty, even the hesitancies, that they seem to carry within their own words. Her 1934 translation of Guillaume of Saint-Thierry is illustrative:

> Therefore the quaking and bewildered soul stands before her God, ready to entreat him, ever holding her very self in the hollow of her hands, as if she were about to make an offering of herself to you. Quaking at the things she is accustomed to, bewildered at things out of the ordinary, she carries a sign of faith in you, in order to find you. But not as yet. . . . She loathes the phantoms that her heart conjures up about you as she would idols . . . and when, burning with a desire for your face, offering you a sacrifice of her piety and justice, oblations and holocaust, she is carried off, she is thrown into confusion all the more. . . . How long, Lord, how Long? If you do not light my lamp, if you do not illuminate my darkness, let me be rescued from this trial, nor except in you, my God, let me step foot across this wall.[92]

Thierry's sermons, according to Davy, portray "in the soul a sense of mystery . . . access to the tabernacle in which a secret knowledge is hidden, impossible to describe, knowledge which causes a change in existence, and a new vision."[93]

In an interview Davy gave the year she died, over fifty years after her experiences in the war, she recalled that her love of the medieval period stemmed from what she saw as its "cosmopolitan character": "Professors from the medieval period moved freely from one country to the other, the monks traveled everywhere, and that seduced me. I love contact with strangers. Race mattered little, the most important thing is the opening of the one to the other."[94] This utopian vision was expressed only with the clarity of retrospection. When she was a young, burgeoning scholar working in the resistance, these were merely hunches and intuitions. She saw in these medieval sources a vision that might counter one that was narrow, authoritarian, closed—whether coming from familial pressures for stability and traditional gendered expectations or the right-wing imagined homogeneity of Christianity. Davy saw fluid borders, texts written by people who she eventually came to love as friends, friends who perforated the neat divisions between Christians and non-Christians, the West and the East, and the medieval and modern, who lived amid the tensions between solitary mysticism with friends, rather than the nuclear family. Davy and her community aimed to reject the strict observance that separated insiders from outsiders, Europe from its colonies, Christians from non-Christians, modernity from the medieval, immigrants from natives, *l'Orient* from *l'Occident*. The lives she saw included authors like Bernard, who penned passages on God of dazzling beauty, while she still admitted his shortcomings and recognized how impossible it is to disentangle some of his sermons from the long history of medieval Christian violence.

In 1955, Davy joined the Centre national de la recherche scientifique as a researcher on religion, which allowed her enormous freedom of research and travel, as the position had no teaching obligations. She lectured throughout Europe, Asia, Africa, the United States, and South America. She spent much time in India and Japan. Her time in those countries deepened the insights she had in earlier decades, the fruit of which was a major 1976 publication, *Le thème de la lumière dans le judaïsme, le christianisme, et l'islam* (The theme of light in Judaism, Christianity, and Islam), and at the end of her life she served as lead director of a four-volume series on comparative mysticism.[95] She would later explain that her goal was not, as she put it, "to confuse Christian apophatism with Buddhist emptiness. One cannot mix the paths, but understand that the traditions overlap and complement one another."[96] Davy's initial approach to her sources, affectively charged and interpersonal, seems to have inoculated her against simplistic and uncritical attachment to them and allowed her to instead see them as complex human beings inhabiting complex religious traditions. But it was not only the medieval monks who Davy bonded with in this period. Her more expansive vision of medieval Western Christianity came from key friendships with people who introduced difference into her academic and personal life.

SPIRITUAL KINSHIP:
DAVY'S BONDS WITH LIVING *AMIS*

During the war and after, few of the priests Davy knew from her days training as a medievalist came to her salon at Fortelle. The exceptions were the
Jesuits Jean Daniélou and Gaston Fessard. According to Davy, Fessard
was "generous in spirit. I loved him and so did everyone else. He had the
benevolence to accept people with other ideas." Davy's goal at Fortelle was to
have a place for discussion of religion in "an atmosphere of free thought."[97]
Davy claimed the success of her seminars was owed to Marcel Moré, an
eccentric wealthy banker, leftist Catholic, friend of Georges Bataille's, and
later contributor to Emmanuel Mounier's journal *Esprit*. Moré held his own
monthly salon, which Davy attended, and the crowds went back and forth
between Davy's and Moré's gatherings. Attendees included Jean Wahl, Pierre
Klossowski, Nicholas Berdyaev, Jacques Lacan, Maurice de Gandillac, Jean
Hyppolite, Jean Burgelin, Jacques Madaule, his wife Suzanne Madaule, Jean
Grenier, and Gilles Deleuze. Deleuze's biographer refers to Davy as Deleuze's
"high priestess" in the war years—the two met when Deleuze was only a
high school senior, but he made a huge splash at Davy's salon for his brilliance.[98] One of Deleuze's first early essays, "From Christ to the Bourgeoisie"
(1946), is dedicated to her.

In this community, Davy found kindred spirits who stammered for the
language to describe their place in relation to organized religion. After her
experiences at the Institut Catholique, she claimed she fled the institutional
church, but her position was never one that could be considered secular. She
forged a community of like-minded thinkers who refused to settle for either
the orthodoxies of the churches or secularism, and among those gathered in
her salon at Fortelle and around journals such as *L'âge nouveau*, friendship
played a particularly important role. Her bond with the Russian philosopher
Nicholas Berdyaev stands out, and she describes him in a way that she might
describe herself by the 1940s: "Although Orthodox in spirit he remained
outside any religious community while regarding the Orthodox church with
respect and affection."[99] As a member of the Russian émigré community in
Paris, Berdyaev introduced Davy to the world beyond the borders of Western Christendom, but he did so personally, face-to-face, and passionately.
Davy would recall their bond as a source of spiritual sustenance even long
after Berdyaev died in 1948. Berdyaev was part of the Russian emigration

abroad in 1917, which helped familiarize Western audiences with Russian religious thought. Berdyaev and Davy carried on a close friendship in Paris in the late 1930s and 1940s. Their travels sometimes overlapped in Berlin and London, where they spent time together, he attended her salon at Fortelle, and they collaborated on the journal *Cahiers de la nouvelle époque*. It seems to have been a genuinely close relationship. Davy describes talks between the two of them that lasted sometimes until dawn, in the car outside his apartment. Davy wrote about Berdyaev's life and thought for French audiences while he was still alive, beginning in 1948 for the Jesuit journal *Esprit* ("Nicolas Berdiaeff ou la lutte de la création contre l'objectivation"), and in 1964, she wrote a book about him, *Nicolas Berdiaev, l'homme du Huitième Jour* (*Nicolas Berdyaev, Man of the Eighth Day*).[100]

Similar to her approach to the medieval mystics, Davy claimed that one needed "to feel a certain kinship" with Berdyaev to understand him.[101] She considered herself part of the "same spiritual family" as the Russian philosopher (her beloved Guillaume of Saint-Thierry often called it "un certaine parenté spirituelle").[102] She describes how "I can think of none whose inner self seemed as wide open to the transcendent as Nicholas Berdyaev. He was inhabited by a presence, and his look, his thought, his voice, bore witness to the mystery within him."[103] These impersonal, modern ways of describing the supernatural common in this community (the "presence of the eternal," the "mystery of God," the "divine dimension") were, for Davy, felt in her concrete, special friends like Berdyaev, who were the *specific* vehicles of a transcendent grace that could be felt among "spiritual kin." She went on:

> When I saw him I always used to think that the Prophets of Israel must have had a similar look, as of a man inspired, a visionary who, while engrossed in his inner life, was at the same time yearning for the future; a look haunted by a presence like a spirit made visible in the form of a dancing flame. Age could not dim the beauty of his look nor extinguish its vivacity. Besides, it is a fact and verifiable that the eyes of a spiritual man even in old age retain a dazzling look of youthfulness, composed of spontaneity and talent. When he talked his deep voice brought out the best in the listener; his presence alone brought one beyond one's normal limits, bringing new dynamism to the spirit and changing time's rhythm; all seemed to be quickened by him. He did not invite confidences; his very presence drained away all inessentials and, strangely enough, when near him, people were taken out of themselves and felt a strange happiness. But was it really happiness, the mysterious feeling in the depth of

your being which you wished would last forever? Something inside you came to life. . . . You felt in some way transfigured and wanted to live in that state always.[104]

If her beloved medieval monks had introduced Davy to a "God who can be seen, touched, contemplated, a God so intimate that he can be felt without any need for elaboration," Berdyaev enabled her to glimpse something of this experience in the present. Davy's passionate language evinces a certainty that Berdyaev both embodies something of that ancient spiritual depth (depths like the prophets of Israel also possessed) *and* carries an ability to pass it on to others near him: through her friend, the spiritual was "made visible"; in his presence one was "brought beyond one's normal limits," "time quickened," and one felt "transfigured."[105]

We see something similar in Davy's friendship with Louis Massignon, who she met at Eranos, where they returned many times together, and he came often to her salon at Fortelle. While their friendship was not as close as hers with Berdyaev, she and Massignon collaborated on projects with the journals *L'âge nouveau* and *Dieu vivant*. After Massignon died in 1962, Davy penned an article on her friend entitled "The Man in Whom God Comes Alive."[106] Again, she was affected not merely by Massignon's ideas about Islam but by what she perceived as the spiritual power of his presence. Massignon was "a fascinating but strange person, and he seemed sometimes to be the prey of a sort of delirium, a type of delirium that accompanies only the great men or the great mystics. He was immersed in an ocean of fullness, like a fire that was kindled and flaming, and it was possible to see it gradually become comparable to the burning bush." At such moments Massignon was "inhabited, swept away, not only by a strange fire, but by a love full of compassion. When we left this sparkling man, we kept some glimmers in ourselves."[107] According to Davy, the holiness she sensed from both Massignon and Berdyaev was something that one could not only observe but rather obtain, as through these friendships the flame was passed on, like a torch, person-to-person.

Davy's intimacies reveal that there has never been a time when intimacy between friends was possible in a context immune from power and politics, although this may be rarely mentioned or even consciously considered by the thinkers themselves.[108] The warmth of spiritually powerful friendship is no safe haven from other kinds of power, no magic circle protected from race, gender, and religious difference, but intimacy and friendship have their own *specific* religious power within these broader societal forces. These bonds take place within the larger dynamics of Western fascination with eastern Europe (Berdyaev) and orientalism (Massignon), and the sacred is made real through the personal spheres of intimacy that happen always within, and alongside, the more diffuse networks of discursive and nondiscursive power.

LIVES AND AFTERLIVES OF
MARIE-MAGDELEINE DAVY

Given the fullness of Davy's life, the prolific nature of her scholarship, and the politics she practiced, it is a wonder that she is not more well known. What do we gain from learning about her today? When Davy's name surfaces in English-speaking scholarship at all, it tends to be allied with the early scholars of comparative religion in Europe and the intellectuals Steven Wasserstrom describes in *Religion after Religion*, such as the Islamicist Henry Corbin, Mircea Eliade, and Gershom Scholem.[109] According to Wasserstrom, from the 1930s to the 1960s, these three comparativists laid the foundation for what we might today consider New Age spirituality. There is nothing contemporary scholars like Wasserstrom loathe more than these founding comparativists' penchant to generalize and breeze past difference, their attraction to bizarre, esoteric texts rather than religious people of flesh and bone, their sentimentality and neglect of power and politics—all of which have become central to the study of religion in recent decades. It is true that Davy at times inhabited those spheres. In the late 1970s, for instance, Davy participated regularly in the meetings of the Université Saint-Jean de Jérusalem (USJJ), which Henry Corbin founded in 1974 after he retired from the École pratique des hautes études. The USJJ was a society of scholars dedicated to comparative studies in spiritual matters, and their yearly colloquium attracted participants connected to the Russian émigré religious thinkers and the field of comparative mysticism.[110] Davy also had been a regular attendee at Eranos. She loved Henry Corbin, whom she was close with, and Davy was a friend of Eliade's and engaged in two major intellectual projects with him, and she translated Scholem's work.

One of the reasons that the reputations of figures like Corbin and Eliade are so damaged today is because despite the putative openness and cosmopolitan nature of their scholarship on religion, deep down it is coming to light that they harbored secret loathing and enemies, and they veered radically to the right. Eliade's alliances with the fascist Romanian movement the Iron Guard (under whose influence he became, according to one historian, "rabidly anti-Semitic") are well known.[111] Eliade said to the press in 1937, "Is it possible that the Romanian nation will end in the most miserable disintegration in history, eaten by poverty and syphilis, invaded by Jews and torn by aliens?"[112] While Davy ran in those circles, though not exclusively, the politics associated with her scholarship could not be more different. In the face of anti-Semitism and authoritarianism, she was an active resister: forging documents for the safe escape of Jews, political prisoners, and airmen; shifting the content of her teaching to include Judaism; and convening conferences that helped ensure Jewish, Russian, and Islamic scholarship was published in the French presses. We are missing a great deal of the politics in the history of the comparative study of religion because stories almost always exclude people on the margins of its intellectual history—that is, women. Davy's work and insights did not emerge from any privileged vantage point as a woman, but her borderland position in relation to the mainstream certainly brought a new perspective.[113] When we include women like Davy in our scholarship, not only do we diversify intellectual history, but familiar fields—comparative religion, theology, philosophy of religion—actually look different. In her realism, scholarship, and political action, she stood with a community that worked *against* both the theosophists and New Agers, who spurned serious linguistic study and careful attention to differences and politics, as well as the militants, nationalists, and xenophobes, who believed in blood purity and were enraptured by the dream of Catholic renewal.

But situating Davy among the scholars of comparative religion, even as it gives a richer genealogy of that field, glides past Catholic theology. Davy's career, even her life, is incomprehensible without the institutions, training, and people connected to Catholic theology in inter- and postwar Europe: her training under Gilson in Cistercian monasticism; her sense, stemming from a Cistercian reading sensibility, that these ancient monks could be awakened, as friends, in the present; the Jesuit, Benedictine, and Dominican journals that published so much of her work; her understanding of God as something sensed from both spiritual friendships and solitude (a theme in the Catholic medieval piety she knew so well); her collaborations with theologians like Jean Daniélou on journals such as *Dieu vivant*; and the reviewers who supported her work, including the Jesuit Henri de Lubac and Dominican Marie-Dominique Chenu. I want to avoid viewing Davy as emblematic of an evolution "from" devout Catholicism "to" something more ecumenical and global because she held these concerns *together* throughout her long life. Layering, rather than developing or evolving, seems a more constructive form of analytic lens for understanding Davy. Her commitment to and training in Catholic theology helped protect Davy from succumbing to the same temptation as many comparative religion scholars: assuming that religious vitality and spirituality are found in the exotic, romantic East, instead of in the Christian West. Moreover, the ways in which, as a woman, she was never an insider in this world transformed her into a connected yet critical voice. Moving outside of the somewhat insular clerical theological atmosphere of *ressourcement*, she formed spiritual friendships with other outcasts in France, kindred spirits like Berdyaev and her friends in the resistance. These relationships opened new horizons. Yet the story of Catholic theology's *ressourcement* movement is always told without people like Davy. Perhaps when we think about the history of "Catholic thought," we can consider the ways in which some of this thinking was forced underground, in a way, only to resurface in new forms. Michel de Certeau describes Christian reflection as always having a here and an "elsewhere, an afterwards, a beyond, this, not that." I think of Davy as a kind of "elsewhere" *within* Catholic theology, a here *and* a beyond.[114]

Drawn inexorably toward difference, in friendships, spirituality, activism, and scholarship, Davy and her community exhibited a commitment to mixed, cosmopolitan solidarities. Bringing Davy to life helps offer an answer to the censure of mysticism as insufficiently political and realist. Davy worked to pull medieval studies and mysticism away from circulation that supported nostalgic tribalism and instead put them to new uses. Mysticism, in Davy's hands, was a religious form of dissent against both Enlightenment rationalism and right-wing, xenophobic Catholic nostalgia. It refused the dream of Christian purity but still felt there was a religious way of engaging with present-day issues. Medievalism was a strong current in the political atmosphere of mid-twentieth-century Europe, and through the spiritual friendships Davy felt with the twelfth-century monks who were the focus of her life's work, she engaged it in a fresh, humane, and more inclusive way. Yet the spiritual bond that was perhaps most important of all for Davy was one that took place almost entirely in the realm of memory, and it is to her friendship with Simone Weil that I now turn.

FIGURE 1. Objects that friends saved of Jacques and Raïssa Maritain: a portrait, a funeral card, and a check (gifts given to the author).

FIGURE 2. Photos of friends alongside holy figures framed in Raïssa Maritain's study. Courtesy of the Archives of the Cercle d'études Jacques et Raïssa Maritain, Kolbsheim, France.

FIGURE 3. Gabriela Mistral in 1938. Courtesy of the Biblioteca Nacional de Chile, Memoria Chilena, Archivo Gabriela Mistral.

FIGURE 4. Davy in solitude. Courtesy of the Archives départementales des Deux-Sèvres, Niort, France, 155 J.

FIGURE 5. Davy and her books. The authors of the countless texts she transcribed, translated, and analyzed were her beloved companions. Courtesy of the Archives départementales des Deux-Sèvres, Niort, France, 155 J.

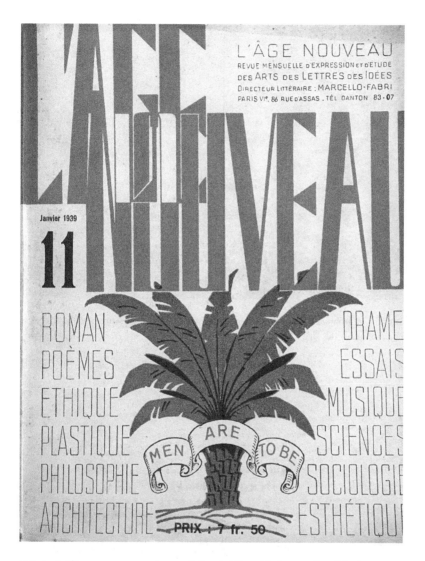

FIGURE 6. *L'âge nouveau* was an ecumenical and philosophical space where Massignon, Davy, and others debated spiritual, social, and political questions outside Catholic ecclesial circles. Courtesy of the Archives départementales des Deux-Sèvres, Niort, France, 155 J.

FIGURE 7. A group of faculty and students at Maison Simone Weil. Courtesy of the Archives départementales des Deux-Sèvres, Niort, France, 155 J.

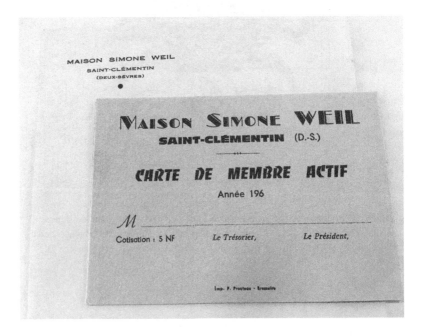

FIGURE 8. Maison Simone Weil stationery. Courtesy of the Archives départementales des Deux-Sèvres, Niort, France, 155 J.

FIGURE 9. Claude McKay portrait, 1941. Courtesy of the Carl Van Vechten Trust.

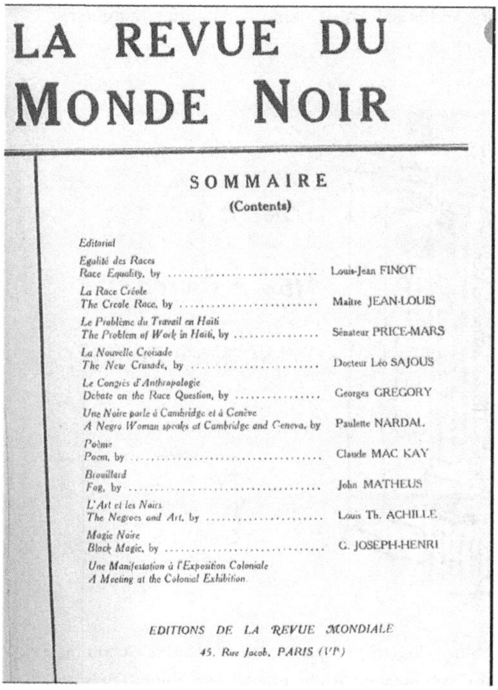

LA REVUE DU MONDE NOIR

SOMMAIRE
(Contents)

Editorial

Egalité des Races
Race Equality, by .... Louis-Jean FINOT

La Race Créole
The Creole Race, by .... Maître JEAN-LOUIS

Le Problème du Travail en Haïti
The Problem of Work in Haïti, by .... Sénateur PRICE-MARS

La Nouvelle Croisade
The New Crusade, by .... Docteur Léo SAJOUS

Le Congrès d'Anthropologie
Debate on the Race Question, by .... Georges GREGORY

Une Noire parle à Cambridge et à Genève
A Negro Woman speaks at Cambridge and Geneva, by ... Paulette NARDAL

Poème
Poem, by .... Claude MAC KAY

Brouillard
Fog, by .... John MATHEUS

L'Art et les Noirs
The Negroes and Art, by .... Louis Th. ACHILLE

Magie Noire
Black Magic, by .... G. JOSEPH-HENRI

Une Manifestation à l'Exposition Coloniale
A Meeting at the Colonial Exhibition

EDITIONS DE LA REVUE MONDIALE
45, Rue Jacob, PARIS (VI⁰)

FIGURE 10. The inaugural issue of the *Revue du monde noir*, the Paris-based journal promoting Black internationalism.

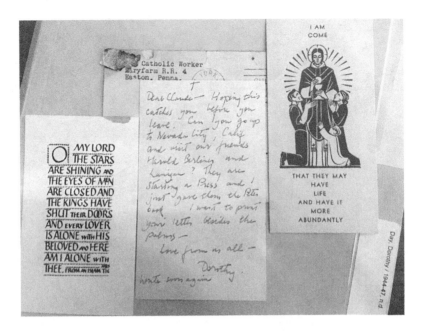

FIGURE 11. Letters from Dorothy Day to Claude McKay with religious cards tucked inside, the gold coin of spiritual friendship. Courtesy of the Dorothy Day Collection, Department of Special Collections and University Archives, Raynor Memorial Libraries, Marquette University.

FIGURE 12. Friendship House brochure. Courtesy of the Ellen Tarry Papers, Schomburg Center for Research in Black Culture, Manuscripts, Archives, and Rare Books Division, New York Public Library.

0
4

THE INTIMACY AND RESILIENCE OF INVISIBLE FRIENDSHIP

Marie-Magdeleine Davy and Simone Weil

I sought but could not feel his presence and sank back into the vestiges of memory until I found him.

PATTI SMITH, *M Train*

Friendship should be considered as the sole legitimate exception to the duty of universal love; that is to say, love should imitate the light of the sun.

MARIE-MAGDELEINE DAVY, *The Mysticism of Simone Weil*

INTRODUCTION

MARIE-MAGDELEINE DAVY'S most intense spiritual bonds were with men: her first *amis* were her beloved medieval monks and her cherished teachers, the friends who introduced her to a world beyond French Catholicism. She acknowledged this openly. Admittedly, Davy was treated terribly by the Jesuits at the Institut Catholique, Charles Journet called her "enfant," and indeed, Marcel Moré seems even more annoying (though he was apparently tolerated by everyone because he had a ton of money and funded everything). But many men supported Davy throughout her long career.

Some, like Bernard of Clairvaux, Guillaume of Saint-Thierry, and Nicholas Berdyaev—despite their gender, or perhaps because of it—became more than just friends; they were unseen, treasured guides long after they had died, part of Davy's inner life.

There was one exception. Davy met a young woman, the activist and philosopher Simone Weil, at the home of Marcel Moré sometime in the 1930s. Davy was six years older than Weil, but they were both young intellectual women with unconventional lives who inhabited similar philosophical circles. Although their time together was not long—Weil died tragically in 1943 when she was only thirty-four—it was enough to change Davy's life. Very soon after Weil died, friends gathered her papers together, and at the grassroots level stories began to circulate attesting to Weil's life of radical solidarity with those on the margins of society and to the unusual depth of her spirituality. Much like the cult of the saints in the history of Christianity, stories attributing a kind of holiness to Weil and the collecting of her writings became the impetus that built up her regional, national, and, eventually, international reputation. Davy was part of this early effort. She knew Weil in the 1930s and researched her life after Weil died in 1943. She developed a friendship with Weil's parents and often, in the late 1940s, went to their house to talk about her.[1] Davy published her first two articles on Weil in 1950 and her first book in 1951, lifting up Weil as a model for a new kind of sanctity in the modern world. Two more books followed. In 1962, Davy created an experimental utopian community for international students in rural France, the Maison Simone Weil, in her friend's honor.

When Davy wrote about Weil, as with Massignon and Berdyaev, she reached for language that signaled a total transformation in her presence: "This extraordinary woman," she marveled, "was overwhelming as soon as she uttered a few words. . . . Her gaze aroused an exit from the self, an opening towards the essential. Even her presence subjugated you."[2] "No one of our age," she noted elsewhere, "has created such an intensity of spiritual radiance as Weil."[3] But unlike Davy's bonds with Berdyaev and Massignon, the vast majority of her experiences with Weil took place in the realm of memory. Theirs was not exactly a friendship in the modern sense (they were together in person only a handful of times). Davy's connection with Weil instead better resembles the bonds of "intimacy and resilience," which Peter Brown describes, that Christians in the ancient world had with holy people, who were viewed as bringing traces of the supernatural into ordinary reality.[4] The saints held the sacred within them, but in the context of their inner bonds with devotees, they shared it with others, spread it around.

Davy's relationship with Simone Weil might be understood as a twentieth-century instantiation of the cult of the saints, not uncommon in their circle. Davy, like many in her network, was far too immersed in leftist skepticism of devotional piety to join the energetic devotional cults around someone like Thérèse of Lisieux, for instance, who was canonized in 1925 in response to devotees who held her relics and read her texts soon after her death in 1897. Yet just as Thérèse was for the men and women assembled around her, for Davy, Weil was much more than a moral exemplar. Davy understood that the grace Weil possessed was something truly contagious that circulated even after Weil's death. We might think of the religious anthropologist William Christian's line: "Very little religious gets permanently thrown away."[5] The religious history of humanity is a dynamic process whereby old attachments to the sacred constantly shift to new places and reappear in new forms. The cult of the saints was part of the religious imagination of Davy and her loosely Catholic network, and in the 1930s and 1940s this piety and theology resurfaced as a compelling way to relate to another human being whose life was sensed as, somehow, extraordinary. A focus on the invisible bond between Weil and Davy is also an opportunity to bring to light the broader social and political dynamics concerning gender in this religious and intellectual world. While neither Weil nor Davy used words typical of feminism, nor did either advance causes specifically for women, they deliberately arranged their lives in radical disjunction to the mainstream norms available to women at the time. If the family and the household have been described by historians of modern Europe as "the relations and institutions that anchored this world," both Davy and Weil cut that anchor rope and sailed on without it, into the waves and wind.[6]

WOMEN AND GENDER, SCHOLARSHIP, AND ACTIVISM

When Davy wrote about Weil she drew from the same metaphors of fictive kinship she used with the Cistercian monks and with Massignon and Berdyaev: Weil was a "kindred spirit," and they were part of the same spiritual family. But Weil was kindred to Davy in ways the men could never be: like Davy, Weil absolutely rejected the paths laid out for modern women, the married housewife with children or the nun. Weil experimented with the most stereotypically masculine kinds of employment, working not only in the fields of philosophy and history, as Davy did, but even in factories and the military. She took a leave from her teaching position in 1934–35 to work in the Renault factory in Boulogne-Billancourt and write about the conditions of the worker. Scornful of domestic tranquility and comforts, Weil famously preferred to sleep in the most uncomfortable, cramped spaces on the floor, moving place to place as a kind of itinerant intellectual and activist. Weil rejected her femininity and signed letters to her mother, "Your respectful son."[7] Davy zeroed in on this, noting that Weil "dressed more like a man or a religious monk than a woman" and that there was "nothing feminine about her."[8] Neither exoticism nor the presence of difference fueled Davy's attachment to Weil, as with her connections to the Islamicist Massignon or the Russian Berdyaev. Rather, Davy saw something of herself in Weil.

Davy began to research Weil's life and writings after the war, around 1947, four years after Weil's death and probably about ten years after they first met in person. At that time, women's vocation as wife and mother was undergoing a resurgence in France. The family found itself elected to the status, according to Claire Duchen, "of a national symbol."[9] The home was seen as disrupted by the war, and it was women's job to set things back in order, a postwar ideal that segued easily from the wartime Vichy model of "Travail, Famille, Patrie" (Work, Family, Country). The spiritually powerful bond Davy felt with Weil must be understood in the context of their shared rejection of these values.

To be sure, Davy and Weil occupied a man's world of religious philosophy and activism, but there were a few other women who had lives quite similar to Davy's, some of whom Davy counted as friends. By looking to the broader context of Catholic women intellectuals in Davy's milieu, we can better see the particularities of Simone Weil's spiritual magnetism and just how different she was. Davy was not the only young, unmarried female intellectual who worked with medieval theological materials in creative ways. Some were also politically active. While Davy was training as a medievalist in the 1930s, for example, in France, England, and North America, other women medievalists were joining the ranks, primarily in secular history, language, or literature departments, and studying medieval theological texts in nontheological settings.[10] One remarkable friend of Davy's, Jeanne Ancelet-Hustache, secured her PhD from the Sorbonne in German literature, with a specialization in the Christian Rhineland mystics. Like Davy, her medieval scholarship at first glance seems innocuous enough, but it, too, had an edge and was similarly groundbreaking in its incorporation of difference into the story of canonical Western Latin Christendom. She brought into the history of medieval Christian mysticism the texts of

women, offering the first translations, annotations, and analyses of Mech-
thild of Magdeburg in 1926, Elizabeth of Hungary in 1947, and Clare of Assisi
in 1953. Ancelet-Hustache was the first scholar to pull the legacies of these
medieval women writers from the confines of hagiography and Catholic
devotional literature and into the realm of scholarly discourse, just as the
ressourcement theologians had done with the patristics, the Maritains with
Thomas Aquinas, and Davy with Guillaume of Saint-Thierry and Bernard
of Clairvaux. Ancelet-Hustache's training in medieval German translation
allowed her to work expertly on the Rhineland mystical texts of women,
but to get ahold of these primary sources, she had to beg the nuns from
particular religious orders, who held the precious manuscripts of these holy
women in their abbeys. In these delicate negotiations, Ancelet-Hustache
offered her Catholic credentials and, often in her written requests for copies
of documents, included holy cards, tiny crosses, rosaries, and promises of
prayers and love in Christ, as if to show that although she was an academic
historian, the nuns would be putting these documents in the hands of someone who would understand them. She was successful. The translations and
annotations Ancelet-Hustache published in the 1940s and 1950s remain, to
this day, foundational.

Like Davy, Ancelet-Hustache's creative work on medieval Christianity
was accompanied by risky political action. In the 1930s, she was a well-
known and influential commentator in *L'Aube* on the refugee crises in
Europe, advocating for just treatment of Jewish refugees in France as early
as 1936. She was active in the group Comité catholique des amitiés françaises
à l'étranger (Catholic committee of French friendships with refugees) during the war. In the postwar period, she took part in German and French
reconciliation efforts, translating for French readership the works of German Christian authors like Franz Stock, the German priest who served
as a chaplain to imprisoned French resisters during the war, and Romano
Guardini. In 1977, Ancelet-Hustache was awarded the Georges Dupau Prize
of the Académie française for her life's work, which included hundreds of
articles, books, translations, commentaries, and a legacy of political activism. As with Davy, her story is virtually unknown in the English-speaking
world.[11] Today, in the works of American medievalists interested in women
and mysticism, like those of Caroline Walker Bynum and Bernard McGinn,
Ancelet-Hustache's efforts surface in voluminous footnotes. Even the theologian Hans Urs von Balthasar, well-known to the English-speaking world,
relied heavily on her works about Elizabeth of Hungary.

Another acquaintance of Davy's, Marie-Thérèse d'Alverny, also came under the spell of Étienne Gilson when he taught at the University of Strasbourg, where she studied medieval philosophy and specialized in the *mentalité* of the twelfth and thirteenth centuries as a young student.[12] She went on to pursue further study of twelfth-century Christianity at the École nationale des chartes, where she defended her thesis in history in 1928, and completed her doctorate in the history section of the École pratique des hautes études.[13] D'Alverny spent most of her career as an archivist at the Bibliothèque nationale, specializing in their medieval holdings and providing sources to countless *ressourcement* theologians and historians, who relied heavily on her expertise. She was also a published scholar, codirector (along with Marie-Dominique Chenu) of the journal *Archives d'histoire doctrinale et littéraire du Moyen Âge*, which Gilson had launched in 1926, and a "master philologist and historian of ideas," according to Giles Constable.[14] Like Davy, d'Alverny reached out to incorporate the presence of difference into the sources of Christianity. She was from a family of French scholars interested in Islam, and her brother André d'Alverny, SJ, was the founder of the Centre religieux d'études arabes and a professor of Arabic literature.[15] Marie-Thérèse d'Alverny published extensively on the interactions between Islam and Christendom in the twelfth and thirteenth centuries and wrote several articles dedicated to the prominent role of the Persian Muslim philosopher and scientist Avicenna in medieval Christian thought. In 1948, d'Alverny published her most widely cited academic article, a detailed comparison of two different twelfth-century Latin translations of the Qur'an.[16] Moreover, d'Alverny, similar to Davy, found just as much to reject within the sources of Christianity as to resurrect. D'Alverny also published an article on the uniform, widely held misogyny among medieval Christian writers, stating plainly that her exposition is "harsh," but the texts are boring: they all say the same derogatory things about women and "lack variety and original ideas."[17] But d'Alverny's attention was drawn primarily to those medievalists who were curious, patient, and open to genuine learning about the other. In her words, the "spirit of a discoverer" is one that "befits a good historian" then and now.[18] One of her former students remembered that she was interested in "internationalizing" the study of Christianity, not only by seeing Islam as part of medieval Christian history but by supporting international students who came to study in Paris. In one of d'Alverny's obituaries, Malgorzata H. Malewicz, a Polish student, recalled a special seminar d'Alverny led in the 1950s that included scholars from fourteen nationalities who were all thinking about Islam and Christianity in the medieval world.[19] D'Alverny died in 1991, her funeral held in Paris at the Arabic-speaking church. Like Davy, d'Alverny offered a powerful alternative to a medievalism that inspired nationalism and xenophobia.

Davy, d'Alverny, and Ancelet-Hustache were among the first to break away from previous generations of female "amateur" intellectuals who studied medieval Christendom, becoming instead "professional" scholars. Professionalized they were, however they still were not yet equal to their male counterparts and never attained top appointments in their fields. D'Alverny finally left the Department of Manuscripts at the Bibliothèque nationale in 1962 after she was not promoted to the head of the department when Jean Porcher retired. She confessed to a friend that she was the "victim of a plot" under circumstances "so scandalous" that she had to realize the "humorous side of the situation."[20] As for Ancelet-Hustache, while she earned the *aggregation*, all the professoriat vacancies she applied for went to men. She spent her career as a highly successful independent scholar. Davy and d'Alverny were both elected to the prestigious Centre national de la recherche scientifique in France, which afforded them enormous freedom in travel and research but did not have the same status as being a member of a university faculty.[21]

One wonders whether such incidents inoculated these women against the many forms of seductive, uncritical attachment to the tradition of the Christian past that we see more commonly in ecclesial apologetic approaches to history. Situated on the edges of the professional Catholic historical, theological, and philosophical disciplines themselves, these women "prowled the borderlands of Christianity," to use Michel Foucault's provocative phrase.[22] From the edges, their minds flourished. Instead of merely piling more details onto Christian history, they laid claim to a refurbished sense of the religious past, one much more complex, dynamic, and attentive to difference.

Moreover, all three had unconventional family lives. Like Davy, d'Alverny never married but carried on close friendships with men and women who became more like kin (Giles Constable told me d'Alverny was like family to him). Davy wrote in her own memoir that she had admired Ancelet-Hustache's unconventional marriage: she was the primary breadwinner, and her husband had been the main caretaker of their beloved daughter Jacqueline, who died tragically at only eight years old from diphtheria.

But despite so much in common, in looking through archival photos, correspondence, and private and public writings of all three women— d'Alverny, Ancelet-Hustache, and Davy—it becomes apparent that Davy's life, looks, and writings more greatly evinced the disposition of a rebellious outsider, and her scholarship, gradually, steered more in that direction after she left the Institut Catholique in 1940. This can be partly explained by the fact that in 1936 Davy branched off from the discipline of secular history and entered the totally male and almost exclusively clerical world of the Catholic seminaries in order to pursue theological, rather than historical, study. Her experiences gave her a more critical perspective on institutional Christianity, and this is an experience Ancelet-Hustache and d'Alverny did not share.

Bonnie Smith's classic work on the gendering of the discipline of history in Europe is also helpful here. Smith argues that from the late nineteenth century until about 1940, just when these women were completing their degrees, women's positions in the discipline of history were coded as masculine, scientific, and objective. Women historians were caught between being viewed as the "feminized amateur" or the "masculine professional." Scholarship that displayed emotion had to be overcome for early women professional scholars to gain respectability. Intimate relationships (especially spouses and children) ideally also needed to be renounced for the "construction of the citizen-scientist" scholar. Hence, many female scholars reputable in the field had to turn themselves into "prim models of sobriety and diligence."[23]

Davy, even from the beginning, wanted nothing of this. Rebellion *against* historicist approaches was at the core of her scholarly identity. Instead of showing scientific objectivity, her historical authors were beloved friends she wanted to summon back to life. If Gilson, Baruzi, and other male professors intimately attached to their subjects (and eventually the clerical theologians like Chenu and de Lubac), there were no signs, at least at the time, that women did or could. Their academic position had to be secure enough before they were able to shed the ideals of an impersonal, scientific approach to the past. Not only did D'Alverny and Ancelet-Hustache remain Catholics committed to and less critical of the institutional church than Davy (she might argue it was because they never spent time inside a seminary!), but their scholarship was also more historicist. We can thus see why Davy considered Weil, like herself, an "academic," as she referred to Weil, trained with a top-notch intellectual formation, even though Weil had, perhaps unusually for the time, managed to avoid what Davy called the "professional deformation which converts the academic woman into something grey and correct and totally devoid of fantasy."[24] Weil embodied something entirely different. It was almost as if Weil came from elsewhere. Furthermore, if Davy found herself on the edges of the institutional church while at the same time drawn irresistibly toward it—the dazzling reflections on God by the mystical theologians, the rigor of its ancient languages—she met her match in

Weil. Davy discovered her voice through Weil, her "kindred spirit," and she released herself within Weil's texts. While it was not the case that there were no other women intellectuals around, for Davy there was perhaps no other quite like Weil, no one who came so close to herself.

ON THE POETICS OF THE OUTSIDER

Davy and Weil shared a poetics, an aesthetic. Their lives and their writings offered a distinctive political and intellectual sensiblity, one that stood away from the mainstream. Davy's other friends, Berdyaev and Massignon, harbored something of this too, a poetics of outsiderness.[25] Weil was the most extreme in this regard, and Davy relished these details about Weil's lack of professional decorum: Davy fastened with delight on Weil's "extreme negligence of her appearance," for instance, and described an unsuspecting young girl who once "had to listen to [Weil's] long and brilliant commentaries on the Upanishads without daring to admit that she was bored to tears."[26] Davy chose as a Christian scripture to illustrate Weil's life Paul's letter to the Corinthians on the foolishness of the cross.[27]

From the liminal space of the margins, Weil, according to Davy, lived a "life closely akin to that of the great mystics. Living as she did in a land shaped by Christianity, the word easily comes to mind, but it would be equally true to speak of Muslim or Vedanic mysticism."[28] By 1951, Davy had been pulling in sources beyond the mystical texts of Latin Christendom for some time. She translated Jewish mystic texts, edited works on Sufism, hosted conferences on Taoism, immersed herself in the world of Eastern churches, and oversaw the publication of dozens of additional works. Weil was an ideal source of spiritual admiration for Davy precisely because her own inner life appeared to have been nourished by an equally staggering range of sources. Weil was trained formally as a philosopher, but in 1938 she became fascinated by the study of mystical texts, with particular attention to Meister Eckhart, John of the Cross, and the Bhagavad Gita. Davy described her in 1951:

> But whether one looks at her interpretations of philosophy, her immense understanding of different religions, her commentaries on Buddhist or Taoist texts, or on the Upanishads or the Paternoster, she is magnificently one. . . . Her spiritual life seems, nevertheless, to be the most difficult to

define because of its great range and fullness. It would be necessary to
be endowed with rare spiritual gifts to be able to grasp her real message
in all its fullness. If, lacking her quality, we sometimes find her thought
eluding us, it is because we are all too eager to apply a label. We are in
love with categories and groups. If we can place someone in a school, a
nation, a part, a religion, it is reassuring, since we can then start taking
dimensions. It gives us a feeling we can measure them, incorporate them
in a given framework. But this is to create an alloy. Simone Weil was
chemically pure.[29]

While Massignon and Berdyaev represented Islam and Russia respectively,
and Bernard of Clairvaux and Guillaume of Saint-Thierry were portals into
the medieval world and the life of the spirit, Weil had apparently fully assimilated all categories, according to Davy, exceeding the boundaries of any
nation, religion, or school. As Davy saw her, not only did Weil understand
these texts that were global in scope, but she also incorporated them into her
inner life. Davy imagined that Weil lived them, embodied them.

Davy offered another glimpse of the bond she felt with Simone Weil's
global mysticism when, in December 1951, the French literary journal L'âge
nouveau posed a series of questions to the public on "The Idea of God and
Its Consequences."[30] The questions steered readers to consider God in decidedly personal ways, as opposed to purely theoretical or historical: "What
does God mean to you? Does God correspond to a particular word? What
importance do you accord to the existence of God? What consequences do
you think follow from your own idea of God, whatever it may be?"[31] Answers
poured in for months and months, and four years later, they selected seventy-
four responses for publication. Davy, serving on the editorial board since
1941, insisted that they publish answers representing not only French and
Catholic individuals but a range of perspectives: Catholic composer Olivier
Messiaen; the scholar of Indo-Iranian studies Abdul Ghafour Farhadi from
Afghanistan; philosophers Jean Wahl and Jean Grenier; Catholic existentialist Gabriel Marcel; Islamicist Louis Massignon; Swami Siddheswarananda,
a monk in the Ramakrishna order; Vladimir Jankélévitch, a Russian-born
philosopher; pacifist Théodore Ruyssen; and many more. Although two
years later, Émile Poulat would criticize the journal for publishing only "religiously nonconformist" artists, writers, and intellectuals and ignoring, for
the most part, "l'homme de la rue," it made a splash.[32] Davy submitted her
own answer, which gives us a window into her sense that God is something
experienced interpersonally:

For me, the word "God" corresponds to flashes of a living presence, gen-
erating a certainty, and this knowledge is irreducible to habitual, ordinary
knowledge. It is an existential experience. I attach neither content nor
importance to the proofs of the existence of God. This is merely a path of
exteriority, which has no meaning for modern man. It seems to me very
difficult for a professor to speak of God effectively. Only someone who
has become "alive" can communicate a "living" sense of God. The latter
manifests itself less in the use of words, than in the tone and voice that
present a *quality of certainty* and signify a contact with God, that hearing
alone can grasp [*saisir*]. The example of Kierkegaard is suggestive here,
and later, Simone Weil. When food is cooked, for example, fire does not
appear in the dish, but one knows that the dish has had contact with the
flame. In human relationships, it is easy to grasp [*saisir*] in others the
traces of this kind of burn.[33]

Davy's answer about God as experience rather than dogma represents something of the era here. Even the young Jacques Derrida was writing at this
time, "One did not prove [*prouver*] the existence of God, but rather felt
[*éprouver*] it."[34] But Davy was unique in her evocation of "human relationships" as the crucial medium for sensing "traces" of the living God in the
present. These traces offered glimpses into the depth of Weil's spiritual life,
firsthand, face-to-face, in her inflections, her tone, her body—evidence that
Weil had been touched (burned, cooked, contacted by the flame) by God.
For Davy, the word *God* is invoked by the traces seen through relationships
with people like Weil. We hear echoes of the intensities of Davy's bond with
medieval monks like Bernard of Clairvaux and Guillaume of Saint-Thierry.

In Davy's other writings on Weil, she goes even further. When sensed by
others, Weil's closeness with God could have a transforming, even disturbing effect on those around her. Weil "shed" a "spiritual radiance" around
herself, as Davy put it: "No character of our age has created such an intensity
of spiritual radiance as Simone Weil."[35] She "carried within herself a flame,"
Davy wrote, "that scorched others. She disturbed the tranquility of things
and troubled the security of bourgeois society. Her lucid gaze stopped men,
institutions, and events of all that was spurious."[36] She spoke "above the most
ordinary octaves" and had "the energy of a hurricane"; "Simone Weil put
herself at the heart of the dough that is humanity, where she worked as a
leaven."[37] Davy sees in Weil something of William James's description of the
saints: "They are the impregnators of the world, vivifiers and animators of
potentialities of goodness which but for them would lie forever dormant. . . .

One fire kindles another, and without the over-trust in human worth which they show, the rest of us would be in spiritual stagnancy."[38] Like the language between Massignon and Kahil, Davy also depicts their friendship as a context for the holy fire of spiritual contagion.

Davy's descriptions of Weil draw deeply from the language of the cult of the saints in Christian history. According to Peter Brown, in ancient Christianity, saints were not merely moral exemplars who could teach about faith or God through their admirable lives, but rather their holiness was actually and really shared *to* others. In a curious way, saints were understood to have a kind of infectious, transformative power that stemmed from the fact that their inner resources were understood to be not their own. Brown describes the saint as an "invisible friend" and an "invisible protector," an exemplar who was "close to both you and his own Exemplar," and through the intimacy with the saint, your own Exemplar drew nearer. Christian hagiographical traditions are replete with portrayals of saints as not only good examples but also embodiments of the divine, who take on its power and then radiate this outward.[39]

This notion of the saint is something that can be generalized as a feature of religion itself, not only Christianity.[40] The late renowned anthropologist Stanley Tambiah characterized saints in East Asian Buddhism "as a radiant person who can cast his blessing upon the laity and transmit part of his charisma to them, very much in the mode of *darsan*."[41] Likewise, saints in Hinduism, according to John Hawley, "differ from us in their exuberance. . . . Moderation is not their secret. They stand apart from ordinary people of good will and offer more than ethics, but emphasize union with God, the transcendent, an experience of that 'something more.'"[42]

Davy saw all of this in Weil, not a paragon of morality but someone "possessed" by God, a "lover of God, of which Bernard of Clairvaux or St. Thierry have spoken." Davy attributed to her a flame, a light, a fire, and that fire spread. Weil addressed this process in her own writings on mystical experience. She described it in terms of the inner transformation whereby God enters one's soul: "What used to be called 'I' and 'me' is destroyed, liquefied; and in place of it there is a new being, grown from the seed that fell from God into the soul."[43] Davy cited extensively from Weil's own reflections on this divine alteration and saw in her its embodiment. Davy had been working on Hindu texts, at least informally, and collaborating with scholars of Asian and Indian religions in Paris since as early as 1940. In her 1951 book on Weil, Davy draws from a recently published book on Hindu meditation by Swami Sivananda Saraswati that her friend Jean Herbert translated into French in 1950.[44] She uses it to describe the process of the individual mind's dissolution and merging with the cosmic as a penetrating, transformative force, like a chick with golden wings which "pierces the eggshell of the world."[45]

As Davy understood it, this holiness was best received face-to-face, in person. She theorized that something so deeply personal and interior could be sensed, as if almost intuitively, by kindred spirits. "It is not enough," Davy wrote, "to know someone. One has to understand them, coincide with them. Besides, we don't talk about our spiritual experiences. They can only be read between the lines, in the inflection of a voice, or perhaps even in an expression in the eyes."[46] But she knew too that once the holy person died, as Weil had so early, we were left with things: texts, objects, memories held in other people's minds. But which ones conveyed the holiness of a departed friend? When reading about religious experiences, Davy argued that those written *to* a friend get closest to their reality and complexity. Davy harked back to her earliest training as a medievalist in the 1930s, when her first research projects focused on medieval texts that were relational in genre, like letters and sermons related to the topic of friendship itself.

For this reason she wrote, "It is only by a lucky accident that we are able to know something of the inner life of Simone Weil . . . thanks to her correspondence with Fr. Perrin." It was "their confidence born of mutual confidence and friendship that allowed her to transmit her experience, with a naked eloquence that was stripped of every mask."[47] Joseph-Marie Perrin was a Dominican priest whom Weil befriended in 1941 in Marseilles, where Weil and her Jewish family had been forced to flee from Paris on account of Vichy laws. Perrin, nearly blind, was not much older than Weil, and they hit it off, engaging in long dialogues about the religious life in the form of conversations and letters. Though she came close to the Catholicism of Perrin's faith, she refused baptism, preferring to remain on the religious margins. In 1950, seven years after Weil's death, Perrin published some of Weil's writings addressed to him as *Attente de Dieu* with a long letter.[48] According to Davy, these writings had the "quality of a revelation" because they were written *to* a friend, not a public presentation about religion. It was like a whispered conversation, a secret disclosure to a trusted confidant. This was one reason Davy highlighted a claim she attributed to Weil, which could just as well be her own: "Friendship should be considered as the sole legitimate exception to the *duty* of universal love; that is to say, love should imitate the light of the sun."[49]

However, there is a danger in ascribing a spiritual experience to these relationships, as that experience then belongs in someone else's hands, and it can ossify and harden the farther removed it is from the source. Perrin, Davy thought, never got Weil quite right. He wrote a preface that was far too "prudent," according to Davy, and missed Weil's intensity and radicalism. "How she would have smiled at Fr. Perrin's cautious preface to the *Attente de dieu*," Davy mused.[50] On the opposite end of the spectrum, Marcel Moré, who also knew Weil, published an essay in *Dieu vivant* accusing Weil of being a "Cathar" who subscribed to an obsessive anti-materialist dualism that led to her refusal to care for her own body and, eventually, her demise.[51] As Davy saw it, Moré rendered Weil's inner life too strange, and Perrin, not strange enough. Davy vehemently disagreed with Moré's analysis, but Moré never allowed her to publish a critique in *Dieu vivant*, and Davy never really moved on. After that, she called the journal *Dieu mort-né* (Dead God).[52] Despite her disapproval of others' views, she never quite trusted her personal interpretation either and filled her own writings on Weil with apologies.

ON THE POLITICS OF "IMPERSONALISM"

Considering the poetics of Davy's and Weil's lives and works on mysticism, it makes sense that their politics would also be off-center from the mainstream. In both of their political essays and correspondence about fascism, Davy and Weil rarely used the language that most French Catholics deployed at the time—the language of human rights, human personalism, and human dignity, like that found in the writings of Paul Valéry, Jacques Maritain, and Henri de Lubac. These intellectuals were the more professional Catholics invited to postwar meetings about human rights in the United States and Geneva. While the discourse of human rights and personalism was not antithetical to Davy's and Weil's visions, they articulated these ideas with distinct phrasing that suggests a slightly different moral and political vision. Instead of discussing human rights, the most direct political writings of Weil and Davy are endowed with a tragic, Dostoyevskian spirit, the literary language of suffering, and the faint possibility of human connection. Weil explicitly created neologisms to counter the language of personalism—*impersonalism* was one—that better envisioned other imaginative potentialities. Davy zeroed in on this.

Weil had discovered her interest in comparative religion by way of politics. As a young thinker, she was active in worker rights campaigns in the early 1930s. Davy focused on the fact that the category of experience was just as important to Weil's politics as it was to her mysticism. Weil claimed that she was unable to write on worker conditions and poverty without first-hand knowledge. Davy explained, "She knew already that nothing has the same quality as actual experience." Weil took time off from teaching high school in the late 1930s to work in the Renault auto factory in 1941 and on a farm in Marseilles. Davy cited a line in which Weil describes her need "to go among people in many different walks of life and identify myself with them."[53] "Experience," Davy added, "is something that is forgotten by statesmen and economists and experts in labor patterns."[54]

Weil's experimental stints in manual labor have since become objects of some mockery and eye-rolling. She was clumsy, and it is doubtful whether she helped much. One wonders what the men and women on the factory line thought of this physically awkward philosopher who joined their ranks to learn about their lives for "experience" and to "identify [herself] with them." It's an easy target. I cannot think of a time when this is mentioned in lectures, and often in articles, without some snickers. But in the late 1930s and early 1940s, Weil was both reflecting on and contributing to a widespread effort, particularly among Catholics, to get a closer, more attentive and realistic approach to the world of the worker. Consider this: In July 1937 in Paris, when Weil was living there, a young Catholic priest celebrated mass for sixty thousand people. The crowd, mostly throngs of worker rights activists and laborers, listened during the homily: "Forgive us, oh Lord, that we have not sufficiently hated injustice and war." A soloist followed the homily, singing for "light in the obscurity of the underground mine, and consolation in the face of ordeals," while a background choir chanted, "Working class of France! Working class of the world! Build up your courage and gain confidence!"[55] But for all that jouissance of solidarity, six years later, in 1943, the priests Henri Godin and Yves Daniel published La *France, Pays de mission?* after studying the industrialized slums on the outskirts of Paris. They realized that Catholicism was virtually absent in the lives of these workers, and the priests and bishops in Paris were so far removed from the actual reality of their lives, that it was as if they were two different countries. They advocated a rethinking of industrial France as a new mission site, and just as in other countries, one was unable to "preach" the Gospel there from the outside without local knowledge gained from living among the people and speaking their language. In order to serve the working class, priests now too must "join its ranks."[56] In 1942, with the help of the cardinal, Godin and Daniel created the seminary Mission de France, which led to a new order of worker priests, who as part of their pastoral role simply worked and lived alongside the laboring class in solidarity and learning. This suggested that theology was not just about ideas but about practice, in how people live, what they do, and how they feel, as evidenced by texts such as Gabriel Le Bras's *Introduction à l'histoire de la pratique religieuse en France*, which came out in 1944. The Dominican theologian Marie-Dominique Chenu became the theological advisor to the seminary and eventually, in 1955, published *Pour une théologie du travail* (*The Theology of Work*).[57]

All of this was in the air when Simone Weil attempted to experience life in the factory and on the farm before she wrote about workers' plights. But what Marie-Magdeleine Davy concentrates on is the fact that Weil's experiments were more than investigative or sociological. They were themselves a kind of mysticism. Davy notes that when Weil lived with the "anonymous masses, their unhappiness entered into her, soul and body, disintegrating her on every level."[58] Some of Weil's later writings describe meeting men and women who were thoroughly on the margins of society: those she calls the "vagabond," the "afflicted," "a torn and bloodied thing," the one who merely "stammers" rather than speaks.[59] She saw a gaping chasm between these "vagabonds" and "afflicted," on the one hand, and the democratic, professional institutions aimed at protecting rights and liberties, on the other.

Instead of personalism or human rights, Weil placed her hope instead in individuals who cultivated the art of radical attention to those easiest to ignore. "Putting ourselves in the place of a being whose soul is mutilated by affliction or is in imminent danger of becoming such a being" is a process she describes not as personalism but its opposite: "the *impersonal*."[60] She had in mind those who set *aside* the personal and widened their view of the world to encompass multiple outsider perspectives. Weil's vision of an egoless attention, her *impersonalism*, was for Davy a sort of holiness. This was not without risk, Davy saw, because the impersonal entails an inner transformation of the self, which leaves you vulnerable to take in that which is outside yourself, whatever it is you attend to with focus and attention. The goal is not only to understand but actually to interiorize the object of attention, and Weil's notion of attention echoed the Cistercian reading strategies in which Davy was trained. Davy admired Weil's "deliberately and consistently maintained effort at attention," but it could be perilous. "With the greatest frankness," Davy notes, "Weil writes, 'If there were twenty or so young Germans in front of me at this minute, singing Nazi songs in a chorus, part of me would immediately become Nazi.'"[61] Weil fought against fascism until her death in 1943, but even she admits that her politics of attention or impersonalism could leave one susceptible to absorbing whatever was around you.

We see something of this style in Davy's own writings in the early post-war period. In 1947, just as she was researching Weil, she published the slim book *Aimer toutes les mains* (Loving every hand). By this time, she had seen medieval Christianity usurped by the Far Right, worked tirelessly and often clandestinely to counteract this, and narrowly escaped arrest, and she had known Weil at least ten years, though Weil had been dead for four. In *Aimer toutes les mains*, Davy descends to the lowest of the low, focusing her attention on those most hated in 1947: the Nazi collaborators. The book was an experimental fiction piece, but the long section "in place of an introduc-tion" was largely a plea against retribution. Davy had witnessed some of the vigilante justice then rampant in Paris. After 1945, roughly ten thousand people accused of collaboration with Nazis were executed, nine thousand of them without trial. Retributions were particularly strong against women, and those accused of sleeping with Nazis were subject to particularly grue-some violence, like having their heads forcibly shaved or swastikas painted on their bare chests and being forced to march openly. These women, known as *femmes tondues*, were the subjects of remarkably symbolic acts of gender-specific punishment.[62] In response, Davy dedicated *Aimer toutes les mains* to "The Living and the Dead." In the book, she acknowledges that the palpable urge for retribution in Paris after the war was something universal: "The ancient Romans knew about it: they burned a hot iron on the breasts of the slanderers."[63] Davy continues, "I too have witnessed it. But," she states,

> there is no point in revenge. Revenge tightens the knots and it becomes impossible to ever untangle them. . . . . The one who was present at the scandal but living now has an arrow in the flesh. But the wound can heal, man can become a new being, can become reborn. Located beyond fear, knowledge can become even more lucid. Anyone who uses brute force simply ignores a more powerful force: that of love . . . *Loving Every Hand*, hands that sow seeds, provide light, heat, but even the hands that sowed distress, death, ignorance. Hands that beg, fill the cemeteries, seek the sun. Open hands.[64]

Davy's words, at first glance, are all Cistercian: the possibility of love as rebirth, knowledge located beyond fear, and knowledge based in love as the most lucid kind of knowledge. Two years earlier, Davy had published a text on Bernard of Clairvaux's theology of mystical love. During the war, Davy taught on love in Bernard. Recall her sudden recitation of his words when the soldiers burst into her classroom unannounced. But here she puts it to new use, offering it as a theological language to resist a universal urge for vengeance in the fraught postwar context. In another setting, for another writer, perhaps these calls for love and nonviolence might have rung hollow (naive, childish, sentimental), especially in 1947, but Davy was there: she had put herself at risk, and she knew the politics and resistance and realism the world required. This was not a naive call for spirituality when political action was necessary. Hers was a spirituality connected to a kind of politics she understood well. I wonder if the religious imagination Weil helped Davy develop also trained her to look past the surface, given reality for subtle, buried alternatives: neither the Right's xenophobic dream of Catholic purity, nor the Left's penchant for what Tony Judt calls "macho realism" after the war (he cites Simone de Beauvoir's line that the only good collaborator is a dead collaborator) or their secularism.[65] Davy's language, blended with the vision of Weil, her inner guide in the late 1940s and 1950s, suggests instead the skill of closely approaching the reality at hand and reading between the lines, something akin, in fact, to knowing a person intimately.

EFFORTS AT AN ANTI-IMPERIALIST SPIRITUALITY

In some of Davy's reflections on Weil, she seems to suggest that Weil's diffuse, cosmopolitan spirituality and the mystical attentiveness of her politics were unique achievements that evolved out of Christianity. "We should not assume that it was only what was visibly Christian that drew Simone Weil to Christianity. No. Greece, Egypt, ancient India, the beauty of the world, the true, authentic reflections of this beauty, the secret depths of human hearts that have no religion—all these drew her to Christianity," Davy reflects, "for she was Christian because she was deeply spiritual."[66] Yet Davy doesn't neatly sort this out. Davy also resists this idea of the pull of religion, including Christianity, toward a kind of cosmopolitanism so vast and universal that it becomes indistinguishable from secularism, having superseded all traces of religious particularity. The problem with the church, for Davy, is not just its particularism or borders (i.e., that the church is not expansive and secular *enough*) but its acquiescing *to* the secular and refusal of the sacred. Unlike Weil's capacious spiritual life, the juridical aspect of Catholicism was a "false religion" and "had allowed itself to become bourgeois . . .

adapted itself to human interests, thus enslaving the holy, prostituting it, and in a sense becoming the gravedigger of the holy within itself."[67] Institutional Catholicism falls short because it is too human, too secular. She would distinguish secular universalism from a kind of cosmopolitan spirituality that is directed at God and, like Weil herself, exists askew with ordinary, secular reality.

In places, the genealogy of this cosmopolitan spirituality is decidedly Christian, but elsewhere Davy tracks it differently. It would be hard to find a modern writer who at once is so hopeful in the possibility that Christianity could be involved in the making of a more humane, interconnected world and at the same time gives such an honest and realistic assessment of its role in fomenting violence. Davy cites Weil's analysis of the North American slave trade undertaken by Christians and the savagery of colonialism when Christian nations "drive out beauty" from every other country and come in with "its arms, its commerce, its religion."[68] In her writing on Weil's analysis of Christian violence, Davy notes that in addition to the Christians of the past who committed atrocities, even the style of the church's hierarchical authoritarianism underwrites totalitarianism in the present. "No intelligent person will be astonished at the obvious fact that some great parties, like Nazism or Communism have been very akin to the church and to the constitution of certain religious orders, both in organization and dogma. The letters of Gregory VI make a very interesting study in totalitarianism, at least in its initial, primitive form," Davy states.[69] She published widely on the symbols of the clown, the dog, and the acrobat in medieval sermons and how they served as vehicles to communicate anxieties about religious and cultural difference. For all the possibilities of transformation presented by the ancient Christian mystics, and those like Weil who embodied them in the present, Christianity was not a monolithic site of uncritical nostalgic yearning. It was her engagement with Simone Weil that gave Davy some of the language and energy for this overtly political and critical writing. Davy was rarely judgmental of Weil, but she did attribute to Weil one great flaw: the failure to realize the depth and beauty of her own Judaism.

MAISON SIMONE WEIL

Davy knew that before Weil died, she dreamed of creating alternative institutions in the world that would allow for new kinds of relationships and new ways to practice attention and build communities. Weil predicted that "institutions that are meant to protect rights, persons and democratic liberties," like the sort Jacques Maritain and other famous philosophers advocated for, would understandably garner much public support and were needed. But she also noted that we need to "invent other ones" too—institutions that might help cultivate selfless practices of listening in order to be attentive to those who "stammer rather than speak."[70] And in 1962, almost exactly twenty years after Weil wrote those words, Maison Simone Weil was born. When Davy's own academic career began to slow down in the 1960s, she moved to the small village of Saint-Clementine in rural western France. Davy had spent some summers there as a child, and from one of her uncles she had inherited an old, decaying twenty-two-bedroom estate in the countryside called La Roche aux Moines. In 1962, Davy turned the chalet into a dormitory to house students from all over the world, who would come to Saint-Clementine for a few weeks to enroll in a program Davy named after her beloved friend, Maison Simone Weil. The goal was for the students—from Ukraine, Russia, Sweden, Holland, Spain, France, and England—to attend workshops and lectures on spirituality, politics, religion, and literature that would be of broad interest and help them forge international ties. Davy enlisted the young Dutch artist and historian Aurelia Stapert to help manage the program and teach classes. It was free for many students; others paid a nominal fee. Davy recruited friends from Paris, Berlin, and London to serve as speakers, and topics for the sessions included things like "The Sense of the Sacred in Shakespeare," "Spirituality and Existentialism," and "Teilhard de Chardin," along with cultural and even athletic events that exhibited the optimistic celebration of the world community in postwar period, like judo and Ukrainian dance performances by the Ukrainian students. Students would also perform Georges Bernanos's play *Le dialogue des Carmélites*. Some participants were simply thrilled to go to France and speak French, and some remembered talking all day about life's biggest ideas and then swimming in the river at night.[71] The local newspaper in Saint-Clementine noted how the summers turned this sleepy country town into a "village européen."[72] People as far away as Argentina heard about it and wrote to Davy wondering how they might replicate the Maison Simone Weil there.

This utopian community was perhaps the last vestige of her experimental salon in the 1930s and 1940s at Fortelle, a reenactment of her early ideals recast decades later with the more optimistic glow of the postwar period. In the 1960s, Saint-Clementine was located in the far northwest region of France, which had become an unlikely epicenter of progressive Catholicism, even in tiny towns.[73] Although Maison Simone Weil couldn't be considered exclusively Catholic, its vibe—with the emphasis on Teilhard, spirituality and existentialism, global community—was pretty close. Davy became, in the little town of Saint-Clementine, something of a beloved local hero. "When she appeared in the village," someone recalled, "always wearing trousers and smoking, she brought sweets for the children who gathered there."[74] She was concerned with improving the lives of young people in the village, not only the international students who visited. Davy saw that students coming from Russia, Sweden, and England could also broaden the horizons of the locals. She started a workshop for young village girls on the theme of courage, although it never really took off (she didn't trust her own maternal instincts, claiming she had none, but she was unable to find the right teachers). To this day, Davy continues to be celebrated in this part of France from time to time, and there is a nice plaque in her honor in the town square. In 2014, the mayor of Saint-Clementine held a festival commemorating Davy's life. They even referred to Davy as having been a "conseillère municipal," a kind of city councilor.[75]

Looking through Davy's archives, particularly the materials connected to Maison Simone Weil, I couldn't help but think about how often intellectuals like Davy, scholars of comparative mysticism or "spiritual but not religious" thinkers, are dismissed as high-modernist romantics who disdained both ordinary people and politics. It is impossible to get that feeling from Davy when we can view her carefully rendered architectural plans for updating the chalet to accommodate the students; flyers made announcing the most exciting events of the week; meticulously planned meal schedules; countless exchanges to settle travel logistics for speakers; and piles of photos from the students who kept up with her afterward and sent her updates about their jobs, marriages, and travels. And this doesn't even address, going back many years before Maison Simone Weil, Davy's much more dangerous work in the resistance that began in 1940, about which she was almost totally silent. Alongside Davy's high-minded modernism, her mysticism, her immersion in long-dead languages, her passion for exotic religions and friends, and even her esotericism, Davy's life is simply full of other people she cared for, risked for. If her aim for Maison Simone Weil was to create a utopian space in honor of her friend, she succeed in including much of Weil's legacy: the global spirituality, the openness to difference, the ecumenism and internationalism, the conversations that were religious but engaged with contemporary philosophy and literature. But missing was an emphasis on economics and justice. The house served in the realm of poetics and the religious imagination, which seems so far removed from Weil's experiments with workers and the afflicted.

It is also worth noting that in her photos, much like those of Simone Weil, Davy is almost always pictured alone, appearing almost haunted and rarely smiling, a book in one hand, a cigarette in another. Despite the power she felt from the bonds of friendship with Weil, the medieval monks, and people like Berdyaev and Massignon, there is an undeniable solitary nature to Davy, a sense that she belongs elsewhere. Davy once described Berdyaev in a way that would have been a good description of herself: "Such a man," she wrote, "needed solitude, isolation, and dreams."[76] Davy chose as the epigraph for her memoir a line from Nietzsche's *Human, All Too Human*: "In solitude, you devour yourself; in company, you are devoured by the many: now, choose!"[77] Davy confessed in her memoir that she "married solitude, as others take a spouse," and detailed her belief that there was an invisible fence that enclosed her soul and God with one another, letting no one else in.[78] This fence protected her from the lot of many women, who were so fully consumed by their relationships that nothing of themselves remained.

SOLITUDE, ISOLATION, AND DREAMS

Davy once explained that anchoring her soul in solitude enabled her to "reach" friends that have passed away, like Simone Weil, whom she began publishing on seven years after Weil's death, or Berdyaev, who was the focus of a book she wrote nearly twenty years after he died. "I must confess," Davy begins, "I never managed to live easily with the deaths of those who were dear to me. I am, each time, deeply disturbed by the disappearance of those whom I have loved." She suggests that the "entry into anonymity," what elsewhere she called solitude and a kind of spiritual detachment, makes it possible for her to "reach the dead and the living, without distinguishing them from one another. An unlimited love reunites them."[79] Davy's world of friends took place in a cosmology that included the living and the dead, that was felt in the realm of memory and dreams and even managed to "[reach] them" in the present. When it came to Weil especially, Davy seems to imply that this intimacy was more appropriate after Weil died and that the bond was possible only then: "Perhaps it was necessary," Davy muses, "to wait for her to die, before we could dare to look into her face, speak of her, wonder at her and listen attentively to her message."[80] In the history of Christianity, the notion of sainthood works to bridge past, present, and future. This may be why the language of sainthood or invisible friendship rather than that of modern friendship seems to most accurately describe the intimacy she felt with Weil.

Other modes of consciousness, including visions and dreams, also played important roles in Davy's bond with loved ones who had passed away. For example, in 1962, almost twenty years after Berdyaev died, Davy wrote about how in 1940 he shared with Davy a religious vision he had in a dream. In the dream, Berdyaev was at an ecumenical council, but everyone kept telling him there was no room for him. So he left the meeting and walked toward a huge rock in the distance and began climbing. Trying to go up the rock, he told her, "I kept on succumbing to weariness and exhaustion and I saw my hands and feet were covered in blood. With agonizing efforts I kept climbing up the rock. And then, I suddenly saw in front of me the figure of Christ crucified, his side pierced and blood flowing from the wound. I fell at his feet utterly exhausted and hardly conscious. Then I awoke, stirred and shaken by this extraordinary vision."[81]

Davy claimed that it would be impossible for a friend to understand these dreams and visions without having had similar experiences. But those who recognize these inner events see within them an "echo," as she put it, of their own sensations. By accessing the inner life of a friend with whom she felt a spiritual kinship, Davy heard an echo of herself. As Davy wrote about Berdyaev's dream, the Second Vatican Council was taking place, from which she herself was, of course, excluded. But Davy only rarely wrote about her own criticisms of the church or sexism, or about specific visions of Christ crucified (like many moderns, she preferred "the eternal" and "mystery"). A religious dream that was not hers but a friend's enabled her to write about both, indirectly. In many friendship circles, dreams were shared in secrecy, visions of Christ whispered about, promises made to God confessed after the fact, and all offered a glimpse of the sacred to one another. From Weil to Eckhart, from Massignon to Bernard of Clairvaux, when Davy wrote on this community, it is as if she presents friendship as experienced in a dream state, where antiquity meets memory and mixes with flashes of transcendence.

To describe her community of spiritual kin, Davy evoked a symbol that suggested movement, migration, and flight between vast distances, especially the distance from the mundane to the sacred. She called her spiritual family "the winged beings of the world," writing, "The winged beings are not always accepted by the majority of people. Their personalities are isolated, they are solitary, and their joy is rooted in their interiority. However, there's a secret communion among them." The winged beings, she continues, "are in a state of love, they can do as they wish, they speak freely of what others dare not think, for they are afraid of nothing. . . . They are like birds in the sky, placed in high, that is, in God, so they know no limitation."[82] Davy's symbol has a long, robust history in Western religious literature, from the biblical descriptions of God as a bird who carries the Israelites on her wings, under whose feathers Israel can take refuge; to Noah's dove; to the hunted composers of the lamentation Psalms, who are attacked on all sides and take flight, like birds; to the raven who delivered bread to the desert fathers of Saint Anthony and Saint Paul. What symbol could be a starker contrast to the religious imagination of the Right, which Davy had resisted since the 1930s, with its stress on land, stability, blood, fixity, borders, roots? The last book Davy wrote was published in 1998, *L'oiseau et sa symbolique* (The bird and its symbolism).[83] She claims she loves the idea that wings, in giving flight, are a method of movement that leaves no trace.

Jacques and Raïssa Maritain also once described their circle of friends with bird metaphors, referring to their intimate community as a "little flock." But Davy's bonds with her friends differed from theirs. There were no framed pictures of friends among her devotional objects, the sorts of artifacts that are everywhere in the archives of the Maritains. The Maritains had a beautiful home, were consummate hosts, and were, in a way, sentimental about each of their friends. But there is nothing sentimental about Davy, no stories of her presiding over elaborate dinners. There is almost, oddly, an *impersonal* quality to Davy's friendships. She saw special friends like the medieval monks, Berdyaev, Massignon, and Weil as powerful vehicles of the transcendent that could become passed on, person-to-person, but it was almost as if this was not about them as people (there was no begging for photos of friends' sweet faces, as was so common with the Maritains) but about the holiness shining *through* them, from afar. We can see this toward the end of Davy's life, when the writer Jean Biès asked her what teaching she wanted to impart to the world. Davy replied, "I am not conscious of having any particular message. From time to time, something filters through me. But it is not from me."[84]

Davy's friend Marc-Alain Descamps shared with me that after Davy's death, there was a colloquium held in Paris in her honor on January 31, 1999. Hundreds were at the gathering, but it was "stupefying," he said, shocking. Davy had given the impression that many were her best friend, the special object of her affections. But Davy carefully separated her different encounters and passed from one to the other without saying so. Her life was typically divided between all these different interests, and she avoided presenting them together or having them get to know one another. At the colloquium there was shock at the extraordinary diversity of her friends. Dominicans wondered how she could have connected with the Jesuits, Benedictines, Carthusians, and so on. And they found in front of them all her agnostic, atheist and irreligious friends. And all of her other Protestant, Orthodox, Jewish, Hindu, Buddhist, Taoist, Shintoist, Tantric, Korean friends were there too. It was too much for everyone who had installed her as a saint in the small niche of their hearts.[85]

Descamps said the experience of seeing all these people was an "intrusion of memory" for them and felt like a kind "of betrayal, and sacrilege." He continued, "Those who believed they had possessed her could not share her, thereby showing that they had understood nothing of what she asked of them."[86] Like almost everyone in her community, she spoke little about the jealousies and grief that hovered around the edges of these bonds. Descamps noted, "Everyone who loved her wanted to claim her as their own."[87] It could be that she imagined her solitude as a protection from all these worries.

It has been impossible to give more than a sampling of Davy's thought here, and there remains so much more to her story. In her old age, for example, she traveled a great deal to India and wrote a book on Henri Le Saux, the Benedictine monk who moved to India, became a disciple of the Hindu sage Sri Ramana Maharshi in 1948 and a pioneer of Hindu-Catholic relations, and changed his name to Abhishiktananda. Davy's friendships, travel, politics, and scholarship seem to go on endlessly, and indeed, living from 1903 to 1998, in many ways she captures something of the *entire* twentieth century in Europe.

Davy once described Weil as "similar to a flame," like the "prophets whose vision is always burning."[88] As we imagine Davy moving close to the light of Weil, we can see so many of the various winds of the twentieth century that propelled Davy toward Weil. We can think just about gender, for instance, though Davy would not want us to view them both as women. But they were, even if neither Davy nor Weil resembled the vast majority of women at the time, or even in the present day: those who perhaps have plans of mystical journeys of their own, or desires for larger political commitments, but are pulled constantly away into the vortex of the everyday—cleaning up the family's breakfast, fetching the children from school, waiting at the doctor. Neither Davy nor Weil worried much about these ordinary cares, and even when they had to attend to them, at least for themselves, it wasn't a priority. Davy was drawn to the flame of Weil in part because of her rebellious mood that rejected such considerations, the freedom from those cares. Weil and Davy were passionately attracted to a world coded as masculine. Davy saw in Weil a brilliant thinker who also pitched her tent outside the seductive safety of the church or the university and refused the more secure vocations of the church archivist and scientific historian, which were beginning to be offered to women. In Weil, Davy found someone who, though she denied much, read the twentieth century tragically, darkly, and also immersed herself with joy in the religious treasures of the past, treasures vast in scope and from all around the globe, and they both dedicated themselves to the rigor of the ancient languages required to read these texts. The flickering light of Weil appealed to Davy because she was a women who had a brilliant mind, and not just the body many emphasized after her death, as is often the case with women intellectuals. So many stressed the starvation that ushered in Weil's tragic demise at age thirty-four; her refusal to indulge in sugar as a young child during wartime privations; her horrible outfits and "her home-liness, her physical clumsiness, her migraines, her tuberculosis" (to draw from Susan Sontag's famous litany).[89] "By the age of fourteen," Mona Ozouf notes of Weil, "she had achieved beyond her wildest dreams her plan not to be attractive."[90] No, Davy loved Weil's intellect. But she did love something about her body too, that her ideas were never only cognitive. They were instead embodied in her life, in the way she dressed, in the places she slept, even, as Davy states in 1951, in the tone of her voice and the "expression in the eyes."[91] This allure was intellectual *and* embodied, and it was a sensual, if not exactly sexual, bond. As Davy saw it, Weil's way of living out her philosophy was so wonderful, so pure, so powerful that it *had* to be close to God—it *was* holiness itself. What else could it possibly be? "God dwells in the secret places," Davy wrote when she reminisced on Weil's life.[92] This holiness spread out, and drawing close to Weil, Davy felt a light that, at least for her, flickered brightly on the dark landscape of the twentieth century.

Whatever Davy's shortcomings, near the presence of Simone Weil, Davy broke with doctrines on the purity of Catholic renewal and moved toward cosmopolitan solidarities beyond the familial, Catholic, and national. This solidarity did not imagine secularism as the only way to cross chasms of difference. With Weil, Davy was attentive to intellectual and religious stirrings from other parts of the world, from India to the industrial slums of France, and her desire for learning about these was not just another hidden scramble for imperialism. She had a lucid grasp on the contemporary reality of her time. It was an alert, less complacent religiosity. Davy held out hope that a revitalization in both modernity and the church would be possible, but she wrote that this "depends more on saints than on theologians."[93] Simone Weil, more than anyone else, was Marie-Magdeleine Davy's invisible friend, her inner guide, and her saint.

05

FRIENDSHIP AND THE BLACK CATHOLIC INTERNATIONALISM OF CLAUDE MCKAY

INTRODUCTION

WHEN THE POET Claude McKay converted to Roman Catholicism in 1944, his old friends were horrified, reacting almost as if he had died.[1] McKay was a Jamaican-born writer of the Harlem Renaissance, active in Black radical circles most of his life. To add to the shock of his baptism, he told his good friend, the Black Catholic writer Ellen Tarry, that he was more of a "European Catholic" than "an American one."[2] Yet McKay was an artist who had made his name in deliberate resistance to European aspirational culture and aesthetics: his writings instead evoked the sounds and sensibilities of voices from the rural Jamaican hill towns where he grew up; the African immigrant dockworkers who made a living in the shipyards of southern France; and Harlem's Black dining car waiters, drifters, street preachers, and sex workers. He was at odds with what he perceived as the elitism of figures like W. E. B. Du Bois and the idea of cultivating a talented tenth to uplift the race. McKay spent his life refusing to wear what he called the "borrowed robes of hypocritical white respectability."[3] But by 1944, Claude McKay had become a *European Catholic*?

In recent years, McKay's connections to Europe as well as to the Caribbean and the United States have drawn the attention of scholars interested in Black cultural expression beyond, according to Brent Hayes Edwards, the more standard "U.S.-bound themes of cultural nationalism, civil rights protests, and uplift in the literary culture of the 'Harlem Renaissance.'"[4] Indeed, McKay offers us a nearly paradigmatic example of Paul Gilroy's notion of transatlantic Black modernism.[5] Born in Jamaica, McKay immigrated to the United States in 1912 and ended up in Harlem in 1914. He was a gifted poet: his collection *Harlem Shadows* (1922) propelled him to become "the most famous poet among black Americans" and is today viewed as one of the texts that inspired the Harlem Renaissance, and in 1928, McKay published one of the first best-selling novels of African American literature, *Home to Harlem*.[6] But like so many African American musicians, artists, and writers, McKay fled American racial violence and set sail across the Atlantic, first to England in 1919, then on to Russia in 1922, then France, Spain, and eventually Morocco. He returned to the United States in 1937, where he remained until his death in 1948. McKay evoked this restless wandering in his art.

Among the strands that tied together what Gilroy terms a "webbed network" of Black diaspora transnationalism, Catholicism has received little attention, especially concerning Claude McKay.[7] Catholicism's role in Black and antiracist internationalism is more difficult to see if we only look at English-speaking countries of the African diaspora, where Protestantism has historically predominated. As an adult, however, McKay spent a lot of time in the Catholic countries of Europe, France and Spain in particular, and there the religion was more than just a cultural backdrop for his traveling. In Europe, and eventually in Harlem and Chicago, McKay connected with a small transnational counterculture of writers, activists, and artists, in whose efforts Catholicism was key as a means to forge interracial, intraracial, and international affiliations that could counter the rise of nationalism, European imperialism, and white bigotry. Of course, mainstream Catholicism also functioned to intensify racism throughout the world, but for a minority counterculture, it presented a worldview and set of practices that fostered new kinds of solidarities across national and racial lines. This counterculture included Catholic journals that published Francophone Black writers in English for American readers, like the *Interracial Review* founded in 1931, which brought together writers like Louis Thomas Achille from Martinique and Ellen Tarry from Alabama. Also notable were French-language journals like *Univers: Bulletin catholique international* and *Esprit*, Emmanuel Mounier's "new Left" alternative to the communist press, which published Frantz Fanon's 1952 *Peau noire, masques blancs* (*Black Skin, White Masks*). This new, numerically small and fragile Catholic antiracist counterculture can be found as well in the emphasis on political and spiritual friendship in the names of many Black and interracial associations from this period, like

Amitié franco-dahoméenne in Paris or the Friendship House, established in Harlem in 1938. When Claude McKay traveled at the edges of these Catholic circles, they were just beginning to lay the foundations for racially conscious Catholicism in the colonial world, which would develop more fully—in fits and starts—in places like Paris in the 1950s, as Elizabeth Foster's *African Catholic* demonstrates, and in Chicago, as Matthew Cressler has uncovered.[8] These journals, associations, and utopian communities were all run by lay Catholics or Catholic-educated activists who centered racial solidarity in their work, often in opposition to more conservative stances or silence on race by bishops and the papacy. While this international Catholic counter-culture was much smaller than that of the more colonial mainstream, the story of interwar transnational Black modernism is incomplete without it.

By the time Claude McKay left for Europe in 1922, he had seen waves of frenzied racial violence sweep through the United States, which gave him a dark read of the concepts of modernity, civilization, and, what he perceived as its ancillary morality, Protestantism. He often used these nouns interchange-ably, and for McKay they were all merely respectable words that covered over the same tribalism and racist violence. McKay had long been interested in forms of recalcitrant resistance to modernity, and non-Protestant religion, in his opinion, offered a critical method for this. Throughout his career, McKay wrote vividly about the folktales from Mozambique that he heard in southern France, the incense and candles from African shrines in Har-lem apartments, and the resilience of peasant Christians in rural Jamaica, as well as about Roman Catholicism: he was fascinated with Black statuary in Catholic Spain and researched Black Catholic history at the new Schomburg library in Harlem, founded in 1925 by McKay's friend Arturo Schomburg. After his conversion, Catholic themes appear more explicitly in his poems, and the initial draft of McKay's final, posthumous book, *My Green Hills of Jamaica*, recovered a Spanish Catholic history of the island.

But most important of all, the Catholic scene McKay encountered in the 1930s and 1940s was a deeply relational culture, decidedly anti-family and focused on friendship. By remaining rather private about actual sex, McKay's Catholic counterculture possessed a muted, though not exactly transgressive, queer sensibility: *no spouse, no kids, no questions.* Like all the protagonists in this book, Claude McKay spurned modernity's traditional anchors: the nation and the nuclear family. A self-described wanderer and "vagabond," McKay felt that friends were the threads that held his world together.[9] McKay dedicated his books to friends, wrote essays on the com-plexities and difficulties of friendships with white people, and rhapsodized on the almost mystical pleasures of Black male friendship in his 1929 novel *Banjo*. McKay's friends, male and female, white and Black, were his lifeline. They floated him money between writing jobs, nursed him through illness, and introduced him to religion. But he also withdrew from them, canceling and dodging commitments, and by the end of his life, he had become paranoid and needy. Friendships were difficult for McKay, but he never stopped his efforts, and he converted to Catholicism because of the connections he had made at an experimental, interracial community in Harlem, the Friendship House. Though France always stayed with McKay, and he called himself a pariah in the United States, in truth it was in Harlem from 1936 through 1944 where he began to claim Catholicism as something of his own, owing to his friendship with Alabama-born, Black Catholic writer Ellen Tarry. While McKay's radical, secular friends thought he had lost his mind when he converted, and his Catholic associates claimed too simply that "at last, this wandering mistral found his sweetest song," neither quite fits.[10] McKay remained a restless wanderer until the very end. After his baptism in 1944, he soon felt enclosed by all the white Catholics who had rushed into a Black poet's life so enthusiastically and so suddenly.

Finally, though McKay was not a born Catholic like Louis Massignon or raised in a Catholic culture like Marie-Magdeleine Davy, Jacques Maritain, and Gabriela Mistral, a look back on McKay's writings before his conversion reveals a nearly lifelong interest in religion. When he converted in 1944, it would have been hard to find another community that better combined the disparate strands of McKay's interests than the US and Francophone Catholics that he met did. They shared a worldview that was counter-culturally religious with an emphasis on the mystical strain of religion, internationally rather than nationally oriented, centered on friendship rather than family, politically antiracist, and (later in McKay's life) virulently hostile toward liberal Protestantism and communism. McKay was an unbound seeker, and his journey culminated in a relational network within a particular religious culture that met his eclectic and unusual sensibilities in the late 1930s and early 1940s, though it, too, was an imperfect container for his desires and beset with its own problems.

McKay's friendships are more difficult to narrate than the others in this book. Religion and the intimacies in his life (both platonic and sexual) were linked in complex ways, and he was reluctant to disclose any details of these relationships, at least in a way that scholars can access today. There are few letters of spiritual ecstasy to friends, either published or archival. We lack florid expressions of the fevered bond of spiritual connection. For McKay, those ways of experiencing religion (common with the Maritains, Massignon, and Marie-Magdeleine Davy) would have seemed very European, bohemian, and Catholic. Yet at the same time, while friendship was central to McKay alongside a kind of interpersonal, anti-institutional Catholicism and leftist politics, much in the way these were for other individuals in these spiritual networks, they hang together slightly differently for McKay, an émigré from the African diaspora who converted to Catholicism as an adult. When he came to New York, although he spoke "French and German and [knew] botany and the science of the stars," he couldn't find work as a writer.[11] He instead worked as a waiter on the rail lines and held odd jobs throughout his life, even spending time in a dilapidated federal work camp in upstate New York in the 1930s. This hustle to secure his well-being was an undercurrent through many of his friendships, and McKay was very forthcoming about the challenges that seemed to beset many of his friendships with white people. Finally, though the themes of religion and friendship can be traced back to even some of McKay's earliest writings, I pay closest attention to unpublished archival materials from 1939 to 1948, the final decade of McKay's life and his most explicitly "Catholic" period.

FORMATIVE JAMAICAN YEARS (1889–1912)

Claude McKay was born in the mountains of the Jamaican countryside in 1889 and named Festus Claudius, after two rulers mentioned in the book of Acts. Jamaica was right in the heart of the Caribbean migratory sphere, a "space of constant religious creation."[12] Revival preachers sometimes passed through the hill towns where McKay grew up, and when people converted, Christianity often blended with the Obeah traditions inherited from the memories of those who arrived from Africa on British slave ships. McKay's mother's family traced its origins to Madagascar and his father's to the Ashanti community of West Africa. His grandparents were enslaved, but his parents were born free, after the abolition of slavery in Jamaica in 1834.[13] McKay's parents were among the few in their community who severed ties with African religious traditions and were strict Baptists, and his father was a church deacon in the lineage of the first missionaries who came to Jamaica in 1814 from the Baptist Missionary Society in London. They were relatively prosperous farmers and landowners, well-respected community leaders. McKay was the youngest of their eleven children, the baby of the family and adored by his mother. His older siblings were also anointed with biblical names like Claude's—Rachel, Thomas, Matthew, Uriah—and acted more like second parents to him, especially Uriah (nicknamed U'Theo), who was an adult by the time Claude was born. U'Theo, a teacher, had grown distant from his parents' Baptist faith and introduced European literature and philosophy to his youngest brother, which planted some seeds for Claude's bohemian, poetic tendencies. McKay left his boyhood Baptist missionary school, Mount Zion Church, and lived with U'Theo for a while, spending much of his childhood absorbed in books of European literature, which were on the island as part of the colonial education of Jamaican children. "Novels, history, bible literature, tales in verse . . . and nearly all Shakespeare's plays," McKay remembered reading in his 1937 memoir, calling this the "great formative period of my life."[14] When McKay wasn't reading, he wandered the Jamaican countryside with boyhood friends, a group of adolescents who had, like him, rejected the missionary Baptist faith on the island. "In one high mountain village there were ten of us boys in a free-thinking band, and most of them were heathen from their own primitive thinking, without benefit of books." "In Jamaica," McKay continues, "boys' friendships are so important. The peasants of Jamaica were always fond and faithful in friendships. Every boy and every man had a best friend, from whom he expected sympathy and understanding even more than from a near relative."[15] This formative period—as McKay rejected parts of Europe that came to Jamaica (the Baptist faith) but embraced others (modernism, European poetry), along with the emphasis on male friendships and the romance of "uncivilized" culture—would create something of the early edifice of McKay's inner life, which countercultural Catholicism would eventually enter and begin to fill.

McKay's adult memories of his childhood veer again and again to religion, often blending it with reflections on sexuality. McKay claimed that the Protestant Christianity of the British missionaries introduced a puritanical morality around sex, in particular a compulsion toward marriage that had been mostly absent in this farming community: babies born of out wedlock were common and unremarkable; open marriages and even, in McKay's words, "free love" were part of the rural Jamaican culture of his childhood. At the same time, he noted how the fervent revival meetings that swept through villages from time to time—people shouting, preaching, praying, crying, hugging, rolling on the ground—were "Protestant" but deeply sexually charged. In the tent revivals, McKay recalled, girls would often end up pregnant and then eventually, now converted, have to get married: "Revival marriages, we called them because in many cases there was nothing of the usual merry making and high feasting. The missionary just got a cheap ring and married the offenders."[16] He was happy to have nothing to do with any of it, marriage or the religion. McKay reviled Protestantism most of his life and spurned domesticity. By 1937, he would describe himself as a "truant by nature, and undomesticated in the blood."[17]

But when McKay writes about the religious culture of his childhood, even among the Christian converts, he paints a more complicated picture than that of passive islanders compliant under missionary compulsion. In one of McKay's short stories, "The Strange Burial of Sue" (published in the 1932 anthology *Gingertown*), the protagonist Sue is an archetypical Jamaican peasant woman: hardworking and committed to the caretaking responsibilities of the community while also in a "free loving" open marriage, one which no one seemed to mind, even her husband. When Sue dies, the town becomes sick with grief, but the Protestant minister claims the unfaithful wife is "going to hell." Her husband forces the minister to step aside, takes over the pulpit, and reclaims the religious space. Inspired by Jesus's words, "I am the resurrection and the life," he calls forth memories of Sue from friends who loved her: "And the hell-fire panic loosened its grip on the crowd. And there was singing of soothing hymns, hopeful hymns, and mingling of farewell tears."[18] McKay's writing often draws from the deep wellsprings of rural Jamaican peasants' religious imagination, despite what he sees as the inadequacy of the Protestant morality they were handed. Though McKay left Jamaica at age twenty-three and never returned, when he writes of the resilience of Black cultural traditions, his nostalgia for the sensuality and simplicity of the countryside, the power of the religious imagination in the African diaspora, or the primacy of friendship—McKay's enduring themes—one has a sense that McKay as a writer is reaching back to these memories of Jamaica.

The friendship in Jamaica that altered the course of McKay's life most was with Walter Jekyll, a white folklorist from England who was living there while writing an ethnography of Jamaican musicians. McKay was eighteen when they met and enthralled by the real bohemian who lived like a peasant but possessed all the books his brother had taught him, as well as even more radical ones. McKay befriended Jekyll and dared to show him his poems. While Jekyll was British, he urged McKay to reject the aspirational aesthetics of British English and continue with the few poems McKay had written in the Jamaican dialect. McKay's channeling of authentic, ordinary

Black voices—first in his Jamaican poems, later in novels about Marseilles and Harlem—eventually became the creative font of McKay's art, and he first honed this in the context of friendship, with both Jekyll and his boyhood friends. At the end of his life, when writing *My Green Hills of Jamaica*, McKay looks back on this time:

> I continued writing poems in the dialect. My association with my comrades seemed to help inspire the writing. Sometimes in the evening as I walked with some companions along the banks of the Rio Cobre, a new poem would pop into my head. Poems seemed to flow from my heart, my head, and my hands. I just could not restrain myself from writing. When I sent them on to Mr. Jekyll, he wrote back to say that each new one was more beautiful than the last. Beauty! A short while before I never thought that any beauty could be found in the Jamaican dialect. Now this Englishman had discovered beauty and I too could see where my poems were beautiful. Also my comrades and sometimes the peasants going to market, to whom I would read some of them, like them. They used to explain, "Why they're just like that, they're so natural." Then I felt that I was fully rewarded for my efforts.[19]

These friendships inspired McKay's first two books of poetry, published in 1912 when he was twenty-three years old, one of which, *Songs of Jamaica*, was widely acclaimed on the island. Though McKay's use of local dialect in poetry helped propel him to literary stardom, one can't help but note how it was the British Jekyll who encouraged McKay to use it, which recalls this line from Mary Gordon: "No one appreciates local color like a colonizer; to fix the colonized in a highly ornamental carapace of the past is to keep them from genuine contemporary power."[20] Yet part of McKay's success can be attributed to the fact that he was thoroughly wary of turning people into exotic "types" for white consumption. "Our Negros were proud though poor," he states in a posthumously published essay. "They would not sing clowning songs for white men and allow themselves to be kicked around by them."[21] In McKay's poems, the Jamaican dialect didn't merely give voice to an exotic or primitive culture. Serious racial themes and his sense of the beauty of Jamaica (the deep-blue Sukee River, the work ethic of its people) combined to resist caricature and stretched beyond simple colonial desire for racial primitivism. Jekyll, however, in the preface to *Songs of Jamaica*, stokes dull primitivist fantasies for readers, assuring them that the author was a "Jamaican peasant of pure black blood," despite the facts that McKay's mother had mixed ancestry and that they were a free, fairly prosperous family, not to mention how he was raised on Shakespeare and modernist poetry from his brother, a local intellectual and educator.[22]

McKay's friendship with Walter Jekyll loomed large over the rest of his life. Jekyll was likely gay, and McKay writes openly that they lived together for a time; Jekyll called McKay his "special friend," whom he mentored and doted on.[23] McKay had a girlfriend while they were friends, but many of McKay's essays about his own life circle back to Jekyll's formative influence. In his correspondence and published writings, McKay was guarded about his own intimate relationships, and he never disclosed whether their relationship was explicitly sexual, but neither does McKay seem ashamed of their bond or try to hide it. McKay talks of what sounds like a crush on the older man, acknowledges the thrill of Jekyll's encouragement, and notes Jekyll's deep sorrow upon McKay's departure from Jamaica. But regardless of the presence or absence of sexual activity, the relationship between a white British man of fifty-one years and a Black Jamaican eighteen-year-old was surely sustained in what Avery Gordon calls the "troubled intersection of sexual desire and colonial power."[24] Here the word *friendship* must include the more pernicious undertow of colonial longing, which echoes the bond between Massignon and Abd-el-Jalil.

Some scholars see in McKay's privacy around his intimate relationships—his male and female lovers, his short-lived marriage—a closeted space of silence and even deceit. Contemporary scholar Gary Holcomb, for example, seeks to open McKay's "confidential interior space—closeted . . . by his own sometimes deceptive descriptions."[25] My approach differs. McKay openly loathed Protestant missionary religion, particularly its sexual morality as matrimonial, reproductive, and familial, and he had no qualms about publicly rejecting it and pursuing an alternative life for himself. Yet he wrote very little on his love life biographically. In response to an early reviewer who tried to see McKay's own sexuality in the protagonist of one of his novels, McKay claimed, "The peeping critic seems to know more about my love life than I do myself. Perhaps it is necessary to inform him that I have not lived without some experience. And I have never wanted to lie about life, like the preaching black prudes . . . but I am entirely unobsessed by sex."[26] The erotics of male friendship combined with his silence on actual sex, along with his condemnation of Protestant "civilized" morality, especially its compulsion toward reproductive matrimony, were crucial pieces in McKay's personal construction of Catholicism decades later.

RACE, RELIGION, AND THE DIFFICULTIES OF
FRIENDSHIP: MCKAY'S EARLY HARLEM YEARS
(1914–1922)

McKay moved to the United States in 1912 and began a nomadic life that would last until his death in 1948—living in Nebraska, Harlem, Russia, France, Spain, North Africa, New York again, Chicago, and New Mexico. After he left Jamaica, one of the central preoccupations in McKay's writing was not simply the desire for friendships but how, in the United States, race will fatally disturb them—interrupting, then warping, dominating, and laying them to waste. When he settled in Harlem in 1914, he joined millions of men, women, and children from the African diaspora who headed north, some arriving like McKay from the West Indies and the Caribbean, others migrating from the American South in search of better opportunities in the cities of the Midwest and the North.[27] As a Jamaican, McKay felt in some sense removed from American Black and white racial politics: while racism did exist in Jamaica (McKay remembered that the darker the skin on the island, the worse police treated you), it was not as stark, nor was it supported by a legal system of segregation as in the United States. Blacks were moreover the majority in Jamaica. In the United States, according to McKay, racism "was like a fist to the face."[28]

McKay's early writings about his arrival to the United States take on the tone of an appalled outsider, a stunned ethnographer. In 1918, he published an autobiographical essay in the British literary journal *Pearson's Magazine* and explained, "It was the first time I had ever come face to face with such manifest, implacable hate of my race, and my feelings were indescribable." He recounted white people's "almost primitive animal hatred towards their weaker black brothers. In the South daily murders of a nature most hideous and revolting, in the North silent acquiescence, deep hate half-hidden under a puritan respectability, oft flaming up into an occasional lynching—this ugly raw sore in the body of a great nation."[29] But McKay's most personal, experiential writings on race took place when he reflected on attempted friendships with white people. In opposition to the liberal ideal that interracial friendship could *solve* the problem of racial inequality, McKay claimed that friendship only surfaced it. McKay titled the third chapter of his memoir *A Long Way from Home* (1937) "White Friends," where he describes his early friendships in Harlem after his arrival: "Friends from the upper class, the middle class, the lower and the very lowest class.

Maybe I have had more white than colored friends. Perhaps I have been impractical in putting the emotional above the social value of friendship, but neither the color of my friends, nor the color of their money, nor the color of their class has ever been of much significance to me."[30] But difficulties were raised at nearly every turn, and he points to white anxieties and boundaries. When he came to the United States, he "had the experience of a fine friendship with a highly cultured white women, a friendship which turned into a hideous nightmare because of the taboos of the dominant white community. I still retain a bitter memory of my black agony, but I can only try to imagine the white crucifixion of that cultured woman."[31] However, it was typically his white liberal friends who made real mutuality and genuine affection almost impossible because they were so naive about the lives of their Black friends. McKay recalled an afternoon trip to the New Jersey countryside with his editor and friend, the Jewish writer Max Eastman, when no restaurant would serve the mixed-race group. The only table they were offered was in the back of a dirty commercial kitchen, which made for an awkward, spoiled afternoon. He went to the theater with another white friend, both as theater critics, but they were forced to sit separately, with McKay in the back of the theater.[32] "On many occasions," he notes, "when I was invited out by white friends, I refused. Sometimes they resented my attitude. For I did not always choose to give the reason. I did not always like to intrude the fact of my being a black problem among whites. For, being born and reared in the atmosphere of white privilege, my friends were for the most part unconscious of black barriers. In their happy ignorance they would lead one into the traps of insult."[33] "My prayer to God is: Save us," McKay would later write in a 1941 poem, "from our friends!"[34] McKay found friendships easier with white people who hewed closer to the world from which he came: rural people who worked in Harlem as day laborers, waiters, rail line workers, even crooks, underdogs of the white world. In the later chapter "Another White Friend," McKay writes fondly of an eccentric white friend, Michael, who made his living pickpocketing rich people in downtown Manhattan but was "profoundly sentimental about friendship, the friends of his friend, and anyone who had befriended him. He could even feel a little sorry for some of his victims after he had robbed them."[35] McKay's white writer friends loved seeing McKay and Michael together, envisioning them as the future of race relations, but that only embarrassed McKay. To him, when compared to other white people he knew, someone like Michael was far more attuned to the landscape of power in the city, the dangers of the police, the need to duck under it all. Most other whites had no idea of this because the races lived in such isolation from one another. McKay explained,

> I think the persons who invented discrimination in public places to ostracize people of a different race or nation or color or religion are the direct descendants of medieval torturers. It is the most powerful instrument in the world that may be employed to prevent *rapprochement* and understanding between different groups of people. It is a cancer in the universal human body and poison to the individual soul. It saps the sentiment upon which friendliness and love are built. Ultimately it can destroy even the most devoted friendship. Only super-souls among the whites can maintain intimate association with colored people against the insults and insinuations of the general white public and even the colored public. Yet no white person, however sympathetic, can feel fully the corroding bitterness of color discrimination. Only the black victim can.[36]

McKay was right to point out that it took something almost supernatural to break taboos around "intimate association" across color lines in the United States in this period. In *Black Metropolis* (1945), the classic anthropological study of race and everyday life in the northern United States, African American sociologists Horace R. Cayton and St. Clair Drake note that segregation laws were most strictly enforced in public places where physical intimacy was more likely. Segregation practices tended to be ignored in spectator events, where the public just sits and watches. But segregation was enforced, violently, in places like beaches, swimming pools, and dance halls.[37] The perceived threat of white and Black intimacy across the spectrum—friendship, sex, dating, marriage—generated the most vicious mob violence in the country.

For example, the summer of 1919, when McKay lived in Harlem, became known as the "Red Summer" when violent race riots swept across the United States. The riots were instigated in July 1919 in Chicago after a Black teenage boy who swam in a whites-only section of Lake Michigan was stoned and drowned by a violent mob of white teenagers. When the cops refused to arrest the instigator, violence in the crowd escalated, and racial rioting ensued.[38] A wave of frenzied violence passed through the country over the next thirteen days. The most gruesome story came from Ellisville, Mississippi, where a gang of white men severely wounded John Hartfield, a Black man accused of raping a white woman. A local white doctor sadistically kept Hartfield alive so that he could die publicly by lynching the next day.

Newspapers announced the time and place, and more than ten thousand "upstanding citizens gathered at the appointed tree, after fervently debating the 'best' way to torture him . . . so they chopped off his fingers, hung, and burned him, and then shot his lifeless body with 2,000 bullets."[39] Parts of Hartfield's body were sold as souvenirs, his fingers preserved in a jar with alcohol. Behind all this cruelty was the taboo of Black and white "intimate association."

These macabre scenes from around the country set the stage for McKay's "If We Must Die," a poem published in 1919, which catapulted McKay to the height of literary stardom and changed his life. The poem became "the anthem of the moment," signaling a new racial awakening among Black Americans.[40] He wrote:

> If we must die, let it not be like hogs
> Hunted and penned in an inglorious spot,
> While round us bark the mad and hungry dogs,
> Making their mock at our accursed lot.
> If we must die, O let us nobly die,
> So that our precious blood may not be shed
> In vain; then even the monsters we defy
> Shall be constrained to honor us though dead!
> O kinsmen! we must meet the common foe!
> Though far outnumbered let us show us brave
> And for their thousand blows deal one deathblow!
> What though before us lies the open grave?
> Like men we'll face the murderous, cowardly pack,
> Pressed to the wall, dying, but fighting back![41]

The poem, McKay later remembered, "exploded out of me" when he was working as a railway porter with other terrified Black workers. It evokes a rich symbolic world tethered to reality with concrete, simple nouns—the mob, penned hogs, barking dogs, blood, a wall, the dead—but the key line comes at the end: "dying, but fighting back!" In 1919, it marked a new era of Black resistance. He recalled, "Ministers ended their sermons with it, and congregations responded, Amen. It was repeated in Negro clubs and Negro schools and at Negro meetings. To thousands of Negros who are not trained to appreciate poetry, 'If We Must Die' makes me a poet. I myself was amazed at the general sentiment for the poem."[42] It is still hailed today as the "symbolic manifesto of the spirit of the Harlem Renaissance."[43]

But at the outer edges of the most fiercely political of McKay's poems, the theme of friendship lingers. In *A Long Way from Home*, McKay describes how white and Black people were all trapped in this insanity together. Racism in the United States was a vast, structural force of power, which no personal feelings, however strong, even between friends, could counter. He recalls,

> There had been bloody outbreak after outbreak in Omaha, Chicago, and Washington, and any crazy bomb might blow up in New York even. I walked over to a window and looked out in the backyard. Michael [McKay's white friend] said, "And if riot broke in Harlem and I got caught up here, I guess I'd be killed maybe." "And if I were downtown and I was caught in it?" said I, turning round. Michael said: "And if there were trouble here like that in Chicago between colored and white, I on my side and you on yours, we might both be shooting at one another, eh?" "It was like that during the war that's just ended," I said, "brother against brother, and friend against friend. They were all trapped in it and they were all helpless." I turned my back again and leaned out of the window, thinking how in times of acute crisis the finest individual thoughts and feelings may be reduced to nothing before the blind brute forces of tigerish tribalism which remain at the core of civilized society.[44]

Because of this tigerish tribalism of "civilized society," McKay criticized liberal solutions such as integration, economic uplift, and education, which he felt could not touch the core of the more sinister force at work in American racial violence. The "civilized" United States (as opposed to "backwater" rural Jamaica, where this kind of violence was unheard of) was for McKay just a label that signaled the triumphal, orderly forms of racialized brutality. This awakened his desire for forms of culture that would be *un*civilized, or "off-modern," to use Svetlana Boym's phrase, which came from somewhere else.[45] It would be almost three decades before McKay began to think seriously about becoming Catholic, but his scathing critique of modernity was another point of entry for his eventual attraction to Catholicism. As Josef Sorett and Madhuri Deshmukh rightfully point out, McKay sensed that Catholicism, like him, harbored something of the anti-modern; it, too, saw something dark at the core of the engine of "progress."[46]

Most critics view the McKay who penned "If We Must Die" as an early radical whose fire faded by the end of his life, as he became more drawn to religion, and disappeared altogether when he became a Catholic in 1944.

"He began as a radical," one critic notes, "and ended as a Catholic."[47] But the French Catholic literary critic Jean Wagner suggests that McKay's early poetry of resistance is a soulful art form that expresses an inner conviction and even a "spirituality" connected to the "mystical feelings" that McKay later claimed Catholicism helped structure.[48] McKay was thinking about spiritual matters as early as 1918, long before his conversion, when he wrote at the time:

> At first I was horrified, my spirit revolted against the ignoble cruelty and blindness of it all. Then I soon found myself hating in return; but this feeling couldn't last long for to hate is to be miserable. Looking about me with bigger and clearer eyes I saw that this cruelty in different ways was going on all over the world. Whites were exploiting and oppressing whites even as they exploited and oppressed the yellows and blacks. And the oppressed, groaning under the lash, evinced the same despicable hate and harshness towards their weaker fellows. I ceased to think of people and things in the mass—why should I fight with mad dogs only to be bitten and probably transformed into a mad dog myself? I turned to the individual soul, the spiritual leaders, for comfort and consolation. I felt and still feel that one must seek for the noblest and best in the individual life only: each soul must save itself.[49]

While we don't know which spiritual leaders are referred to here, some of McKay's other poems from this period indicate that when McKay describes an inner kernel that can inspire rebellion in the face of death, he often evokes the language of religion. He draws on biblical themes of new life and revitalization, themes that would have been familiar to McKay as a boy in Mount Zion Church and, later, as a reader of modernist literature. In his poem "Exhortation, Summer of 1919," McKay picks up the image of a new awakening in the Black world:

> O my brothers and my sisters, wake! Arise!
> For the new birth rends the old earth and the very dead are waking,
> Ghosts are turned flesh, throwing off the grave's disguise,
> And the foolish, even children, are made wise;
> For the big earth groans in travail for the strong, new world in making—[50]

This poem uses a range of biblical idioms: with the ghosts turned flesh emerging from the grave, McKay gestures toward the scene in the Gospel of Matthew (28:52–53) when the tombs open after the resurrection of Jesus ("And many bodies of the saints who had fallen asleep were raised, and coming out of his tombs after his resurrection they went into the holy city and appeared to many"). The "foolish . . . made wise" points to Paul's letter in 1 Corinthians, which depicts the radical reversal of hierarchy in the new community of disciples. The feel of the poem itself suggests the rich symbolic world of the book of Revelation and the promise of the new world in the making.

Indeed, McKay's most vivid early poems of resistance drew deeply from the symbolic well of Christianity, including a poem he published one year later in 1920. "The Lynching" links American lynching to the crucifixion of Jesus, as McKay's friend Langston Hughes would similarly do in his 1931 poem "Christ in Alabama." McKay writes,

> His spirit is smoke descended to high heaven.
> His father, by the cruelest way of pain,
> Had bidden him to his bosom once again.

He goes on to describe the lynched body and the demonic cruelty of the white crowd. The body

> Hung pitifully o'er the swinging char.
> Day dawned and soon the mixed crowds came to view
> The ghastly body swaying in the sun:
> The women thronged to look, but never a one
> Showed sorrow in her eyes of steely blue;
> And little lads, lynchers that were to be,
> Danced around the dreadful thing in fiendish glee.[51]

McKay's religious imagery functions to frame racial violence in deeper, probing ways, but his theologizing never makes his politics drift lazily into old familiar tropes. The racial violence is never redeemed, even in some future. This violence also refuses the theological aesthetic that would turn it into something mournful, mysterious, or unresolved. There is instead an icy clarity of vision.

In these early poems, I imagine McKay channeling the voices of the people he grew up with in Jamaica—not passively, quietly accepting the white minister's version of Protestantism but moving the minister aside to reclaim the religious language in one's own voice, "proud," "fighting back." In his early years in Harlem, from 1914 to 1922, McKay was an avowed agnostic, but Christianity remained an apt vehicle for McKay's turbulent thoughts. The people he spoke to and for were far too steeped in religion ("Children don't forget easily," as the writer Abbigail Rosewood notes).[52] By evoking traditional religious imagery for creative, even radical ends in these early poems of resistance, McKay also aligns himself with fellow Caribbean immigrants in Harlem in this period. While neither secular nor within the Protestant Black church, McKay's creative elicitation of religion and eventual conversion to a minority religion joined him to scores of other Caribbean immigrants in Harlem in the 1920s and 1930s who, as Judith Weisenfeld describes, refused the dominant religious and racial categories in an effort to create new religious and racial identities.[53] In addition to the Caribbean Harlem context, McKay's religious imagery in this period also echoes the white modernist poets to whom his brother and Jekyll introduced him when he was an adolescent in Jamaica. McKay claimed these poets created art by digging deep into one's *own* past, not by imitating European sensibilities. "Of all the poets I admire," he states in *A Long Way from Home*, "Byron, Shelley, Keats, Blake, Burns, Whitman, Heine, Baudelaire, Verlaine and Rimbaud and the rest—it seemed to me that when I read them—in their poetry I could feel their race, their class, their roots in the soil, growing into plants, spreading and forming the background against which they were silhouetted. I could not feel the reality of them without that. So likewise I could not realize myself writing without that conviction."[54] In following the lead of the Europeans, who were so clearly fixed within the specifics of their European culture, class, and whiteness, one similarly plants oneself in one's own past. For McKay, to work in the spirit of Whitman was to "realize myself" as *Jamaican* as possible and connect with the voices from home.

When we recall McKay's early religious imagination in Harlem until 1922, I believe that he would want readers to remember not just the racism and the art of resistance but also the many pleasures of this time. He was called McKay the "playboy of the New Negro Renaissance," and McKay made no secret that he spurned domesticity.[55] He had a brief, failed marriage to a Jamaican woman who left Harlem and returned to Jamaica when she was pregnant with McKay's child. She raised their daughter Hope on her own. Though Hope and McKay began a correspondence when she was an adult, she never met her father in person. Sadly for Hope, McKay had friends instead, white and Black, as well as other lovers. One of McKay's few close Black friends from the early Harlem days was Hubert Harrison, who like McKay was a fellow West Indian émigré and prominent Black radical writer. Harrison published prolifically and gave speeches on philosophy, politics, and sexuality; he collected erotica, wrote openly about the gay scene in Harlem, and spoke about birth control, sexual freedom, and the hypocrisy of white preaching on sexual morality. ("Harlem was surely queer as it was black," Saidiya Hartman writes of this period.)[56] McKay never wrote on these topics as explicitly as Harrison, and certainly not in relation to his own life. He, too, lived in Harlem's queer world, but in his own writing, he traversed it more quietly—some might say more closeted—but also simply more privately. Saidiya Hartman offers one explanation for African Americans who were quieter about sexual transgression in Harlem at the time: "Those who dared refuse the gender norms and social conventions of sexual propriety— monogamy, heterosexuality, and marriage— . . . [were] targeted as potential prostitutes, vagrants, deviants, and incurable children. Immorality and disorder and promiscuity and inversion and pathology were the terms imposed to target and eradicate these practices of intimacy and affiliation."[57]

Perhaps there is something of a self-protective instinct against these threats in McKay's reluctance to write about his own intimate life or his sexual politics. But when Hartman describes young women whose lives refused conformity, much like McKay's, she also depicts them as "wayward: to wander, to be unmoored, adrift rambling, roving, cruising, strolling, and seeking. *To claim the right to opacity*."[58] I wonder if McKay's relative silence about his own intimate life is similarly a refusal to disclose, a reclamation of privacy. To affirm for oneself space *unavailable* for the analysis and gaze of the public suited McKay's private temperament, and it also cohered with his understanding of the artist: "I must not forget," he once wrote to Alain Locke, "the artist is a self-protective animal."[59] Additionally, McKay had a shy side: one of McKay's most beautiful poems from the early Harlem days, "Courage," offers a glimpse:

> O lonely heart so timid of approach
> Like the tropic flower that shuts its lips
> To the faint touch of tender finger tips.[60]

His writing often evokes the furtive emotions of someone outside the mainstream.

But amid literary success and quiet pleasures, Claude McKay went abroad looking, like so many other Black writers and artists in the United States, for a place to be treated like a human being. He left shortly after publishing his collection of poetry *Harlem Shadows* in 1922. He first set sail for England, then Russia, returned briefly to New York, then joined a group of Black expatriates in Berlin and, eventually, in France. Abroad, he wrote, worked, and stayed in touch with friends in New York. "Correspondence with friends," he noted from abroad, "is one of the special interests of living for me."[61] He partied, wrote, went to dance clubs, grew sick and exhausted, and was nursed back to health, eventually, by friends. Though he was deeply attuned to the difficulties of friendships, especially with white writers he met in Harlem, it was his friends, at home and abroad, white and Black, male and female, who always seemed to come through for him.

A "TIE . . . TO BETTER KNOW EACH OTHER, TO LOVE ONE ANOTHER": BLACK CATHOLIC INTERNATIONALISM IN FRANCE (1922–1929)

Like many African American artists and writers in the interwar period, Claude McKay ended up in Paris, which was, as James Baldwin described it, a "refuge from the American madness."[62] Paris had long been seen as a sanctuary from the racism Black artists experienced in the United States, and in interwar Paris, "money flowed like wine," McKay recalled, enough to support a rich culture of jazz musicians, dancers, writers, and artists on the eve of World War II and just after.[63] Richard Wright, Langston Hughes, Sidney Bechet, Countee Cullen, and Marian Anderson were all part of the Black émigré community there. Paris is a key landmark in the emergence of a distinctively Black Catholic culture in the twentieth century as well. Mary Lou Williams converted to Catholicism in Paris, as did Josephine Baker. In 1924, Alain Locke wrote to Langston Hughes, urging him to come the City of Light: "You can, and will, love Paris. Be spiritually Catholic."[64] According to Locke's biographer Jeffrey C. Stewart, Locke had gotten to know several Catholics in Paris, including the African American Catholic sculptor Richmond Barthé, who became Locke's sometime lover (Barthé later produced sculptures of prolific Catholic subjects like *Mary* [1945], *The Mother* [1935], *Head of Jesus* [1949], and *Crucifixion* [1948] and was awarded the James J. Hoey Award by the Catholic Interracial Council in 1945).[65] Though infrequently acknowledged, in the interwar period, Black artists and writers were important protagonists in the culture of Catholic creativity in Paris.

While Claude McKay knew Black Catholic artists like Barthé in Paris in 1923, he was drawn more to the country's immigrants from other parts of the African diaspora: men from Mozambique and Algeria making a living down in Marseilles, the waiters and sex workers in Paris from Dakar, and the elite male and female students from French colonial countries like Martinique in the Caribbean who had been selected for study in Paris, the colonial metropolis. All these people, in McKay's view, were more like him, fellow underdogs living in the shadows of the City of Light. In interwar Paris, it would not have been difficult for McKay to connect with others from the African diaspora. According to Jennifer Boittin, during World War I, half a million soldiers from French colonies—mostly countries in West and North Africa—were conscripted into France's war. Many stayed there to look for work after the war ended, and the vast majority were manual laborers and service workers in Paris and dockworkers and shipyard laborers in southern France. McKay also made contact with the much smaller population of African students who were chosen to leave their home countries to pursue a university education in Paris.[66] If not all practicing Catholics, these people would have at least been what Tracy Fessenden helpfully calls "trained Catholics," educated in French Catholic missionary schools in the African diaspora.[67]

For example, in Paris, McKay connected with the famous Nardal sisters from Martinique, Jane and Paulette, who traced their ancestry to West Africa. Their great-great-grandparents had been enslaved and taken to Martinique to work the sugar plantations. Paulette and Jane were born three generations later, when their family was by then genteel, devout French-speaking Catholics. Paulette won a prestigious scholarship to the Sorbonne in 1920 to study English literature, where she completed a thesis on Harriet Beecher Stowe. Paulette Nardal was the Sorbonne's first Black student and the first student in France to write on race as a doctoral thesis subject.[68] In Paris, she and her sister Jane hosted an important salon in their house in Clemart, just outside Paris, which McKay attended. The Nardal salon helped set in motion the newly emerging movement of *l'internationalisme noir*, the subject of a 1928 essay Paulette published in Paris. The aim of *l'internationalisme noir* was to forge solidarities among people from the African diaspora, particularly between those from the English-speaking and French-speaking worlds. As Brent Hayes Edwards explains, the Nardal sisters were "key in the formation of an 'elsewhere' to counter European imperialism" and the creation of "the possibility of an alliance of intellectuals of African descent that might 'shadow' and speak against the creeping domination of European imperialism around the world."[69] The context of multinational and multicultural interwar Paris was critical.

The Paulette sisters were the ideal intellectuals to draw the Black diaspora community together in Paris: fluent in both French and English, Paulette was a Caribbean-raised, French-educated scholar of race in American literature. McKay may have been particularly drawn to Paulette, who learned English from a year spent in Jamaica. Paulette was often the translator between the English and French speakers, Black and white, who passed through their salon. "My God! They made me translate everything," she recalls in her memoir. "I was knocked out afterwards! And the one thing I remember is that those people surely appreciated a lot of wine."[70]

Paulette was a member of the Association universitaire catholique des laïques missionnaires in Paris, and like many Catholics in this period look- ing for new, more expansive modes of international solidarity, the Nardal sisters drew upon the language of friendship to describe their salon, pre- ferring to call it a "cercle d'amis."[71] When they launched the new journal *Revue du monde noir* in 1931, inspired by these *amitiés*, their mission state- ment promised not only to promote ideas about Black internationalism but also to cultivate relational experiences and forge affective bonds that would go beyond national identity: the *Revue du monde noir* aimed "to create among Negroes of the entire world, regardless of nationality, an intellec- tual, and moral tie, which will permit them to better know each other to love one another, to defend more effectively their collective interests and to glorify their race."[72] Their first issue appeared in 1931 with McKay's poem "To America" published in French and in English, and his "Spring in New Hampshire" appeared in the 1934 issue.[73] As one of Paulette's biographers describes, "Above all in her salon fostering transnational friendships and collaborations, that has secured her place as an essential figure to know in the study of Black internationalism in Paris."[74] There was not only the element of racial solidarity and international politics at the salon, Paulette recalled, but something circulated among the *cercle d'amis* that was "surely deeper! There was the racial element, but there was something more, the expression of a black soul. It was a revelation!"[75]

The Nardal sisters' salon of *amitiés* was also interracial and included in particular other non-native French immigrants. Clemart was an important center of Russian and eastern European immigration (Berdyaev also had a famous salon in Clemart in roughly the same period). Paulette remembered joining with these men and women too, mainly as *amis*: "We had Russian friends . . . a lot of Slavic friends too who really interested us. Curiously, we found ourselves on the same page with them, much more than with the French." Creativity around religious and racial identity emerged amid these new encounters. Paulette explained that she was Catholic, but "I was trying to learn what my religion even *was*" among all this cultural, spiritual, and political experimentation in Paris, and the *cercle d'amis* took place in "a moment that corresponded to a kind of conversion, without ever having left the Catholic religion."[76] In Paris, some progressive white Dominican French priests, like Father Joseph-Vincent Ducatillon, became Paulette's confidants and spiritual directors, part of what she called "my Catholic family."[77] In the 1930s in Paris, Dominicans were at the vanguard of progressive theology, and Marie-Magdeleine Davy, too, worked closely with them at the time. Interracial progressive Catholicism was only a small minority within interwar Parisian culture, which saw Catholicism not as the main topic or point of their efforts but as one cultural and spiritual strand making up a tapestry that brought people together, providing at least some language for that something "deeper! . . . something more." This interreligious and interracial culture included both lay Catholics and clergy, and so in the 1930s, when McKay later came to know a similarly interracial Catholic scene in Harlem that also focused on friendship, with a decidedly Francophile and international vibe, it would have been culturally familiar.

The Nardals' *cercle d'amis* and the *Revue du monde noir* served as McKay's first introduction to the politics and spirituality of friendship in the Black Catholic culture in Paris, but others followed. In Paris, McKay befriended the writer and activist Kojo Tovalou Houénou, born in the French colonial country Dahomey. While he was not a practicing Catholic like the Nardal sisters, Houénou had been educated at a Catholic boarding school in Bordeaux.[78] In 1923, Houénou formed the solidarity group Amitié franco-dahoméenne. The group's name traced its lineage to the Société des amis des Noirs led by the Jesuit Abbé Grégoire in Paris in 1790, which worked to end slavery in the French colonies.[79] McKay was fascinated with Houénou and wrote an article about him in *The Crisis* in 1922. While the aim of the Nardal sisters' *cercle d'amis* was the cultivation of actual bonds of friendship, for Amitié franco-dahoméenne friendship was a metaphor directed at more explicit political work. Houénou explained their mission to McKay: "Our chief aim is to give wide publicity in France to every act of aggression or lawless exploitation that the French Colonials may commit against the natives. By doing this we will keep a constant check on the Colonial administrations and thus we hope to prevent the worst abuses in the French colonies that are the most common. . . . Our business is to watch and prevent."[80] In this context, *amitié* between those in Paris and those in African colonies signaled equality and care and demanded the sober-minded work of surveilling, documenting, and making public colonial violence. An antiracist and internationalist notion of *amitié* offered new modes of affiliation beyond the familial, the national, and the racial.

McKay was never charmed by the cathedrals of France's Catholicism or its liberal literati, but he seemed to love meeting these men and women from the Catholic Francophone African diaspora like Houénou. His own formative education in modernist literature by his brother and Jekyll led McKay to recognize similarities between these individuals and himself: a brilliant, literary child from a colonized African country, a local prodigy nourished in colonial culture and aesthetics who made it north but never severed ties with home. Writers like McKay, the Nardal sisters, and Houénou all knew the ravages of colonialism but still drew sustenance from European traditions of culture and thought. As someone long skeptical about "civilized" puritanical morality, and Protestantism most of all, McKay may have felt that the Black Catholic scene in Paris, at least among the immigrants, also possessed an aura of rebellion: for someone raised under British colonialism by Baptist parents, who then came to the United States (where the KKK would target not only Blacks but also Catholics and Jews), Black Francophone Catholicism would have presented an entirely different, "off-modern" world. Catholicism, even this early in his life, was close to McKay's aesthetic sensibility, which inclined toward the old, the ancient, and the dead. In 1918, he described his poetry in this way: "I have adhered to such of the older traditions as I find adequate for my most lawless and revolutionary passions and moods. I have not hesitated to use words which are old, and in some circles considered poetically overworked and dead, when I thought I could make them glow alive by new manipulation."[81]

Eventually, McKay met other African intellectuals like Lamine Senghor who were even more critical of French colonialism and likely gave McKay a more skeptical read of race in France than many of the Black émigrés in Paris. According to Michel Fabre, McKay grew more resistant to the allure of Paris, differing from many of the Black writers and artists who came there from the United States. McKay was the first Black writer to "break with the 'French myth'—the image of a non-racist France," as Fabre notes.[82] McKay would later write that the French loved to talk about their openness on race, but this "had little to do with reality."[83] In his 1934 series "Cities," he writes,

> Paris never stormed my stubborn heart
> And rushed like champagne sparkling to my head

Whirling me round and round till I am spent
To fall down like a drunkard at her feet.[84]

McKay left Paris and headed south for Marseilles in 1928, and here he seems to have found what James Baldwin said so many African Americans often futilely sought in Paris: that "longed-for, magical human contact."[85] McKay wrote a novel based on the people he met in Marseilles, *Banjo: A Story without a Plot* (1929), which endeared him to the Negritude intellectuals in the 1930s and 1940s. The novel takes place in the dockyards and dilapidated bars of Marseilles, where a motley crew of immigrant laborers lives on the edges of the shipping industry, eking out a living, sleeping on the beach, playing music, going to sketchy bars. While the dockworkers were poor, McKay didn't see in their culture misery or suffering. They were rowdy, fun-loving, irreverent types, like the people he knew growing up in Jamaica. In Marseilles, McKay discovered Nardal's *l'internationalisme noir* in the flesh: the protagonist Roy (based on McKay himself) notes, "In no other port had he ever seen such a picturesque variety of Negroes. Negroes speaking the civilized tongues, Negroes speaking all the African dialects, black Negroes, brown Negroes, yellow Negroes. It was as if every country of the world where Negroes lived had sent representatives to drift into Marseilles." McKay's writing relishes the aesthetic pleasures of meeting these people; their skin is not just Black but "coffee black," "gold-brown," "chestnut colored," "sealskin brown, tantalizing brown, teasing brown, velvet brown, chocolate brown." It is above all "black skin warm with the wine of life, the music of life, the love and deep meaning of life."[86] Just like the Nardal sisters' *cercle d'amis*, a form of *amitié* was at the heart of this culture: Roy might have a "rough and tumble laboring life," but the "most precious souvenirs of it were the joyful friendships that he had made among his pals."[87] Nothing else compared. The difficulties of friendships with white people McKay described in Harlem, at least for a time, lifted.

McKay zeroes in on the pleasures and intimacies of Black male friendship in this waterfront town of drifters with almost no women (and when they do come, it's not nearly as fun): in one Senegalese-owned bar, "music is on, the Senegalese boys crowd the floor, dancing with one another, they dance better male with male than with the girls, putting more power in their feet, dancing more wildly, more natively more savagely. Senegalese in blue overalls, Madagascan soldiers in khaki, dancing together."[88] The novel ends when Roy and Banjo commit to their friendship and life of vagabondage and insist Banjo's girlfriend stays behind. There are very few women or traces of "civilized" culture anywhere, and only a handful of white people here and there, who, like everyone else, are just riff-raff—people like McKay's friend Michael from Harlem, drifters out for a good time. The world McKay creates in *Banjo* is certainly more bawdy, drunk, and male than the Nardals' *cercle d'amis*, but both share something crucial: *l'internationalisme noir* tied together not by familial or romantic affections but by a special transnational kinship made of friends. These relationships were meant to evoke new kinds of alliances and solidarities and, ultimately, new affective experiences of one another, of the world, and even of themselves. McKay often wrote how here in this motley crew at Marseilles—in their exuberance, their weird religion, their proletarian and vulgar selves—he found something he claimed he never found in Harlem or Paris: "That simply natural warmth of a people believing in themselves, such as he had felt among the rugged poor and socially backwards blacks of his island back home." He continues,

> Only when he got down among the black and brown working boys and girls of country did he find something of that instinctual ability to react spontaneously, like Banjo, the protagonists who could respond to the emotions of pleasure or pain, joy or sorrow, kindness or hardness, charity, anger, and forgiveness. Only within the confines of his own world of color could he be his true self. But so soon as he entered the great white world, where of necessity he must work and roam and breathe the larger air to live, that entire world, high, low, middle unclassed, all conspired painfully to make him conscious of color and race. Should I do this or not? Be mean or kind? Accept, give, withhold? In determining his action he must be mindful of his complexion. Always he was caught up short by the thought of color, as if some devil's hand jerked a cord to which he was tethered in hell. Regulate his emotions by a double standard. Oh it was hell to be a man of color, intellectual and naturally human in the white world. Except for a superhuman, almost impossible. But of one thing he was resolved: civilization would not take the love of color, joy, beauty, vitality and nobility out of his life.[89]

Indeed, there is a kind of religious exuberance in the way McKay depicts Black friendships outside the gaze of the white world. His descriptions of the male characters in *Banjo* have a mystical strain, while not exactly "religious": Banjo has "a hot crazy-drunk manner. He was a type that was never sober, even when he was not drinking. These were the delirious fever days of Marseilles." This mystical vibrance surfaces in the novel in moments of intimate sensual, if not explicitly sexual, vitality, fun, and rowdiness between men: "Shake that thing!" is not merely dancing but something transcendent that happens on barroom floors among friends "in the face of the shadow of Death. Treacherous hand of murderous Death, lurking in sinister alleys, where the shadows of life dance, nevertheless to their music of life. Death over there! Life over here! Dance down the Death of these days, the Death of these ways in shaking that thing. Shake that thing! . . . eternal rhythm of the mysterious, magical, magnificent—the dance divine of life . . . Oh Shake That Thing!"[90]

Spiritual vitality emerges most of all in the context of male ecstatic camaraderie, but religious idioms appear elsewhere in *Banjo* too. Just as in his first books of poetry, McKay writes the dialogue in the local dialect, and Banjo describes the stories of the street preachers, boys who share Senegalese folktales of witch gods, and stories of dead children reappearing as crocodiles. Catholicism also functions here as part of Marseilles's "uncivilized" religious landscape. McKay depicts the old Catholic hospital where the sick go for help, called the Hotel Dieu, at which each Sunday a "gloriously macabre picnic" is held.

> It loomed like a great grey rock of Refuge on the hill above the Ditch. The ultimate hope of salvation for the afflicted. Below it was a church with a wooden Christ nailed to a cross in the yard. . . . Patients who were not bedridden flocked out on the two tiers of verandas. Girls of the Ditch with bandaged eyes and broken mouths and noses with knife wounds and arms in slings, hobbling on crutches, all victims of the bawdy riot; hollow-cheeked youths limping by; poor pimply children of leaky, squinting eyes; ulcerous middle-aged men and women, the old ones learning to creep again. From the beds against the windows, red naked stumps of arms and legs were stuck up like grotesqueries. Into this scene entire proletarian and bawdy families, as well as friends, had come to share the sacred Sunday dinner with the patients. Their children were with them and each group gathered around the bed of the patient to gorge and guzzle red wine amid the odors of ether and iodine.[91]

In this grotesque scene, McKay revels in a surreal litany of obscene ailments and injuries among the patients, all made visible at this frightful Catholic picnic that offers "salvation for the afflicted." Although his politics were decidedly leftist, and he had spoken in Russia in 1922 at the Congress of the Communist International, scenes like this give us a glimpse of McKay's worldview, which refuses to accept religion as the main obstacle in the lives of the afflicted.

Published in French in 1931 by Éditions Rieder, *Banjo* entered the scene at just the right time.[92] The Senegalese scholar Ousmane Socé's 1937 *Mirages de France* notes that Banjo was on the shelves of all the politically active Black students living in Paris at the time. McKay was considered by some as the true "inventor of Négritude," and Aimé Césaire was said to have known entire passages of *Banjo* by heart and praised McKay for creating a hero out of the "ordinary Negro . . . drawn seriously and passionately."[93] Until the interwar period, Black students in the Francophone world were educated on white European civilization alone (only white European authors were taught in missionary schools, and all the pictures in children's books had white skin). But contact with *American* Black artists and writers in Paris caused both white and Black people to begin to see Black culture with new eyes for the first time.[94] As Paulette Nardal recalls in her memoir, "I cannot even tell you how happy and proud I was to see how the Parisians and the French could be thrilled by these black productions."[95] McKay's *Banjo* fit right in here, not as a depiction of either an exotic other or a "back to Africa" political aesthetics. For French readers, it was a celebration of Black skin, Black music, Black dancing, and, most of all, the erotics of Black male friendship outside the white gaze, which still drew from some parts European modernism and aesthetics. Roy's rhapsodies in *Banjo* about Tolstoy, his valorization of the "mysticism of Jesus," and the Catholic hospital picnic together signaled an emerging appreciation for Black arts as distinct from, but connected to, Europe.[96] McKay's writing summoned something of that new racial consciousness in which white and Black cultural materials would enrich one another. While *Banjo* by no means entered this landscape as a Catholic text (it would still be fifteen years before he converted), its sensibility nevertheless resonated deeply with Black Catholic Francophone writers like the Nardal sisters, Louis Thomas Achille, and Léopold Senghor. Like McKay, who had been to Russia by this point, they all rejected communism. Crucially, McKay did not view non-Protestant illiberalism as necessarily an obstacle to any kind of emancipation. Descriptions of Paulette Nardal could similarly, by the 1940s, describe McKay himself: she had "anti-racist commitments, the virulent hatred of communists, Catholic fervor: Paulette finds it difficult to fit into an ideological box."[97]

Ever the wanderer, McKay moved from Marseilles to Spain in 1929, and like so many radical thinkers who came to Spain from elsewhere—Simone Weil, George Orwell, Gabriela Mistral—he was taken by what he saw there. Spain was the first place where he claimed to have begun thinking more personally and seriously about Catholicism. McKay lived for several months in Barcelona and saw the Black Madonnas of Spain, most likely in the rugged mountains of nearby Montserrat, with their shrine to "La Maronita," the Black statue of Mary and child that has drawn pilgrims from around the world since the eighth century, and still does today.[98] The Black Madonna appears so different from the blue-dressed, white-skinned Mary popular in American and European iconography. McKay wrote his friend James Weldon Johnson from Spain, "If you ever come to Europe soon, you must be sure to visit Spain. . . . It is the only European country that touches me emotionally."[99] After McKay converted to Catholicism in 1944, fifteen years later, he published an essay referring to this time in Spain as a key stepping stone on his religious itinerary. In Spain, he explains, "I fell in love with Catholicism. I discovered in Spain that Catholicism had made of the Spanish people the most noble and honest and humane of any in the world." Spain was "Catholic and not Puritan," which "had made of the Spanish people the most noble and honest and humane of any in the world, while Protestantism had made of the Anglo-Saxons and their American cousins the vilest, hoggish and most predatory and hypocritical people in the world. . . . Spain taught me that progress was not with the 'Progressives.'"[100]

When McKay eventually returned to Harlem in 1934, Europe had given him glimpses of what could be considered a live alternative to "civilized modernity" and "progress." Some parts of European Catholic culture, like what he found in Spain, McKay himself would point to, in retrospect, as foundational for his eventual conversion. Other links between Europe and McKay's turn to Catholicism were those he could not or did not articulate, but scholars, when taking a wider view, can connect more dots. Understanding his conversion requires a backward glance at his friendship with Black Catholics in Paris, such as the Nardal sisters' *cercle d'amis*, and the new modes of nonfamilial and nonnational affiliation they envisioned, along with the mystical exuberance and erotics of quietly queer Black male friendship he describes in *Banjo*. We can follow the thread further back still to Jamaica, where McKay's early formation steeped in modernist aesthetics and anticolonial, anti-Protestant materials gave him a bohemian attraction to "uncivilized" religion. This all helped prepare the soil of McKay's inner life, in which a certain kind of Catholic counterculture of the late 1930s would eventually take root.

CATHOLIC HARLEM AND THE FRIENDSHIP HOUSE
(1934–1940)

Though women never appear in *Banjo*'s most ecstatic relational scenes, in real life McKay's female friends were crucial supports and softened his landing from Europe back to Harlem in 1934. He had been gone for many years and spent all his royalties from his books, and in the midst of the Great Depression, much of the money that had driven the earlier Harlem Renaissance had dried up. To survive, he worked odd jobs and reconnected with old friends like the writer Dorothy West, who mailed him a little extra cash from time to time.[101] ("I'm maternal," she explained to him. "I must go fussing about this and that. I love best the people who need me most.")[102] His old editor Max Eastman sent him money too and helped him find places to crash. McKay eventually developed a relationship with the African American model and sculptor Selma Burke, who like McKay had spent time in Europe and returned to New York. She recalled, "I used to eat at Dick Heweys's and one night a man in a great coat and a cap came in. And Dick said, 'I can't give you another dinner on credit Claude.' I asked if it was McKay and said, 'Make that dinner for two.' . . . McKay had just returned from Europe and was practically penniless. He told me his plight. His landlady had locked him out and he had been sleeping on the subway for a couple of days. He was absolutely filthy. So I took him home, washed his clothes."[103] McKay and Burke's friendship eventually became more intimate, and they lived together on and off that year.

It was a new friend of McKay's, the Black Catholic writer Ellen Tarry, who would enter his life and change it most drastically. Tarry was also an outsider in Harlem who had arrived with ambitions to write. She was born in 1906 in Alabama, and after her father's death, she was sent to a Catholic boarding school, St. Francis de Sales High School, in Rock Castle, Virginia. The school was run by the Sisters of the Blessed Sacrament, the religious order founded by Mother Katharine Drexel in 1891 to serve African American and Native American children. It was a decidedly mystical, erotic faith the sisters instilled in Tarry. She later noted, "It was through the Sisters of the Blessed Sacrament, founded by Mother Katharine, that I discovered the Prisoner of Love who waits in the tabernacle throughout the world for men to come to Him so that He may open the door to His Father through the teachings of Holy Mother the Church."[104] When she was a student, the nuns doted on Tarry, setting high academic standards for her and sending her on a retreat with mystical books like Thomas á Kempis's *Imitation of Christ*. With her mother's written permission, Tarry converted to Catholicism while there. Tarry would later write a laudatory book about Drexel and was even involved with her canonization in 1965. She always thought of herself as part of the Drexel family and claimed that "she shares a certain kinship" with everyone who had been educated in one of Drexel's schools.[105]

At St. Francis de Sales, Tarry's fellow students and nuns were supportive when she cut out a magazine clipping for a writer's course after her high school graduation and mailed it in.[106] The boldness of her dream is striking—for an African American girl to make concrete plans for a writing career in the American South in 1920, when the vast majority of girls like her faced a future of what Saidiya Hartman calls "the broom and the mop," cleaning white people's dirty houses and caring for children.[107] In a parallel way, Tarry's dreams and plans as a young girl evoke something of the regalness that Tracy Fessenden explains was noticed by everyone in New York about the singer Billie Holiday. Like Tarry, Holiday was raised for a time in a Catholic boarding school for African American girls in roughly the same period (though Holiday was in Baltimore, Tarry in Virginia), and the nuns trained the girls in a similar sort of mystical piety. This mysticism was surely ignored as much as it inspired, but at least in some cases, and maybe in Tarry's and Holiday's, it cultivated a sense of dignity, depth, and aspiration beyond the presented ordinary reality. Tarry's mother was more schooled in the ways of the world than her daughter, however, and arranged for Ellen to become trained as a schoolteacher after graduation. Tarry tried it, quickly grew bored, and eventually headed north for Harlem in 1929 to follow her dreams.

Tarry first encountered McKay in a writing group in 1935, who was intrigued to meet a Black Catholic in New York. He told Tarry how communists had deeply penetrated the Black writer scene in Harlem and noted that their anti-Catholic attitude would surely prevent her from getting more writing opportunities. McKay vowed to help her. ("I was grateful," she recalled, "but he forbade me to say the word. Gratitude, 'I *hate* the word!'")[108] In 1936, he gave her a job. McKay had been hired as a supervisor for the Federal Writers' Project, a federally funded Depression-era public works effort that paid writers to compose on-the-ground local histories around the country. In 1936, the New York City project gathered forty writers, mostly Black but some white, to work on the "Negro History of New York." Over a period of fifteen months, they documented New York's Black history from the seventeenth century until 1935—arts, churches, activism, even local dialect and language and mainstream civic leaders and eccentricities—analyzing materials mainly from those newly housed at the Schomburg library, which was opened in 1925 by Arturo Schomburg, a friend of McKay's.[109] This project fit within a much larger energetic movement among scholars, journalists, and amateur collectors in the interwar period to gather primary sources of African American history and lay claim to a past that had been denied by mainstream historical narratives. McKay especially appreciated histories that disrupted the traditional narratives of Black elites as Protestant and American. McKay wrote favorably of Schomburg's skill at finding these surprising, unusual sources for the new library's holdings, such as a 1573 volume of poetry published by Juan Latino, the first Black Spanish poet. Through historical materials such as these—poetry from the African diaspora in Spain—McKay's beloved Europe, and Spain in particular, appeared more entangled with Black history, and Black history looked more European. These early efforts to explore the complex history of the Black diaspora in Europe worked to dismantle prevailing notions that, in the words of Kennetta Hammond Perry and Kira Thurman, "Black people's place in Europe is transient and that their fates and futures lie somewhere else," which "perpetuates the false paradox that it is impossible to be Black and European."[110] In the 1930s, when McKay returned from Europe, where he saw Black internationalism thriving, he was drawn to material that complicated narratives of a white Europe.

McKay hired Tarry to work on his team and cover the topics of religion and the Underground Railroad in New York history. For McKay, Tarry would have been the ideal person to write on religion. With allegiances neither to communism nor to the more dominant Protestant Black church, she saw the religious landscape with a different set of eyes than most writers in New York. Though McKay had exhibited some interest in religion earlier—the biblical poems, the mystical exuberance of *Banjo*, the Catholic Nardal sisters' *cercle d'amis*, the fascination with Spanish Catholicism—he drew on research from Tarry and others he supervised at the Federal Writers' Project for his next two books, both of which centered Harlem's unusual religious landscape. In *Harlem: Negro Metropolis* (1940) and *Amiable with Big Teeth* (1941), the dominant theme is the deep, almost intractable religiosity of the people from the African diaspora in Harlem, which was difficult to map onto the political landscape of the 1930s. The religious sensibilities of Harlem's Black community fascinated and perplexed McKay, challenging him to think about Black culture and politics in unconventional ways. For example, in *Harlem: Negro Metropolis*, McKay explains how the "religion of the Negro people stirs and swells and rises riotously over the confines of the Negro church." In Harlem, this religious excess finds expression in places like the "mystic shops," as he calls them; the little basement chapels presided over by priestesses who blend Christian and Orisha traditions; and the household shrines where people go to light candles, speak with the dead, and bring solace or good luck. The "lavish use of incense, oil, candles" in "an atmosphere of a rosary of meaningless words" may "appease the obscure yearnings of their minds, which civilized religion cannot satisfy." He confessed going to some of these "mystic chapels" with friends and enjoying them. McKay claimed that both the Harlem intellectuals and the respectable members of the Black churches, however, saw these African shrines as an embarrassment. "Educated Negroes might delude themselves that there is no difference between black folk's religion and white folk's religion," McKay notes, but this fundamentally overlooks the persistence of the religious imagination from Africa.[111] McKay writes very little autobiographically about this period, but his friendship with Tarry had by then grown close, and his description of African-inflected household religion in Harlem of 1940 is so "Catholic" (rosaries, incense, candles, meaningless words, speaking with the dead) that one can envision how McKay may have begun to see Catholicism as the more apt container for African religious practices.

But McKay refused to romanticize the Black religious cultures of Harlem that he was increasingly drawn to, pointing out how easily these overflowing religious instincts became usurped by people in power, particularly those who seemed more "modern" or who adhered to Marxism or more "civilized" religion, eager to steer the religious masses into more evolved, respectable directions. "The Communists," he wrote, "under the pretense of modernism and progressivism . . . appealed directly to the primitive religious instincts of the masses."[112] But the vast majority of the Black poor remained religious, he claimed, usually in an "uncivilized" way—a mix of Christianity and these underground African mystic chapels. The problem was that among Harlem's more "uncivilized" religious leaders there were many charlatans who alienated people from understanding the political reality of their lives. McKay describes at length the profound, almost ecstatic appeal of Father Divine and the Muslim convert Sufi Abdul Hamid, who channeled Harlem's religious fervor: "Dominating the Harlem scene, Father Divine herded thousands of bewildered, helpless Negroes into his kingdoms and made them contented with singing and dancing. . . . The Sufi appeared envious of the almost miraculous Divine success and announced that he too would return to the black magic of mysticism, where he could always make a comfortable living."[113] Some religiously disillusioned youth joined the Communist Party,

while others joined the workers' alliances, which gave them a political frame
for their lives but, according to McKay, ignored the religious imagination
and acceded too much to "progress." In McKay's view, what he called the
"religious instincts" were the noncompliant seeds of resistance to civilized
modernity, which were inherently appealing to McKay. But how to write
about religion, tap into it, use it, without advocating charlatan mysticism or
essentializing Black people as modernity's exotic other? He knew how often
Black religiosity was turned into an exotic spectacle for whites. McKay was
onto something: the lingering sense that African American religious experience is seen by whites as the most "real" because African Americans are
innately spiritual and naturally "un-modern," which reproduces the racialized essentialism of the "perpetual primitive."[114] McKay comes close to this
position and raises further questions.

McKay's novel *Amiable with Big Teeth: A Novel of the Love Affair between
the Communists and the Poor Black Sheep of Harlem* (written in 1941, published posthumously) puts these tensions on display. It takes place in Harlem, just after the Italian invasion of Ethiopia in the mid-1930s. African
Americans who had developed transnational Black alliances in the interwar
period saw the Italian invasion of Ethiopia as a direct assault on Black sov-
ereignty. McKay frames the problem using biblical imagery, starting with
the title, which comes from chapter 53 of the book of Isaiah, "All we like
sheep have gone astray." He compares Harlem's Black community to sheep
lured away by white communists, who had formed organizations in Harlem
"with the sole purpose of milking the poor credulous colored people."[115] The
communists in the novel urge African Americans to reframe the Italian
invasion as an issue not of Black autonomy but of the rising global threat of
fascism. McKay gives them the fictional name the "White Friends of Ethiopia" (which recalls the chapter in his memoir about "white friends" and the
problems they bring). The "Friends" try to entice Black Harlemites into their
cause, but as McKay describes it, the communists miss the deep, almost
religious tie Black people have with Africa: "To the emotional masses of the
American Negro church the Ethiopia of today is the wonderful Ethiopia
of the Bible," a reference to Psalm 68:31, "Ethiopia shall soon stretch out
her hands to God," which forms the title of the novel's first chapter.[116] The
novel unfolds as a tragicomic tale that orbits around a handful of eccentric
characters in Harlem, all of whom are engaged in back-and-forth between
the Black-led charity Hands to Ethiopia and the White Friends of Ethiopia,
with the latter never coming to understand the religious imagination and
racial history of the former.

As McKay was preparing *Amiable with Big Teeth* in the late 1930s or 1940, back in Europe, his old friend Paulette Nardal was also engaging with the issue of Ethiopia and had emerged as a key leader, working with French-speaking Catholics and enlisting them to support Ethiopia's claim to independence, as well as spearheading another group that evoked the friendship metaphor: Amis du peuple éthiopien (Friends of the Ethiopian People). Its name almost mirrored, in French, McKay's satirical association in Harlem. But Nardal's group shared McKay's sympathies. Working with Catholics, it aimed to provide an alternative to communist internationalism and was more akin to Houénou's solidarity group Amitié franco-dahoméenne. Nardal's Amis du peuple éthiopien documented political problems faced by Ethiopians and rallied other Catholics to publish a manifesto on the inequality of the races in the Parisian daily newspaper *Le Journal*. It also advocated international aid to Ethiopia, in defiance of the pope, who supported Italy.[117]

When McKay finished *Amiable with Big Teeth* in Harlem, he had been friends with Ellen Tarry for five years. She was less paranoid about communism than he but shared some of his misgivings. Tarry remembered going to a meeting where the communists urged Black activists to send money to the antifascist fight in Spain: "What about Alabama?" she asked. "The crackers are still killing my people down there and nobody is lifting a finger."[118] Tarry was nearly alone in her combination of Catholicism, antiracism, and anticommunism. Most white leftist activists were only concerned with fascism in Europe, and when Tarry first moved to Harlem in the 1920s, there were no Catholics in her circles of racially conscious Black writers and activists, and the political orientation of white Catholics focused primarily on charity. The vast majority of white Catholics were uncomfortable with Black newcomers to the city and had fled Harlem for the suburbs, and the parish system mostly functioned as structures for segregated enclaves. After failing to find a single Catholic interested in addressing the issue of racism in New York City, Tarry wrote a letter to a nun with whom she had been close in Virginia, a former teacher, and the nun advised her to connect with Father Michael Mulvoy, CSSP, who ran St. Mark's parish in Harlem. Mulvoy was rare—a white priest who had built up a Black Catholic parish in Harlem and was also involved in racial justice work, such as putting pressure on Harlem's white businesses to employ the community's Black residents. "He knew that we did not want pity or charity," Tarry remembered of Father Mulvoy, "but an equal chance to acquire for us the necessities of life and to preserve human dignity."[119] This relationship is evidence of the webbed, albeit rare, connection Catholic structures could create between races: a Blessed Sacrament nun in Virginia connecting a white Irish priest from the Congregation of the Holy Spirit in Harlem to a Black Alabama-born woman and turning them, eventually, into something like unlikely kin, after Tarry and Father Mulvoy grew close. "When he was transferred," she recalled, "it was like papa had died over all over again."[120] Father Mulvoy's actions as a radical Catholic priest were successful because his work was actually (briefly, cautiously) supported by the diocese, which in the 1930s was heavily investing in raising a Black Catholic culture in Harlem. After the white Irish and Italian parishioners fled Harlem for the suburbs during the Great Migration, the massive infrastructure of Catholic church buildings was abandoned. The cardinal did not want Protestants taking over Harlem, so they decided to put major money and muscle into evangelizing African American residents of Harlem to fill the churches again with local residents. According to Cecilia Moore, religious orders dedicated specifically to African American evangelization descended into the city, like the Sisters of the Blessed Sacrament, who had taught Tarry, and opened parochial schools meant to bring Black families into the church by providing a good education to their children.[121] These efforts were largely successful and marked what Josef Sorett calls the "dawn of a uniquely catholic (and catholicizing) moment in African American culture."[122] This set in motion a wave that would swell, and the number of Black Catholics in the United States tripled from 296,988 in 1940 to 916,854 in 1960.[123]

Father Mulvoy introduced Tarry to a new, small, experimental interracial Catholic community in Harlem called the Friendship House, which was founded by Russian émigré Catherine de Hueck in 1938.[124] Like McKay, de Hueck was an immigrant and outsider in the United States, and she, too, was stunned by the racial inequality she witnessed there. America has "ghettos like Hitler's Jewish ghettos in Warsaw," she wrote in 1946. De Hueck was a charismatic writer and speaker who described American racism in dramatic, theological terms. Racism for de Hueck was Americans' "Veil . . . that suffocates and enfolds all those who want to lift it and pass beyond its light-killing darkness. Lucifer's hands are seen rearranging the Veil. Is Lucifer himself the Veil?"[125]

The Friendship House evolved over the years as leadership changed and new outposts opened in other parts of the country, but it was primarily an intentional community of lay Catholics, live-in volunteers dedicated to addressing the problem of race in the United States, who organized their lives around prayer, service, and community. As they grew, the community posed questions about their mission: "What is the Friendship House? This is, of course, difficult to answer since we are many things to many people," but at its core, an early pamphlet explains, "Friendship House is a pioneer group of Catholic laymen who are attempting to bring about an end to racial separation."[126] Friendship House shared some similarities with Dorothy Day's Catholic Worker House of Hospitality, which had opened farther downtown five years earlier. Depending on local leadership, there were often tensions around the meanings and purpose of interracial "friendship." Was friendship—largely interpersonal between Blacks and whites—their goal or only the starting point for greater solidarity? One approach viewed interracial friendships as ends in themselves, along with works of charity (the Harlem Friendship House had a clothing and food bank and held after-school programs for children). But leaders like Ellen Tarry rightfully claimed this approach to friendship and charity gave white volunteers what she called a "fairy godmother" sense of themselves and kept the Black residents powerless.[127] Tarry preferred more collaborative and activist methods, similar to the French associations of *amitié*, like Amitié franco-dahoméenne.

While leaders like de Hueck advanced a vision of charity and personal connection with the Friendship House, Tarry became involved in more activist engagement. While she served as a director of the Friendship House in Chicago in 1942, for example, Tarry and the African American Catholic lawyer Harold A. Stevens gathered a list of legal grievances (such as discrimination in housing and employment) from African American residents of the Friendship House neighborhood, which white and Black activists from the Friendship House brought to city officials and bishops, whom they urged to put pressure on the city.[128] Stevens also cited an important event in the summer of 1947 when an interracial group of Friendship House volunteers in protested discriminatory practices at a public beach, which led to threats of court action by the local police until the owner ended the discrimination. Stevens claimed the Friendship House protest was key to the reversal.[129] Betty Schneider, another longtime director of the Friendship House, who first became involved as a student volunteer from the College of Saint Benedict in 1938 at the Harlem chapter, eventually brought two African American female students, Kathleen Yanes and Gertrude Danay, with her back to college in the fall, beginning the project of racial integration at the college. Schneider dedicated the rest of her life to racial justice in the United States, working in the Chicago Public Schools as a college placement counselor and volunteering with Chicago's Friendship House.[130] Initially, the mechanism for these efforts was bringing white people into Black neighborhoods like Harlem in 1938 and the South Side of Chicago in 1942, and later in Washington, DC, in 1948. Most of the Friendship House volunteers lived on-site, and in cases where there weren't enough rooms in the Friendship House headquarter buildings, like in Harlem, white volunteers lived with Black Catholic families.[131] Although today the language of friendship may seem like a naive approach to racial justice, this direct relational method was not without merit. Karen Johnson notes how the Chicago community at its best, "with its simple solution of interracial relationships—contextualized by concern for economic, legal, and religious discrimination—struck a blow at segregation's stronghold."[132] But the goal of friendship as a starting point for bolder political work was not uniformly supported.

Tarry and Stevens were among the few Black leaders in this period's Catholic antiracist work, both active in the Catholic Interracial Council (1934–64) and with the Friendship House.[133] Many of the early volunteers who gathered at Friendship House were white Catholics, mostly young women dissatisfied with the insular immigrant piety of their childhood and compelled by charismatics like de Hueck and Day, who urged Catholics to not only pray but adopt lives that implemented the radical ideals of the Gospel.[134] Ann Harrigan, a longtime volunteer from an Irish Catholic family, remembered her reasons for joining Friendship House (first in Harlem and eventually in Chicago, where she codirected a Friendship House outpost briefly with Tarry):

> We Catholics were a cowed and sheep-like lot, sons and daughters of immigrants, low on the totem pole of politics, education, culture. I was fed up with the teaching of religion as I had experienced it—dullsville, boring, often incompetent. Yes, I was American, a Christian and one who had the great good fortune to be in New York then in the thick of the ferment of new ideas and movements. But American, Christian and knowledgeable as I thought I was, I began to get in Friendship House an education on an entirely new plane, as it was with the rest of the white middle class students, professionals, workers who came to help at Friendship House. Just for starters, none of us had ever spoken to a Negro except on a service basis. Those first real contacts showed us truly it was we who had been deprived—another revelation in itself accompanying the realization that it was a white problem, not a Negro problem. We were exposed to the whole new world of Negroiana—lectures, books, discussions, and especially people, showing dramatically how much we whites had missed in our education. For me, the Friendship House library was a magnet, a vibrant collection of almost 1,000 really important books the

Baroness [de Hueck] had gleaned over the years on art, social sciences, poetry, biography, Negro history, theology, spirituality and so on. It was always much harder to attract Negroes as full-time staff, partly because they are always suspicious of Uncle Toms and do-gooders (as many saw the Baroness and us whites); partly because there were so few Negro Catholics, and finally because of the economic crunch, Negroes not having that much free time to volunteer their services.[135]

Black neighbors had good reason to be skeptical of young white Catholics coming into their communities looking for a ticket out of "dullsville."[136] Jack Kerouac in *On the Road* describes going to a Black neighborhood in Denver in 1949 as a tourist, walking around and "wishing I were a Negro, feeling that the best the white world had offered was not enough ecstasy for me, not enough life, joy, kicks, darkness, not enough night."[137] Certainly many white Catholic radicals who moved into Black neighborhoods brought with them their own fantasies. Ellen Tarry eventually parted ways with the Friendship House for some of the issues she raised about white "fairy godmother" syndrome (and her desire, at last, to get back to writing, her first love). Late in life, Tarry reminisced in a letter to Betty Schneider about the Friendship House, noting how she learned through white Catholics like Catherine de Hueck what *not* to do when it came to racial reconciliation and justice.[138]

Before she left for Chicago, Tarry brought Claude McKay to Harlem's Friendship House in 1940, when he was ill, still broke, and needed to be nursed back to health. In a letter to Max Eastman on August 13, 1942, he recalled, "The only hands that ministered to me were those of strangers from the Catholic Mission, stretched out to snatch me from the Shadow of Death."[139] His encounter with Catholicism deepened considerably there, beyond just their care for him. McKay never wrote any in-depth reflection on the Friendship House or his direct experience of Catholic antiracist work, but we know this was his final stop before his conversion in 1944. McKay would share some of Tarry's critiques of the Friendship House (in a 1944 letter to the white Catholic activist Daniel Cantwell, McKay argued that too much emphasis on interpersonal relationships in the Friendship House missed the economic dimensions of racism).[140] But what was it about the Friendship House that might have appealed to McKay? What tensions were alive that he might have appreciated seeing in action?

In 1940, the culture at the Friendship House pulled together many different threads of McKay's own biography and interests, including its anti-Protestantism, anticommunism, and antiracism, as well as its privacy on matters of sex and anti-family values, European aesthetics and culture, and attention to mystical possibilities of friendship. In his 1937 memoir *A Long Way from Home*, McKay describes how social taboos preventing friendship across lines of racial difference "descended from medieval torturers," and only the "super-souls" could break them.[141] By actually *trying* to break these taboos in the practice of their actual lives, rather than simply discussing them, most of the volunteers understood the difficulty of this work and how much resistance came from both the white and Black communities. This realism would have appealed to McKay.

Admittedly, the Catholic press occasionally portrayed the Friendship House as a panacea of interracial joy, but this was an almost comical white fantasy: "Like a searchlight," one 1940 profile reads, the Friendship House "has gone into the dark places of Harlem and has brought in sunshine and cheer. The happy laughter and gaiety of workers and members both young and old make for a haven of joy and happiness."[142] The longer-term volunteers McKay got to know—white volunteers like Mary Jerdo Keating, Ed Chambers, and Ann Harrigan or Black volunteers like Tarry—were much more realistic about the complexities, failures, challenges, and even serious dangers posed to Blacks and whites affiliated with Friendship House. Ed Chambers, for instance, who began working at Friendship House in Harlem as a young adult and later became a professional community organizer, claimed that at Friendship House, "I lost my romantic idealism and began my entry into the real world of power struggles, conflict, and ambiguity." It "got me off the world as it should be and radicalized me to the world as it is" and moved him "from do-gooderism to organizing."[143] Many of the volunteers were honest about how truly frightening it was to cross racial boundaries. White bigots and Black skeptics alike unnerved them. This honesty would have resonated with McKay. Ann Harrigan, for example, recalled that when she first considered moving to Harlem, her mother would read her stories of violent rapes and murders in the city to scare her away from going. "Have you gone mad?" she remembered her mother's voice. "Have I read you all these stories in vain?"[144] Another volunteer who became a close friend of McKay's, Mary Jerdo Keating, was seriously threatened by a group of Black teenagers who she had asked to leave the center. After de Hueck opened a Friendship House in Chicago in 1942, a group of Black and white volunteers—Betty Schneider, Bill Flynn, Monica Smith Cox, and Ed Adams—were beaten by a white mob as they walked down a street together. The priest Father Joseph Gremillion invited Friendship House volunteers to come to Shreveport, Louisiana, but they had to close the center down after they were threatened several times by whites who left them ominous notes at home: "Attention Nigger Lovers . . . we mean business."[145] To prepare themselves for these attacks, and to keep calm in the face of agitators, the volunteers were taught to "use spiritual weapons."[146] The theology of the mystical body of Christ was the weapon of choice for these Catholics, in which people of all races were understood to be connected as members of Christ's body. The theology was "like our Bible," Ann Harrigan remembered.[147] They prayed it, incorporated it into liturgies, talked about it, and tried to internalize it as a counter-narrative to American racial violence and as a source of spiritual sustenance. In a short essay about his baptism, McKay, too, evokes this theology: "I do believe in the mystery of the symbol of the Mystical Body of Jesus Christ, through which all of humanity may be united in brotherhood."[148]

In addition, McKay and the Catholic radicals surrounding Friendship House shared a yearning to work toward the goals of racial justice outside the logic of secularism or communism. By the late 1930s, McKay's anticommunism was bordering on a near obsession. The tone of this small minority of antiracist Catholics differed—if only slightly—from the hysteria of the mainstream Catholic press, which painted a stark picture of bad communism "out there" and good Catholicism "in here." For the Friendship House Catholics, white racism and complacency was a main reason communism rather than Christianity increasingly appealed to Black Americans. De Hueck once wrote to her local bishop elaborating on this idea: "Communists, Your Grace, are not born—they are made by hypocritical Christians, Catholics included, who render to Christ lip-service only."[149] In early 1940, Ellen Tarry emerged as the leading Black Catholic voice on this topic. In an April 1940 issue of *Commonweal*, Tarry notes, "The time has come for Christian America to shed its coat of hypocrisy and admit its sin." Tarry describes for *Commonweal*'s largely white Catholic readership the appeal of communism among African Americans. She details childhood memories in Alabama: seeing the KKK ride past her window at night, witnessing two teenage boys pulled from their cars and brutally beaten by the police for no reason, hearing that a close family friend with a learning disability was shot by a police officer in a case of mistaken identity. While no group, she argues, "can breathe life back into the dead," these stories must be told to white Catholics "not to spread hatred, stir up sectional strife, or arouse ill feeling. Neither have they been easy to share with you." She adds, "Some of my most highly esteemed friends are white. But my nice white friends, who are thoroughly familiar with these conditions, allow public officers to brutalize and murder helpless and inarticulate Negroes. It is this silence of kindly intentioned America that is causing Negroes everywhere to demand that those who call themselves our friends take their stand and let the world know about it." There is a "harvest of hate that White America has, perhaps unwittingly, sown." For a Black person to want nothing to do with "nice white friends" like the Catholics who comply with the status quo and instead yearn for something more radically transformative, she asks, "Can you honestly blame him?"[150] Tarry does not frame the problem of racial violence for Catholics as merely "out there" rather than "in here," and she takes to task her "nice white friends" in New York. McKay loathed the same tendency in the French, who viewed racism as an "American" problem, and like Tarry, McKay had plenty of his own "nice white friends."

Though located in the United States, the culture around the Friendship House was also thoroughly international, even antinationalist, which fit well for McKay, who once described himself a "poet without country."[151] Its aim to forge affiliations across lines of difference harked back to the Nardals' *cercle d'amis*. De Hueck herself was Russian and educated by French nuns in Egypt. Ann Harrigan's parents came from Ireland, some of the Black families that came through the Friendship House were Caribbean like McKay, and there were even some French-speaking Haitian Catholics who had made their way to Harlem during the Great Migration. Tarry thought such internationalism would be ideal for a rootless wanderer like McKay: "With someone who has travelled the world like you have, why not be a Catholic?"[152] In his unpublished 1945 essay "Right Turn to Catholicism," McKay notes that it was precisely Catholicism's internationalism that appealed to him, describing it as a "vast world organization of true brotherhood."[153] We see some of this Catholic internationalist approach to race in the *Interracial Review*, a journal that provided a platform for Catholics on the left like Ellen Tarry and Dorothy Day. Day, whom McKay had known earlier when they were both writers in the city, was also a fixture in New York's Catholic countercultural journalism in the 1930s and 1940s.

Day and McKay shared a writing style that pressed in as close as possible to the underworld of New York City: a propensity toward the broken, the crooks, and the plain old ugly that evinced a skepticism of the too-smooth surface of the cool. Though most articles in the *Interracial Review* displayed what Matthew Cressler identifies as the missionary tone of "we" (white) Catholics reaching out to "them" African Americans, a few Black Catholics wrote for the *Interracial Review*, including Americans like Tarry and Harold

Stevens. Authors appeared from the Black Catholic Francophone world too. For example, Louis Thomas Achille, the Nardals' cousin, published a 1940 essay in which he states, "In spite of the trend away from churches, masses of Negroes are still so clamoring for religion that they accept it even in disguise and travesty, in falsification and heresy." However, Achille adds, "they will not fail to respond if the Catholic message is delivered to them in its dramatic extremeness and universal adaptability. In this respect one may expect a better response from the working classes, yet unspoiled by a 'liberal' pride-breeding education and by the debilitation of comfort, than from many of the educated well-to-do class."[154] Achille evokes ideas that McKay had long wrestled with, including the almost natural instinct for religion that gets usurped by a false prophet or modernized away in the march toward civilization. (This was how McKay described communism, and Tarry also wrote, "Spit out the vultures who tempt them.")[155] McKay and Achille both saw that any power in modern religion lies in its "dramatic extremity" rather than in its acquiescence to "civilization." Where else could one find these threads of McKay's sensibilities, all gathered at once? The anti-Protestant and anti-communist fervor, the internationalism, and the antiracism, in addition to the connection to Europe, while still in a sense perceiving this culture as "uncivilized," and the focus on friendship rather than family—all of this coalesced around the Friendship House.

Although the link between France and Harlem was key within Black Catholic internationalism, some of this culture stretched farther and included materials from the global south. Tarry's former teacher and nun Sister Timothy mailed Tarry a holy card with the face of the Blessed Martín de Porres (1579–1639), the mixed-race friar from Peru whose cult was emerging in the 1930s among antiracist and Black Catholics in different pockets of the United States. In New York, John Chrysostom Kearns, a Dominican brother, published in 1937 *The Life of Blessed Martín de Porres: Saintly American Negro and Patron of Social Justice*, and when Father Michael Mulvoy pastored St. Mark's from 1932 to 1940, he held the Blessed Martín de Porres devotions each Friday.[156] In France, Giuliana Cavallini's 1957 book *Les "Fioretti" de saint-Martin de Porrès: Apôtre de la charité* (*St. Martín de Porres: Apostle of Charity*) joined the international, interracial chorus to spread Martín's successful cause for canonization in 1962. Martín de Porres was an important member of the "spiritual family" gathered at the Harlem Friendship House in the early 1940s when McKay came: "Blessed Martin," Ann Harrigan wrote, "has been a mother and father to us since we started."[157]

While this would have been a new experience for McKay, the international-ism and the materiality of "uncivilized," even "medieval," religion outside the world of Anglo-Protestantism would have resonated.

By the late 1930s and early 1940s, McKay was developing his own inter-est in Black religious statuary and the history of African Catholicism. He recalled seeing at the Schomburg library "a photograph of a nephew of one of the popes who is unmistakably Negro."[158] McKay told some Catholics about the Black Madonnas he had viewed in Spain, and he began research-ing the African history of Christianity. People associated with the Friend-ship House were a ready audience for such thinking. Betty Britton, a white volunteer, wrote to McKay in 1947 about the "historical suppression of the dark Christ." She explained, "The handsome, pretty Christ is just another watering down of true Christianity during the Reformation. It is also due to the sentimentalizing of religion. Intelligent Catholics, aware of the radical that Christ was, want no more of this sissy art. Of course Christ was darker than the Anglo, Nordic people."[159] In a perhaps desperate effort to connect with her Black friend, Britton wrote with excitement from Mexico about the Black Christs she had discovered there, just like the statuary he had described from Spain. By this point, in 1942, McKay's life was full of women like Britton, who did small research projects for him, edited his work, and found him places to stay. When he moved closer to the Catholic world, such individuals came out in droves.

In fact, perhaps the most important thing about the Catholic racial justice scene was that it was, like McKay, focused on the intimacies of friendship as an alternative form of kinship but silent on actual, physical sex. Friend-ship House aimed to forge an unconventional community of friends—most volunteers refused to marry and tried to stay celibate, although this proved difficult. They didn't take vows like religious orders, and it wasn't quite clear what kind of affiliation they represented. Much like a House of Hospital-ity, they were neither a family nor a monastery, functioning without such legalism and structure. Some volunteers fell in love with one another and with neighbors, and interracial marriages occasionally emerged out of the community. But the longer-term volunteers like Ann Harrigan attempted to remain celibate, living like monastics but immersed "in the world" rather than the cloister. The lack of structure may have complicated the effort. Only in her private journal could Harrigan write, in 1942, "O Lord, I'm such a hypocrite, writing one thing and doing another. I, whose (sexual) desires have a million tongues, each clamoring for more and more attention, must be put down as they come, not putting off the day and time."[160] This kind of struggle remained mainly underground in the community. For their part, neither McKay nor Tarry ever committed to celibacy (and no evidence suggests they were even tempted by it). While McKay was openly bisexual, he never wrote as explicitly on transgressive sexuality as others in New York at the time. Tarry was married briefly and had a baby, but she raised her child without a partner. While this wasn't easy, she was never alone: "I was with friends," she explains in her memoir.[161] Catherine de Hueck briefly married, had it annulled, and had a son who seems to have been involved only around the edges of her life. In 1943, de Hueck shocked Friendship House volunteers when she married again, to journalist Eddie Doherty. When other volunteers responded with disappointment, the reaction was one of the final straws that caused de Hueck to end her formal ties with Friendship House. Eventually, just like Jacques and Raïssa Maritain, the Dohertys took a vow of celibacy in their own marriage in 1955. This muted anti-familial and queer sensibility suited McKay's fiercely private temperament. Tarry recalled one time McKay was offered a faculty position at a historic Black college. According to Tarry, he turned down the job rather than explain that he would not bring a wife and family to fill the apartment they had set aside for him. This Catholic scene, while certainly not openly queer friendly, was a world where one could remain unmarried without having to explain why. We should not assume that McKay was therefore necessarily closeted, full of shame and self-loathing (he could find plenty of that among Catholics too, if he was looking), rather that he was just more private. He wrote to Max Eastman in 1934, "People are never satisfied unless they can grab you by the guts and make you puke out your soul."[162] In *A Long Way from Home*, he mentions that the white appetite for sordid details and fantasies about Black sexuality is an "old bugaboo."[163]

Above all, McKay drew closer and closer to Catholicism because the women he befriended in this counterculture, like Ellen Tarry, Dorothy Day, and Mary Jerdo Keating, knew how to work around his moods and never asked too many questions about his private life. They understood just the right tone to take with men like McKay, who could be grouchy and needy, with jagged edges and sweet sides that only blossomed under exactly the right conditions. Women, especially Catholic women, have long been trained to anticipate the needs of moody men in advance, to smooth out roughness. "I had learned to meet Claude's storms with calmness," Tarry noted, an absolute pro. "Claude was pouting," and "when I could ignore his sullen glances no longer, I asked if anything was wrong." She concluded that "Claude took his bad moods out on me, but I was grateful he showed his charming side to others."[164] These women learned to give McKay silence and space for work (this was a culture where silence and solitude were held in high esteem) and gently welcomed him into the faith. Keating loaned him a cottage in Connecticut in 1943, where he spent weeks alone and wrote a series of poems entitled "The Cycle." He had not yet converted, but the religious themes of these poems show he was close. He describes, for instance, how political leaders set themselves up as false gods, something he had already done in *Amiable with Big Teeth*, but here McKay turns instead to Jesus: "Boldly the flag of love His life unfurled."[165] Dorothy Day arranged for him to take a retreat with her in 1944. He visited a monastery in Indiana, St. Meinrad's, and wrote of the experience, "If I were in search of a true from of communism, I would go to the monasteries of the Catholic church, whose beginnings are older than the Church more antique than the republic of Rome, as ancient as ancient Egypt."[166] And when Day started sending him letters with little holy cards tucked in—the gold coin of this global network of spiritual friendship—the gesture was just right, sending an appropriate signal without making too much of it.[167] Famously direct, Day instinctively avoided the postures of sappiness or sentimentality that McKay despised. Tarry was the same way. She thought too much talk of spirituality sounded phony. Unlike others we have seen, McKay's relational modes were matter-of-fact and understated. McKay would have recoiled under the exuberant love letters of the Maritains and Massignon. But as with them, it was his friends above all who transformed his inner life. "I'll have to say," he wrote to Tarry, "I owe my conversion to you."[168] Tarry's language of spiritual kinship was more mellow, but in McKay, she recognized a new kind of bond, maybe simple, even mundane, but still different from what they had before: "I will pray for you," she wrote him, "and you pray for me."[169] Claude McKay was baptized in Chicago on October 11, 1944.

The antiracism, internationalism, anti-Protestantism, and the muted sexuality centered on friendship were all crucial stones in Claude McKay's pathway to baptism. McKay felt he had found a thread that could weave people together, across lines of difference: "Jesus Christ rejected the idea of any special, peculiar or chosen race or nation, when he charged his apostles: Go ye into all the world and preach the gospel. Not the gospel of Imperialism, Feudalism or Capitalism, or Socialism, Communism or a National Church. . . . I find in the Catholic Church that which doesn't exist in Capitalism, Socialism or Communism—the one true International of Peace and Good Will on earth to all men."[170] But he highlighted most of all what he called "a little of that mystical world of the spirit" that finally drew him in, the mystical world we can glimpse in McKay's early poems of resistance, in the transcendent descriptions of dancing on the barroom floors in Marseilles, in the candles and incense he admired in Harlem's basement shrines, in the longings he claimed to have discerned in Harlem's "uncivilized" religious imagination.[171]

WHITE MALE FRIENDS IN CHICAGO

McKay's baptism took place in Chicago, where Mary Jerdo Keating had helped McKay get a new job with Bishop Sheil's Catholic Youth Organization (CYO) in 1943. In Harlem, he had been broke, sick, and in need of a fresh start. The move to Chicago reinvigorated him. For a time, McKay taught adult night courses at the CYO on Negro literature and poetry. He moved into an apartment just down the street from the St. Martín de Porres House and close to Tarry, who had also decamped in Chicago. However, just as McKay was settling in, Tarry returned for good to Harlem, exasperated by the disagreements she often had with her white codirector, Ann Harrigan, and eager to get back to writing. But other women still came by to check in on him while he still struggled with illness: one woman, Mary Widman, came to his room in the evenings "and made sure he lacked nothing."[172] Yet for the most part, the antiracist Catholic scene in Chicago was much more masculine than New York's, where McKay had so many women friends. McKay seemed comfortable in this world of scruffy white Catholic men. He seems to have appreciated guys like Bishop Sheil, Edward Marciniak, and Father Daniel Cantwell, as well as the old Jesuit Arnold Garvey, an archivist at Loyola University Chicago who guided McKay even deeper into the history of African Catholicism.[173] These friendships appeared to be easier for McKay than his white friendships from earlier years. "I like you," he wrote to Marciniak, "because you are a natural. If you like a Negro you liked him as a person not because you feel you ought to mortify yourself to like one."[174] These men were all deeply involved in interracial work in 1940s Chicago, and Father Cantwell made it clear that interracial friendship was not the end in and of itself in the fight against racism but only the starting point for something more. "When you meet one Negro who you know as a friend a person who means something to you," Cantwell explained, "then he becomes, for you, the victim of every injustice you see done to any Negro." He added, "You work to get rid of the thing."[175]

Of all of them, McKay evidently developed the greatest affections for Bishop Sheil after he converted, even if from a distance. He kept a framed portrait of Sheil in his little apartment, along with a picture of the sacred heart.[176] Ammon Hennacy remembered how McKay once shared with him his sense that Sheil had a "vision of love in his eyes."[177] McKay was extremely private and rarely disclosed much to friends about his own inner life, including the intimacies of his crushes and loves as well as his own spiritual life. It felt invasive for McKay to reveal too much about either. To talk about his new faith would be "letting the world in on a quiet ceremony between a man and his God." He explained, "This would have something of the odor of an interracial marriage touted by the newspapers to make an American sensation. . . . Religion is not a sensation to titillate the appetite of the public. It is a sacred thing to keep and to hold fast between him and his God."[178] Of course, the relationship between him and God was never entirely private but was a space crowded with other people, friends, and maybe lovers too.

After learning he had become a Catholic, McKay's white radical friends from his earlier days assumed he had lost his mind. Max Eastman wrote him in September 1946, "Whether you are sick or whether you are economically dependent, or for whatever reason you are letting a little ignorant-minded neurotic like Dorothy Day do your thinking for you, it is a tragic fact. Again I ask you, for the sake of your pride, if not human civilization, keep it to yourself. Keep mum before the public. Let your heroic record stand."[179] Most secular radicals like Eastman could not fathom how Catholicism might offer anything to Black leftist thinkers like McKay.

Indeed, once he converted, McKay was one of very few Black Catholic writers, and white Catholic radicals couldn't get enough of him (here it is hard not to think of Jack Kerouac's racialized erotic primitivism). Everyone was always asking him to meet them for beers or come to this or that parish, and sometimes he just never showed.[180] After a couple of years in Chicago, this "vagabond lover of life" started itching to leave.[181] He had gotten sick again, suffering from the effects of a stroke, diabetes, and heart troubles. In May 1947, he set his sights on New Mexico, longing for sunshine, and reconnected with Ammon Hennacy, who had recently relocated there. Soon, Hennacy invited McKay down and immersed him into yet another scrappy network of Catholic care. Sister Agnes de Sales, a friend of Hennacy's, secured for McKay a bed on the porch of St. Joseph's Hospital. Hennacy had been experimenting with breathing exercises and spiritual healing, and in one instance he laid his hands on McKay's ailing body, aiming to heal the writer by channeling energy from God. "Whether it was those prayers or those of Sister Agnes or what," after about six weeks, Hennacy recalled, McKay's health improved.[182] But just like McKay's white friendships in Harlem, friendships here mattered little in the broader context of American racism. Hennacy and his friends couldn't find a landlord in New Mexico to rent to a Black tenant, so the local monsignor, José Garcia, set up a bed for McKay in his office for a few weeks. Later, they located an apartment for him in a Mexican part of town.

In this world of scruffy white Catholic men skeptical about modern civilization, McKay fit in just fine. Hennacy remembered nights at Monsignor Garcia's apartment: priests would pass through, and McKay would join them to play cards and drink late into the night. When a priest once realized they were drinking past midnight (and thus violating the old rule to fast after midnight before morning mass), he got up and turned the clock's hand back a couple of hours so they could resume drinking. This purely male sphere—without any women at all—is greatly reminiscent of *Banjo*'s world of bawdy, drinking men on the margins of civilized modernity. There were plenty of characters and misfits in Ammon Hennacy's Catholic New Mexico who McKay likely would have loved, although the crucial difference is that these men were all white. "I'm around so many Catholics," he wrote to Tarry, "no Negroes in sight."[183] Perhaps because these white Catholics claimed, like McKay, to be both radical and illiberal, they seemed different than his earlier white friends. One of the last poems he wrote before he died put it starkly: "And no white liberal is the Negro's friend."[184]

At the end of his life, it remains unclear what McKay thought of all these white Catholics. In a poem he wrote after his conversion, he evokes the disparity between the richness of Black religion and the dullness of white Christianity, where even Jesus is bored and lonely. It's hard to see where exactly his newfound faith would map onto this racialized religious binary:

> While white folk have a special place for God
> On Sunday when they cease from Satan's strife,
> And go to church—ostentatiously parade
> To the grey-stoned, cold-white church—and for whites only
> Where upon their knees they may command God's aid,
> Where Jesus Christ, our Lord, would be very lonely,
> And desire to tumble down these soulless stones
> Useless and nude of life as piled-up bones.[185]

Was this a critique of his new church—soulless and dull, for whites only? Or did he somehow see Catholicism as not quite "white" because it stood apart from Anglo-Protestantism and remained an immigrant church in the United States?

While living among white Catholic radicals like Hennacy, McKay did regain his health, but he still needed help writing, and twice a week he would dictate the book he was working on to Hennacy, a new project on his Jamaican childhood, published posthumously as *My Green Hills of Jamaica*.[186] In his first autobiography, *A Long Way from Home*, McKay had described "home" as New York, an ideal place for his wandering and his ambitions as a writer. Jamaica, he explained then, "was too small for high achievement."[187] Yet in New Mexico, as a recently baptized Catholic among so many new people, his thoughts returned to the island of his childhood, which he portrayed in a way he never could have when he first left in 1912. Thirty-five years of voracious collecting, reading, traveling, and writing, as well as the friendships formed in that period, had taught him much about the world. He looked back at home with new eyes. McKay excavated a *Catholic* history of Jamaica, before it became a British colony. He remembered how the oldest architecture in Jamaica looks like the "old cities of Barcelona, or Seville or Cordova."[188] Most likely drawing on research materials from the Schomburg library, his friendship with the Loyola archivist Arnold Garvey, and more historically dubious materials he picked up at Friendship House, McKay narrates how the island was first colonized by Spain, with the priests and nuns arriving after the Spanish colonists to care for the souls of the islanders. He wrote of "a Negro priest of the Catholic Church in Spanish Town, the original capital of Jamaica." His aim was to recover an early Black Spanish Caribbean Catholicism, and he depicts the sensuality and simplicity of Jamaican rural life in a way that echoes the Catholic culture he had come to know. For the peasants, "the spirits of their dear dead relatives were always around." He wrote disparagingly about the British Anglican colonists like Cromwell who arrived in Jamaica in 1833, armed, McKay notes, with hatred of Catholics in Jamaica and Ireland "like Hitler's hatred of Jews." Because of either the limitations of his sources or his enthusiasm as a convert, McKay was unwilling or unable to see the entanglements between Catholicism, colonialism, and slavery. He made astounding, absurd claims, including the idea that pre-Reformation Catholicism was free of racism and the notion that the church made so few statements on race because they had no racist ideas to begin with. He loved Catholicism's internationalism but never considered that this was due to its participation within colonial endeavors founded on Catholic Europe's sense of civilizational and racial superiority.

None of this made it into the final, posthumously published version of *My Green Hills of Jamaica*. It's possible that his identity as a Catholic Jamaican radical prevented him from being distilled into a comprehensible type, therefore making him too odd and risky to publish. When the book appeared later in 1967, the Catholic materials were for the most part scrubbed out, and today they remain only in an archival draft found at the Schomburg Center. Bishop Sheil wrote a preface to McKay's book, but it, too, didn't make the final cut. In it, he describes McKay's baptism as a kind of homecoming: "Claude McKay has come home."[189] While that may sound like Catholic propaganda from a bishop, McKay did summon memories of a Black Catholic Spanish island from a sickbed in New Mexico for his last writing project, and he also said of his journey, "I came home."[190] This blend of nostalgia, memory, fantasy, and history created a home in his mind that he could now claim as *his*: Black, Catholic, both Caribbean and European, and founded on a new sense of international, "uncivilized" religion that stubbornly refused the tribalism at the heart of "progressive" modernity, an identity forged thanks to his friends.

In 1947, McKay's health finally recovered, and he returned to Chicago. But it was a tough reentry. The weather was cold there, and new friendships were difficult, as always. McKay was convinced that Catholics from Bishop Sheil's CYO were spying on him and opening his mail (and maybe they were). He even wanted people to write him with a seal on the envelope, so he could check if it had been opened.[191] He was fixated on getting *My Green Hills of Jamaica* published. From New York, his old friend Ellen Tarry was trying to help him with this, but McKay was impatient. She was one of the few writers in this circle who had a baby she actually cared for, and the labor delayed her other projects. When McKay asked her what was taking so long, she wrote to him about her baby's fever and her move to a new apartment, asking sarcastically, "Now am I forgiven?"[192] Indifferent or oblivious, he replied with another request, this time to help sell some of the new albums he made with recordings of his poems. Her response: "If you read my last letter about the baby having chicken pox and then the measles, maybe you'd understand?"[193] One cannot help but laugh when reading her memoir as she jokes about why she and McKay never married, which people often wondered about, considering they were close friends, both single, and had absolutely everything in common. "Reason number one is: I'm not ready to go to jail for killing a distinguished Negro poet!"[194] But she always held her own.

By the spring of 1948, McKay had become seriously sick again but never told Tarry. He instead agreed, enthusiastically, to come to New York from Chicago in June 1948 to reconnect with old friends and read poetry at a celebration in honor of the African American poet James Weldon Johnson that Tarry had organized. Johnson had been friends with both McKay and Tarry, and the celebration was planned for the tenth anniversary of his death. Though Johnson was not Catholic, a celebration like this was an important cultural practice African Americans of all faiths and Catholics of all races had in common: marking extraordinary lives who have passed on, in order to reconnect with their spirit in some way. These occasions seemed to express that the sacred is never simply found "out there" but is experienced through specific lives, identified on distinct days in the calendar year, celebrated in particular places. Noting those events and remembering the dead in concrete ways forged a counter-narrative to secular, American histories that had for too long taken a dim view of both Catholic and African American practices. Against the denial of a Black past and the assertion of a warped Catholic "dark age", Tarry's celebration of Johnson professed a different narrative. McKay loved reclaiming the insults about backward-looking Catholics for himself. In one of his poems published in the *Catholic Worker*, he describes the Middle Ages as "dark like me."[195] Yet there was no way, sadly, he could have made a trip from Chicago to New York to celebrate Johnson, and on May 22, 1948, Claude McKay passed away.

When your life has been spent amid a network of caring friends, who deals with your death? Who deals with your body, your belongings? In Chicago, Bishop Sheil presided over the funeral mass, but McKay's body was shipped back to New York. Catholics paid for everything. Ellen Tarry went to the *Catholic Worker* and waited for the body. An anonymous writer published a short essay in June 1948:

> We sat waiting in the small chapel of the funeral parlor on Seventh Avenue in New York for the body of Claude McKay to be brought in. He had died on May 22 in Chicago. As we waited, the organist played softly, the music like a benediction, an assurance in symbolic and life eternal. We were thinking of the voice that is now silent. An American voice. A Negro voice. A great voice. . . . While we waited and the organ played, his body was brought in. In deep reverence we filed past the bier to have a brief last look on a dark face that had known the light of God's freedom in a land [the United States] darkened in spirit and culture. . . . As we knelt beside the still face and recited the Rosary asking God to rest his soul in peace,

we asked also that other souls be filled with the inspiration to voice the need for freedom that Claude McKay lived for.[196]

Reading these lines, one can imagine these Catholic radicals, some African American like Tarry but likely many white, praying over the radiance of this "dark face" with the hopes of one's own inner flame being kindled. McKay here serves as a sort of Magical Negro meant for white redemption, endowing the white people in the room with some of the "mystical negritude" that Roxane Gay describes, which inspires so much of white culture: the Black friend, especially a dead one, who enters the white world to teach racial awareness and forgiveness.[197] McKay would have certainly recoiled at many things in this scene. He wouldn't have liked to be called an American voice, and especially a Negro voice. He hated being referred to as either a Negro poet (literary critics, he said, always want to keep the "Negro in a racial grove")[198] or a Catholic poet ("I happen to be a Negro who is a writer and a converted Catholic").[199] Another *Catholic Worker* writer published a poem about McKay's funeral, where a white person read McKay's poem "If We Must Die" but rushed through it too quickly, as if it was too dangerous to touch, like dynamite.[200]

But there were friends in attendance who mourned McKay, like Tarry, and wouldn't have described him in these ways, aware of the complexities of his life, the struggles he had with his white friends, and the difficulties of realizing his ideals. The year he died, his old acquaintance from Paris Paulette Nardal had still been at work on issues of racial justice and Catholicism from Martinique. But like him, she was sick late in life and walked with a cane. She gave a speech in 1947 to the United Nations that evoked the "mystical body of Christ" as a Catholic way to imagine human unity across difference, the one theology McKay claimed he believed in.[201]

In the end, Claude McKay's conversion took place within a unique moment in Black Catholic history, between the 1920s and 1960s, when more than three hundred thousand African Americans became Catholics in the United States. That same period witnessed the emergence of a racially conscious Catholicism among a small counterculture of Black and white artists, writers, and activists in the United States and the Francophone world, especially Paris. McKay's baptism also belongs with stories of other seemingly unlikely religious conversions to traditions outside the conventional religious communities of African American Baptists, Methodists, and Pentecostals in this period. Along with McKay, we could consider artists such as the poet Robert Hayden, who converted to Bahaism in the early 1940s and was later joined by fellow poet Margaret Danner, as well as conversions by Malcolm X to the Nation of Islam, the beat poet Bob Kaufman to Buddhism, and jazz musician Yusef Lateef to Islam in 1950.[202] They point to, in the words of James Hall, an "exhaustion with received forms," emblematic of "a more general dis-ease or disappointment" with the white Christian legacy in the United States.[203] The story of Claude McKay's turn to Catholicism can be understood as a desire to signal Blackness through new terms, rejecting the mainstream narratives on offer: the nation, the family, the established Protestant church. He yearned for modes of kinship that were international, antiracist, anticommunist, mystical, and anti-family. The friendship culture of radical Catholicism gestures to what Paul Gilroy describes as a hallmark of Black transatlantic art: the "invocation of anteriority as anti-modernity, a look into the past that can create new space for critique in the present."[204]

We can also situate McKay's story alongside Wallace Best's work on Langston Hughes, who views Hughes as a deep religious seeker whose story gives us "a much broader reach for the history . . . of American and African American religion. They became untethered from the conventional Protestant narratives . . . making room for the perspectives, insights, and practices of the doubtful, the skeptical, the disillusioned, and the unsure."[205] McKay was likewise an eccentric, a wanderer, a vagabond, constantly cultivating his own view of things, and for a time, he found in Catholicism something that met both his desires for and condemnations of the modern world. But crucially, McKay's belief that Catholicism embodied his sensibilities did not apply to Catholicism in general; the local experiences he had among friends only suggested to him that it could be. Catholicism was an apt container for many things that McKay glimpsed in his journeys in both Europe and the United States, including the Nardal sisters' *cercle d'amis*, the mystical transcendence among the boys in Marseilles, the culture of Spain, and the world in Harlem that the Friendship House and Ellen Tarry introduced to him. It is important to also note the stubborn, confident illiberalism and skepticism of modernity that abounded in this Catholic counterculture, which McKay entered and claimed as his own. Also located in this matrix was the strange appeal of the new bawdy male friends who were quiet about their sexuality but eschewed convention who McKay met late in life, like Bishop Sheil, Ammon Hennacy, and Father Cantwell, anti-establishment, anti-bourgeois white men who came from the colonial world but disparaged it just like he did, greatly resembling his first special friend, Walter Jekyll.

EPILOGUE

Kindred Spirits as Fragments of Modernity

I SPENT A COLD, rainy week one March alone in Niort, France, a remote town in the western part of the country where the archives of Marie-Magdeleine Davy are held. I trudged to the archives each morning from my hotel to see what kind of narrative I might be able to piece together about her, under the gray sky and wet sidewalks, past shuttered dreary buildings (Niort has seen better days). But inside, Niort's archives of Davy were the most beautiful, inviting things I had ever laid my hands on. The care and attentiveness the archivists have dedicated to Davy is rare, especially considering Davy was a woman neither attached to a famous man nor a saint or a nun. The archivists have treated Davy's legacy like a massive, elaborate collection of gems, immaculately organized with a beautiful printed catalog to guide researchers through each tiny source. This is the work mainly of the fabulous archivist Armelle Dutruc, who has tended to these records with a dedication and tenderness that offers a beacon of hope for humanity.[1] It is precious, but not too precious. They're eager to have others come take a look, explore, touch, photograph, ask questions, and chitchat a bit. In my experience in French archives, that's incredibly unusual. Other than the fact that they're in Niort, it's a dream.

After a long day, one evening I had dinner at a bar by myself. I brought a *New Yorker* with me so I could relax with some English words and look less lonely while I ate and drank my wine. I stumbled upon a piece of fiction by Zadie Smith about Billie Holiday, told in the second person, which Smith wrote after seeing Jerry Dantzic's photographs of Holiday. Smith imagines, in Holiday's voice, thoughts Holiday may have had after giving a series of interviews:

> They never want to know about the surprise you feel in yourself, the sense of being directed by God, when something in the modulation of your threat leaps up, like a kid reaching for a rising balloon. . . . No, they never ask about that. They want the cold, hard facts. They ask the dull questions about the songs, about which man goes with which song in your mind, and if they're a little more serious they might ask about Armstrong or Bessie or Lester. If they're sneaky with no manners, they'll want to know about your run-ins with the federal government of these United States. They'll want to know if you hated or loved the people in your audience, the people who paid your wages, arresting you once for fraternizing with a white man, jailed you for hooking, jailed you for being, and raided your hospital room, right at the end, as you lay conversing with God. They are always very interested to hear you don't read music. Once, you almost said—to a sneaky fellow from the Daily News, who was inquiring—you almost turned to him and said *Motherfucker I AM music*. But a lady does not speak like that, however, and so you did not.[2]

When I read these words, my heart leapt. In them, I recognized the women I have come to know in this project: Marie-Magdeleine Davy, Raïssa Maritain, Simone Weil, Mary Kahil, Ellen Tarry. It was this swirl of images that did it for me: a woman whose sense of her own artistic power was entangled with a certain mystical sensibility—"conversing with God"—but also the toughness in a thought as fabulous as "*Motherfucker I AM music*." The combination of holiness and grit magnetically draw people in but is still too much, too strange to approach directly, so Holiday is guided by questions that clean her up and quickly place her within established narratives of national myth, civil progress, celebrity, and morality. Or else she is kept dirty and pinned down, and others swoon over her suffering and proximity to death. All of this struck me as familiar.

We want the cold, hard facts about these historic figures in order to shuttle them into our own plotlines: Why didn't she marry? She *did* marry, but they didn't have sex? Was she a lesbian? Why wasn't she just a nun? What do you mean she was Jewish *and* Catholic? How is that possible? You mean she dedicated her life to Muslims but was still a Francophile who loved the culture of the colonizers? About Ellen Tarry, one may demand what role, as a Black writer, did she have in laying the groundwork for civil rights. Of

a knowledgeable scholar, if they're Catholic, one will interrogate their relationships with de Lubac or Daniélou; if they aren't, then with Bataille and
Deleuze. The questions might be more philosophical or theological rather
than political: Isn't there implicit Christocentrism in this theory of comparative religion? Isn't there an inherent violence in the appropriation of non-
Christian texts? *Cold, hard facts.* Of course these are desired, and to the best
I can in this narrative, I give them.

But I imagine them: Davy chain-smoking, looking ragged as hell as
always; Raïssa, sick of the whole damn thing, with her shades down, lying
in bed surrounded by books; Ellen Tarry ditching the entire scene—the
activism, the praise—and hiding somewhere, away from them all, where
she can just write, alone at last; Gabriela Mistral closing her eyes, imagining
she and Teresa of Ávila together, barefoot, walking on the rocky countryside
of Spain, until suddenly, she opens her eyes and out comes a poem; Simone
Weil ready to literally go off and die: *Motherfucker we ARE God.* But a lady
does not speak like that, and so they did not.

———————————————

Not long after I read Zadie Smith's essay, I discovered Tracy Fessenden's
book *Religion around Billie Holiday.*[3] Fessenden's research enabled me to
see that the intuitive connection I sensed between Holiday and the women
in this book was not only an impression. As a child, Billie Holiday attended
a Baltimore girls' school run by the Oblate Sisters of Providence, the first
religious order of consecrated women of color, started by the French-born
priest James Joubert. Compelled by a potent combination of French colonial
ambition and mystical zeal, nuns with ties to France structured the inner
lives of youngsters all around the world, including Holiday's Baltimore as
well as the Caribbean, Canada, and Maine. The Oblate Sisters of Providence
worked alongside other missionary nuns who educated children globally,
from Cairo and Chile to Jerusalem and Africa. Several of the women in this
book were educated by this system, but like Holiday, because of race, class,
or temperament, some never really fit, and as soon as they were old enough,
they left to pursue art or writing. Fessenden explains in *Religion around Billie Holiday* how global French piety resulted from colonialism and how it
lingers in the lives of so many mystical and artistic "trained Catholics" and
becomes visible in their art. And like the story of Billie Holiday, we, too, can
see how easily these artists are swept into broader national, civic narratives
over which they have little control.

In the case of this book's protagonists, colonial piety and its aesthetics created a shared Francophile spirituality among people from places as distant as Morocco, Martinique, Russia, Spain, Harlem, Chile, and beyond that emphasized mysticism, friendship, and privacy about sex. But just as in the story of Billie Holiday, the inner lives of these individuals was not only determined by this colonial backdrop. The men and women in this book lived through decades of horrendous violence, both fleeing it and dedicating themselves to its undoing as active critics of those in power and advocates for its victims. This includes the mob violence of the Red Summer of 1919 against Black Americans, which inspired Claude McKay's poem "If We Must Die"; the Spanish Civil War of the 1930s, which pulled Gabriela Mistral and Jacques Maritain together; the anti-Semitic savagery of World War II, to which Marie-Magdeleine Davy organized resistance and which exiled the Maritains in New York; and the violence against Algerian Muslims in their war of independence from 1954 to 1962, which provided the context for Louis Massignon's considerable political evolution. These individuals saw connections among these events too: Ann Harrigan, a volunteer at the Friendship House, wrote in her diary in June 1942 that the "force behind anti-Semitism, anti-Negro, Communism, Fascism, War, is Hate—To hold back this tide, our love must be strong."[4] The love they tried to generate as a counterweight was not an existing abstract universal principal that they could reach for and grab but something that they had to work to create and sustain, with letters, visits, gifts, objects, memories, and photos. In friendships with writers (medieval or modern), their bonds were upheld through translations, books, and essays about friends both living and long dead, writings that they crafted and circulated as expressions of their love and loyalty. Friendship nurtured the energy that propelled their resilience, resistance, and artistic creativity. The practice of friendship facilitated the back-and-forth between theologians, activists, and artists, creating the spaces and circuits for the cultivation and flow of Catholic resistance to fascism, racism, and xenophobia. The matrix of friendship was also the place where ideas about alternative possibilities for the world were generated, held, and spread, in person, letters, memories, and imaginations. Emotions are contagious, and it was through one another that these men and women together gathered the courage to dedicate their talents toward something other than recognition by the status quo, even, for some, at great risk to their own lives. These friendships happened in what Natalie Zemon Davis calls "the cracks" in society, "the fault lines that shake people up to change things."[5] Friendships were not always ends in themselves and could just as often disappoint and fail to realize the hopes people had for them. Sometimes bonds of friendship would simply embody the inequalities of the world, problems which were far too big for friendships alone to solve. McKay wrote contemptuously of his "white friends," similar to Tarry's "nice white friends," who knew all about police brutality and did nothing about it. But there were times, for each writer in this book, when a special friendship provided such balance to the world around them that it evoked something of the transcendent, beyond the ordinary and the given. It was between friends that God was occasionally made real and Love was manifested in such a way that it had to be capitalized, sacralized, as a "great fire of Love between friends," in Massignon and Kahil's words.

When we resurrect the lives of these unusual people, can we simply add them to the existing narratives of twentieth-century Catholic thought before Vatican II, which is otherwise cast as a male and clerical world without desire or love? Can our knowledge of the history of European Catholic thought include thinkers from the African diaspora, like Claude McKay, or from Latin America, like Gabriela Mistral, and at what point do the seams of Catholic intellectual history in Europe break? When we move from the realm of theological ideas to the embodied experience of friendship, are we still concerned with intellectual history? Right now, European Catholic intellectual history is enjoying something of a renaissance, and scholars in disciplines outside of church history are producing extraordinary works that detail how early and midcentury Catholics, once little known outside of the church, were key figures in crucial developments in modernity: founding Christian democracy movements in Europe, centering phenomenology within postwar continental thought, placing the doctrine of human rights at the heart of Western democracy.[6] New scholarship illustrates how thinking and activism in Europe have drawn from and engaged with the world outside Europe—not only for imperial conquest.[7] And there is still so much room to further bring the contributions of women thinkers, artists, and activists into the narrative and to examine African and Latin diasporic writers' connection to Europe's Catholicism. Too often, white Catholics are accustomed to seeing men and women from Latin America who emerge in historical narratives either as sufferers ("the poor") or, according to Natalia Imperatori-Lee, as practitioners of "exotic rituals on the margins of Northern European 'magisterial' Catholicism, which has been construed as the norm," instead of as creative agents of culture, art, aesthetics, and ideas.[8] By noting how figures like Claude McKay and Gabriela Mistral were distinct from and yet still connected to European religious thought, we begin to break apart the long-held assumption that Catholic theological creativity in the years before Vatican II was almost exclusively French and male.[9] While these thinkers did all have some connection to France, with many circulating in and out of interwar Paris as part of an international motley crew of exiles and wanderers, they also had roots and lives all over the world.

If we start to take seriously the international, exilic nature of so much twentieth-century thinking, as Edward Said suggests in his 1984 essay "Reflections on Exile," then friendship becomes central.[10] As McKay explained to a friend in 1924, it takes the experience of going "abroad to know how welcome even a card of recognition is from friends when one is lonely and sick."[11] Seeing the vast geographical space in which most of the protagonists in this book lived their lives—they were all truly iterant, exilic, global thinkers—I came to realize in my research that Paris was just one locale of collaboration and creativity for these Catholic writers and artists in this span of decades. New narratives of a diasporic, international Catholic avant-garde could equally be told from elsewhere in the world, like Montevideo, Cairo, or Jerusalem (to name only a few places that surfaced in my own research as clear epicenters of Catholic creativity in the early and mid-twentieth century), and I hope one day future researchers take on these locales.

With their different vantage points around the world, these artists, poets, and writers cannot rightly be called theologians, but they each grappled with God, truth, reality, and modernity in creative ways that are deeply theological. I appreciate how Paul Mendes-Flohr describes Martin Buber and his world of Jewish thinkers and dreamers from this same period as a member of "the non-academic literati . . . 'free-floating intellectuals' who lived on the margins of academia."[12] It was people like Léon Bloy, Claude McKay, Gabriela Mistral, Ellen Tarry, Raïssa Maritain, Simone Weil, and Paulette Nardal who were Buber's contemporaries, making up Catholicism's own "non-academic literati" of educated thinkers at some distance from the institutional powers of the university and the church. I consider Jacques Maritain and Louis Massignon as part of this world too, but I recognize that they can hardly be considered nonacademic. As white European men, they lived their professional lives at the absolute center of academic power (Massignon held the chair of Muslim sociology at the Collège de France in Paris, and Maritain had positions at the Institut Catholique in Paris and later in the United States at Princeton and the University of Chicago). But

their hearts were with not the professional academic Catholics but the seekers, artists, poets, and mystics, those who trod the back roads through the
tradition. And in this community of exilic, nonacademic literati, we can see
how Catholicism looked for people who inhabited the tradition outside of
the clerical structures and the parish. Like Julie Byrne's study of independent Catholics, this community of poets and writers were "deeply continu-
ous with the family of Catholicisms" but enable us to better see, as Byrne
puts it, the "thoughts and unthinkables, centers and peripheries, flows and
fault lines" of the tradition.[13] I know too that there existed a great range
of relationships with the institutional church within this network: Jacques
Maritain was close friends with Pope Paul VI and served as the ambassador
to the Holy See, while Marie-Magdeleine Davy called the Vatican the place
where the sacred went to die.

    As nonacademic intellectuals, these artists and writers were often ahead
of clerical theologians and professional philosophers, laying the subsequent
foundations for their work. The poet Gabriela Mistral was writing about the
experiences of the poor and the indigenous in Latin America and trying to
forge a Catholicism that contended with the reality of their lives in as early
as 1920. This was decades before the inauguration of Latin American liberation theology and even before her friend Jacques Maritain had untethered
Catholic political philosophy from the politics of the Far Right. When we
include Gabriela Mistral within the narrative of intellectual history, however, not only does it suddenly have greater gender diversity or a wider
chronology, but it's as if the temperature in the room changes, the mood
is different. Though many emerging Catholic leftists after Mistral would
write about social Catholicism, democracy, and the concerns of the poor,
she evokes them uniquely: in Mistral's poems, she depicts an unwed mother
nursing on the sidewalk, for instance, and she gives a dreamlike voice to
babies talking to their mothers. "With the richest blood you watered me,
like watering the buds of the hyacinth, hidden beneath the earth. My feelings are yours and by borrowing your body, I wander the world," she said
in a speech to poor mothers in Mexico in 1924.[14] She endows her take on
the twentieth century with a poetic sensibility, one that also moves closer
to the experience of the women she knew in Chile and in Mexico. Or we
could consider Marie-Magdeleine Davy, who wrote about the glimmers of
truth contained in other religious traditions and researched the historical
ties between Christians and Jews full decades before Vatican II promulgated
Nostra Aetate. Claude McKay described the complexity of race and the religious imagination before the first generation of Black theologians.[15] Artists

did not always pave the way for theologians, and some theologians in this
period were also right there in the mix. Just as Davy became active in the
French resistance in 1940 in Paris, for example, the Jesuit theologian Henri
de Lubac was giving clandestine speeches in Lyon that were a "crucible of
ideas and initiatives" for the resistance.[16] He urged Catholics to contend
seriously with the theology and ideology of the "bloody filth" of Nazi anti-
Semitism and helped French Catholics understand the spiritual ties between
Jews and Christians.[17] In response to the Aryan theologians who worked to
excise Judaism from Christianity, de Lubac wrote, "We will no longer allow
them to tear it away from us."[18]

    If we include clerical theologians like Henri de Lubac alongside people
like Gabriela Mistral, Claude McKay, Jacques and Raïssa Maritain, and Louis
Massignon, we can see how together these theologians, artists, and writers
all rejected the old model of neo-scholasticism that confined the sacred to
small, specific places under the control of the priesthood. In 1941, de Lubac
claimed that clerics treated theology as if they were "curators in a museum,
a museum in which we have inventories, ordered and labeled everything."
By guarding the sacred behind glass, "little by little," he wrote, "it was left to
die in our care."[19] Nazi myths and symbols, according to de Lubac, attracted
people by tapping into their desire for intensity and contracting with something sacred, which people no longer sensed within the church because it
was protected, quarantined, and had withered away. For de Lubac, Nazis
were the ultimate "sacred usurper."[20] This community of theologians, artists, and activists experimented with new ways to imagine the sacred for the
twentieth century, but they did so differently than post–Vatican II Catholics a generation later. In the years following Vatican II, many Catholics
began to conceive of the sacred as more expansive and diffuse, beyond the
spaces traditionally governed by clerical control, like the sacraments. They
envisioned the holy as an immanent part of all the world: in all humanity,
including in the lives of the poor, modern art, and even science. Catherine
Osborne vividly describes this new radical understanding of transcendence
as immanence among Catholics in the 1960s: "Immanence doesn't need,
strictly speaking, to refer to anything beyond itself, not because the world is
self-sufficient but because the world is already filled with God's grace, present in every kingfisher and every particle of steel rebar."[21]

    The men and women who created a culture of spiritual friendship from
1920 to 1960 experimented with immanence and transcendence in a slightly
different way. They were all looking for what many Catholics of this period
called "la sève" (the sap), a spiritual lifeblood that could bring vitality and

holiness into an ossified Catholicism and into a century they deemed badly in need of repair and renewal. But for this community, transcendence could still be found in *specific* bodies, texts, and people—*here*, not there, or *there*, not here. Grace was no longer contained in a glass but flowed from special holy friends who generated and circulated holiness; friends harbored what Robert Orsi calls "real presence" and were not separated by the absolute boundaries between the natural and supernatural.[22] For some, like Mary Kahil and Massignon, these friends were known in the present, face-to-face, while for others, they were the remembered dead, like Simone Weil and Davy, or the beloved authors of ancient sacred texts, perceived as friends by the scholars who read, translated, and transcribed them. This longing for contact with the transcendence of ancient texts meant that their herme-neutic for reading was not historicist or philological but founded on affec-tion, intimacy, even love. We see this particularly monastic way of reading when de Lubac spoke of the fraternal bond he felt with the patristics, when Davy wrote of her friendship with Bernard of Clairvaux and Guillaume of Saint-Thierry, and when Raïssa Maritain described Thomas Aquinas as an author to whom she was fused in a kind of rapturous ecstasy. Many others stretched the hermeneutic of friendship with ancient materials to include non-Christian and non-European sources. Massignon bonded with al-Hallāj, and Claude McKay not only researched the medieval period but identified with it: the "Middle Ages" were "dark like me," McKay stated in a 1946 poem.[23]

Taken together, this worldview did not affirm the radical immanence of transcendence and its indwelling throughout the world but was instead decidedly nonuniversal in its apprehension of holiness. Louis Massignon used a phrase that may sit uneasily with readers today when he called these harbingers of the holy the spiritual or "real elites."[24] These artists, theologians, philosophers, and writers all shared this somewhat rarefied elitist sensibil-ity. When they looked around at their century of war, genocide, and racial violence, they could not perceive the radical immanence of God's presence. Holiness shone, dimly and quietly, in rare, special, specific people. By 1962, certain sectors within the institutional church were prepared to entertain ideas like those generated in these creative prophetic networks. But in my mind, Vatican II is not the most interesting part of this story. These radicals never had their sights set on Rome, and they were never waiting to see when the church's hierarchy would catch up to them. Instead, they used their con-siderable resources to imagine and sustain alternatives themselves.

FRIENDSHIP AND DIASPORIC MODERNITY

When considering how to conceptualize the defining features of this network of artists and activists, I have taken cues from the work of trailblazing scholars in African and African American studies on the practices of diasporic cultures in modernity. Studies on the global circulation of ideas in modernity have examined the slave trade, the global history of the notion of race, and the making of transnational Black cultures all as key to the formation of the modern world. In his classic work *The Black Atlantic*, Paul Gilroy argues that writers and artists whose histories are rooted in forced diaspora (the slave trade, displacements, involuntary migrations) often reclaim this uprootedness in their artistic work and use it to further a more expansive, critical global perspective. "The expressive cultures of the black Atlantic world," he argues, "have been dominated by a special moment of restlessness." Gilroy continues, "What was initially felt to be a burden—the curse of homelessness or the curse of a forced exile—gets repossessed."[25] He cites artists such as Toni Morrison and W. E. B. Du Bois who extended notions of Blackness by appropriating cultural materials from both African diasporic and white European and American philosophical and literary traditions, creating a hybrid "counterculture of modernity" and a new kind of transatlantic modernism. This is one reason Black artists connect to so many different people from around the world: Gilroy remembers feeling enthralled when Jimi Hendrix's "Purple Haze" broke into the London airwaves in 1967, as if Hendrix was speaking to and for all the Black British teenage boys like him, who listened in awe. Pushing Gilroy's insights further, Brent Hayes Edwards in *The Practice of Diaspora* analyzes how this internationalism among Black writers and artists came about in the interwar period, examining what practices made diasporic Black literature, activism, and art possible in places like France and Harlem. He notes, for example, the role of bilingual intellectuals throughout the Francophone and Anglophone worlds, whose writings and translations created spaces in journals where transnational Black solidarity materialized.[26]

Inspired by these scholars, I have tried to argue that in the context of the Catholic diasporic Left, spiritual friendship did the work of smoothing, cultivating, and sustaining various modes of internationalist belonging. During the century of massive exile, war, and genocide, these people were spread around the world, and through letters and memories, and sometimes face-to-face, these friends offered connection, roots, community, and the possibility of transcendence. The words of the biographer of the Uruguayan poet Esther de Cáceres apply just as well to Jacques Maritain from Paris, Mary Kahil from Cairo, Mistral from Chile, Davy from France, McKay from Jamaica: "To know her life," her biographer states, "you have to understand her almost religious feeling for friendship."[27] Friends made God's presence real and gave purpose and reason to their work. Spiritual friendship was the stuff of global theology, spirituality, politics, and art, and as I wrote this book, it felt, at times, like I was peering into a fragmented secret history never intended to be made public. I was uncovering and piecing together a history whose remains I found in letters, etched on tombstones, preserved in funeral eulogies, glimpsed in dedications to books, confessed in diaries. But elsewhere this history was visible, communal, and open: friendship was obvious in the scholarly and activist associations they founded all over the world, like the Maison Simone Weil in Saint-Clementine, the *cercle d'amis* at the center of international noir in Paris, Amitié chrétienne during World War II, the Friendship House in Harlem and Chicago, and the scholarly associations like Amis de Gandhi, Amis de Charles Péguy, and the Asociación de Amigos de Léon Bloy. Spiritual friendship was readily apparent as well in the many books these figures wrote about their friends: Raïssa Maritain's *Les grandes amitiés*, Davy's books on Weil and Berdyaev, Massignon's essays on Charles de Foucauld, and so many more.

In the end, the story of spiritual friendship, gleaned from both private archival documents and public materials, has also had to include its failures. Spiritual friendship sometimes served to obfuscate a realistic assessment of the problems that beset the world and endowed political efforts with an interpersonal mystical poetics that ran counter to historical, sober-minded analysis of the world. In his book on Jacques Maritain and Emmanuel Mounier, Joseph Amato claims this network fell short of offering real solutions since they so often evoked broad, sweeping claims in vague spiritual and civilizational terms, offering little more than an "interior sense of the crisis" of modernity.[28] In their friendships and in their methods of engaging with the world, they summoned poetry, metaphor, and symbol rather than legislative plans. They were brilliant readers but not great historians or political analysts. And spiritual friendship sometimes steered them to loathe those who were biological rather than spiritual kin: they routinely and troublingly shook off the kids they brought into this world, their perplexed elderly parents, and their spouses, like so much dust on their shoes. Nor were these friendships themselves purely harmonious. Recall Mary Kahil, whose intense bond with Louis Massignon came with a world of pain and confusion. Sometimes such troubles pushed them to a breaking point. By the end of her life, Davy had had enough with friendships, spiritual or otherwise. She entered her final years more or less alone. Claude McKay's approach was similar. When he felt smothered and crowded out, especially by white liberals and their plans for him, he simply packed up and moved on. Some of McKay's own writings were about the use of the word *friendship* among white liberals as simply another term for domination. I think too of Abd-el-Jalil, who never really recovered from his Moroccan Muslim family's abandonment after he became a Catholic, taken in by his "spiritual father," the French Islamicist Massignon, when he was a young man studying in Paris. To be sure, studying these friendships is not an invitation to celebrate a lost art of connection, nor is it a romantic paean to those at the margins of Catholic theology. Instead, this work examines one crucial means for the dissemination and expansion of some of the most creative Catholic thinking in the middle of the twentieth century. It places these ideas in their inter-relational contexts, which were charged with complex spiritual and political ambition, dreams, and desire.

These Catholics, of course, did not invent friendship and have no monopoly on that term. Ali Shariati told Louis Massignon that he loved him so much that his heart raced when he thought of him. Was Shariati like that with all his friends? Was there an Islamic conception of friendship among the diasporic Muslim intellectuals who overlapped with the men and women in this particular community? Did Shariati's approach mirror that of Maritain's acquaintance Muhammad Iqbal or of Talal Asad's father, the Jewish convert to Islam who became known as Muhammad Asad? More-over, the Jewish thinkers connected to this community remain today some of the most preeminent philosophers of friendship in the West, including Jacques Derrida and Hannah Arendt. We could also count here works like Martin Buber's 1923 *I and Thou*, which proposes a theology of relationality. For Buber, God is understood not in abstract, intellectual terms but as manifest in moments of pure relationality, when neither subject is dominated or objectified. When I was an undergraduate student more than twenty years ago, an independent study on Buber shined a light on the pathway of the power of intersubjectivity in modernity, and in some ways, with this book I'm continuing to walk down that trail. Not only Muslims and Jews but Protestants, too, have their own histories of the spiritual intensities of rela-tionality and friendship. One of the best studies on spiritual friendship is Carroll Smith-Rosenberg's classic 1975 essay "The Female World of Love and Ritual: Relations between Women in Nineteenth-Century America."[29]

So much of the world that Smith-Rosenberg describes reminds me of the Catholics I have come to know: the women's correspondence with expressions of feverish love, the mailing of sacred treasures to one another (in their case, locks of hair).

That said, when seen in their broader context, the distinctively Catholic meanings with which this community endowed friendship come into greater focus. Their neo-medieval, anti-family sensibility and their connections to theologies of sainthood were particular, uniquely Catholic takes on something that is otherwise universal. The spiritual friendships of Marie-Magdeleine Davy are particularly illustrative. Theologies and practices of the "invisible friendship" of sainthood were part of the established cultural repertoire through which she formed her friendships. Theologies of sainthood came into view, for instance, when Davy sought to make sure those who she called her "spiritual kin" were not just put to work in narratives of ordinary morality and politics. She endowed her friends with an elsewhere quality, something of the taboo, the excessive. In her 1966 *Purity and Danger*, anthropologist Mary Douglas, herself a Catholic, theorizes that in the realm of ordinary reality we work to excise death, danger, and weakness from our lives. But in the religious domain, what is taboo carries what she calls a "symbolic load" in our psyches that can serve as a powerful source of relief, regeneration, and resistance.[30] Friends described holy friends through these kinds of moral taboos, emphasizing their messiness, lack of decorum, rudeness, inscrutability, disorganization, and strangeness. Drawing from the theology of the "fools for Christ" (1 Corinthians 4:10) that has long animated devotion to saints, they referred to friends as possessing a special, spiritual charisma. Davy said that Weil's holiness was actually disturbing rather than straightforwardly inspiring. This God was sensed not as an ethical teaching or even a feeling of love but as something much more unsettling, mysterious, and strange. "Friends," wrote Georges Bernanos in 1947 about his imagined friendship with Léon Bloy, "stirred our faith for reasons we don't always understand."[31]

These distinctively Catholic approaches to spiritual friendship also included their sense that friendship was cultivated in deliberate, explicit contrast to the rise of the nuclear family and in imitation of Christian monastic life, since the Benedictines were intentionally a radical distinction from biological family arrangements. This, too, differs from a world like the one Smith-Rosenberg describes among Protestants, an intense culture of intimacy where cousins, siblings, children, and friends were entangled, and the lines between biological and spiritual kin were deliberately blurred.

These Catholics embraced notions of kinship that explicitly rejected biological conceptions for spiritual, volitional ones.

I have come to believe that there are at least two ways to think about the implications of the anti-family, and largely anti-sex, culture of Catholic avant-garde spiritual friendship, which emphasize either the history of the Catholic closet or the complexity of the relationships formed in this community. Nearly every person in the preceding chapters refused reproductive heterosexual matrimony. Their general silence on sexuality and the promotion of friendships as an alternative to family are both part of a long Catholic history. Catholics' relative comfort with forgoing marriage and children has meant that the tradition has always provided spaces, like the seminary, convent, and monastery, where people could still find all sorts of experiences while they rejected heterosexual marriage. Homosocial worlds offered ways of living outside marriage that were culturally sanctioned and provoked no questions or qualms. Those same worlds, however, also served as closets, which engendered a culture of silence and, certainly for some, shame that twisted into self-loathing and homophobia. Mark Jordan crystallizes this dilemma: "How can we begin to talk about the institutional paradox of a church that is at once so homoerotic and so homophobic, that solicits same-sex desire, depends on it, but also denounces and punishes it?"[32] When it comes to Catholicism and intimacy, secrecy and grief pervade so many sources that are just coming to light, which are riddled with heartbreaking stories of secret, illicit longings, closeted consummation, and abuse.[33] The silence on sex that ran through this community cannot be entirely disentangled from the larger context of Catholic deceit, cover-up, and shame.

But does this relative privacy regarding actual sex mean that these individuals solely felt repression, self-loathing, and shame (as if to say that while they were "spiritual friends," nobody *really* just wanted friendship), as Frédéric Martel claims in *In the Closet of the Vatican*? Though Martel conflates them, I think that the world of spiritual friendship among these laywomen and men is rather different from that of the male clerical system he describes, an all-male world where silence and celibacy was enforced and regulated with juridical injunctions and punishments. Spiritual friendship among these laypeople certainly had problems, but when compared with the culture of the priesthood, I believe these circulations of desire possessed less shame, violence, and repression. One huge difference is that this was a world populated by men as well as women, together. In the largely clerical world Martel examines, there are almost no women at all, and when they do appear in his narrative, they do so only as "beards" or covers for male homoerotic love, which is how he interprets Raïssa's role in Jacques's life. It is only possible, however, to narrate the role of women in this world as mere cover for male homosexuality if one never encounters the reality of these women's lives. Nineteenth-century cultural associations between friendship and femininity made it more acceptable for someone like Raïssa Maritain to write a memoir in 1941 called *Les grandes amitiés* than it would have been for her husband.[34] But her book merely represented a vast underworld of inten-sive, affective bonds between women and men, men and men, women and women. In this network of spiritual friends, erotic desire flowed in homosex-ual and heterosexual directions, between trios, pairs, and communities that included individuals, living and dead, of all genders. Reducing this world of desire to the familiar tropes of Catholic repression disregards the variety of loving bonds and erotic expressions that were not only not repressed but readily admitted as the hot center of their religious lives. This enforcement of binaries—gay or straight, repressed or fulfilled—cannot contain the com-plexities of the erotics of this world. Was there repression here? Shaming? No doubt. But there was a great deal more to their experiences, which old narratives and clerical fixations threaten to blot out of memory.

The people in this community of *amis* were also laypeople. They were freer than most priests. Priests and seminarians have long been discouraged from developing "special friendships," but these laity could come and go as they wished and had private lives under the surveillance of no one.[35] Their sexual lives could and did remain private, and many details are for the most part inaccessible to scholars today. We do know that alongside or within these spiritual friendships, some, like McKay and Mistral, did have sexual lives, though they said very little about them. But their silence does not mean they felt shameful, repressed, or self-loathing: sometimes it just means they were private. Recall Claude McKay's annoyance that so many white readers and interviewers salaciously prodded him about his sex life, insisting on questioning it all the time. Brent Hayes Edwards takes a different route in his scholarship on McKay, content to conclude that McKay's sexuality "remains a mystery" and "can't quite be explained or filed away according to the usual categories."[36] Though the queer energy of this community was greater than I ever would have anticipated, this elusive and persisting mystery of their sexuality aptly describes each of them. Perhaps their form of Catholic spiri-tual friendship was a world in which these mysterious parts of themselves could be protected by a culture that was at once countercultural *and* quiet.

The insistence that the "real" meaning of spiritual friendship lies in repressed sexuality relies too heavily on the logic of secularism and with it the assumption that secular societies do not have as great a taboo around sexuality and therefore have no need for this elaborate panoply of excessive spiritual friendship. Unearthing this archive of love among friends shows that sex—especially its repression—was not the sole underlying facet to these relationships and opens up new ways to imagine forms of Catholic intimacy that do not focus on secrecy, shame, and self-loathing.[37] These stories help us think our way out of what Janet Jakobsen and Ann Pellegrini call the "complacent consensus" of secularism, its promise of an inevitable moral and political advancement around issues of intimacy and sexuality.[38] Instead of assuming that secularism is the only site where love can at last freely express itself, this community hints at a wider range of possibilities for what constitutes a meaningful, flourishing life. For example, Doris Dana was Gabriela Mistral's lover from 1948 until Mistral's death in 1957, and although Mistral never talked about her publicly in that way, they lived and did everything together, and Mistral never seemed, as far as I can see, ashamed of this relationship.[39] Invitations always included both of them. In this network, it was normal, arguably more normal than it is in the modern day United States, for a woman to forgo marriage and children. When Gabriela Mistral was sick, Jacques Maritain wrote to Dana and thanked her for being Mistral's "sister and her angel."[40] No doubt there is something prudish in his language, but when I think about the tacitly sanctioned love between Mistral and Dana that took place within a much wider context of love among friends in Mistral's life—the Maritains, Victoria Ocampo, and the wider eclectic community of Spanish-, French-, and English-speaking people who gathered around her in Europe, Brazil, New York, and all her constant travels—their lives and loves seem expansive and full. Shame, silence, and sublimation are not the first things that come to mind.

The devotion that these men and women had to the realm of friendship has also helped me think beyond how we tend to frame liberal and conservative Catholics. We typically consider Catholics who align politically with the Left as adhering to a mode of relationality that is more communal and public, while viewing the Right as obsessed with private sexual lives and issues like abortion and marriage. But the people in this network refused that binary. Yes, they were committed to the public good (antifascism, antiracism, anticommunism), but they also lavished attention and care on their private lives, which they organized almost entirely around friendships, visible and invisible. To be sure, Catholics have always been considered corporatists who oppose Protestant individualism, which is often because Catholics are seen to have church or commitments to social teaching or the common good. But in practice, I saw that corporatism in this community was something more intimate and interpersonal. Friends offered another form of association and relationality that was still personal but went beyond the familial, the instrumentally reproductive, the national, and the abstract. Indeed, it was these friendships that make me wonder whether anyone, really, at the end of the day, is truly motivated by abstractions like the common good.

The unambiguously anti-family sensibility in this community has made it jarring to see some of these men and women marshaled for the promotion of conservative family-based Catholic gender ideology. Pope John Paul II, for example, lists Jacques Maritain among the "great Christian thinkers" in his 1998 encyclical *Fides et Ratio (Faith and Reason)*.[41] John Hellman sees Pope John Paul II as a "reincarnation" of Jacques Maritain, and Brooke Williams Deely, in her introduction to a collection of John Paul II's writings on women, argues that the pope "advances discourse in continuity with the groundwork laid by Maritain . . . on the centrality of *relation* to our understanding of the person."[42] Pope John Paul II certainly draws from Maritain's concepts of Catholic personalism, especially its relational anthropology, in his publications *Love and Responsibility* (1960, published in English in 1981) and *The Theology of the Body: Human Love in the Divine Plan* (1997). But this is a different Maritain, a Maritain laced with the pope's ideas about sexual difference and gender complementarity.[43] John Paul II situates the procreative ends of sex closer to the center of Maritain's understanding of relationality. The pope's documents sexualize the relational emphasis of Maritain's personalism, or more specifically he *heterosexualizes* it. As Camille Robcis claims, "He redefined the social as fundamentally heterosexual."[44] This emphasis on procreative heterosexuality as the telos of a relational anthropology is simply absent in the work of Jacques Maritain.

The people in this book offer radical new constructs to the depressing and dull vision of gender and human intimacy as pronounced by leaders at the Vatican. But their modes of love also counter more subtle aspects of our culture. Contemporary capitalism functions largely on the premise that the world is awful, and the most we can hope for is pleasure in our private lives, pleasure organized around our nuclear families. As Kathryn Lofton points out, "There is a constant hum of one truth: practicing parenting is central to American life and determinate of the American moral imagination. However much family might be reorganized or queered, it endures as the story within every story."[45] "The challenge," Lofton notes, is that today "you can't imagine how to exit it. The difficulty is that you worry you will be left with nothing if you do: no good, no family, no country."[46] Part of my hope for this project is that it contributes to the efforts to imagine alternative modes of belonging and love and a politics fueled by something more pleasurable than duty. This community of thinkers, writers, and artists arranged their lives and their loves outside the confines of the nuclear family and the nation, and yet, look at all they had. They never merely pointed out problems. They summoned living, breathing, alternatives.

But what happened to these people and to their friendships? From one perspective, this world has disappeared. Dar-el-Salam in Cairo closed in 1962, and Maison Simone Weil shuttered its doors only a few years after it opened in 1960. The Friendship House in Harlem shut down in the late 1940s, and even the more successful one in Chicago, though it lasted longer, sold its property to the Black Panthers in 1980. The *Revue du monde noir*, the journal of Black internationalism in Paris that the *cercle d'amis* gathered around, only lasted six issues, its final issue appearing in 1932 after funding dried up. The Maritains' salon disbanded during World War II. In France, one urban historian recently described walking around the docks of Marseilles carrying a copy of Claude McKay's *Banjo* (1929), saying it was like walking around with an amputated arm. Because of the book, he could *feel* the Marseilles of *Banjo*, full of drifters and revelers from all over the African diaspora connected by rowdy friendship, but after so much of the city's destruction during the war, and its later changes from the pressures of tourism and gentrification, the cultural setting of *Banjo* has vanished.[47] Even beyond the now-shuttered institutions and transformed geographies, the interpersonal, emotional scenes I encountered would be hard to imagine today without raising eyebrows. Can we picture the world's most prominent Catholic philosopher kissing the president of Chile after holding his face in his hands, expressing love and affection, as Eduardo Frei recalled Jacques doing outside the Chilean embassy one night in 1950?

Yet, in all honesty, when I think about the legacy of this community, I am struck not so much by its failure to last but by the fact that they got anything off the ground in the first place. Most of these men and women were seen to embody a spiritual charisma because they lived in such radical distinction to the mainstream norms of professionalization and institutionalization. Claude McKay lost the manuscript of a novel in the truck of someone's car in the 1940s, which he never recovered, in part perhaps because he doesn't seem to have tried. It turned up, randomly, in a folder in the New York Public Library only in 2017. Gabriela Mistral said she preferred to have her writings "scattered" in random bits and in various languages, deliberately unsystematized.[48] She only relented after Frederic de Onís of Columbia University insisted. Although Louis Massignon was at the center of the professional academy at the Collège de France, he had an approach to research so bizarre and so personal that it is impossible to imagine him setting up any sort of school of thought or actual program for others. These were eccentrics. Not only were they all mystically inclined, but several actually relished in the thought that they might disappear. Ellen Tarry, the African American Catholic writer and friend of Claude McKay's, published massively in Black and Catholic publications in New York and Chicago, but she died in relative obscurity in 1990. In an interview toward the end of her life, she stated, "I gave up all my connections to the literary world. Here I am now; all my editors are dead. . . . I don't know anybody. I'm lost, so to speak, as far as the literary world is concerned. But God takes care of fools and babies, and he'll take care of me somehow. I'm not the kind of person who would say, 'I want to be remembered in this fashion.'"[49] Likewise, Gabriela Mistral, in one of the last poems she wrote before she died, imagines her own death and offers herself, for those who need her, as if sacramentally:

EL REPARTO (DISTRIBUTION)

If I am put beside
The born blind,
I will tell her softly, so softly
With my voice of dust,
'Sister, take my eyes.'

Eyes? Why do I need them where all is brightness?

. . .

Let another take my knees
If hers have grown
Stiff and unbending
With snow or frost
Let another take my arms

If hers have been sundered.
And others take my senses
With their thirst and hunger.
Let me finish thus, consumed,
Divided like a loaf of bread.
Thrown to the South or to the North,
I shall never again be one.

This dismantling of myself will be
Like the pruning of branches
That drop from me and lighten my burden
As with a tree.[50]

This offering of herself, as a kind of scattering to the winds, was prescient. Though Mistral is revered and beloved in the literary world, her legacy in the world of Catholicism after her death in 1957 slipped away from her control and went in a direction that would have been unfathomable to her. In Chile, Mistral's image was taken up to advance the narratives of conservative Catholic ideology, particularly under the Chilean military dictatorship of General Augusto Pinochet, who put her face on one of their peso bills. She was more than the beloved Chilean Nobel laureate; she was a handy Catholic alternative to Chile's other Nobel laureate, the conspicuously communist Pablo Neruda. But because she wrote so frequently about motherhood and children, she was vulnerable to co-optation by the Right, and Pinochet regularly held up Mistral as a symbol of the natural, divinely ordained and Chilean notion of womanhood as maternality.[51] Under Pinochet, she was packaged as a symbol of order and submission.

Indeed, in studying this community, you have to push *against* their desires to disappear into someone else's plans for them, to simply fade into the night, to keep their notes messy and inscrutable, to let their manuscripts gather dust in some crazy Catholic attic or end up buried in an old pontifical pamphlet, lost in the trunk of someone's car, abandoned in an apartment.[52] You must refuse their wish to be left alone and instead insist on the importance of their story. But they may first need to be coaxed and given room for their weird moods; you cannot force things too much, pry too hard about topics they don't want to disclose, but should instead help them dust things off, insist that they matter, and put their work out into the world to see what, if anything, takes root. You must treat them, in other words, like a friend.

The stories of their lives are largely forgotten not only because of their

almost mystical impulse to disappear but also due to their eclectic formation. They all had distinct origins from their clerical intellectual contemporaries, like the Dominicans Marie-Dominique Chenu and Georges Anawati
and the Jesuits Henri de Lubac and Jean Daniélou. Mistral, McKay, Davy,
Weil, Massignon, and the Maritains were products of more heterogeneous
and difficult to categorize influences. They were all oddly brilliant, able to
pull together sources from an incredible range of traditions and frequently
gifted in multiple languages. They were rare, unusual people. Unlike the
clergy, they didn't belong to specific religious orders that established and
clarified their legacy. Their identities were less stable. When compared to
not only the clergy but even some of the more famous American Catholic
countercultural figures like Dorothy Day, the religious identities of these
men and women were much more fluid than the label *Catholic* suggests. As
an adult in 1905, Raïssa Maritain converted to Catholicism from the Russian
Judaism of her childhood. She considered herself Jewish-Catholic before
her death in 1960. They were often divided people. In some cases, this was
reflected in their scholarly work, like the convert Anawati's fixation on the
"question Orient-Occident."[53] Davy, for her part, veered from the Catholic
tradition to Eastern Orthodoxy in 1950, but after she realized, to her disappointment, that just as many boring people were Orthodox as Catholic, she
stopped short of conversion. Late in life, she was a widely well-regarded
scholar of comparative mysticism, and no one was certain where to place
her religiously. Ibrahim Madkour called Massignon "the greatest Muslim
among Christians and the greatest Christian among Muslims."[54] A Catholic
scholar of Islam, in 1950 Massignon became a Melkite Catholic priest, of the
Eastern rather than Western tradition of Christianity that uses Arabic as its
liturgical language. To me, they all exhibit an insider-outsider relationship
with Roman Catholicism, which recalls the writings of Jean Baruzi, one of
Davy's very first teachers: "The demands of my thinking being what they are,
I do not feel I have the right to say I am a Catholic, although by this I am not
declaring I am a stranger to everything in the Church."[55] In this community,
atheism was not a settled locale either, as Davy's friend Gershom Scholem
notably expressed, "My secularism is not secular."[56] When Claude McKay
insisted to his American friends that he was more of a European Catholic
than like those in the United States, it was a way of saying to his American
friends, "Yes, Catholic, but . . ."

The men and women of this community remind us that we may need a
more capacious understanding of the term *Catholic*. We have much to learn
from Jewish colleagues on this topic. Amos Oz and Fania Oz-Salzberger, for

instance, write about "Jewish non-orthodoxy" in *Jews and Words*. They are interested in a cohort of Jewish writers who

> kept the tradition in its own ways, steering its variegated courses between Moses and modernity. Linked together in this modern string of Jewish learning, openly and joyfully interacting with the non-Jewish world, fraught with frictions, plural of minds, this modern continuum incorporates Mendelssohn (the third great Moses after the prophet and Maimonides), Gershom Scholem, Franz Rosenzweig, Martin Buber. . . . All of these thinkers still belong, by their own lights, to the great chain of Jewish scholarship, mythically and textually launched on Mount Sinai by Moses, the first teacher. Farther away, no longer part of a self-professed chain, but with some learned rabbi or bookish mother or synagogue canticle still flickering on their biographical horizon, stand Heine and Freud, Marx and the Marx Brothers, Einstein and Arendt, Hermann Cohen and Derrida. We are listening to them here not just because they were Jewish—we are not in the business of smug stocktaking—but because it is evident that these thinkers and artists were etched by something intimately and textually Jewish.[57]

To follow this line of thinking, what might a Catholic non-orthodoxy look like? Someone who is "etched by Catholicism" and "keeping the tradition in their own ways" belongs to a softer kind of Catholicism than that of the professionals and the clergy. It is an intensely relational form of Catholicism (no finding transcendence within, alone) centered not on the parish but around a more mystically inclined sensibility that is less programmatic when it comes to politics. We might begin to work our way toward a new language that could open up more possibilities for scenarios like Carolyn Forché's, when someone asked her, "'You are a Catholic, aren't you?' No one had asked me this question for a long time," she reflects, "and I wasn't sure of the answer."[58] Many can relate.

Yet we must be careful and not make too much of their faith. These individuals avoided categories of race, class, nation, and even, in some sense, religion. Though they were not secular, they were essentially humanists. But they joined the chorus of those humanists who denied secularism its optimism and innocence. Their refusal of secularism, their connections to Europe, and their humanism have made them more difficult to assimilate into the subsequent generations' more strident political climate. In comparison, they seem almost quaint. A biographer of Aimé Césaire wondered why Paulette Nardal, the founder of the *Revue du monde noir* in 1932, is much lesser-known than her male counterparts from the *négritude* movement, concluding that she is "trop mulâtres, trop assimilés, trop catholiques" (too light skinned, too assimilated, too Catholic) for the political landscape that followed this generation.[59] Even their invocation seems to invite the backlash of firmer identities. The experimental jazz age gave way to harsher political climates around the world: according to Denis Pelletier and Jean-Louis Schlegel, after the global events of 1968, official Catholicism became more and more conservative, and leftist Catholics multiplied and radicalized, distancing themselves from religion.[60] Tanella Boni, a scholar of Nardal from Côte d'Ivoire, also highlights how Nardal's framing of her intellectual and political work in terms of her *amis* obscured their power dynamics and suggested a relationship of equals, but this so-called friendship was exploited by those who later claimed the mantel of *négritude* without her and rendered it an almost exclusively male story.[61]

For these reasons these thinkers have remained obscure, but I bring their stories, their works, and their relationships back to life not only because they are Catholic but because without them we miss so much of the true narrative of the twentieth century. McKay was the first Black author with a best-selling novel, whose poem "If We Must Die" was *the* anthem of Black resistance; Marie-Magdeleine Davy was the first woman to study at the Institut Catholique; Gabriela Mistral was the first person from Latin America to win a Nobel Prize in Literature; Paulette Nardal was the first Black student at the Sorbonne; Louis Massignon was the first scholar to study Sufism in the West as a tradition inseparable from Islamic religion. But none of these were individual achievements: friendship powered their resolve, and their focus was energized by love and longing. Today, however, their humanism, their creative, non-orthodox Catholicism, their attention to friendship, and their avoidance of the topic of sex all appear a little stuffy, bourgeois, naive, romantic.

Dipesh Chakrabarty contextualizes leftist intellectuals' squeamishness around anything that seems poetic, mystical, or romantic. He notes, "The experience of fascism has left a certain trauma in leftist intellectuals in the West. They have ceded to fascists all moments of poetry, mysticism, and the religious and mysterious in all the construction of political sentiments and communities (however transient or inoperative). Romanticism now reminds them only of the Nazis." In India, Chakrabarty continues, "It would be sad if we ceded this entire heritage . . . out of a fear that our romanticism must be the same as whatever the Europeans produced under that name.

What, indeed, could be a greater instance of submission to a Eurocentric imagination than that fear?"[62] The men and women in this book were all connected to Europe in the years leading up to Nazism, and while they gravitated toward the mystical and romantic in their scholarship, they were also active in the resistance against both Nazism and European colonialism. The poetic, the mystical, and the interpersonal were central to their political work and to their goals of making a more humane and multicultural world. These somewhat esoteric artists were anti-modernists but not fascists. Their interest in spirituality, moreover, did not mean they were escapists. Nor did this particular set of friendship-obsessed medieval modernists necessarily pave the way for the therapeutic distillation of life into the pursuit of personal fulfillment and intense individual experience.[63]

Their mystical inclination, rather than didacticism, complicates the consideration of what kind of politics follows their tradition, and they have admittedly inspired a wide range of political commitment in their afterlives, on both the right and the left. But there are noteworthy, buried genealogies worth mentioning. The legacy of Catholic spiritual friendship is still with us in surprising and unexpected places. When I was a graduate student, for example, I worked for three years at the Greater Boston Interfaith Organization (GBIO), which was at the time led by the wonderful late Jim Drake. GBIO was a community organization affiliated with the Industrial Areas Foundation (IAF). Jim Drake would always say that terms like *the people* or *the poor* were abstractions, and we instead needed to keep *reality* in mind, which was only possible through relationships with real people, an idea central to IAF organizing principals. Within the broad umbrella organization of GBIO, I served at the Catholic parish of St. Peter's in Dorchester, a low-income Boston neighborhood, which was led by the inimitable Sister Sally McLoughlin and Father John Doyle. Father Doyle had spent time in Latin America in the 1980s and brought to the parish a vision of politically active Catholicism centered on the powerless. But as a member parish of GBIO, any campaign that St. Peter's became involved with began not with politics but by building what they called "relational power" in meetings between neighbors and stakeholders, referred to as "one-to-ones," who would simply get to know one another, learn about one another's values, and forge connections. From the ground up, these relational meetings helped turn the neighborhood surrounding St. Peter's into a powerful *community* where people knew one another, interpersonally, rather than a neglected urban context of powerless, isolated individuals. When I joined the parish, I talked to Sister Sally and Father Doyle about wanting to help and to empower, and they just smiled: *Just get to know our people first, just wait on all that. There is nothing you can do here without personal relationships.* So I did.

Jim Drake, Father Doyle, and Sister Sally taught me that personal relationships are *the* way to amass grassroots power. Relationships are not ends in themselves but the irreplaceable first step to change, and this is a belief that GBIO shares with all the community organizations today affiliated with the IAF, including many of the United States' most powerful networks of community organizing, like Faith in New York or PICO in Philadelphia. While it is not often acknowledged, the relational commitment at the heart of IAF traces its lineage to this Catholic culture of spiritual friendship from 1920 to 1960. The Industrial Areas Foundation was founded in the dock-yards of Chicago under the leadership of the Jewish organizer Saul Alinsky in Chicago, who was friends with Jacques Maritain. After Alinsky stepped down as head of the IAF in 1959, the young Catholic organizer Ed Chambers took over. The son of Irish immigrants, Chambers had been preparing for the priesthood in the Midwest and gone to France as a seminarian, where he was inspired by the creative, socially active Catholicism he encountered there. He met Henri de Lubac and many other leading thinkers of the Catholic avant-garde, and they left their mark.[64] When Chambers returned to the United States and reentered the seminary, he realized that the clerical system would never be the radical source of social change he then envisioned, so he left the seminary. He moved to Harlem and joined the Friendship House as a volunteer, a space so unlike the seminary and more akin to the radical Catholic utopianism he encountered in Paris and Lyon. While Chambers would eventually move on after feeling that the Friendship House, when under the leadership of Catherine de Hueck, was too "do gooder," the insights about the power of interpersonal relations as the foundational edifice for political power never left him. Chambers quickly discovered that some of the Friendship House's work, like passing out free clothing and shoes, did nothing to change the situation of Harlem's low-income Black community. But by building relationships with the people in Harlem (which was, after all, the main goal of FH), he learned about what would: better housing, safer neighborhoods, employment opportunities. Chambers gradually moved from direct service to community organizing, but it was real, on-the-ground relationships with actual neighbors in Harlem that sparked his insight, and the relationships forged at the Friendship House gave the neighborhood more power. When Chambers stepped in as the head of the IAF, he put relational meetings ("one-to-ones") at the core of the organization—and this meant real, interpersonal connection.

Chambers advises community organizers in *The Power of Relational Action* (2016), which he wrote before his death, "If you want one skill, you have to be disciplined to build relationships in public life, to be vulnerable, know what makes you tick, listen to what makes others tick, and there is initially a very low rate of return but you build up trust, connection, community that becomes the foundation of grassroots power." The language of Catholic spiritual friendship is everywhere in his framing of relational power, which unmistakably draws on his early years in Paris and Harlem: "The relational meeting," Chambers explains, "is not a science, not a technique, but an art form in which one spirit goes after another spirit to create connection, confrontation, and an exchange of talent and energy, eventually leading to some kind of joint action. Perhaps one-to-ones would be better named 'the mixing of human spirits.' Body and spirit, charms and personality, compassion and wit, humor and anger—in short, intense, human focused encounters."[65] His experiences as a community organizer were thoroughly interfaith rather than Catholic, but the former seminarian and volunteer never understood relationality in secular terms. Chambers notes,

> In the Abrahamic traditions of Judaism, Christianity, and Islam, humans are made in the *imago dei*, in the image and likeness of God, and as such are infused with divinity itself. It is a gift we are all given at birth. We have a spiritual inclination to interact with others and with the world, to reach out, to change, to correct, to build, to create, to procreate, to exercise power. With this relational power and mix inside of us, with divine power grounded in us, why don't we act more, make changes more often, relate more effectively, and start transforming the world?[66]

The way Chambers speaks of the spiritual and political power of interpersonal relationships can only be understood in the larger matrix of Catholic spiritual friendship in which Chambers was immersed in the 1940s and 1950s, both in France and at the Friendship House. This is one hugely important legacy of the culture of Catholic spiritual friendship.

Other examples are less direct. In researching this book, I traveled to archives, convents, and monasteries and corresponded with older men and women for whom these people are still a living memory. I had the distinct sense that there remains, in some ways, an underground Catholic holy geography and cosmology lit up by memories of the men and women in this book. There are people—never in the media and rarely present in academia—all over the world who feel spiritually bonded to the individuals

I came to know in my research. I would hear from them on the anniversary of Massignon's death or McKay's baptism. Relatives sought me out to give me small precious objects that were important to their aunts and uncles, who were perhaps spiritual friends with Massignon or the Maritains, which they couldn't quite throw it away. People have handed me pictures of Jacques Maritain, a signed check from Raïssa Maritain, and funeral cards, items that were treated like relics and, at least for someone, sometime, accessed the grace of the departed.

The fact that some of these strong feelings still linger means that this world is only now transitioning from living memory to history. Sometimes, the power of these living memories have actually made it harder to study this community and assimilate them into mainstream scholarship. The feelings are so strong that they wall people out. Elizabeth Horan, the preeminent scholar of Gabriela Mistral in the United States, claims that Doris Dana had the rights to all Mistral's papers after her death, but because she was paranoid and possessive and did not have Mistral's gifts in the arts of friendship, Dana was never able to establish a legacy for Mistral. Now that Doris Dana's nieces have given these papers to a publicly accessible archive in Chile, this is changing. Once I received an email from a wealthy French farmer who wanted to see me in New York. He came to my office and said that before Jacques Maritain died, he gave 1,400 letters written between him and Raïssa to a monk of the Little Brothers of the Poor. This monk loved Jacques so much that he only gave them to one person who promised secrecy, and they are not publicly available. The farmer wondered if I can help get them. The passionate friendship between Mary Kahil and Louis Massignon was so divisive and, for Kahil, painful that she burned most of their correspondence. These strong feelings circulating in this world, then and now, have made it in some places impenetrable.

More impressionistically, one recent book that surprisingly exhibits something akin to this world of spiritual friendship is Patti Smith's extraordinary *Just Kids*, which discusses her friendship with the Catholic-raised artist Robert Mapplethorpe that began in 1967. Their bond defied categorization: briefly lovers, creative collaborators, Mapplethorpe and Smith were soulmates, kindred spirits, and muses for one another. Their bond had an artistic and mystical dimension that countered the mainstream modes of relationality and identity. Despite its experimental, ephemeral nature, traces of Catholic spiritual friendship continue to surface unexpectedly in sources like this.

But even for the parts of this movement that did flop, fade, and fail, I think of David Tracy's new theological work *Fragments*. He returns to the notion of the fragment as that which is buried, forgotten, and exiled in Christian history, which can alert people to unknown fragments in their own traditions that can, if recovered, become resources for their lives and their thinking.[67] By unearthing people and communities that have been ignored and dismissed as failures and sentimental, unrealistic dreamers, we can exhume these alternatives to conventional understandings of success in our own society. By finding histories that are merely fragments, weak, exiled—stories that do not lead us directly to the centers of power in our own day—we resist conforming to what is already celebrated.[68] Tracy also uses *fragment* in another sense, as in some buried aspects of history are *fragmenting* and possess the capacity to break things open. I love the boldness of Tracy's invitation to try and "blast the marginalized fragments of the past alive with the memories of suffering and hope" and release them from their "seeming coherent place in the grand narratives we have imposed upon them. Learn to live joyfully, not despairingly, with and in the fragments of traditions we *do* in fact possess."[69] Tracy identifies Walter Benjamin and Simone Weil as the quintessential intellectuals who were geniuses at the art of recovering lost, even repressed, fragments in modernity, which they hoped could point to new ways of being in the world. I think all the men and women in this book—Weil and Benjamin's contemporaries and, in some cases, friends—were also mining for lost fragments: Mistral's poetry about Saint Francis and Teresa of Ávila; Maritain's work on Thomas Aquinas; Davy's studies of Cistercian mystics and her translations of Gershom Scholem's kabbalah writings, which broke apart a purely ethical reading of religion; McKay's writing on the beach-dwelling dockworkers of Marseilles and his late-in-life interest in recovering the African history of Christianity; Louis Massignon's scholarship on al-Hallāj; Ellen Tarry's recovery of the stories of people like Pierre Toussaint, a formerly enslaved man who became a philanthropist and hero in New York City and potential future Catholic saint. They mined for the fragments of past kindred spirits who, once recovered through writing, might offer spiritual and ethical alternatives to the violent undertow of modernity. All the while, they did this work in the context of their own lives that were thoroughly and utterly saturated with friendship.

The relational lives of these women and men came to me mostly in fragments as well, through bits and pieces in letters, on tombstones, in out-of-print journals and books, but eventually I saw that these fragments pointed to a vast, underground relational religious worldview and practice that was central to a particularly creative and global strain of Catholic modernity. But they were also *fragmenting*, in Tracy's sense, and offer a striking alternative to many of the ideas that prevail in our own time: the modern ideology of isolation that prioritizes the self-made man or woman, a bottled-up version of masculinity, and a world where we are better left alone, with our border sealed and gates locked, left to find pleasure in our own private family lives.[70] The lives and relationships of these men and women worked against this skimpy kind of love. These fragmenting stories of spiritual friendship bring us beneath the surface of the formal history of ideas to the sensuous undercurrent of this entire culture. To consider the intimacies of spiritual friendship turns our attention from Catholic ideas and institutions and directs it toward something more vital. Friendship was the stuff of life, action, vivid feeling, and sensuality. It endowed their world with a sense of the sacred and helped them imagine another world beyond it.

ACKNOWLEDGMENTS

My students at Fordham University coaxed this book out of me, and it is my pleasure to thank them here. When I began teaching, I gathered from my undergraduates that the thinkers of early and midcentury Catholicism were difficult to connect with. I would admit to the students that yes, Jacques Maritain's Thomism could be a bit dry and Henri de Lubac's homilies did seem to belong to another era, but their *lives* were so full and interesting, especially their friendships. My students, of course, loved if I filled up class time by rhapsodizing about the spiritual and political meanings these people gave to friendship (instead of asking them what the readings meant). So I started experimenting with assigning things that gave them glimpses into the world of friendship, like letters and eulogies, and writing short lectures about them. It shifted things. I sensed that for my college-aged students friendship was among the most important things in their own lives too, but they never considered that it was anything other than an escape from the pressures of family and school. My students also picked up on the queerness that ran through this whole world, and they invited me to give a lecture on spiritual friendship at the inaugural IgnatianQ Conference held at Fordham in 2014, a student-led conference that focuses on the intersections of faith, sexuality, and social justice in a Jesuit campus. At the time, I had abandoned the thought that my scholarship—focused on dusty archival boxes in France and weird mystical literature—would ever have meaning to student activists. But my students held my ideas as I nervously handed them over and helped show *me* why they were important to people who feel boxed in by the existing relational options of the contemporary landscape. I would never have dared to think that these stories mattered without them, and for that I will always be deeply grateful.

I am so thankful to friends, mentors, colleagues, generous acquaintances, and archivists who helped me turn these ideas into a book. Constance Furey above all has been an incredibly caring mentor, a generous friend, and a creative, energizing interlocutor over the years. She assured me I have the seeds of a book when I felt like I had a mess of notes fueled only by intuition. She helped me figure out logistics at critical stages and encouraged me to the finish line when I was certain I would never ever cross it. She read the entire manuscript and offered feedback. It's not that the book would be different without Constance, but there would be no book without her, and I'm deeply grateful. The scholarship and friendship of Bob Orsi is evident in the preceding pages too, above all his insight long ago about the importance of relationships in the study of religion. And more than that I am grateful to Bob for so many meaningful conversations and for his care for John and me over the years, and for inviting me to reflect publicly on these ideas: first as a contributor for his "Real Presences: Catholic Prayer as Intersubjectivity" forum, and then at Northwestern where I presented these ideas and benefited from thoughtful and incisive feedback. Conversations with Bob more recently about sexuality in Catholicism have pushed me, and I'm thankful for the ways he challenged me. My profound thanks also extend to Stephen Schloesser, who early on supported my work, sometimes even describing my projects to me in ways that were much better than I did. Steve remains such a light in the world of twentieth-century Catholic intellectual history: his creativity and generosity are without parallel. Amy Hollywood, years ago, gave me the names of some of the medievalist women who appear in this book, assuring me that there were stories waiting to be told. I'm always so grateful for conversations with Amy.

I have been fortunate to study Catholic intellectual history when so many scholars are stretching our field, working to create more diverse and inclusive narratives. I'm grateful to my friend Michael Lee at Fordham with whom I co-taught a class on global Catholicism among Latin America, the United States, and France, which gave us both a completely new understanding of the international circuits of thinking and activism in the middle of the twentieth century. Thanks also to Luc Schokkaert, Jos Claeys, and Gerd-Rainer Horn, who organized a conference on progressive Catholicism between Latin America and Europe at Leuven University. From the conference, I'm especially grateful to Susana Monreal from Uruguay and José Zanca from Argentina for pointing me to key resources. Many thanks too to Kathleen Cummings and Peter Cajka for the wonderful Global Catholic History Conference at Notre Dame, where I was fortunate to present a portion of this work and get valuable feedback. Thanks especially to Ruth Harris and Hillary Kaell for their insights there, and to my wonderful friends Florian Michel and Jane Doering for conversations about our shared work and for Jane's magnanimous hospitality. Thank you to Thomas Kselman for his hospitality as well, and for his generous response to my work on Massignon's friendships. I'm also grateful to Atalia Omer for the religion and modernity conference she organized and for being such a smart and caring interlocuter. Special thanks to J. Kameron Carter who, at that conference, offered timely advice and encouragement on my work on Claude McKay right when I needed it. Richard Crane, Vicki Caron, Sister Celia Deutsch, and Father Lawrence Frizzell have been valued colleagues about Catholic anti-Semitism and resistance in Europe. I learned so much from fellow panelists on Black Catholic internationalism at the American Catholic Historical Association conference: Vaughn Booker, Alexia Williams, and James Padilioni. I'm thankful to a whole crew of other people who study religion in the twentieth century, who have enlivened my work with fun and discussion over the years: Marian Ronan, Niloofar Haeri, Michelle Molina, Julie Byrne, Catherine Osborne, Elayne Oliphant, Kathleen Cummings, Paula Kane, Maggie McGuinness, Katie Holscher, Sarah Shortall, and James Chappel.

My research has relied on so many guides into distant lands. Many thanks to Anthony O'Mahony in England, who truly guided me through the labyrinthine world of Louis Massignon and the Catholic approaches to Islam. Anthony's generosity with his own wealth of knowledge has been profound and transformative, something for which I am deeply grateful. I'm thankful also to Anthony for his hospitality in London and for connecting me to Christian Krokus and Sister D. Agnes Wilkins, from whom I also learned so much about Massignon. Along similar lines, Elizabeth Horan has been an extraordinary guide into the complex, fascinating world of the Chilean writer Gabriela Mistral. Her own scholarship is so rich that it set me on my path, and she also kindly read my chapter and offered many generous comments. Marc-Alain Descamps of Paris was an incredible correspondent about Marie-Magdeleine Davy. I'm so grateful for the time he spent sharing his knowledge about his late friend, and especially for sending me to the Archives départementales des Deux-Sèvres in Niort, France. In addition to the archivists at Deux-Sèvres, my thanks go to archivists and librarians elsewhere, whose correspondences and professionalism made this book possible: the Claude McKay Collection at Yale's Beinecke Rare Book and Manuscript Library, the Schomburg Center for Research in Black Culture, the Ann Harrigan Makletzoff Papers at the University of Notre Dame Archives, and the Archivo Gabriela Mistral at the Biblioteca Nacional Digital de Chile.

Closer to home, it has been wonderful to be a part of the Class 200 series at the University of Chicago Press, especially due to Kyle Wagner and series editors Katie Lofton and John Modern, who have all been fabulous each step of the way. The creativity they bring to our field has alighted me with inspiration. Tracy Fessenden read the entire manuscript at the early and the late stages, and she responded so generously and incisively to my evolving ideas. Tracy's feedback along with her own scholarship were absolute gems, and I'm very grateful to her. Thank you also to the two other anonymous readers for their careful reports. My sincere thanks also to Elizabeth Ellingboe and Barbie Halaby for their wonderful editing work.

At Fordham, I am so thankful to have participated in reading group discussions about critical theory and theology over a period of many years with colleagues George Demacopoulos, Brad Hinze, Ben Dunning, Telly Papanikolaou, Bob Davis, and Sam Haddad. I learned so much from them, and they each generously thought with me aloud as I worked through tangles in my thinking and panicked, especially about sexuality and friendship, for which I am thankful to Ben in particular. Our department chair, Patrick Hornbeck, is a champion for all of us, and I'm so grateful for his support and leadership while I worked on this project. It is a pleasure also to thank Kathy Kueny, who generously read my Massignon chapter and offered valuable feedback. Our department has not been the same without our beloved friend Jim Fisher, but I'll always be grateful to Jim for his encouragement on this book and for showing me what another kind of scholarly presence might look like. In our department, I'm grateful also for conversations with Kathryn Reklis, Bryan Massingale, Sarit Kattan Gribetz, and Jeannine Hill Fletcher. More recently, several wonderful women at Fordham outside of my department enriched my scholarly life while I finished the book and buoyed me with encouragement and inspired me in their dedication to our students and community, especially Sara Lehman, Orit Avishai, Rachel Annunziato, Eve Keller, and Ava Gagliardi. I have been fortunate to have had excellent student research assistants at Fordham, including Eric Martin and Mary Kate Holman, along with Menios Papadimitriou, who helped with the endnotes. I also thank Rohini Parthasarathy, who served as an undergraduate researcher on the life of Claude McKay and the Friendship House, and I'm thankful to Fordham's Office of Undergraduate Research for the support of Rohini's work. Thank you also to the Ames Foundation for travel funds at Fordham, and to the American Philosophical Society and the American Academy of Religion Travel Grant.

I thought about Natalia Imperatori-Lee and Maureen O'Connell often as

I wrote. Their love and care over the years have constantly been a center of gravity: when I bring these two the chaos and uncertainty of my book, my life, and the world, I come away feeling relief, clarity, and a renewed sense of purpose, and I thank them for everything. In this way I'm also grateful to our house church community too, Natalia, Michael Lee, Brad Hinze, and Christine Hinze, for their friendship and love. I am thankful for the friendship of Mara Willard, Tamsin Jones, and Rachel Smith, especially for their help early on with the ideas in the book at the "Smith Symposiums" we created so long ago. Mary Dunn and Carrie Fuller have been such beloved companions for reflection on the topics I explore and so, so much else. I thank all these people for their love and support.

I am also grateful to several contemplative communities who have welcomed me over the years, providing desperately needed stretches of silence for thinking and writing, spaces that also connected me, in a way, to the monastic-loving people I was writing about. Thanks especially to the Benedictine Abbey of Regina Laudis in Bethlehem, CT; the Benedictines of Stanbrook Abbey in York, England; the Anglican Benedictine nuns of St. Mary's Abbey in West Malling, England; the convent of St. Birgitta in Darien, CT; the Dominican Sisters of Hope of the Center at Mariandale in Ossining, NY; and the Sisters of St. Ursula at the Linwood Spiritual Center in Rhinebeck, NY. I am utterly useless on my own, so I truly could not have written this book without these communities structuring my quiet focus. And in a different way, the Little Sisters of the Assumption, an order more active than contemplative, are founders of the amazing organization LSA Family Services in East Harlem, which has been a welcome place where I see the ideals of the book embodied in another context. I'm grateful especially to Sister Margaret Leonard's creative thinking on the topic of mutuality and for all the staff at LSA for welcoming us in.

Deep thanks too to friends and family outside of the worlds of religion and the academy, who have been such a steady stream of adventure, care, and laughter, renewing my spirits as I was in the tough slog of writing: Courtney, Jeanne, Louisa, Leslie, and their families make parenting and *life* so much more fun and meaningful, along with Francesca and Kendra, and the Lynch family, who made our time in London so memorable. Love and gratitude to my own family, our parents, Tim, Keasha, Art, Neal, and Barb, for their support, encouragement, and love of our kids, along with Jamie, Janel, Chris, Jylene, Matt, Anita, and their children. Heartfelt thanks too to my wonderful cousins Emily and Sara, lifelong sources of laughter and support.

Above all, a sky-high mountain of thanks and love to John Seitz, who made this book possible and enriched everything in my life outside it too. He read the chapters several times in their entirety, helped me unravel lines of argument, and tightened my prose with utter candor and complete grace. He encouraged me when I doubted, reminding me that these stories were important and that I should tell them. He protected my solitude when I needed it, and because of his sense of adventure, his love, and his care, he has helped create a life that feels so abundant in the best way. It is a joy to parent with John our two wonderful children Tavia and Jonah. The book seemed to move so slowly, but everything with Tavia and Jonah moved quickly, and as they grew bigger each year, they occasionally asked about the book and waited for me when I had to slip away to tend to it. But to my great joy, they mercifully filled my heart and mind with so many other things, just the wonderful stuff of their lives. My deepest devotion and gratitude to John, Tavia, and Jonah.

Finally, my thanks to the community of people I describe in this book, for giving me secondhand the pleasures of the creativity and courage of the lives. I began writing in earnest after the 2016 election, a context of rising xenophobia around the world. I was grateful to immerse myself in the stories of their resistance in the 1930s and 1940s. Now, I am finishing the book in the midst of two new contexts of total upheaval: the nation and the globe rising in rebellion to centuries of oppression of Black lives, sparked by the killing of George Floyd and so many others, and the COVID-19 pandemic. The men and women in this book speak again. Claude McKay and Ellen Tarry, in chapter 5, wrote about race and police brutality eighty years ago in language that could describe our own world with detailed precision. Men and women in other chapters lived lives that were thrown off course by the disasters and violence of wars and the Holocaust in the past century. Friendships were their center of gravity, but when many could no longer see one another face-to-face, they threw themselves into letter-writing and the pleasures of memory, which fueled their work. The wonderful late scholar Bernard Doering once told me that that best thing about becoming a scholar of Jacques and Raïssa Maritain and their community is that they will be lifelong companions, in an inner sense. This has been so true, and despite their imperfections and shortcomings, I hold a spot of profound respect and affection for each of the men and women in this book. I am grateful for the companionship they have provided me, and it is an honor to finally share their stories.

NOTES

When not otherwise noted, translations are my own.

INTRODUCTION

1. William Christian, *Divine Presence in Spain and Western Europe 1500–1960: Visions, Religious Images and Photographs* (Budapest: Central European University Press, 2016), 91.
2. Christian, *Divine Presence*, 92.
3. Peter Brown, *The Cult of the Saints* (Chicago: University of Chicago Press, 1981), chap. 3; Peter Brown, "The Saint as Exemplar in Late Antiquity," in *Saints and Virtues*, ed. John Stratton Hawley (Los Angeles: University of California Press, 1987), 3–14.
4. Marie-Magdeleine Davy's name is often spelled Marie-Madeleine and abbreviated simply as "M.M." I follow the guide of Davy archivist Armelle Dutruc and use Marie-Magdeleine throughout. See Armelle Dutruc, *Marie-Magdeleine Davy (1903–1998) ou l'Orient intérieur: Répertoire numérique détaillé des archives de Marie-Magdeleine Davy* (Niort: Archives Départementales des Deux-Sèvres, 2012), 8. For more on Davy, see her memoir, Marie-Magdeleine Davy, *Traversée en solitaire*, ed. Marc-Alain Descamps (Paris: Albin Michel, 1989). See also Marc-Alain Descamps and Jacques d'Ares, *Marie-Magdeleine Davy, ou la liberté du dépassement* (Paris: Le Miel de la Pierre, 2001), along with the shorter but useful Étienne Fouilloux, "Marie-Magdeleine Davy," in *Destins de Femmes: Religion, culture, et société (France, XIXe–XXe siècles)*, ed. Anne Cova and Bruno Dumons (Paris: Letouzey et Ané, 2011), 144–45. For some brief works in English, see Bernard McGinn, "'The Violent are Taking It by Storm' (Mt. 11:12): Reflections on a Century of Women's Contributions to the Study of Mystical Spirituality," *Spiritus: A Journal of Christian Spirituality* 13, no. 1 (2013): 17–35; Brenna Moore, "Into the Catacombs of the Past: Women and Wartime Trauma in the French Catholic *Ressourcement* Project (1939–1945)," in *God's Mirror: Renewal and Engagement in French Catholic Intellectual Culture in the Mid-Twentieth-Century*, ed. K. Davies and T. Garfitt (New York: Fordham University Press, 2015), 186–209.

5. Paul Elie, *The Life You Save May Be Your Own: An American Pilgrimage* (New York: Farrar, Straus and Giroux, 2004).

6. Michel de Certeau, "Massignon pèlerin et professeur," *Libération*, December 2, 1983.

7. Jean Sarocchi, "Louis Massignon et Gabriel Marcel," in *Massignon et ses contemporains*, ed. Jacques Keryell (Paris: Karthala, 1997), 211.

8. My thinking here is indebted to Constance Furey, *Poetic Relations: Intimacy and Faith in the English Reformation* (Chicago: University of Chicago Press, 2017), 4–20.

9. Tracy Fessenden, *Culture and Redemption: Religion, the Secular, and American Literature* (Princeton, NJ: Princeton University Press), 64. For helping me think about friendship in this more expansive way, I am indebted to Frédéric Gugelot's innovative work on the "spiritual families" created by the European intellectuals who converted to Catholicism in the early twentieth century, "Le temps des convertis, signe et trace de la modernité religieuse au début du xxe siècle," *Archives de sciences sociales des religions* 119 (2002): 45–64. My thinking is also shaped here by Robert A. Orsi's work on religion as relationship in *Between Heaven and Earth: The Religious Worlds People Make and the Scholars Who Study Them* (Princeton, NJ: Princeton University Press, 2005), 1–19; and Constance Furey, "Body, Society, and Subjectivity in Religious Studies," *Journal of the American Academy of Religion* 80, no. 1 (March 2012): 7–33. See also Robert Orsi, *History and Presence* (Cambridge, MA: Harvard University Press, 2016), especially 72–112. I initially explored these materials in Brenna Moore, "Friendship and the Cultivation of Religious Sensibilities," *Journal of the American Academy of Religion* 83, no. 2 (May 2015): 237–63.

10. Pierre van der Meer de Walcheren, *Rencontres* (Paris: Desclée de Brouwer, 1961), 37.

11. My thinking on the political power of these mixed friendships has been influenced by Leela Gandhi, *Affective Communities: Anticolonial Thought, Fin-de-Siècle Radicalism, and the Politics of Friendship* (Durham, NC: Duke University Press, 2005), 12, 116.

12. For more on the language of homogenous kinship and conservative politics in France, see Camille Robcis, *The Law of Kinship: Anthropology, Psychoanalysis, and the Family in France* (Ithaca, NY: Cornell University Press, 2013). See also Lloyd S. Kramer, "Religion, Sacrifice, and National Life," in *Nationalism in Europe and America: Politics, Cultures, and Identities since 1775* (Chapel Hill: University of North Carolina Press, 2011), 81–101.

13. Claude McKay, *Amiable with Big Teeth: A Novel of the Love Affair between the Communists and the Poor Black Sheep of Harlem* (New York: Penguin, 2017). For more on the incredible story of the recent discovery of this unpublished manuscript, see Jennifer Wilson, "A Forgotten Novel Reveals a Forgotten Harlem." *Atlantic*, March 9, 2017, https://www.theatlantic.com/entertainment/archive/2017/03/a-forgotten-novel-reveals-a-forgotten-harlem/518364/.

14. Ann Harrigan, "A Study in Fear," box 3, folder 22, Ann Harrigan Makletzoff Papers (MAK), University of Notre Dame Archives, Notre Dame, IN.

15. "B [the Baroness, Catherine de Hueck Doherty's nickname] taught me so much, especially what not to do. I often marvel that B had the nerve to venture out on an uncharted course with no knowledge of the people she was supposed to serve." Letter from Ellen Tarry to Betty Schneider, dated 1988, box 1, folder 28, Ellen Tarry Papers, Schomburg Center for Research in Black Culture, New York.

16. For more on this issue, see Barbara Caine, ed., *Friendship: A History* (London: Equinox Press, 2009).

17. Arvind-Pal S. Mandair, *Religion and the Specter of the West: Sikhism, India, Postcoloniality, and the Politics of Translation* (New York: Columbia University Press, 2009), xv.

18. For biographical information on Mary Kahil, see Jacques Keryell, *Mary Kahil, une grande dame d'Egypte (1889–1979)* (Paris: Geunther, 2010); Margot Badran, *Feminists, Islam, and Nation: Gender and the Making of Modern Egypt* (Princeton, NJ: Princeton University Press, 1995), 96–114; Agnes Wilkins, "Mary Kahil and the Encounter Between Christianity and Islam," *Downside Review* 135, no. 3 (2017): 131–43.

19. College Notre Dame de Nazareth, "Historique," accessed September 10, 2016, http://www.ndn.edu.lb/?q=page/historique.

20. Letter from Louis Massignon to Mary Kahil, February 9, 1935, in *L'hospitalité sacrée*, ed. Jacques Keryell, with a preface by René Voillaume (Paris: Nouvelle Cité, 1987), 101.

21. See Elizabeth Horan's introduction to Gabriela Mistral, *Motivos: The Life of St. Francis*, ed. and trans. Elizabeth Horan (Tempe, AZ: Bilingual Review Press, 2013). I am grateful to Dr. Horan's correspondence and guidance on the issue of Mistral's education and encounter with French literature.

22. Gabriela Mistral and Victoria Ocampo, *This America of Ours: The Letters of Gabriela Mistral and Victoria Ocampo*, ed. and trans. Elizabeth Horan and Doris Meyer (Austin: University of Texas Press, 2003).

23. Samuli Schielke and Liza Debevec, eds., *Ordinary Lives and Grand Schemes: An Anthropology of Everyday Religion* (New York: Berghahn Books, 2012).

24. Carolyn Forché, *Twentieth Century Poetry of Witness* (New York: Norton Press, 1993), 31.

25. Elisa Camiscioli, *Reproducing the French Race: Immigration, Intimacy, and Embodiment in the Early Twentieth Century* (Durham, NC: Duke University Press, 2009), 1.

26. Langston Hughes, *Collected Works*, edited by Christopher C. De Santis (Columbia: University of Missouri Press, 2002), 9:31, quoted in Michael Goebel, *Anti-Imperial Metropolis: Interwar Paris and the Seeds of Third-World Nationalism* (Cambridge: Cambridge University Press, 2015), 1. See also Jennifer Anne Boittin, *Colonial Metropolis: The Urban Grounds of Anti-Imperialism and Feminism in Interwar Paris* (Lincoln: University of Nebraska Press, 2010); for an analysis of the postwar period, see Félix F. Germain, *Decolonizing the Republic: African and Caribbean Migrants in Postwar Paris, 1946–1974* (East Lansing: Michigan State University Press, 2016). For a more conceptual overview, see Rita Chin, *The Crisis of Multiculturalism in Europe* (Princeton, NJ: Princeton University Press, 2017).

27. Paula Hyman, *The Jews of Modern France* (Berkeley: University of California Press, 1998).

28. Goebel, *Anti-Imperial Metropolis*, 29. I am also deeply grateful for correspondence with Elizabeth Horan on the details concerning Spanish-speaking networks in interwar Paris.

29. Gotz Nordburch and Umar Ryad, "Introduction: Toward a Translational History of Islam and Muslims in Interwar Europe," in *Transnational Islam in Interwar Europe: Muslim Activists and Thinkers*, ed. Gotz Nordburch and Umar Ryad (London: Palgrave Macmillan, 2014), 3.

30. Bekim Agai, Umar Ryad, and Mehdi Sajid, *Muslims in Interwar Europe: A Transcultural Historical Perspective* (Leiden: Brill, 2016).

31. Transcript reprinted in James Baldwin and Raoul Peck, *I Am Not Your Negro: A Companion Edition to the Documentary Film Directed by Raoul Peck* (New York: Vintage Books), 88.

32. Boittin, *Colonial Metropolis*, 93.

33. Brent Hayes Edwards, *The Practice of Diaspora: Literature, Translation, and the Rise of Black Internationalism* (Cambridge, MA: Harvard University Press, 2003), 4.

34. I am indebted here to Edward Said's "Reflections on Exile" in *Reflections on Exile and Other Essays* (Cambridge, MA: Harvard University Press, 2000), 173.

35. Letter from Gabriela Mistral to Victoria Ocampo, August 1937, in Mistral and Ocampo, *This America of Ours*, 45.

36. Quoted in Michael Fabre, "Claude McKay and the Two Faces of France," in *From Harlem to Paris: Black American Writers in France, 1840–1980* (Champaign: University of Illinois Press, 1991), 96. See also William Shack, *Harlem in Montmartre: A Paris Jazz Story between the Great Wars* (Berkeley: University of California Press, 2001).

37. Anson Rabinbach, "Paris, Capital of Anti-Fascism," in *The Modernist Imagination: Intellectual History and Critical Theory: Essays in Honor of Martin Jay*, ed. Warren Breckman, Peter E. Gordon, A. Dirk Moses, Samuel Moyn, and Elliot Neaman (New York: Berghahn Books, 2011), 184.

38. Dorothy West, *Where the Wild Grape Grows: Selected Writings, 1930–1950* (Amherst: University of Massachusetts Press, 2004), 207.

39. Quoted in Patricia Rubio, "Constructions of the Self: The Personal Letters of Gabriela Mistral," in *Gabriela Mistral: The Audacious Traveler*, ed. Marjorie Agosín (Athens: Ohio University Press, 2003), 204.

40. Letter from Raïssa Maritain to Charles Journet, January 24, 1940, in Charles Journet and Jacques Maritain, *Journet–Maritain Correspondance*, vol. 3, *1940–1949* (Paris: Éditions Saint-Augustin, 1996), 42–44.

41. R. Maritain, *Les grandes amitiés*, in J. Maritain and R. Maritain, *Oeuvres complètes* (Paris: Saint-Paul, 1995), 14:625–26.

42. Stephen Schloesser, "From Mystique to Théologique: Messiaen's 'ordre nouveau,' 1935–1939," in *God's Mirror: Renewal and Engagement in French Catholic Intellectual Culture in the Mid-Twentieth Century*, ed. Katherine Davies and Toby Garfitt (New York: Fordham University Press, 2014), 129–61; Stephen Schloesser, "The Rise of a Mystic Modernism: Maritain and the Sacrificed Generation of the Twenties," in *The Maritain Factor: Taking Religion into Interwar Modernism*, ed. Rajesh Heynickx and Jan De Maeyer (Leuven, Belgium: Leuven University Press, 2010), 28–39; Stephen Schloesser, *Jazz-Age Catholicism: Mystic Modernism in Postwar Paris, 1919–1933* (Toronto: University of Toronto Press, 2005).

43. Joseph Roth, *Report from a Parisian Paradise: Essays from France, 1925–1939* (New York: W. W. Norton, 2005), 99.

44. Vicki Caron, *Uneasy Asylum: France and the Jewish Refugee Crisis, 1933–1942* (Stanford, CA: Stanford University Press, 1998), 216–17, 288–89.

45. Mark Antliff, *Avant-Garde Fascism: The Mobilization of Myth, Art, and Culture in France, 1909–1939* (Durham, NC: Duke University Press, 2007); see also Romy Golan, *Modernity and Nostalgia* (New Haven, CT: Yale University Press, 1995).

46. Bernard Wall, "Tradition and Social Justice," *Dublin Review*, April 1937, 258, 261; Jay P. Corrin, "Catholic Writers on the Right," *Chesterton Review* 25, no. 1/2 (1999): 81–101; Antliff, *Avant-Garde Fascism*; see also Golan, *Modernity and Nostalgia*. For a recent tracing of interwar neo-medievalism and nationalism to our own time, see the excellent essay, Andrew Elliot, "A Vile Love Affair: Right Wing Nationalism and the Middle Ages," *The Public Medievalist*, February 14, 2017, http://www.publicmedievalist.com/vile-love-affair/.

47. Antliff, *Avant-Garde Fascism*, 111.

48. Matthias Koening and Wolfgang Knobl, "Religion, Nationalism, and European Integration," in *Religion and National Identities in Enlarged Europe*, ed. Willfried Spohn, Matthias Koening, and Wolfgang Knobl (New York: Palgrave Macmillan, 2015), 120; Martin Blinkhorn, *Fascists and Conservatives: The Radical Right and the Establishment in Twentieth-Century Europe* (New York: Routledge, 1990), 14. Italy's well-known 1920s nationalist agenda and its embrace of Catholic neo-medieval aesthetics accompanied the Fascists' ban of literature on birth control and increased penalties for abortion in 1926, declaring both crimes against the state.

49. James Chappel, *Catholic Modern: The Challenge of Totalitarianism and the Remaking of the Church* (Cambridge, MA: Harvard University Press, 2018), 64.

50. Chappel, *Catholic Modern*.

51. Brent F. Nelsen and James L. Guth, *Religion and the Struggle for European Union: Confessional Culture and the Limits of Integration* (Washington, DC: Georgetown University Press, 2015). The Catholic genealogy of human rights has been celebrated by many Catholics; see, for instance, Mary Ann Glendon, "The Influence of Catholic Social Doctrine on Human Rights," *Journal of Catholic Social Thought* 10, no. 1 (2013): 69–84. For Samuel Moyn and others, however, this betrays the deep conservatism of human rights discourse and policy. Samuel Moyn, *Christian Human Rights* (Philadelphia: University of Pennsylvania Press, 2015).

52. Ralph Schor, *L'immigration en France, 1919–1939* (Nice: Université de Nice, 1986), 73.

53. Bernard Comte, *Initiatives de théologiens face à la persécution antisémite à Lyon en 1941–42* (Lyon: Institut Catholique, 1993), 15–16.

54. Darcie Fontaine, *Decolonizing Christianity: Religion and the End of Empire in France and Algeria* (Cambridge: Cambridge University Press, 2016), 5, 47. Fontaine also has a great section on the role of friendship more generally among Christian activists in Algeria and France who supported Algerian independence; see Fontaine, *Decolonizing Christianity*, 126.

55. On the Friendship House, see Karen J. Johnson, *One in Christ: Chicago Catholics and the Quest for Interracial Justice* (Oxford: Oxford University Press, 2018).

56. D. P. Resnick, "The Société des Amis des Noirs and the Abolition of Slavery," *French Historical Studies* 7 (1972): 558–69.

57. Thanks to Hillary Kaell for pointing me to this history, Dorothy R. Scheele, "The Friendship Train," accessed October 14, 2019, http://www.thefriendshiptrain1947.org/.

58. Dana Robert, "Cross-Cultural Friendship in the Creation of Twentieth-Century World Christianity," *International Bulletin of Missionary Research* 35 (2011): 100–107.

59. Claude McKay, "The Middle Ages," *Catholic Worker* 13 (May 1946).

60. Léon Bloy, *Lettres à ses filleuls, Jacques Maritain et Pierre van der Meer de Walcheren* (Paris: Stock, 1928), 78.

61. Jacques Maritain and Julien Green, *The Story of Two Souls: The Correspondence of Jacques Maritain and Julien Green*, ed. Henry Bars and Eric Jourdan, trans. with an intro. and rev. notes Bernard Doering (New York: Fordham University Press, 1988).

62. These extracts are taken from a work by Ali Shariati entitled "Kavir," quoted in Michel Cuypers, "Une rencontre mystique: Ali Shariati–Louis Massignon," *Mélanges de l'Institut dominicain d'études orientales* 21 (1993): 23. See also Anthony O'Mahony, "Mysticism and Politics: Louis Massignon, Shi'a Islam, Iran and Ali Shari'ati—A Muslim-Christian Encounter," in *University Lectures in Islamic Studies*, ed. Alan Jones (London: Oxford University Press, 1998), 2:113–34.

63. Letter from Mistral to Ocampo, September 1951, in Mistral and Ocampo, *This America of Ours*, 181.

64. Roland Barthes, *Roland Barthes* (New York: Hill and Wang, 2010), 64.

65. Frédéric Martel, *In the Closet of the Vatican: Power, Homosexuality, Hypocrisy* (New York: Bloomsbury Continuum, 2019).

66. Frédéric Martel, "Response: Catholics Don't Like the Truth," Syndicate Symposium for *In the Closet of the Vatican*, May 28, 2019, https://syndicate.network/symposia/theology /in-the-closet-of-the-vatican/. The full symposium and response is an excellent discussion of Martel's book.

67. Wesley Hill, *Spiritual Friendship: Finding Love in the Church as a Celibate Gay Christian* (Grand Rapids, MI: Brazos Press, 2015).

68. For more on the relationship between Jacques and Raïssa, see Brenna Moore, *Sacred Dread: Raïssa Maritain, the Allure of Suffering, and the French Catholic Revival, 1905–1944* (South Bend, IN: University of Notre Dame Press, 2013), chap. 5; Brenna Moore, "Out of the Shadows: Raïssa Maritain on Poetry and the Visibility of Violence," *The Wisdom of Youth: Essays Inspired by the Early Work of Jacques and Raïssa Maritain*, ed. Travis Dumsday (Washington, DC: Catholic University of America Press, 2016), 51–66.

69. Amy Hollywood, *Acute Melancholia and Other Essays: Mysticism, History, and the Study of Religion* (New York: Columbia University Press, 2016), 149–62.

70. Anthony Pinn, "Embracing Nimrod's Legacy: The Erotic, the Irreverence of Fantasy, and the Redemption of Black Theology," in *Religious Intimacies: Intersubjectivity in the Modern Christian West*, ed. Mary Dunn and Brenna Moore (Bloomington: Indiana University Press, 2020).

71. Louis Bayard, "So What If Lincoln Was Gay?," *Paris Review*, April 16, 2019, http://www .theparisreview.org/blog/2019/04/16/so-what-if-lincoln-was-gay/.

72. Claude McKay, *A Long Way from Home* (New Brunswick, NJ: Rutgers University Press, 2007), 88.

73. Saidiya Hartman, *Wayward Lives, Beautiful Experiments: Intimate Histories of Social Upheaval* (New York: W. W. Norton, 2019), 227. Emphasis added.

74. Paulette Nardal and Phillipe Grollemund, *Fiertés de femme noire: Entretiens / Mémoires de Paulette Nardal* (Paris: Éditions L'Harmattan, 2019), 43.

75. Maggie Nelson, *The Argonauts* (Minneapolis: Graywolf, 2016), 74.

76. Letter from Louis Massignon to Abd-el-Jalil, August 26, 1933, in *Massignon–Abd-*

el-Jalil: parrain et filleul, 1926–1962, ed. Françoise Jacquin (Paris: Éditions du Cerf, 2007), 99.

77. Kate Hennessy, *Dorothy Day: The World Will Be Saved By Beauty* (New York: Scribner, 2017).

78. Davy, *Traversée en solitaire*, 113.

79. Ann Harrigan Makletzoff, Unpublished Memoirs, box 3, Ann Harrigan Makletzoff Papers (MAK), University of Notre Dame Archives, Notre Dame, IN.

80. Mark Jordan, *Telling Truths in Church: Scandal, Flesh, and Christian Speech* (Boston: Beacon, 2003), 22.

81. Hannah Arendt, "Walter Benjamin 1982–1940," in *Men in Dark Times* (New York: Harvest, 1968), 203.

82. The phrase "utopian margins" comes from Avery F. Gordon, *Letters from the Utopian Margins: The Hawthorn Archive* (New York: Fordham University Press, 2017).

83. Kolbsheim replica, Jacques and Raïssa Maritain Archives, Kolbsheim, France.

84. Conversations with J. Michelle Molina at Northwestern University helped me see the significance of materiality in religious relationships, along with her own scholarship. See J. Michelle Molina, "Making a Home in an Unfortunate Place: Phenomenology and Religion," in *An Anthropology of Catholicism*, ed. Kristen Norget, Valentina Napolitano, and Maya Mayblin (Oakland: University of California Press, 2017), 256–72, and J. Michelle Molina, "Father of My Soul: Reason and Affect in a Shipboard Conversion Narrative," *Journal of Jesuit Studies* 2 (2015): 641–58.

85. For an excellent exception, see a new volume that includes essays about the legacies of scholars such as Mary Douglas, Caroline Walker Bynum, Wendy Doniger, and others to the study of religion, Sarah J. Bloesch and Meredith Minister, *Cultural Approaches to Studying Religion: An Introduction to Theories and Methods* (London: Bloomsbury Academic, 2019).

86. For histories of this theological movement, see Gregory Baum, ed., *The Twentieth Century: A Theological Overview* (Maryknoll, NY: Orbis, 1999); Brian E. Daly, "Knowing God in History and in the Church: *Dei Verbum* and '*Nouvelle Théologie*,'" in *Ressourcement: A Movement For Renewal in Twentieth-Century Catholic Theology*, ed. Gabriel Flynn and Paul D. Murray (Oxford: Oxford University Press, 2014); Joseph Famerée, *L'ecclésiologie d'Yves Congar avant Vatican II: Histoire et Église* (Leuven, Belgium: Leuven University Press, 1992), 107; Gabriel Flynn, "*Ressourcement*, Ecumenism, and Penumatology: The Contribution of Yves Congar to *Nouvelle Théologie*," in Flynn and Murray, *Ressourcement*; Étienne Fouilloux, *Une Église en quête de liberté: La pensée catholique française entre modernisme et Vatican II (1914–1962)* (Paris: Desclée de Brouwer, 1998); Paul McPartlan, "*Ressourcement*, Vatican II, and Eucharistic Ecclesiology," in Flynn and Murray, *Ressourcement*; Jürgen Mettepenningen, "*Nouvelle Théologie*: Four Historical Stages of Theological Reform towards *Ressourcement* (1935–1965)," in Flynn and Murray, *Ressourcement*. Though the narrative tends to be clerical, there are still buried histories of understudied priests and theologians that still need to be told; see, for example, the important work of Mary Kate Holman, "The Signs of the Times in the Life and Thought of Marie Dominique Chenu" (PhD diss., Fordham University, 2020).

87. See Ann Braude, "Women's History Is American Religious History," in *Retelling U.S. Religious History*, ed. Thomas A. Tweed (Berkeley: University of California Press, 1997), 87–107; Judith Weisenfeld, "Invisible Women: On Women and Gender in the Study of African American Religious History," *Journal of Africana Religions* 1, no. 1 (2013): 133–49; Mia Bay, Farah Griffin, Martha Jones, and Barbara Savage, eds., *Toward an Intellectual History of Black Women* (Chapel Hill: University of North Carolina Press, 2015)

88. Marie-Lise Gazarian-Gautier, *Gabriela Mistral: The Teacher from the Valley of Elqui* (Chicago: Franciscan Herald Press, 1975), 132.

89. Recent books on *ressourcement*—the otherwise excellent work of Jurgen Mettepenningen, *Nouvelle Theologie: Inheritor of Modernism* (London: T&T Clark, 2010), and Hans Boersema, *Nouvelle Théologie and Sacramental Ontology: A Return to Mystery* (Oxford: Oxford University Press, 2009)—set the stage for further investigation of women's contributions.

90. Kennetta Hammond Perry and Kira Thurman, "Black Europe: A Useful Category of Historical Analysis," *Black Perspectives*, December 20, 2016, http://www.aaihs.org/black-europe-a-useful-category-of-historical-analysis.

91. Tyrone Tillery, *Claude McKay: A Black Poet's Struggle for Identity* (Amherst: University of Massachusetts Press, 1992).

92. Quoted in Tillery, *Claude McKay*, 145.

93. Claude McKay, "The Cycle," *Complete Poems*, ed. William J. Maxwell (Champaign: University of Illinois Press, 2004), 253.

94. Raïssa Maritain, "Deus excelsus terribilis," *Commonweal* 40, no. 24 (September 29, 1944): 563–66.

95. Michael Rothberg, *Multidirectional Memory: Remembering the Holocaust in the Age of Decolonization* (Stanford, CA: Stanford University Press, 2009).

96. John Connelly, *From Enemy to Brother* (Cambridge, MA: Harvard University Press, 2012).

97. Gabriela Mistral, "Footprint," in *Selected Poems of Gabriela Mistral*, ed. and trans. Ursula K. Le Guin (Albuquerque: University of New Mexico Press, 2003).

98. Maureen O'Connell, Ignatian Family Teach-In Address, November 8, 2015, Washington, DC, https://ignatiansolidarity.net/wp-content/uploads/2015/12/OConnell-IFTJ-address-.pdf.

99. Hilton Als, *White Girls* (San Francisco: McSweeney's Publishing, 2014), 138.

100. Hollywood, *Acute Melancholia*, 47. For a good resource questioning the fixation on trauma in contemporary theory, see Tamsin Jones, "Traumatized Subjects: Continental Philosophy of Religion and the Ethics of Alterity," *Journal of Religion* 94, no. 2 (April 2014): 143–60.

101. My thinking here is indebted to Paul Gilroy, *The Black Atlantic: Modernity and Double Consciousness* (New York: Verso, 1993).

102. Furey, *Poetic Relations*, 18.

103. Gandhi, *Affective Communities*, 12, 116.

104. Joel Martin, "Almost White: The Ambivalent Promise of Christian Missions among the Cherokees," in *Religion and the Creation of Race and Ethnicity*, ed. Craig Prentiss (New York: New York University Press, 2003), 43–60.

105. Robert Bartlett, *The Making of Europe: Conquest, Colonization, and Cultural Change, 950–1350* (Princeton, NJ: Princeton University Press, 1993); Ann Taves, "Sexuality and American Religious History," in *Retelling U.S. Religious History*, ed. Thomas A. Tweed (Berkeley: University of California Press, 1997), 36; Jennifer Snow, "The Civilization of White Men: The Race of the Hindu in *United States v. Bhagat Singh Thind*," in *Race, Nation, and Religion in the Americas*, ed. Henry Goldschmidt and Elizabeth McAlister (New York: Oxford University Press, 2004).

106. My thinking here is indebted to Robert Orsi, who has long claimed that the religions we study "continue to be imagined and treated as conglomerations of religious individuals, rather than as thick contexts of intersubjective exchanges among humans and between humans and special others (gods, ghosts, angels, ancestors and so on). . . . By ignoring the web of relationships in which the subject comes to be and always exists, the individual as a multi-dimensional reality disappears as well into the mass. . . . The individual becomes a cypher of discourse, discipline, and power in much writing on religion." Robert Orsi, "What Are Our Academic Assumptions About Religion?," in *Proceedings: Second Biennial Conference on Religion and American Culture* (Purdue: Center for the Study of Religion and American Culture, Indiana University), 9–11.

107. Marci Shore, "Can We *See* Ideas? On Evocation, Experience, and Empathy," in *Rethinking Intellectual History*, ed. Darrin M. McMahon and Samuel Moyn (Oxford: Oxford University Press, 2014), 194–211.

CHAPTER ONE

1. "Como dos poetas cristianos": Eduardo Frei Montalva, *Memorias (1911–1934) y Correspondencias con Gabriela Mistral y Jacques Maritain* (Santiago: Planeta, 1989), 14; "about God, life, and death": quoted from Marie-Lise Gazarian-Gautier, who was also present with Mistral at the end of her life. Marie-Lise Gazarian-Gautier, *Gabriela Mistral: The Teacher from the Valley of Elqui* (Chicago: Franciscan Herald Press, 1975), 104.

2. Telegram from Jacques and Raïssa Maritain to Doris Dana, January 7, 1957, digitized, Archivo Gabriela Mistral, Biblioteca Nacional de Chile.

3. Letter from Doris Dana to Jacques Maritain, December 28, 1956, published in *Cahier Jacques Maritain* 74 (2017): 15. My thanks to Florian Michel for pointing out this letter to me.

4. Mistral's close friends Olaya and Radomiro Tomic from Chile described the events to Doris Dana, Mistral's caretaker, lover, and the executor of her will. Letter from Olaya and Radomiro Tomic to Doris Dana, January 27, 1957, in *Gabriela Mistral's Letters to Doris Dana*, ed. Velma Garcia-Gorena (Albuquerque: University of New Mexico Press, 2018), 356–57.

5. Hjalmar Gullberg, "Award ceremony speech," given on December 10, 1945, Nobel Prize.org, Nobel Media AB 2019, http://www.nobelprize.org/prizes/literature/1945/ceremony-speech.

6. María Laura Picón, "Gabriela Mistral y Jacques Maritain: Una amistad a través del

océano," *Notes et documents* 42 (April 2019): 78–93; María Laura Picón, "Jacques Maritain y Victoria Ocampo: A propósito de la guerra civil española en la revista Sur," *Notes et documents* 35/38 (September 2016–December 2017): 72.

7. I am grateful for correspondence with Elizabeth Horan on this point.

8. There are several excellent biographies of Gabriela Mistral, and this section draws from these studies, including the introduction to Gabriela Mistral and Victoria Ocampo, *This America of Ours: The Letters of Gabriela Mistral and Victoria Ocampo*, ed. and trans. Elizabeth Horan and Doris Meyer (Austin: University of Texas Press, 2003); Licia Fiol-Matta, *A Queer Mother for the Nation: The State and Gabriela Mistral* (Minneapolis: University of Minnesota Press, 2002); Gabriela Mistral, *Selected Poems of Gabriela Mistral*, ed. and trans. Ursula K. Le Guin (Albuquerque: University of New Mexico Press, 2003); Marjorie Agosín, *A Gabriela Mistral Reader* (Fredonia, NY: White Pine Press, 1993); Karen Patricia Peña, *Poetry and the Realm of the Public Intellectual: The Alternative Destinies of Gabriela Mistral, Cecília Meireles, and Rosario Castellanos* (Leeds: Legenda, 2007); Elizabeth Horan, *Gabriela Mistral: An Artist and Her People* (Washington, DC: Organization of American States, 1994). The University of Chile maintains an extraordinary Spanish-language website with up-to-date secondary literature on Mistral, a detailed biography, and photos (http://www.gabrielamistral .uchile.cl).

9. Elizabeth Horan points out that Mistral's early essays from 1919 and her poem "Al pueblo hebreo" suggest Mistral's early philo-Semitic commitments, though they were not without their own paradoxes.

10. Patricia Rubio, "Constructions of the Self: The Personal Letters of Gabriela Mistral," in *Gabriela Mistral: The Audacious Traveler*, ed. Marjorie Agosín (Athens: Ohio University Press, 2003), 204.

11. Anne Fremantale, preface to Gazarian-Gautier, *Gabriela Mistral*, xii.

12. Elizabeth Rosa Horan, "Sor Juana and Gabriela Mistral; Locations and Locutions of the Saintly Woman," *Chasqui* 25, no. 2 (1996): 90.

13. Martin C. Taylor, *Gabriela Mistral's Struggle with God and Man: A Biographical and Critical Study of the Chilean Poet* (Jefferson, NC: McFarland, 2012), 53–55.

14. Randall Couch, introduction to *Madwoman: The "Locas mujeres" Poems of Gabriela Mistral, a Bilingual Edition* (Chicago: University of Chicago Press, 2008), 5.

15. Horan, "Sor Juana and Gabriela Mistral," 90.

16. Pablo Neruda, *Memoirs*, trans. Hardie St. Martin (New York: Penguin, 2000), 21.

17. Pericles Lewis, "Modernism and Religion," *The Cambridge Companion to Modernism* (Cambridge: Cambridge University Press, 2011), 181.

18. Gabriela Mistral, *Motivos: The Life of St. Francis*, ed. and trans. Elizabeth Horan (Tempe, AZ: Bilingual Review Press, 2013), 133.

19. Elizabeth Horan, introduction to Mistral, *Motivos*.

20. Horan, "Sor Juana and Gabriela Mistral," 94.

21. Gabriela Mistral, "Silueta de Sor Juana Inés," published later in Gabriela Mistral, "Silueta de Sor Juana Inés," *Ábside* 15 (1951): 506.

22. Mistral, *Motivos*, 147.

23. Mistral, *Motivos*, 149.

24. Gabriela Mistral, *Antología Mayor: Prosa* (Santiago: Cochrane, 1992), 556.

25. Mistral, *Antología Mayor*, 150.

26. Matilde Ladrón de Guevara, a friend of Mistral's, records Mistral saying this in Matilde Ladrón de Guevara, *Gabriela Mistral, "Rebelde Magnifica"* (Santiago: Imprenta de la Central de Talleres del S.N.S., 1957), 45.

27. Gabriela Mistral, "Social Question," in the documentary source book, *A History of Christianity in Asia, Africa, and Latin America, 1450–1990*, ed. Klaus Koschorke, Frieder Ludwig, Mariano Delgado, and Roland Spliesgart (Grand Rapids, MI: Eerdmans, 2007), 201–13.

28. Mistral, "Social Question," 201–13.

29. Denis Pelletier and Jean-Louis Schlegel, *À la gauche du Christ: Les chrétiens de gauche en France de 1945 à nos jours* (Paris: Éditions du Seuil, 2012); Gerd-Rainer Horn and Emmanuel Gerard, eds., *Left Catholicism, 1943–1955: Catholics and Society in Western Europe at the Point of Liberation* (Leuven, Belgium: Leuven University Press, 2001); Gerd-Rainer Horn, *Western European Liberation Theology 1924–1959: The First Wave* (New York: Oxford University Press, 2008).

30. Quoted by Marie-Lise Gazarian-Gautier, who was also present with Mistral at the end of her life. Gazarian-Gautier, *Gabriela Mistral*, 121.

31. Mistral, *Motivos*, 133.

32. St. Francis of Assisi, "The Canticle of Brother Sun," in *Francis and Clare: The Complete Works*, trans. and with an introduction by Regis Armstrong and Ignatius Brady (Mahwah, NJ: Paulist Press, 1982), 39–40.

33. Letter from Gabriela Mistral, June 14, 1925, in Mistral, *Motivos*, 162.

34. Letter from Mistral to Doris Dana, December 17, 1949, in Garcia-Gorena, *Mistral's Letters to Doris Dana*, 129.

35. Letter from Mistral to Victoria Ocampo, in Mistral and Ocampo, *This America of Ours*, 47. Letter is undated, and no envelope survives, though due to references of events, editors estimate it was written sometime between 1933 and 1938.

36. Picón, "Gabriela Mistral y Jacques Maritain," 79.

37. I am grateful for correspondence with Elizabeth Horan for clarifications on this point.

38. For more on the Maritains' conversion to Catholicism, see Raïssa Maritain, *Les grandes amitiés* (New York: Éditions de la Maison Française, 1941), translated into English by Julie Kernan as *We Have Been Friends Together* (New York: Longmans, Green, 1942). A second volume was published along with the first in the French edition, *Les grandes amitiés: Les aventures de la grâce* (New York: Éditions de la Maison Française, 1944). For more on the life of Raïssa Maritain, see Judith D. Suther, *Raïssa Maritain: Pilgrim, Poet, Exile* (New York: Fordham University Press, 1990); Brenna Moore, *Sacred Dread: Raïssa Maritain, the Allure of Suffering, and the French Catholic Revival, 1905–1944* (South Bend, IN: University of Notre Dame Press, 2013).

39. On the relationship between Bloy and the Maritains on this issue, see Brenna Moore, "Gold Fillings into Crocodiles' Teeth: Christian Fear, Imagination, and Politics in Léon Bloy," in *Saving Fear: The History of Fear in Christianity*, ed. Ann Astell (South Bend, IN: University of Notre Dame Press, 2019).

40. For more on Mistral's Jewish background and the theme of Judaism in her writing, see

Martin C. Taylor, "The Hebraic Tradition," in *Gabriela Mistral's Struggle*, 115–45. On the theme of Judaism in Raïssa Maritain, see Brenna Moore, "Philosemitism under a Darkening Sky: Jews and Judaism in the French Catholic Revival (1900–1940)," *Catholic Historical Review* 99, no. 2 (2013): 262–97. Brenna Moore and Richard Crane, "Cracks in the Theology of Contempt: The French Roots of Nostra Aetate," *Studies in Christian-Jewish Relations* 8, no. 1 (2013): 1–28.

41. Letters from Mistral to Jacques and Raïssa Maritain, October 3, 1939, and November 24, 1944, Archivo Gabriela Mistral, Biblioteca Nacional de Chile; and Mistral to J. and R. Maritain, September 2, 1947, in Frei Montalva, *Memorias*, 11.

42. Letter from Mistral to J. and R. Maritain, November 24, 1944, Archivo Gabriela Mistral, Biblioteca Nacional de Chile.

43. Letter from Mistral to J. and R. Maritain, January 13, 1949, reprinted in María Laura Picón, "J. Maritain y Esther de Cáceres: Una amistad spiritual," *Notes et Documents* 24 (September–December 2012): 86.

44. Letter from J. Maritain to Mistral, dated August 13, 1939, Archivo Gabriela Mistral, Biblioteca Nacional Digital de Chile.

45. Jacques Maritain, *Three Reformers: Luther, Descartes, Rousseau* (London: Sheed and Ward, 1928), 9, 171–75.

46. Martin Luther, "On the Estate of Marriage," in *Faith and Freedom: An Invitation to the Writings of Martin Luther*, ed. John F. Thornton and Susan Varenne (New York: Random House, 2002), 251. During their marriage, the Maritains guarded their vow of celibacy with secrecy, but after Raïssa died, Jacques opened up a bit about it in the initially privately circulated *Journal of Raïssa*, and later in Jacques Maritain, "Love and Friendship," in *Notebooks* (New York: Magi Books, 1984), 228.

47. James Chappel, *Catholic Modern: The Challenge of Totalitarianism and the Remaking of the Church* (Cambridge, MA: Harvard University Press, 2018).

48. For more on the national promotion of marriage and family in this period, see Claire Duchen, *Women's Rights and Women's Lives in France 1944–1968* (London: Routledge, 1994), 64–66.

49. Elizabeth Horan, "California Dreaming: Gabriela Mistral Lucid Cold War Paranoia," *White Rabbit: English Studies in Latin America* 3 (August 2012): 2–34.

50. Cocteau quoted in Claude Arnaud, "The Angel's Dream," in *Jean Cocteau: A Life* (New Haven, CT: Yale University Press, 2016), 391.

51. Florian Michel, "Jacques and Raïssa Maritain: Reputation for Holiness and Spiritual Fruitfulness," in *The Wisdom of Youth*, ed. Travis Dumsday (Washington, DC: Catholic University of America Press, 2016), 2–21.

52. Jacques Maritain and Julien Green, *The Story of Two Souls: The Correspondence of Jacques Maritain and Julien Green*, ed. Henry Bars and Eric Jourdan, trans. with an intro. and rev. notes Bernard Doering (New York: Fordham University Press, 1988), 144.

53. J. Maritain and Green, *The Story of Two Souls*, 211.

54. R. Maritain, *Les grandes amitiés*, 99.

55. Maurice Sachs, Jacques Maritain, and Raïssa Maritain, *Maurice Sachs, Jacques Maritain, Raïssa Maritain Correspondance (1925–1939)* (Paris: Gallimard, 2003), 22.

56. I am grateful to René Mougel at the Jacques and Raïssa Maritain Archives, Kolbsheim, France, for showing me these preserved objects.

57. Kolbsheim replica, Jacques and Raïssa Maritain Archives, Kolbsheim, France.

58. R. Maritain, *Les grandes amitiés: Les aventures de la grâce*, 41.

59. See correspondence in Frei Montalva, *Memorias*.

60. Letter from Mistral to J. Maritain, March 14, 1938, reprinted in Picón, "J. Maritain y Esther de Cáceres," 80.

61. Quoted in Frei Montalva, *Memorias*, 14.

62. Letter from Mistral to Ocampo, undated (sometime between 1926 and 1938), in Mistral and Ocampo, *This America of Ours*, 104.

63. Victoria Ocampo, *This America of Ours*, 300.

64. For more on the anti-family history of Catholicism, see Mary Dunn, *Cruelest of All Mothers: Marie de L'Incarnation, Motherhood, and Christian Tradition* (New York: Fordham University Press, 2016), 97–99.

65. Brian McGuire, *Friendship and Faith: Cistercian Men, Women, and Their Stories 1100–1250* (Burlington, VT: Ashgate, 2002); Jodi Bilinkoff, *Related Lives: Confessors and Their Female Penitents, 1450–1750* (Ithaca, NY: Cornell University Press, 2005); Constance Furey, *Erasmus, Contarini, and the Religious Republic of Letters* (Cambridge: Cambridge University Press, 2006); and Alan Bray, *The Friend* (Chicago: University of Chicago Press, 2003).

66. Bray, *The Friend*, 294–95.

67. Georges Bernanos, "Dans l'amitié de Léon Bloy," appendix to *Présence de Bernanos* (Paris: Plon, 1947), 1232.

68. Charles Journet and Jacques Maritain, *Journet–Maritain Correspondance*, vol. 4, *1950–1957* (Paris: Éditions Saint-Augustin, 1998), 922.

69. R. Maritain quotes Bloy in *Les grandes amitiés*, in J. Maritain and R. Maritain, *Oeuvres complètes* (Paris: Saint-Paul, 1995), 14:754.

70. Pierre van der Meer Walcheren, *Journal d'un converti* (Paris: Georges Cres & Cie, 1917).

71. Walcheren, *Journal d'un converti*.

72. Léon Bloy, *Lettres à ses filleuls, Jacques Maritain et Pierre van der Meer de Walcheren* (Paris: Stock, 1928), 122.

73. Bloy, *Lettres à ses filleuls*, 138–39.

74. See, for example, Charles Journet and Jacques Maritain, *Journet–Maritain Correspondance*, vol. 3, *1940–1949* (Paris: Éditions Saint-Augustin, 1998), 386.

75. Thomas Merton, *Turning toward the World: The Pivotal Years: The Journals of Thomas Merton* (San Francisco: Harper Collins, 1996), 145.

76. J. Maritain and Green, *The Story of Two Souls*.

77. Bernanos, "Dans l'amitié de Léon Bloy," 1232.

78. R. Maritain, *Les grandes amitiés: Les aventures de la grâce*, 41.

79. Denis Pelletier and Jean-Louis Schlegel, *À la gauche du Christ: Les chrétiens de gauche en France de 1945 à nos jours* (Paris: Éditions du Seuil, 2012).

80. Jennifer Ann Boittin, *Colonial Metropolis: The Urban Grounds of Anti-Imperialism and Feminism in Interwar Paris* (Lincoln: University of Nebraska Press, 2010).

81. Boittin, *Colonial Metropolis*, xvii.

82. Elizabeth Horan, in Mistral, *Motivos*, 111. Boittin, *Colonial Metropolis*, describes Paris as an international, cosmopolitan setting resisting and reliant on French colonialism.

83. Waldo Frank, "Chuquicamata," in *Impressions of Latin America*, ed. Frank McShane (New York: William Marrow, 1963), 289.

84. Bernard Doering, "Jacques Maritain and the Spanish Civil War," *Review of Politics* 44 (October 1982): 489.

85. John King, "Towards a Reading of the Argentine Literary Magazine *Sur*," *Latin American Research Review* 2 (1981): 57–78; John King, *Sur: A Study of the Argentine Literary Journal and Its Role in the Development of a Culture, 1931–1970* (Cambridge: Cambridge University Press, 1986); Mark Falcoff, "Intellectual Currents," in *Prologue to Perón: Argentina in Depression and War, 1930–1943*, ed. Mark Falcoff and Ronald H. Dolkart (Berkeley: University of California Press, 1976), 110–35.

86. Jacques Maritain, "Carta sobre la independencia," *SUR* 22 (1936): 54–86; Jacques Maritain, "Conferencia de Jacques Maritain a propósito de la 'Carta sobre la independencia,'" *SUR* 27 (1936): 7–41; Jacques Maritain, "Con el pueblo: De un nuevo humanism," *SUR* 31 (1937): 7–21; Jacques Maritain, "Sobre la guerra santa," *SUR* 35 (1937): 98–117.

87. J. Maritain, "Con el pueblo," 8. For a more thorough analysis, see Doering, "Maritain and the Spanish Civil War," 489–522.

88. Letter from Mistral to Eduardo Frei, 1937, in Frei Montalva, *Memorias*, 111.

89. For good introduction to this network, see Victoria Ocampo, *Testimonios: Tercera serie* (Buenos Aires: Editorial Sudamericana, 1946); Enrique Anderson Imbert, "Victoria Ocampo: 'Testimonios. Tercera serie' (Buenos Aires, 1946)," *SUR* 139 (1946): 72–73; Doris Meyer, *Victoria Ocampo: Against the Wind and the Tide* (Austin: University of Texas Press, 1990).

90. King, *Sur*, 64. I am grateful to conversations with fellow conference participant José Zanca from Argentina on the topic of Catholic antifascist activism in Argentina, along with his excellent book, José Zanca, *Cristianos antifascistas: Tensiones en la cultura católica argentina (1936–1959)* (Buenos Aires: Siglo XXI, 2013). See also Mario C. Nascimbene and Mauricio Isaac Neuman, "El nacionalismo católico, el fascismo y la inmigración en la Argentina (1927–1943): Una aproximación teórica," *Estudios Interdisciplinarios de América Latina y el Caribe* 4, no. 1 (1993): 115–40.

91. Picón, "J. Maritain y Esther de Cáceres," 54–63.

92. Picón, "J. Maritain y Esther de Cáceres," 54–63.

93. Picón, "J. Maritain y Esther de Cáceres," 62.

94. Quoted in Picón, "J. Maritain y Esther de Cáceres," 54–63.

95. Picón, "J. Maritain y Esther de Cáceres," 54–63.

96. Prologue to Frei Montalva, *Memorias*, 11

97. Letter from Eduardo Frei Montalva to Mistral, dated 1934, in Frei Montalva, *Memorias*, 13.

98. Frei Montalva, *Memorias*, 35.

99. Letter from Mistral to Ocampo, dated 1938, in Mistral and Ocampo, *This America of Ours*, 38. On this bond between Ocampo and Mistral, see Alicia Jurado, "La amistad

entre Gabriela Mistral y Victoria Ocampo," *Boletín de la Academia Argentina de Letras* 54 (1989): 523–61.

100. Picón, "J. Maritain y Esther de Cáceres," 54–63.

101. Thank you for correspondence with Elizabeth Horan.

102. Garcia-Gorena, *Mistral's Letters to Doris Dana*, 356–57.

103. Mistral, *Selected Poems*, 317.

104. Raïssa Maritain, *Marc Chagall* (New York: Éditions de la Maison Française, 1943); Jacques Maritain and Raïssa Maritain, *Oeuvres complètes de Jacques et Raïssa Maritain* (Paris: Éditions Saint-Paul, 1995), 15:551–52.

105. Undated letter from Mistral to R. Maritain, in Picón, "Gabriela Mistral y Jacques Maritain," 87.

106. R. Maritain, *Les grandes amitiés*, 626.

107. Journet and Maritain, *Journet–Maritain Correspondance*, 3:42–44.

108. Undated letter from Mistral to R. Maritain, in Picón, "Gabriela Mistral y Jacques Maritain," 87.

109. Letter from J. Maritain to Mistral, March 18, 1949, in Picón, "Gabriela Mistral y Jacques Maritain," 89.

110. Letter from Mistral to Maritain, January 13, 1949, reprinted in Picón, "J. Maritain y Esther de Cáceres," 86. French translation reprinted in Alejandro Serani and Ian Henriquez, "Lettres de Jacques, Raïssa, et Gabriela Mistral: jalons pour une histoire," *Cahiers Jacques Maritain* 74 (2017): 5–16.

111. Letter from Mistral to J. Maritain, October 4, 1941, in Frei Montalva, *Memorias*, 19.

112. Frei Montalva, *Memorias*, 157–61.

113. Frei Montalva, *Memorias*, 157–61.

114. Olivier Compagnon argues that the hostility between Jacques Maritain and the conservative church in Argentina was due to the deep and pervasive anti-Semitism of so many in the hierarchy. Raïssa was born Jewish, and the Maritains (along with Mistral) contributed to Catholic efforts in philo-Semitism in the early 1930s and for the rest of their lives. Gourdon Vincent, *Olivier Compagnon, Jacques Maritain et l'Amérique du Sud: Le modèle malgré lui* (Villeneuve-d'Ascq: Presses Universitaires du Septentrion, 2003), 110–88.

115. Letter from Mistral to J. Maritain, October 4, 1941, in Frei Montalva, *Memorias*, 163–64. For more on the controversies between Pérez and Maritain, see Otto Boye, "El Pensamiento de Maritain en Chile," paper presented at "Primer Coloquio del Pensamiento Contemporáneo. Jacques Maritain," Viña del Mar, Chile, September 9, 2007, http://www.jacquesmaritain.com/pdf/15_PRE/07_PR_OBoye.pdf.

116. Edward Lawrence, "In This Dark Hour: Stefan Zweig and Historical Displacement in Brazil, 1941–1942" (master's thesis, University of New Orleans, 2017).

117. Leo Carey, "The Escape Artist: The Death and Life of Stefan Zweig," *New Yorker*, August 27, 2012; Marion Sonnenfeld, ed., *Stefan Zweig: The World of Yesterday's Humanist Today, Proceedings of the Stefan Zweig Symposium* (Albany: State University of New York Press, 1983).

118. "Letter by Gabriela Mistral to Eduardo Mallea about the death of Stefan Zweig," trans.

C. M. Lorenz, digital copy in Charlotte Marie Lorenz Collection at Lawrence University Archives, Appleton, WI.

119. Letter from Mistral to J. Maritain, October 4, 1950, in Frei Montalva, *Memorias*, 33.

120. Gabriela Mistral, "Lámpara de catedral," *Religious Faith and World Culture*, ed. William Loos (New York: Prentice Hall, 1951), 281–83.

121. The journal of the Sembradores de Amistad association (founded in Monterrey, Mexico, in 1936) published some works on Gabriela Mistral; see Gloria Riestra, "La influencia de Tagore en Gabriela Mistral," *Sembradores de Amistad* (May 1965): 5–9.

122. For more on these groups, see Vicki Caron, *Uneasy Asylum: France and the Jewish Refugee Crisis, 1933–1942* (Stanford, CA: Stanford University Press, 1999), 216–17, 288–89; Folder 44, Archives Jeanne Ancelet Hustache, Saulchoir Seminary, Paris; Bernard Comte, *Initiatives de théologiens face à la persécution antisémite à Lyon en 1941–42* (Lyon: Institut Catholique, 1993), 15–16.

123. Letter from the Church of Peace Union with the World Alliance for International Friendship through Religion to Mistral, April 1951, Archivo Gabriela Mistral, Biblioteca Nacional de Chile.

124. Mistral, "Lámpara de catedral," 281–83.

125. Jacques Maritain, "A Faith to Live By," *The Nation* 164, no. 20 (May 17, 1947), 568–70.

126. J. Maritain, "A Faith to Live By."

127. Jacques Maritain, *Peasant of the Garonne* (New York: Wipf & Stock, 2013), 232.

128. Letter from J. Maritain to Saul Alinsky, October 1947, in *The Philosopher and the Provocateur: The Correspondence of Jacques Maritain and Saul Alinsky*, ed. Bernard Doering (South Bend, IN: University of Notre Dame Press, 1994), 34.

129. Letter from Alinsky to J. Maritain in Doering, *The Philosopher and the Provocateur*, 17.

130. Gabriela Mistral, "La palabra maldita," published as an editorial in Costa Rica in 1951 and reprinted in Chile in Ladrón de Guevara, *Gabriela Mistral*, 107–10; and in Diamela Eltit, *Crónica del sufragio femenino en Chile* (Santiago: SERNAM, 1994), 90–93.

131. Gabriela Mistral, "The Fall of Europe," in *Lagar* (Santiago: Editorial del Pacifico, 1954), reprinted in Mistral, *Selected Poems*, 285–86, and in Diane E. Marting, ed., *Spanish American Women Writers: A Bio-bibliographical Source Book* (Westport, CT: Greenwood, 1990), 109–13.

132. "Annual Convocation of the Academy of American Franciscan History," *The Americas* 7, no. 3 (1951): 361–61.

133. Taylor, *Gabriela Mistral's Struggle*, 222.

134. Card from Jacques and Raïssa Maritain to Mistral, 1953, digitized collection, Archivo Gabriela Mistral, Biblioteca Nacional de Chile. See also card from Jacques and Raïssa Maritain to Mistral, 1954, Archivo Gabriela Mistral, Biblioteca Nacional de Chile.

135. Letter from R. Maritain to Mistral, May 1954, Archivo Gabriela Mistral, Biblioteca Nacional de Chile.

136. Letter from Mistral to J. and R. Maritain, November 4, 1945, Archivo Gabriela Mistral, Biblioteca Nacional de Chile.

137. Letter from Mistral to J. and R. Maritain, November 4, 1945, Archivo Gabriela Mistral, Biblioteca Nacional de Chile.

138. Waldo Frank, "Gabriela Mistral," *The Nation*, January 26, 1957, 84.

139. Gabriela Mistral, *Selected Prose and Prose-Poems*, ed. and trans. Stephen Tapscott (Austin: University of Texas Press, 2004), 207.

140. For studies on Mistral and religion, I am indebted to the works of Elizabeth Horan and Martin C. Taylor. See Horan's introduction to Mistral, *Motivos*, and Taylor, *Gabriela Mistral's Struggle*.

141. Letter from Doris Dana to Radomiro Tomic, November 3, 1966, Archivo Gabriela Mistral, Biblioteca Nacional de Chile.

142. Story recounted in J. Maritain and Green, *The Story of Two Souls*, 199.

143. J. Maritain and Green, *The Story of Two Souls*, 211.

144. Sadly, no one else really did! *The Peasant of the Garonne* was critical of Vatican II because Jacques saw the council as eclipsing a contemplative spirituality that Raïssa embodied for him. She was a mystic; it makes sense that this was "her" book.

145. J. Maritain and Green, *The Story of Two Souls*, 211.

146. Picón, "J. Maritain y Esther de Cáceres," 62.

147. Arnaud, *Jean Cocteau*, 473.

148. See the overall tone in the Mistral-Ocampo correspondence in *This America of Ours*.

149. Telegraph from Jacques Maritain to Mistral, 1955, digital copy, Archivo Gabriela Mistral, Biblioteca Nacional de Chile.

150. Sachs quoted in Arnaud, *Jean Cocteau*, 476.

151. Eduardo Frei Montalva, "Aniversario de muerte de Gabriela Mistral," January 10, 1967, Archivo de Prensa Casa Museo Eduardo Frei Montalva, Santiago, Chile.

152. Frank, "Chuquicamata," 289.

153. Story told to Velma García-Gorena in the introduction to *Mistral's Letters to Doris Dana*.

154. John Howard Griffin, *Jacques Maritain: Homage in Words and Pictures* (New York: Magi Books, 1974), 22.

155. Arnaud, *Jean Cocteau*, 391.

156. David Tracy, "On Naming Saints," *Saints: Faith without Borders* (Chicago: University of Chicago Press, 2011), 102.

157. Dorothy Day, *All the Way to Heaven: The Selected Letters of Dorothy Day*, ed. Robert Ellsberg (New York: Image Books, 2012).

158. Michel de Certeau, *The Mystic Fable, Volume One: The Sixteenth and Seventeenth Centuries*, trans. Michael B. Smith (Chicago: University of Chicago Press, 1995).

159. Jane Bennett, *The Enchantment of Modern Life: Attachments, Crossings, and Ethics* (Princeton, NJ: Princeton University Press, 2001), 4.

CHAPTER TWO

1. Anthony O'Mahony, "Louis Massignon: A Catholic Encounter with Islam and the Middle East," in *God's Mirror: Renewal and Engagement in French Catholic Intellectual Culture in the Mid-Twentieth-Century*, ed. K. Davies and T. Garfitt (New York: Fordham University Press, 2015), 250.

2. Dominique Avon, *Les Frères prêcheurs en Orient: Les dominicains du Caire (années 1910–années 1960)* (Paris: Éditions du Cerf, 2005), 25.

3. Several excellent overviews of the life and works of Massignon exist in both English and French: Christian Krokus, *The Theology of Louis Massignon: Islam, Christ and the Church* (Washington, DC: Catholic University of America Press, 2017); Albert H. Hourani, *Islam in European Thought* (Cambridge: Cambridge University Press, 1990), 43–49; Anthony O'Mahony, "The Influence of the Life and Thought of Louis Massignon on the Catholic Church's Relations with Islam," *Downside Review* 126 (2008):169–92; Anthony O'Mahony, "Our Common Fidelity to Abraham Is What Divides: Christianity and Islam in the Life and Thought of Louis Massignon," in *Catholics in Interreligious Dialogue: Studies in Monasticism, Theology and Spirituality*, ed. Anthony O'Mahony and Peter Bowe (Leominster: Gracewing, 2006), 151–92; Mary Louise Gude, *Louis Massignon—The Crucible of Compassion* (South Bend, IN: University of Notre Dame Press, 1996); Guy Harpigny, *Islam et Christianisme selon Louis Massignon* (Louvain: Université Catholique de Louvain, 1981).

4. Agnes Wilkins, "Mary Kahil and the Encounter Between Christianity and Islam," *Downside Review* 135, no. 3 (2017): 133.

5. Massignon occasionally referred to himself as a *"catholique ami de l'Islam"* as a way to sidestep politics—merely a "friend," not an advocate of Islam nor one who comes to it with ulterior motives. See, for example, the 1938 letter from Massignon to the Lebanese scholar Youakim Moubarac in Jacques Keryell, ed., *Louis Massignon et ses contemporains* (Paris: Karthala, 1997), 270.

6. Herbert Mason, *Memoir of a Friend* (South Bend, IN: University of Notre Dame Press, 1988), 81.

7. Edward Said, *Orientalism* (New York: Pantheon, 1978), 268. For more of Said on Massignon, see Edward Said, "Islam, the Philological Vocation and French Culture: Renan and Massignon," in *Islamic Studies: A Tradition and Its Problems*, ed. Malcolm H. Kerr (Malibu: Undena, 1980), 53–72.

8. Marie-Magdeleine Davy, "L'homme en qui Dieu verdoie," *Question de* 90 (1992): 218–19.

9. Jacques Maritain, *Cahier de l'Herne* (Paris: 1962), 451–52.

10. Louis Massignon, "An Entire Life with a Brother Who Set Out on the Desert: Charles de Foucauld," in *Testimonies and Reflections*, ed. Herbert Mason (South Bend, IN: University of Notre Dame Press, 1989), 22. The Massignon-Foucauld correspondence has been published in Jean-François Six, *L'aventure de l'amour de Dieu* (Paris: Éditions du Seuil, 1993).

11. Gude, *Louis Massignon*, 139.

12. Jean Jacques Waardenburg, *Muslims as Actors: Islamic Meanings and Muslim Interpretations in the Perspective of the Study of Religions* (New York: Walter de Gruyter, 2007), 178.

13. For understanding the delicacy of the issue of the Kahil-Massignon friendship, I am grateful for conversations with Father Patrick Ryan, SJ, and Sister Agnes Wilkins, OSB, as well as to Jacques Keryell for Louis Massignon, *L'hospitalité sacrée*, ed. Jacques Keryell, with a preface by René Voillaume (Paris: Nouvelle Cité, 1987).

14. Michel de Certeau, "Massignon pèlerin et professeur," *Libération*, December 2, 1983.

15. Susannah Heschel and Umar Ryad, introduction to *The Muslim Reception of European Orientalism: Reversing the Gaze* (London: Routledge, 2019). Other works revising this narrative about orientalism include Suzanne L. Marchand, *German Orientalism in the Age of Empire: Religion, Race, and Scholarship* (Cambridge: Cambridge University Press, 2009), and Bekim Agai, Umar Ryad, and Mehdi Sajid, *Muslims in Interwar Europe: A Transcultural Historical Perspective* (Leiden: Brill, 2015).

16. For basic biographical data of Massignon's childhood, I rely on Gude, *Louis Massignon*, Krokus, *Theology of Louis Massignon*, O'Mahony, "Our Common Fidelity," and Keryell, *L'hospitalité sacrée*, 33–73.

17. For more on the orientalist scholarly field Massignon had entered and transformed, see Richard King, *Orientalism and Religion: Postcolonial Theory, India, and the "Mystic East"* (London: Routledge, 1999); Marchand, *German Orientalism*; Dana S. Hale, *Races on Display: French Representations of Colonized Peoples 1886–1940* (Bloomington: Indiana University Press, 2008); Roger Benjamin, *Orientalist Aesthetics: Art, Colonialism, and French North Africa, 1880–1930* (Berkeley: University of California Press, 2003).

18. Massignon, "An Entire Life," 22; Jacques Keryell, "Louis Massignon et l'Association Charles de Foucauld," in *Louis Massignon au coeur de notre temps*, ed. Jacques Keryell (Paris: Karthala, 1999), 173–93; Lucienne Portier, "Louis Massignon et Charles de Foucauld," in *Louis Massignon*, ed. Jean-François Six (Paris: Éditions de l'Herne, 1970), 35.

19. Massignon, "An Entire Life," 21. Emphasis added.

20. Massignon, "An Entire Life," 28.

21. Louis Massignon, preface to *The Passion of al-Hallāj: Mystic and Martyr of Islam*, trans. Herbert Mason (Princeton, NJ: Princeton University Press, 1982), xxi.

22. Quoted in Krokus, *Theology of Louis Massignon*, 27. For an excellent discussion of Massignon's textual method, see Krokus, "Louis Massignon: Method," in *Theology of Louis Massignon*, 18–45.

23. Quoted in Krokus, *Theology of Louis Massignon*, 26.

24. This dramatic story appears throughout the Massignon bibliography. For Massignon's own account, see Louis Massignon, *Parole donnée* (Paris: Éditions du Seuil, 1983), 25–41. Secondary sources include Daniel Massignon, *Le voyage en Mésopotamie et la conversion de Louis Massignon en 1908* (Paris: Éditions du Cerf, 2001); Krokus, *Theology of Louis Massignon*, 11–14; and Gude, *Louis Massignon*, 27–56.

25. It also propelled within him a kind of conversion to the Catholicism of his childhood (Massignon had come from a Catholic family but had never been particularly devout). But it was a Christian conversion experience that happened in a totally Islamic setting: in Iraq, with everyone speaking Arabic around him, and facilitated by a vision of the Muslim martyr al-Hallāj.

26. Letter from Louis Massignon to Mary Kahil, March 25, 1938, in Keryell, *L'hospitalité sacrée*, 206.

27. Louis Massignon, preface to *La Passion d'Al-Hallâj*, 4 vols. (Paris: Gallimard, 1975), xxvii.

28. Ian Latham, "The Conversion of Louis Massignon in Mesopotamia in 1908," *ARAM* 20 (2008): 254–55.

29. Louis Massignon, *Essay on the Origins of the Technical Language of Islamic Mysticism*, ed. and trans. Benjamin Clark and Herbert Mason (South Bend, IN: University of Notre Dame Press, 1997).

30. Massignon, *Origins of Technical Language*, 6.

31. Massignon, *Origins of Technical Language*, 33.

32. For a contemporary take on the issue Massignon addressed, see Rozina Ali, "The Erasure of Islam from the Poetry of Rumi," *New Yorker*, January 5, 2017.

33. Carl Ernst, "Between Orientalism and Fundamentalism: Problematizing the Teaching of Sufism," in *Teaching Islam*, ed. Brannon Wheeler (Oxford: Oxford University Press, 2002), 108–23.

34. For more on the differences between Massignon and Palacios in their approach to Sufism, see Anthony O'Mahony, "Eastern Christianity and Jesuit Scholarship on Arabic and Islam: Modern History and Contemporary Theological Reflections," in *Philosophy, Theology and the Jesuit Tradition: "The Eye of Love,"* ed. Anna Abram, Michael Kirwan, and Peter Gallagher (London: Bloomsbury T&T Clark, 2017), 169–72. For more on Palacios, see Paul Nwyia, "Ibn 'Abbad de Ronda et Jean de la Croix: À propos d'une hypothèse d'Asin Palacios," *Al-Andalus* 22 (1957): 113–30.

35. Omid Safi, "Is Islamic Mysticism Really Islam?," *Huffington Post*, updated May 29, 2011, https://www.huffingtonpost.com/omid-safi/is-islamic-mysticism-real_b_841438 .html.

36. Ernst, "Between Orientalism and Fundamentalism," 119, and Safi, "Is Islamic Mysticism Really Islam?"

37. Massignon, *Origins of the Technical Language*, 33–34.

38. Keryell, *L'hospitalité sacrée*, 207.

39. Massignon, *The Passion of al-Hallāj*, 22.

40. O'Mahony, "Eastern Christianity and Jesuit Scholarship," 173.

41. Quoted in Krokus, *Theology of Louis Massignon*, 184. Emphasis added.

42. Waardenburg *Muslims as Actors*, 161.

43. Roger Griffin, *Fascism's Modernist Revolution: A New Paradigm for the Study of Right-Wing Dictatorships* (Leiden: Brill, 2016).

44. Mark Antliff, *Avant-Garde Fascism: The Mobilization of Myth, Art, and Culture in France, 1909–1939* (Durham, NC: Duke University Press, 2007); Griffin, *Fascism's Modernist Revolution*.

45. Gotz Nordburch and Umar Ryad, "Introduction: Toward a Translational History of Islam and Muslims in Interwar Europe," in *Transnational Islam in Interwar Europe: Muslim Activists and Thinkers*, ed. Gotz Nordburch and Umar Ryad (New York: Palgrave Macmillan, 2014), 31; Matthias Koening and Wolfgang Knobl, "Religion, Nationalism, and European Integration," in *Religion and National Identities in Enlarged Europe*, ed. Willfried Spohn, Matthias Koening, and Wolfgang Knobl (New York: Palgrave Macmillan, 2015), 120.

46. Tony Judt and Timothy Snyder, *Thinking the Twentieth Century* (New York: Penguin, 2013), 172.

47. Henri Massis, *Defense of the West*, preface by G. K. Chesterton (London: Harcourt, 1928), 8–10.

48. G. K. Chesterton, *The Flying Inn* (San Francisco: Ignatius Press, 2017).

49. Adam Gopnik, "The Back of the World: The Troubling Genius of G. K. Chesterton," *New Yorker*, June 7, 2008, 59.

50. See the voluminous references to Massignon in Joseph Maréchal, *Studies in the Psychology of the Mystics* (Mineola, NY: Dover Publications, 2004), 33–50. Originally published as *Études sur le psychologie des mystiques*, 2 vols. (Leuven, Belgium: Brugis Bevaert, 1926, 1937).

51. For a useful overview of the history of *la nouvelle théologie*, see Jürgen Mettepenningen, *Nouvelle Théologie–New Theology: Inheritor of Modernism, Precursor of Vatican II* (London: Continuum, 2010); Gabriel Flynn and Paul Murray, *Ressourcement: A Movement for Renewal in Twentieth-Century Catholic Theology* (Oxford: Oxford University Press, 2014); Étienne Fouilloux, *Une église en quête de liberté: La pensée catholique française entre modernisme et Vatican II, 1914–1962* (Paris: Desclée de Brouwer, 1998).

52. Letter from Marie-Dominique Chenu to Father Gillet, February 8, 1939, in Avon, *Les frères prêcheurs*, 340.

53. It made sense that the Dominicans were the pioneers to follow in Massignon's lead when, after all, their "turn to the sources" led them back to dig more deeply into Thomas Aquinas, who was himself immersed deeply in Arabic thought.

54. Jean-Jacques Pérennès presents an accessible portrait of Anawati in Jean-Jacques Pérennès, *Georges Anawati (1905–1994): Un chrétien égyptien devant le mystère de l'Islam* (Paris: Éditions du Cerf, 2008).

55. Pérennès, *Georges Anawati*, 114.

56. Georges Anawati, *L'ultimo dialogo: La mia vita incontro all'Islam* (Venice: Marcianium Press, 2010), 64. Pérennès emphasizes how rare it was for Dominicans to study Islam and the importance of Massignon for Anawati's vocation as an Islamicist. Pérennès, *Georges Anawati*, 1, 33.

57. Anawati, *L'ultimo dialogo*, 111.

58. Islamicist David Burrell describes the Institut dominicain d'études orientales's long-standing, renowned reputation in Cairo as an "apostolate of friendship." David Burrell, *Questing for Understanding: Persons, Places, Passions* (Eugene, OR: Wipf & Stock, 2012), 94.

59. Naomi Davidson, "Muslim Bodies in the Metropole: Social Assistance and 'Religious' Practice in Interwar Paris," in Agai, Ryad, and Sajid, *Muslims in Interwar Europe*, 105–54. This analysis also helps give historical framing to Elayne Oliphant's excellent forthcoming study of the process by which Catholicism in France has become marked as "banal" and assimilable to secularism, whereas Islam has never been granted the privilege of banality. See Elayne Oliphant, *The Privilege of Being Banal: Art, Secularism, and Catholicism in Paris* (Chicago: University of Chicago Press, forthcoming).

60. Mayanthi Fernando, *The Republic Unsettled: Muslim French and the Contradictions of Secularism* (Durham, NC: Duke University Press, 2014).

61. Davy, "L'homme en qui Dieu verdoie," 218–19.

62. Jean Lacouture, "Un prophète dans le siècle," *Le Monde*, November 8, 1962.

63. Victor and Edith Turner, *Image and Pilgrimage in Christian Culture* (New York: Columbia University Press, 2011), 34.

64. King, *Orientalism and Religion*; Elizabeth Ezra, *The Colonial Unconscious: Race and Culture in Interwar France* (Ithaca, NY: Cornell University Press, 2000).

65. Richard Wheeler, "Louis Massignon and Al-Hallâj—An Introduction to the Life and Thought of a 20th Century Mystic," *ARAM* 20 (2008): 232.

66. This is discussed in detail in Jeffrey Kripal, "The Passion of Louis Massignon: Sublimating the Homoerotic Gaze in *The Passion of al-Hallâj* (1922)," in *Roads of Excess, Palaces of Wisdom* (Chicago: University of Chicago Press, 2001), 98–155. See also Gude, *Louis Massignon*, 21–25.

67. Letter from Louis Massignon to Abd-el-Jalil, in *Massignon—Abd-el-Jalil: Parrain et filleul, 1926–1962*, ed. Françoise Jacquin (Paris: Éditions du Cerf, 2007), 99.

68. Maurice Borrmans, preface to Jacquin, *Massignon—Abd-el-Jalil*, 11.

69. Biographical information here comes from Jacquin, *Massignon—Abd-el-Jalil*, 99, and Mehdi Sajid, "A Muslim Convert to Christianity as an Orientalist in Europe—The Case of the Moroccan Franciscan Jean-Mohammed Abdeljalil (1904–1979)," in Heschel and Ryad, *Muslim Reception of European Orientalism*).

70. Sajid, "Muslim Convert to Christianity."

71. Telegram to the minister of foreign affairs in Morocco, June 24, 1928, in Jacquin, *Massignon—Abd-el-Jalil*, 285.

72. Jacquin, *Massignon—Abd-el-Jalil*, 28.

73. Jacquin, *Massignon—Abd-el-Jalil*, 28.

74. Quoted in O'Mahony, "Our Common Fidelity," 175.

75. Jacquin, *Massignon—Abd-el-Jalil*, 40.

76. First quote from letter from Abd-el-Jalil to Massignon, September 8, 1942; and the second from Massignon to Abd-el-Jalil, April 23, 1948, in Jacquin, *Massignon—Abd-el-Jalil*, 101.

77. Letter from Massignon to Abd-el-Jalil, May 1, 1951, in Jacquin, *Massignon—Abd-el-Jalil*, 189.

78. Letter from Massignon to Abd-el-Jalil, August 26, 1933, in Jacquin, *Massignon—Abd-el-Jalil*, 98.

79. Jacquin, *Massignon—Abd-el-Jalil*, 87, 111.

80. Mason, *Memoir of a Friend*, 88.

81. Borrmans, preface to Jacquin, *Massignon—Abd-el-Jalil*, 23–29.

82. Quoted in Mehdi Sajid, "Muslim Convert to Christianity."

83. Avon, *Les Frères prêcheurs*, 30.

84. Letter from Abd-el-Jalil to Massignon in Borrmans, preface to Jacquin, *Massignon—Abd-el-Jalil*, 27.

85. Letter from Abd-el-Jalil to Massignon in Borrmans, preface to Jacquin, *Massignon—Abd-el-Jalil*, 29.

86. See this issue discussed in a letter dated September 2, 1934 from Massignon to Abd-el-Jalil, *Massignon—Abd-el-Jalil*, 119.

87. Jacques Keryell, "Notice biographique de Mary Kahil," in *L'hospitalité sacrée*, 77–98.

88. Quoted in Gude, *Louis Massignon*, 132.

89. Margot Badran, *Feminists, Islam, and Nation: Gender and the Making of Modern Egypt* (Princeton, NJ: Princeton University Press, 1995), 96–100, 113–14.

90. Badran, *Feminists, Islam, and Nation*, 100.

91. Badran, *Feminists, Islam, and Nation*, 96.

92. Avon, *Les Frères prêcheurs*, 125.

93. Avon, *Les Frères prêcheurs*, 125.

94. Keryell, *L'hospitalité sacrée*, 98.

95. Keryell, *L'hospitalité sacrée*, 100.

96. Keryell, *L'hospitalité sacrée*, 101.

97. Keryell, *L'hospitalité sacrée*, 13. See also Wilkins, "Mary Kahil," 133.

98. Keryell, "Notice biographique de Mary Kahil," 77–98.

99. Guy Harpigny's influential analysis divides Massignon's life into the Hallājian, Arba-hamic, and Gandhian cycles. Harpigny, *Islam et Christianisme*. See also Camille Dre-vet, who gathers passages of Massignon's and Gandhi's writings for a compendium of overlapping themes in Camille Drevet, *Massignon et Gandhi: La contagion de la vérité* (Paris: Éditions du Cerf, 1967); see also Gude, *Louis Massignon*, 127–30; and Christian Krokus, "Christianity, Islam, and Hinduism in Louis Massignon's Appropriation of Gandhi as Modern Saint," *Journal of Ecumenical Studies* 47, no. 4 (2012): 525–40.

100. Letter from Massignon to Mary Kahil, February 10, 1934, in Keryell, *L'hospitalité sacrée*, 175.

101. Letter from Massignon to Kahil, April 2, 1934, in Keryell, *L'hospitalité sacrée*, 134, 184–85. Mary Louise Gude's text first alerted me to this important passage, and I have relied on some of her translation and translated some of it my own. Gude, *Louis Massignon*, 137.

102. Letter from Massignon to Kahil, January 1, 1935, in Keryell, *L'hospitalité sacrée*, 196.

103. Letter from Massignon to Kahil, June 26, 1947, in Keryell, *L'hospitalité sacrée*, 240.

104. Letter from Massignon to Kahil, April 32, 1934, in Keryell, *L'hospitalité sacrée*, 186.

105. Letter from Massignon to Kahil, March 20, 1934, in Keryell, *L'hospitalité sacrée*, 183.

106. Wilfred Cantwell Smith, *The Meaning and End of Religion* (London: SPCK, 1978), 142.

107. Keryell, *L'hospitalité sacrée*, 175. Emphasis added.

108. Keryell, *L'hospitalité sacrée*, 218.

109. For more on the connections between human and divine love in Islamic mystical tradi-tions, see Omid Safi, "Introduction: Islam's Path of Radical Love," *Radical Love* (New Haven, CT: Yale University Press, 2018), xix–xxvi; Fatemeh Keshavarz, "The Ecstatic Faith of Rumi," *On Being* podcast, original air date March 1, 2007, last updated March 8, 2012, https://onbeing.org/programs/fatemeh-keshavarz-the-ecstatic-faith-of-rumi/.

110. Keryell, *L'hospitalité sacrée*, 187.

111. Keryell, *L'hospitalité sacrée*, 187.

112. Keryell, *L'hospitalité sacrée*, 101.

113. Keryell, *L'hospitalité sacrée*, 327.

114. Jeffrey Kripal, *Roads of Excess, Palaces of Wisdom* (Chicago: University of Chicago Press, 2001), 145.

115. Dipesh Chakrabarty, *Provincializing Europe: Postcolonial Thought and Historical Dif-ference* (Princeton, NJ: Princeton University Press, 2002), 78.

116. Constance M. Furey, "Sexuality," in *The Cambridge Companion to Christian Mysticism*, ed. Amy Hollywood and Patricia Beckman (Cambridge: Cambridge University Press, 2012), 330.

117. Maggie Nelson, *The Argonauts* (Minneapolis: Graywolf, 2016), 9.

118. Nelson, *Argonauts*, 9.

119. Nelson, *Argonauts*, 9. Emphasis added.

120. Elliot Wolfson, *A Dream Interpreted within a Dream: Oneiropoiesis and the Prism of Imagination* (New York: Zone Books, 2011), 3.

121. Anthony M. Petro, "Celibate Politics: Queering the Limits," in *Queer Christianities: Lived Religion in Transgressive Forms*, ed. Kathleen T. Talvacchia, Michael F. Pettinger, and Mark Larrimore (New York: New York University Press, 2014), 45. For a similar line of questioning, see also Benjamin Kahan, *Celibacies: American Modernism and Sexual Life* (Durham, NC: Duke University Press, 2013).

122. Furey, "Sexuality," 330.

123. Bernard McGinn, "Mysticism and Sexuality," *The Way Supplement* 77 (1993): 47.

124. Teresa of Ávila's celebrated vision of God is one in which an angel appeared before her and "thrust a lance to pierce my very entrails, when he drew it out, he seemed to draw them out also and to leave me all on fire with a great love of God. The pain was so great that it made me moan; and yet so surpassing was the sweetness of this excessive pain that I could not wish to be rid of it. The soul is satisfied now with nothing less than God." Teresa of Ávila, *Book of Her Life*, ed. and trans. Jodi Bilinkoff, Kieran Kavanaugh, and Otilio Rodriguez (London: Hackett, 1999), 22.

125. Private notes transcribed in Keryell, *L'hospitalité sacrée*, 130.

126. Keryell, *L'hospitalité sacrée*, 187.

127. Keryell, *L'hospitalité sacrée*, 221.

128. For an excellent new overview of Massignon and Kahil's Al-Badaliya association (along with new translations of several of Massignon's letters to the association), see Dorothy C. Buck, ed., *Louis Massignon: Pioneer of Interfaith Dialogue and the Badaliya Prayer Movement* (Clifton, NJ: Blue Dome Press, 2017).

129. Massignon was also influenced by French Catholic revival literary works on substitutionary suffering and vicarious suffering. See François Angelier, "Douleur, substitution, intersignes: Aux sources littéraires de la pensée de Louis Massignon," in *Louis Massignon et le dialogue des cultures*, ed. Daniel Massignon (Paris: Éditions du Cerf, 1996), 155–70; Paolo Dall'Oglio, "Louis Massignon and Badaliya," *ARAM* 20 (2008): 329–36.

130. Buck, *Louis Massignon: Pioneer*, 21.

131. Jean-François Six, "L'Union, la Badaliya et autres associations foucaldiens," *Bulletin des Amis de Louis Massignon*, no. 19 (2008): 55.

132. Avon, *Les Frères prêcheurs*, 175.

133. Avon, *Les Frères prêcheurs*, 175.

134. Quoted in Keryell, *L'hospitalité sacrée*, 33.

135. Avon, *Les Frères prêcheurs*, 109.

136. Georges Anawati provides a list of several conference titles in "Louis Massignon et le dialogue islamo-chrétien, Souvenirs personelles," in D. Massignon, *Louis Massignon et le dialogue des cultures*, 271, 278–80. See also Avon, *Les Frères prêcheurs*, 564.

137. Avon, *Les Frères prêcheurs*, 567.

138. These ideas have not faded. For example, see Roger Cohen, "Islam and the West at

War," *New York Times*, November 16, 2015, https://www.nytimes.com/2015/02/17/opinion/roger-cohen-islam-and-the-west-at-war.html.

139. Avon, *Les Frères prêcheurs*, 575, 130.

140. Waardenburg, *Muslims as Actors*, 167.

141. Paolo Dall'Oglio, "Massignon and *jihad* in the Light of de Foucauld, al-Hallâj and Gandhi," in *Faith, Power, and Violence*, ed. John J. Donohue and Christian W. Troll (Rome: Pontificio Istituto Orientale, 1998), 103–14. For more on Massignon on the issue of Israel and Palestine, see Anthony O'Mahony, "Le pèlerin de Jérusalem: Louis Massignon, Palestinian Christians, Islam and the State of Israel," in *Palestinian Christians, Religion, Politics and Society in the Holy Land*, ed. Anthony O'Mahony (London: Melisende, 1999), 166–89.

142. Wheeler, "Louis Massignon and Al-Hallâj," 229, 239.

143. Keryell, *L'hospitalité sacrée*, 300.

144. Keryell, *L'hospitalité sacrée*.

145. Étienne Fouilloux, "Une vision eschatologique du christianisme: *Dieu vivant* (1945–1955)," *Revue d'histoire de l'Église de France* 57, no. 158 (1971): 47.

146. For a firsthand description of some of these early marches that mention Massignon's participation, see "Hommages aux morts de la place de la Nation," *Le Monde*, July 23, 1957.

147. Letter from Kahil to Massignon, December 1960, in Keryell, *L'hospitalité sacrée*, 330.

148. Letter from Massignon to Kahil, August 5, 1956, in Keryell, *L'hospitalité sacrée*, 298.

149. Louis Massignon, "L'Occident devant l'Orient: Primauté d'une solution culturelle," *Politique étrangère*, 17, no. 2 (1952): 13–28.

150. "Un Appel de M. Massignon pour que des sépultures décentes soient données aux victimes des manifestations musulmanes," *Le Monde*, November 9, 1961, http://www.lemonde.fr/archives/article/1961/11/09/un-appel-de-m-massignon-pour-que-des-sepultures-decentes-soient-donnees-aux-victimes-des-manifestations-musulmanes_2273290_1819218.html.

151. Letter from Kahil to Massignon, Keryell, *L'hospitalité sacrée*, 329.

152. Letter from Massignon to Kahil, January 16, 1950, in Keryell, *L'hospitalité sacrée*, 265.

153. Krokus, *Theology of Louis Massignon*, 102.

154. Address of Massignon to the Badaliya Association, June 7, 1957 reprinted in Buck, *Louis Massignon: Pioneer*, 138.

155. Newsletter from Massignon to the Badaliya Association, June 1958, in Keryell, *L'hospitalité sacrée*, 494.

156. Keryell, *L'hospitalité sacrée*, 404.

157. Keryell, *L'hospitalité sacrée*, 404.

158. Mahmud al-Mas'adi interview in Ziad Elarmsafy, *Sufism in the Contemporary Arabic Novel* (Edinburgh: University of Edinburgh Press, 2012), 68.

159. Hatsuki Aishima, *Public Culture and Islam in Modern Egypt: Media, Intellectuals and Society* (London: I. B. Tauris, 2016), 33.

160. These extracts are taken from Ali Shariati, "Kavir," quoted in Michel Cuypers, "A Mystical Encounter: Ali Shari'ati—Louis Massignon," in Keryell, *Massignon et ses contemporains*. See also Anthony O'Mahony, "Mysticism and Politics: Louis Massignon, Shi'a

Islam, Iran and Ali Shari'ati—A Muslim-Christian Encounter," in *University Lectures in Islamic Studies*, ed. Alan Jones (London: Oxford University Press, 1998), 2:113–34.

161. Sheikh Ibrahim, political leader in Algeria, quoted in Thierry Hentsch, *Imagining the Middle East* (Montreal: Black Rose Books, 1992), 175.

162. Massignon wrote a lengthy letter to the Badaliya association reflecting on the year of 1959, in Keryell, *L'hospitalité sacrée*, 414.

163. Letter from Massignon to Kahil, February 2, 1957, in Keryell, *L'hospitalité sacrée*, 299.

164. Letter from Massignon to Kahil, April 17, 1962, in Keryell, *L'hospitalité sacrée*, 319.

165. Mason, *Memoir of a Friend*, 117. For more on the topic of Massignon, Islam, and Vatican II, see Anthony O'Mahony, "Catholic Theological Perspectives on Islam at the Second Vatican Council," *New Blackfriars* 88 (July 2007): 385–98; O'Mahony, "Life and Thought of Louis Massignon"; Neal Robinson, "Massignon, Vatican II and Islam as an Abrahamic Religion," *Islam and Christian Relations* 2 (1991): 182–203; Andrew Unsworth, "Louis Massignon, the Holy See and the Ecclesial Transition from 'Immortale Dei' to 'Nostra Aetate': A Brief History of the Development of Catholic Church Teaching on Muslims and the Religion of Islam from 1883 to 1965," *ARAM* 20 (2008): 299–316.

166. Massignon never published this talk, but it is partially transcribed in Jacques Keryell, *Jardin donné: Louis Massignon à la recherche de L'Absolu* (Paris: Éditions Saint-Paul, 1999), 152.

167. Letter from Massignon to Kahil, April 17, 1962, in Keryell, *L'hospitalité sacrée*, 319.

168. Letter from Kahil to Georges Anawati, August 10, 1962, in Avon, *Les Frères prêcheurs*, 575.

169. Keryell, *L'hospitalité sacrée*, 333. Wilkins, "Mary Kahil," also offers a wonderful analysis of this passage.

170. Keryell, *L'hospitalité sacrée*, 333, 336.

171. Keryell, *L'hospitalité sacrée*, 80.

172. J. Maritain, *Cahier de l'Herne*, 451–52.

CHAPTER THREE

1. For more on Davy, see her memoir *Traversée en solitaire*, ed. Marc-Alain Descamps (Paris: Albin Michel, 1989); Marc-Alain Descamps and Jacques d'Ares, *Marie-Magdeleine Davy, ou la liberté du dépassement* (Paris: Le Miel de la Pierre, 2001); and Étienne Fouilloux, "Marie-Magdeleine Davy," in *Destins de Femmes: Religion, Culture, et société (France, XIXe–XXe siècles)*, ed. Ann Cova and Bruno Dumons (Paris: Letouzey et Ané, 2011), 144–45. For some brief works in English, see Bernard McGinn, "'The Violent Are Taking It by Storm' (Mt 11:12): Reflections on a Century of Women's Contributions to the Study of Mystical Spirituality," *Spiritus: A Journal of Christian Spirituality* 13, no. 1 (2013): 17–35; Brenna Moore, "Into the Catacombs of the Past: Women and Wartime Trauma in the French Catholic *Ressourcement* Project (1939–1945)" in *God's Mirror: Renewal and Engagement in French Catholic Intellectual Culture in the Mid-Twentieth Century*, ed. Katherine Davies and Toby Garfitt (New York: Fordham University Press, 2015), 186–209.

2. Davy, *Traversée en solitaire*, 42.

3. For more on Davy's role in the resistance (a topic about which she was very reticent to discuss at length in her own writings), see Margaret L. Rossiter, *Women in the Resistance* (New York: Praeger, 1985), 111; Anne Thoraval, *Paris, les lieux de la Résistance: La vie quotidienne de l'armée des ombres dans la capital* (Paris: Parigramme, 2007), 66; Ian Darling, *Amazing Airmen: Canadian Flyers in the Second World War* (Toronto: Dundurn, 2009), 195; and Jean-Dominique Durand and Régis Ladous, eds., *Histoire religieuse: Histoire globale, histoire ouverte: Mélanges offerts à Jacques Gadille* (Paris: Bibliothèque Beauchesne, 1992), 40.

4. Durand and Ladous, *Histoire religieuse*, 40.

5. Resistance awards and memorabilia are found in box 154, Marie-Magdeleine Davy Archives, Départementales des Deux-Sèvres, Niort, France.

6. For a useful overview of the history of *la nouvelle théologie*, see Jürgen Mettepenningen, *Nouvelle Théologie–New Theology: Inheritor of Modernism, Precursor of Vatican II* (London: Continuum, 2010); Gabriel Flynn and Paul Murray, *Ressourcement: A Movement for Renewal in Twentieth-Century Catholic Theology* (Oxford: Oxford University Press, 2014); and Étienne Fouilloux, *Une église en quête de liberté: La pensée catholique française entre modernisme et Vatican II, 1914–1962* (Paris: Desclée de Brouwer, 1998).

7. Marie-Magdeleine Davy, *Bernard de Clairvaux, Saint Bernard* (Paris: Aubier, 1943), 121.

8. John Connelly, *From Enemy to Brother: The Revolution in Catholic Teaching on the Jews, 1933–1965* (Cambridge, MA: Harvard University Press), 33.

9. Davy, *Traversée en solitaire*, 19.

10. See Marc Étienne Fouilloux, "Marie-Magdeleine Davy," in Cova and Dumons, *Destins de Femmes*, 144–45.

11. Davy, *Traversée en solitaire*, 111.

12. Quoted in Eric Edelmann, "L'instant ultime entretien avec Marie-Magdeleine Davy," *Question de* 36 (May–June 1980): 5.

13. Florian Michel, *Étienne Gilson: Une biographie intellectuelle and politique* (Paris: Vrin, 2018).

14. Philip Daileader and Philip Whalen, eds., *French Historians 1900–2000: New Historical Writing in Twentieth-Century France* (London: Wiley, 2010), xix. Raïssa Maritain offers a vivid depiction of the Sorbonne at the time in "Récit de ma conversion," *Cahiers Jacques Maritain* 7–8 (1983): 77.

15. Quoted in Étienne Gilson, *The Mystical Theology of St. Bernard*, trans. A. H. C. Downes (Collegeville, MN: Cistercian Publications, 1990), xiv.

16. Émile Poulat, *L'université devant la mystique. Expérience du Dieu sans mode. Transcendance du Dieu d'Amour* (Paris: Éditions Salvator, 1999), 3.

17. Marie-Magdeleine Davy, *Bernard de Clairvaux* (Paris: Albin Michel, 2001).

18. Davy, *Bernard de Clairvaux*, 121.

19. Edelmann, "L'instant ultime," 5.

20. Davy, *Traversée en solitaire*, 73.

21. Marie-Magdeleine Davy, *Un traité de la vie solitaire: Epistola ad fratres de Monte-Dei* (Paris: Vrin, 1940), 8.

22. Marie-Magdeleine Davy, *Les chemins de la profondeur* (Paris: Éditions du Relié, 2014).

23. Rachel Smith, "Language, Literacy, and the Saintly Body: Cistercian Reading Practices and the Life of Lutgard of Aywières (1182–1246)," *Harvard Theological Review* 109, no. 4 (October 2016): 586–610.

24. Albrecht Classen, *Friendship in the Middle Ages and Early Modern Age: Explorations of a Fundamental Ethical Discourse* (Berlin: Walter de Gruyter, 2010).

25. Davy, *Un traité de la vie solitaire*, 23.

26. Jean Leclercq, *L'amour des lettres et le désir de Dieu: Initiation aux auteurs monastiques du Moyen-Age* (Paris: Éditions du Cerf, 1991).

27. Davy, *Un traité de la vie solitaire*, 23.

28. Amy Hollywood, introduction to *The Cambridge Companion to Christian Mysticism*, ed. Amy Hollywood and Patricia Z. Beckman (Cambridge: Cambridge University Press, 2012), 25.

29. Marie-Magdeleine Davy, "Guides et méthodes de la vie intérieure chrétienne," *Question de 9*, no. 4 (1975).

30. Davy's role in the BEC is found in the Marie-Magdeleine Davy Archives, 155 J 67, Départementales des Deux-Sèvres, Niort, France. The BEC is also mentioned as a resistance site in Thoraval, *Paris, les lieux de la Résistance*, 66.

31. Marie-Magdeleine Davy, *Les Dominicaines* (Paris: Grasset, 1934) (vol. 18 of Les grands ordres monastiques et instituts religieux).

32. Marie-Dominique Chenu, "Un religion contemplative," review of *Les Dominicaines*, by Marie-Magdeleine Davy, *VS* 43, no. 187 (April 1935): 86–89.

33. Marie-Dominique Chenu, "M.-M. Davy.—Guillaume de Saint-Thierry. Deux traités sur la foi: Le miroir de la foi. L'énigme de la foi," *Cahiers de civilisation médiévale* 3, no. 12 (1960): 498.

34. De Lubac cites Davy's works on Guillaume of Saint-Thierry's discussion of the *Song of Songs* in vol. 2 of his *Medieval Exegesis: The Four Senses of Scripture*, trans. E. M. Macierowski (Grand Rapids, MI: Eerdmans, 2000), 239, 240, 329, 332, 397, 403, 408. See also Henri de Lubac, *Corpus Mysticum: The Eucharist and the Church in the Middle Ages*, trans. Gemma Simmonds, with Richard Price and Christopher Stephens (South Bend, IN: University of Notre Dame Press, 2007), 167–69.

35. For Marie-Magdeleine Davy's works in this time published by religious orders' publishing houses, see *La psychologie de la foi d'après Guillaume de Saint-Thierry: Extrait des "Recherches de théologie ancienne et médiévale"* (Louvain: Abbaye du Mont César, 1938); *Traité de la vie solitaire, Guillaume de Saint-Thierry* (Paris: Vrin, 1940); *Saint Bernard, oeuvres traduites et préfacées* (Paris: Aubier, 1945); *Guillaume de Saint-Thierry, Deux traités de l'amour de Dieu* (Paris: Vrin, 1953); *Théologie et mystique de Guillaume de Saint-Thierry* (Paris: Vrin, 1954); *Guillaume de Saint-Thierry: Commentaires sur le Cantique des Cantiques* (Paris: Vrin, 1958); *Guillaume de Saint-Thierry: Deux traités sur la foi: Le miroir de la foi, l'énigme de la foi* (Paris: Vrin, 1959).

36. Michel de Boüard, review of *Un traité de l'amour du XIIe siècle. Pierre de Blois*, by Marie-Magdeleine Davy, *Revue d'histoire de l'Église de France* 20, no. 86 (1934): 111–12.

37. Davy, *Traversée en solitaire*, 111–13.

38. Davy, *Traversée en solitaire*, 111–13.

39. Davy, *Traversée en solitaire*, 99.

40. Davy, *Traversée en solitaire*, 99.

41. Descamps and d'Ares, *Marie-Magdeleine Davy*, 22. For a useful overview of gender and higher education in this context, see Toril Moi, *Simone de Beauvoir: The Making of an Intellectual Woman* (Oxford: Oxford University Press, 2008), 23–27.

42. Like Davy, Elisabeth Behr-Sigel, a Russian Orthodox, sat in and followed free courses at St. Sergius Orthodox Theological Institute in Paris, which, at that time, did not allow women.

43. Jean Daniélou, "Les orientations présentes de la pensée religieuse," *Études* 249 (1946): 5–21.

44. "The return to the sources is to history what the return to principles is to philosophy: the same spiritual power, the same rejuvenation, the same fertility, the one reinforces the other." M.-D. Chenu, *Une école de théologie: Le Saulchoir* (Paris: Éditions du Cerf, 1983), 127.

45. Quotations from the classic *ressourcement* essay by Jean Daniélou, "Les orientations présentes de la pensée religieuse," *Études* 249 (1946): 5–21.

46. Davy, *Traversée en solitaire*, 65. Other women medievalists came to similar conclusions about the hierarchy's treatment of the *ressourcement* theologians. See Marie-Thérèse d'Alverny's obituary of Chenu, "In Memoriam M.D. Chenu, O.P. (1895–1989)," *Archives d'histoire doctrinale et littéraire du Moyen Âge* 57 (1990): 9–10. Medievalist Beryl Smalley, for example, converted to Protestantism when Chenu was silenced.

47. Davy, *The Mysticism of Simone Weil*, 74.

48. Yves Congar, "The Brother I Have Known," *Thomist* 49 (1985): 495–503.

49. Davy, *Traversée en solitaire*, 111.

50. For more on the role of Jeanne Ancelet-Hustache, see Vicki Caron, *Uneasy Asylum: France and the Jewish Refugee Crisis, 1933–1942* (Stanford, CA: Stanford University Press, 2002), 216–17, 288–89.

51. Timothy Snyder, "The Test of Nazism That Trump Failed," *New York Times*, August 18, 2017, http://www.nytimes.com/2017/08/18/opinion/the-test-of-nazism-that-trump-failed.html?mcubz=1.

52. Rossiter, *Women in the Resistance*, 111; Thoraval, *Paris, les lieux de la Résistance*, 66; Darling, *Amazing Airmen*, 195; Durand and Ladous, *Histoire religieuse*, 40.

53. Thoraval, *Paris, les lieux de la Résistance*, 66.

54. Quoted in Robert Gildea, *Fighters in the Shadows: A New History of the French Resistance* (London: Faber & Faber, 2016), 157.

55. Descamps and d'Ares, *Marie-Magdeleine Davy*, 44.

56. For Davy's work in the resistance and her scholarship as a medievalist in this period, see 155 J 26–27, 65, in box 12, Marie-Magdeleine Davy Archives, Départementales des Deux-Sèvres, Niort, France.

57. Mark Antliff, *Avant-Garde Fascism: The Mobilization of Myth, Art, and Culture in France, 1909–1939* (Durham, NC: Duke University Press, 2007); see also Romy Golan, *Modernity and Nostalgia* (New Haven, CT: Yale University Press, 1995). Françoise Meltzer shows similar logic of medievalism and right-wing nationalism at work earlier,

in mid-nineteenth-century German Romantic thinkers such as Friedrich Schlegel. Françoise Meltzer, "Unity under Christendom: German Romanticism's Middle Ages," *Cadernos de Literatura Comparada* 16 (2007): 20.

58. Roger Griffin, "Fascism's Modernist Revolution: A New Paradigm for the Study of Right-Wing Dictatorships," *Fascism* 5 (2016): 105–29.

59. Hilaire Belloc, *Jeanne d'Arc*, trans. Marguerite Faguer, preface by Henri Massis (Paris: Frimin-Didot, 1930), xvii.

60. Bernard Wall, "Tradition and Social Justice," *Dublin Review* 401 (1937): 258, 261; Jay P. Corrin, "Catholic Writers on the Right," *Chesterton Review* 25, no. 1/2 (1999): 81–101.

61. Sandrine Sanos, *The Aesthetics of Hate: Far-Right Intellectuals, Antisemitism, and Gender in 1930s France* (Stanford, CA: Stanford University Press, 2012), 68.

62. "Interview with G. K. Chesterton," *Jewish Chronicle*, September 22, 1932.

63. G. K. Chesterton, *Saint Thomas Aquinas: The Dumb Ox* (New York: Doubleday, 1974), 22. For a Far-Right use of these ideas for today, see William Kilpatrick, "Chesterton's Islamic England," *Crisis Magazine*, December 9, 2014, http://www.crisismagazine.com /2014/chestertons-islamic-england.

64. Étienne Gilson, "Letter to Chesterton's Editor," in Josef Pieper, *Guide to Thomas Aquinas* (San Francisco, Ignatius Press, 1991), 6–7.

65. Quoted in Seth D. Armus, *French Anti-Americanism 1930–1948* (Lanham, MD: Lexington Books), 67.

66. Quoted in Olivier Wieviorka, *The French Resistance*, trans. Jane Marie Todd (Cambridge, MA: Belknap Press, 2016), 95.

67. Davy, *Traversée en solitaire*, 31, 34.

68. Davy, *Traversée en solitaire*, 82–83.

69. Davy, *Traversée en solitaire*, 37.

70. Davy, *Traversée en solitaire*, 99.

71. Étienne Fouilloux, "Instruments, relais, et cadres du regime: Clerge catholique et regime de Vichy," presented to the colloquium "Le regime de Vichy et les Français" of the Institute d'Histoire du Temps Présent, Paris, June 11–13, 1990; François Marcot, Bruno Leroux, and Christine Levisse-Touzet, *Dictionnaire historique de la Résistance* (Paris: Robert Laffont, 2006), 871.

72. Henri de Lubac, *At the Service of the Church: Henri de Lubac Reflects on the Circumstances That Occasioned His Writing*, trans. Anne Englund Nash (San Francisco: Ignatius Press, 1992), 50.

73. Henri de Lubac, *Paradoxes of Faith*, trans. P. Simon, S. Kreilkamp, and E. Beaumont (San Francisco: Ignatius Press, 1987), 57–58.

74. Henri de Lubac, "Un Nouveau 'Front' Religieux," in *Israël et la foi chrétienne* (Fribourg: Éditions de la Librairie de l'Université de Fribourg, 1942).

75. This lecture was published as Henri de Lubac, "Le fondement théologique des missions," *Bibliothèque de l'Union mission du clerge de France* (1941): 3–29; and partially reproduced and translated in Henri de Lubac, *Theology in History*, trans. Anne Englund Nash (San Francisco: Ignatius Press, 1996), 367–88. For more on de Lubac's activities in the resistance, see Renée and François Bédarida, *La Résistance spirituelle, 1941–1944:*

Les cahiers clandestins du Témoignage Chrétien (Paris: Albin Michel, 2001); Étienne Fouilloux, *Les chrétiens français entre crise et libération, 1937–1947* (Paris: Éditions du Seuil, 1997); Henri de Lubac, *Christian Resistance to Anti-Semitism: Memories from 1940–1944*, trans. Elizabeth Englund (San Francisco: Ignatius Press, 1990).

76. Bernard Comte, *Initiatives de théologiens face à la persécution antisémite à Lyon en 1941–42* (Lyon: Institut Catholique, 1993), 15–16.

77. On Amitié chrétienne, see François Delpech, *Sur les juifs; Études d'histoire contemporaine* (Lyon: Presses Universitaires de Lyon, 1983), 238–49.

78. Henri de Lubac, *Christian Resistance to Anti-Semitism: Memories from 1940–1944*, trans. Elizabeth Englund (San Francisco: Ignatius Press, 1990), 16.

79. Alexander Altmann, "Georges Vajda (1908–1981)," *Proceedings of the American Academy for Jewish Research* 50 (1983): xix–xxiii.

80. See also Susanna Heschel, *The Aryan Jesus: Christian Theologians and the Bible in Nazi Germany* (Princeton, NJ: Princeton University Press, 2009).

81. Davy, *Saint Bernard*, 8.

82. Davy, *Saint Bernard*, 9.

83. Meltzer, "Unity under Christiandom," 20.

84. *Cahiers de la nouvelle époque* found in 155 J 60, Marie-Magdeleine Davy Archives, Départementales des Deux-Sèvres, Niort, France.

85. Inside cover of all issues of *L'âge nouveau*, found in 155 J 48-51, Marie-Magdeleine Davy Archives, Départementales des Deux-Sèvres, Niort, France.

86. 155 J 18, Marie-Magdeleine Davy Archives, Départementales des Deux-Sèvres, Niort, France.

87. "Obituary Notices—Henri Maspéro," *Journal of the Royal Asiatic Society of Great Britain and Ireland* 1 (1946): 95.

88. Kenneth G. Zysk, *Medicine in the Veda: Religious Healing in the Veda: with Translations and Annotations of Medical Hymns from the Ṛgveda and the Atharvaveda and Renderings from the Corresponding Ritual Texts* (Delhi: Motilal Banarsidass Publishers, 2009). At the Collège de France, a chair in Sanskrit was established in 1814, and the chair of Islamic sociology in 1903. See Edmund Burke III and David Prochaska, eds., *Genealogies of Orientalism: History, Theory, Politics* (Lincoln: University of Nebraska Press, 2008), 165.

89. Étienne Fouilloux, *Christianisme et Eschatologie Dieu Vivant (1945–1955)* (Paris: CLD, 2015), 22.

90. There is a similar methodology in Leigh Schmidt's description of the role of sympathy in the study of religion. Leigh Schmidt, "On Sympathy, Suspicion, and Studying Religion: Historical Reflections of a Double Inheritance," in *The Cambridge Companion to Religious Studies*, ed. Robert Orsi (Cambridge: Cambridge University Press, 2012), 15–35.

91. Marie-Madeleine Davy, "Le thème de la vengeance au moyen âge," in *La vengeance: Études d'ethnologie, d'histoire et de philosophie*, ed. R. Verdier (Paris: Cujas, 1991).

92. Marie-Madeleine Davy, *Guillaume de Saint-Thierry, Méditative orationes* (Paris: Vrin, 1934).

93. Quoted in Descamps and d'Ares, *Marie-Magdeleine Davy*, 44.

94. Quoted in Armelle Dutruc, *Marie-Magdeleine Davy (1903–1998) ou l'Orient intérieur: Répertoire numérique détaillé des archives de Marie-Magdeleine Davy* (Niort: Archives Départementales des Deux-Sèvres, 2012), 10n8.

95. Marie-Magdeleine Davy, *Encyclopédie des mystiques*, vol. 1, *Chamanisme, Grecs, Juifs, Gnose, Christianisme primitif*; vol. 2, *Christianisme occidental, ésotérisme, protestant-isme, islam*; vol. 3, *Egypte, Mésopotamie, Iran, hindouisme*; vol. 4, *Bouddhismes tibétain, chinois, japonais, Yi-King, tch'an, zen* (Paris: Petite Bibliothèque Payot, 1996).

96. Quoted in Edelmann, "L'instant ultime," 5.

97. Davy, *Traversée en solitaire*, 131–33.

98. François Dosse, *Gilles Deleuze and Félix Guattari: Intersecting Lives*, trans. Deborah Glassman (New York: Columbia University Press, 2011), 91–93. See also Joshua Ramey, *The Hermetic Deleuze: Philosophy and Spiritual Ordeal* (Durham, NC: Duke University Press, 2012).

99. Marie-Magdeleine Davy, *Nicolas Berdyaev: Man of the Eighth Day*, trans. Leonara Siepman (Paris: Flammarion, 1964), 10.

100. Marie-Magdeleine Davy, "Nicolas Berdiaeff ou la lutte de la création contre l'objectivation," *Esprit* 147, no. 8 (August 1948): 162–78, and *Nicolas Berdiaev, l'homme du huitième jour* (Paris: Flammarion, 1964).

101. Davy, foreword to *Nicolas Berdyaev*, 2.

102. Davy, *Nicolas Berdyaev*, 44. Guillaume de Saint-Thierry, *Deux traités de l'amour de Dieu: De la nature et de la dignité de l'amour*, ed. Marie-Magdeleine Davy (Paris: Vrin, 1953), 55.

103. Davy, *Nicolas Berdyaev*, 2.

104. Davy, *Nicolas Berdyaev*, 47.

105. Davy, *Nicolas Berdyaev*, 47–49. Davy had also come in contact with Russian Orthodox monks in Paris, and between these monks and the power of Berdyaev, Davy considered converting to Orthodox Christianity. But she said she heard so many Russian Orthodox priests saying horrible things about the Catholic Church that she assumed there was just the same amount of small-mindedness as the Western hierarchy (who she regarded as mere civil servants). On Berdyaev, see Michel Alexander Vallon, *An Apostle of Freedom: Life and Teachings of Nicolas Berdyaev* (New York: Philosophical Library, 1960), 139; and Donald A. Lowrie, *Rebellious Prophet: A Life of Nicolai Berdyaev* (Westport, CT: Greenwood, 1974). See also Donald Lowrie, *Saint Sergius in Paris: The Orthodox Theological Institute* (London: SPCK, 1954); Catherine Gousseff, "Une intelligentsia chrétienne en exil: Les orthodoxes russes dans la France des années 20," in *Intellectuels chrétiens et esprit des années 1920, Actes du colloque*, ed. Pierre Colin (Paris: Éditions du Cerf, 1997), 119; Mark Corrado, "Orientalism in Reverse: Henry Corbin, Iranian Philosophy, and the Critique of the West" (master's thesis, Simon Fraser University, 2004). For an excellent overview of Berdyaev's thought in its international context, see Lisa Holsberg, "Nikolai Berdyaev and the Spiritual and Intellectual World of a Russian Philosopher in Exile, 1922–1948" (PhD diss., Fordham University, 2021).

106. Marie-Magdeleine Davy, "L'homme en qui Dieu verdoie," *Question de* 90 (1992): 218–19.

107. Davy, "L'homme en qui Dieu verdoie," 219.

108. Richard King, *Orientalism and Religion: Postcolonial Theory, India, and the "Mystic East"* (London: Routledge, 1999); Elizabeth Ezra, *The Colonial Unconscious: Race and Culture in Interwar France* (Ithaca, NY: Cornell University Press, 2000).

109. Steven M. Wasserstrom, *Religion after Religion: Gershom Scholem, Mircea Eliade, and Henri Corbon at Eranos* (Princeton, NJ: Princeton University Press, 1999).

110. Torrance Kirby, Rahim Acar, and Bilal Baş, eds, *Philosophy and the Abrahamic Religions: Scriptural Hermeneutics and Epistemology* (Newcastle upon Tyne: Cambridge Scholars Publishing, 2013), 353.

111. Mihail Sebastian, *Journal, 1935–1944: The Fascist Years* (Lanham, MD: Rowman & Littlefield, 2012), xiv.

112. Quoted in Sebastian, *Journal, 1935–1944*, xiv.

113. For a parallel argument that has influenced my own on women's scholarship and the discipline of history, see Bonnie Smith, *The Gender of History: Men, Women, and Historical Practice* (Cambridge, MA: Harvard University Press, 1998).

114. Michel de Certeau, "How Is Christianity Thinkable Today?," in *The Postmodern God*, ed. Graham Ward (Oxford: Blackwell, 1997), 151.

CHAPTER FOUR

1. Marie-Magdeleine Davy, *Traversée en solitaire* (Paris: Albin Michel, 1989), 112–14.

2. Davy, *Traversée en solitaire*, 112.

3. Marie-Magdeleine Davy, *The Mysticism of Simone Weil*, trans. Cynthia Rowland (Whitefish, MT: Kessinger, 2010).

4. Peter Brown, "The Saint as Exemplar in Late Antiquity," in *Saints and Virtues*, ed. John Stratton Hawley (Los Angeles: University of California Press, 1987), 3–14.

5. William Christian, *Divine Presence in Spain and Western Europe 1500–1960: Visions, Religious Images and Photographs* (Budapest: Central European University Press, 2016), 246.

6. Jennifer L. Palmer, *Intimate Bonds: Family and Slavery in the French Atlantic* (Philadelphia: University of Pennsylvania Press, 2016), 5.

7. Mona Ozouf, "Simone Weil: Simone, or Asceticism," in *Women's Words: An Essay on French Singularity*, trans. Jane Marie Todd (Chicago: University of Chicago Press, 1997), 199.

8. Marie-Magdeleine Davy, *Introducion au message de Simone Weil* (Paris: Librairie Plon, 1954), 3, box 34, Marie-Magdeleine Davy Archives, Départementales des Deux-Sèvres, Niort, France.

9. Claire Duchen, *Women's Rights and Women's Lives in France 1944–1968* (New York: Routledge, 2003), 23.

10. Judith M. Bennett, "Medievalisms and Feminism," *Speculum* 68, no. 2 (1993): 309–31.

11. This information about Ancelet-Hustache's fascinating life comes from days spent in her archives at the Bibliothèque du Saulchoir in Paris. I am thankful to the director,

Frère Jean-Michel Potin, OP, for guidance and permissions. I wish I could have done more with Ancelet-Hustache in this book and hope to write more on her in a future research project.

12. Charles Burnett, "Marie-Thérèse d'Alverny," in *Women Medievalists and the Academy*, ed. Jane Chance (Madison: University of Wisconsin Press, 2005).

13. For her full bibliography, see *Archives d'histoire doctrinale et littéraire du Moyen Âge* 149 (1991): 279–89.

14. Giles Constable, "Marie-Thérèse d'Alverny (25 January 1903–26 April 1991)," *Proceedings of the American Philosophical Society* 136, no. 3 (September 1992): 418–42. See also Laurence K. Shook, *Étienne Gilson* (Toronto: Pontifical Institute of Mediaeval Studies, 1984), 44. D'Alverny also held a series of prestigious grants and visiting appointments, including several in the United States at Berkeley and Columbia, and was awarded an honorary doctorate at Smith College in 1984.

15. On André d'Alverny, see Christian W. Troll, "On Being a Servant of Reconciliation," in *Christian Lives Given to the Study of Islam*, ed. Christian W. Troll and C. T. R. Hewer (New York: Fordham University Press), 118.

16. Marie-Thérèse d'Alverny, "Deux traductions latines du Coran au moyen âge," *Archives d'histoire doctrinale et littéraire du Moyen Âge* 22–23 (1947–48): 69–131.

17. Marie-Thérèse d'Alverny, "Comment les théologiens et les philosophes voient la femme," *Cahiers de civilisation médiévale* 20 (1977): 105–29.

18. Marie-Thérèse d'Alverny, "Translations and Translators," in *Renaissance and Renewal in the Twelfth Century*, ed. Robert L. Benson, Giles Constable, and Carol D. Lanha (Cambridge, MA: Harvard University Press, 1982), 430.

19. Malgorzata H. Malewicz, Jean Jolivet, Charles Burnett, and Jean Vezin, "Nécrologie: Marie-Thérèse d'Alverny (1903–1991)," *Cahiers de civilisation médiévale* 35, no. 139 (1992): 287–93.

20. Marie d'Alverny to Giles Constable, quoted in Constable, "Marie-Thérèse d'Alverny," 418–22.

21. I am grateful for conversations with Giles Constable on this.

22. Quoted in Michel de Certeau, *Heterologies: Discourse on the Other* (Manchester: Manchester University Press, 1986), 182.

23. Bonnie M. Smith, *The Gender of History: Men, Women, and Historical Practice* (Cambridge, MA: Harvard University Press, 1998), 195.

24. Davy, *The Mysticism of Simone Weil*, 16–17.

25. Jonathan Judaken and Robert Bernasconi, eds., *Situating Existentialism: Key Texts in Context* (New York: Columbia University Press, 2012), 259.

26. Davy, *The Mysticism of Simone Weil*.

27. Davy, *The Mysticism of Simone Weil*, 21.

28. Davy, *The Mysticism of Simone Weil*, 18.

29. Davy, *The Mysticism of Simone Weil*, 16–17.

30. "L'idée de Dieu et ses consequences," *L'âge nouveau* 90 (January 1955), in box 12, Marie-Magdeleine Davy Archives, Départementales des Deux-Sèvres, Niort, France.

31. "L'idée de Dieu."

32. Émile Poulat, "Dez (André) L'Age Nouveau," *Archives de sociologie des religions* 1, no. 1 (1956): 199–200. Ordained as a priest in 1945, Poulat joined the ranks of the "worker priests" who departed from traditional ways of exercising the ministry and went to share the lives and fortunes of workers in factories and on docks. Rome ordered the experiment ended in 1954, and Poulat left the priesthood and married a year later and went on to become a prominent scholar of French history and sociology.

33. "L'idée de Dieu."

34. Quoted in Edward Baring, *The Young Derrida and French Philosophy, 1945–1968* (Cambridge: Cambridge University Press, 2011).

35. Davy, *The Mysticism of Simone Weil*, 5.

36. Davy, *The Mysticism of Simone Weil*, 13.

37. Davy, *The Mysticism of Simone Weil*, 14, 84.

38. William James, *The Varieties of Religious Experience: A Study in Human Nature* (London: Longmans, Green, 1902).

39. Brown, "Saint as Exemplar," 11.

40. On the making of saints, Kenneth Woodward argues that in the history of Christianity, the church uses saints to demonstrate virtue and teach morality, while the laity use it to access supernatural power. See Kenneth Woodward, *Making Saints: How the Catholic Church Determines Who Becomes a Saint, Who Doesn't, and Why* (New York: Touchstone, 1996).

41. Quoted in John A. Coleman, "Conclusion: After Sainthood?," in Hawley, *Saints and Virtues*, 218.

42. Hawley, *Saints and Virtues*, 218.

43. Davy, *The Mysticism of Simone Weil*, 47.

44. For more on Jean Herbert the Indologist, see Gopal Stavig and Swami Shuddhidananda, *Western Admirers of Ramakrishna and His Disciples* (Belur Math, India: Advaita Ashrama, 2010), 80, 214–15, 561.

45. Davy, *The Mysticism of Simone Weil*, 80.

46. Davy, *The Mysticism of Simone Weil*, 12.

47. Davy, *The Mysticism of Simone Weil*, 17.

48. Simone Weil, *Attente de Dieu*, with an introduction and notes by J.-M. Perrin (Paris: Éditions du Vieux Colombier, 1950).

49. Davy, *The Mysticism of Simone Weil*, 23.

50. Davy, *The Mysticism of Simone Weil*, 9.

51. Marcel Moré, "La Pensée religieuse de Simone Weil," *Dieu vivant* 17 (1950): 47–54.

52. Davy, *Traversée en solitaire*, 129.

53. Davy, *The Mysticism of Simone Weil*, 28.

54. Davy, *The Mysticism of Simone Weil*, 14.

55. Gerd-Rainer Horn, *Western European Liberation Theology: The First Wave (1924–1959)* (Oxford: Oxford University Press, 2009), 29.

56. Piotr H. Kosicki, *Catholics on the Barricades: Poland: France, and "Revolution," 1891–1956* (New Haven, CT: Yale University Press, 2018), 205.

57. Marie-Dominique Chenu, *Pour une théologie du travail* (Paris: Éditions du Seuil, 1955).

58. Davy, *The Mysticism of Simone Weil*, 6.

59. Simone Weil, "What Is Sacred in Every Human Being?," in *Late Philosophical Writings*, ed. Eric Springsted (South Bend, IN: University of Notre Dame Press, 2015), 190.

60. Simone Weil, "Human Personality," in *Simone Weil: An Anthology*, ed. Siân Miles (New York: Grove Press, 1986), 71.

61. Marie-Magdeleine Davy, *Simone Weil* (Paris: Éditions Universitaires, 1956), 68.

62. Duchen, *Women's Rights*, 13–14, 41.

63. Marie-Magdeleine Davy, *Aimer toutes les mains* (Paris: Au Masque d'Or, 1947), 10.

64. Davy, *Aimer toutes les mains*, 4.

65. On "macho realism," see Tony Judt in Tony Judt and Timothy Snyder, *Thinking the Twentieth Century* (New York: Penguin, 2013), 216.

66. Davy, *The Mysticism of Simone Weil*, 110.

67. Davy, *The Mysticism of Simone Weil*, 74

68. Davy, *The Mysticism of Simone Weil*, 68.

69. Davy, *The Mysticism of Simone Weil*, 70.

70. Weil, *Late Philosophical Writings*, 190.

71. Maison Simone Weil box 155 J 66, Marie Magdeleine Davy Archives, Départementales des Deux-Sèvres, Niort, France.

72. Quoted in Joclyn Simms, "The Tomb of the Tomboy," *Deux-Sèvres Monthly*, October 2015, 15.

73. Gerd-Rainer Horn, *The Spirit of Vatican II: Western European Progressive Catholicism in the Long Sixties* (Oxford: Oxford University Press, 2015).

74. Simms, "Tomb of the Tomboy."

75. "Un square pour Mademoiselle Davy," *La Nouvelle République*, October 18, 2015, http://www.lanouvellerepublique.fr/Deux-Sevres/Actualite/24-Heures/n/Contenus /Articles/2015/10/19/Un-square-pour-Mademoiselle-Davy-2505230.

76. Marie-Magdeleine Davy, *Nicolas Berdyaev: Man of the Eighth Day*, trans. Leonara Siepman (Paris: Flammarion, 1964), 55.

77. Right after the war in 1946, the French Society for Nietzsche was founded, and Davy and Gabriel Marcel played significant roles.

78. Davy, *Traversée en solitaire*, 213.

79. Quoted in Armelle Dutruc, "Marie Magdeleine Davy," *Cahiers d'Orient et d'Occident* (November–December 2010): 4.

80. Davy, *The Mysticism of Simone Weil*, 14

81. Davy, *Nicolas Berdyaev*, 44.

82. Davy, *Traversée en solitaire*, 223–32. Rebecca Solnit helped me think about bird symbols in Davy; Rebecca Solnit, "Wild Goose Chase," in *A Book of Migrations: Some Passages in Ireland* (London: Verso, 2011), 185–95.

83. Marie-Magdeleine Davy, *L'oiseau et sa symbolique* (Paris: Albin Michel, 1998).

84. Interview cited in Marc-Alain Descamps, "La Vie Marie-Magdeleine Davy," http:// www.europsy.org/pmmdavy/davymm.html.

85. Marc-Alain Descamps, email correspondence with author.

86. Marc-Alain Descamps, email correspondence with author.

87. Marc-Alain Descamps, email correspondence with author.

88. Marie-Magdeleine Davy, "L'idée de Dieu."

89. Susan Sontag, "Simone Weil," *New York Review of Books*, February 1, 1963.

90. Ozouf, "Simone Weil," 182.

91. Davy, *The Mysticism of Simone Weil*, 17.

92. Davy, *The Mysticism of Simone Weil*, 49.

93. Davy, *The Mysticism of Simone Weil*, 74.

CHAPTER FIVE

1. I thank the wonderful work of my former undergraduate research assistant, Rohini Parthasarathy, who helped with the Claude McKay chapter, assisted in finding and analyzing materials, and wrote her own excellent undergraduate research paper on McKay, "Spirit of the Vagabond," in December 2018. Thank you to the Fordham College at Rose Hill deans for supporting Rohini's research assistance. There is some scholarly discrepancy about McKay's date of birth. I follow Wayne Cooper, "Claude McKay's Birthday and the Unfinished Business of African-American Scholarship," *Caribbean Quarterly* 38, no. 1 (1992): 1–4. On the issue of old friends' reactions to McKay's conversion, see the McKay and Max Eastman correspondence. Claude McKay "stopped living years ago," Elena Eastman, Max's wife, said after learning McKay had died. Christopher Irmscher, *Max Eastman: A Life* (New Haven, CT: Yale University Press, 2017), 305. Irmscher's excellent biography analyzes some of the Eastman-McKay correspondence, but you can find the full correspondence in the Claude McKay Collection, Yale Collection of American Literature, Beinecke Rare Book and Manuscript Library, New Haven, CT.

2. Quoted in Ellen Tarry, *The Third Door: The Autobiography of an American Negro Woman* (Tuscaloosa: University of Alabama Press, 1992), 250.

3. Claude McKay, *A Long Way from Home* (New Brunswick, NJ: Rutgers University Press, 2007), 176.

4. Brent Hayes Edwards, *The Practice of Diaspora: Literature, Translation, and the Rise of Black Internationalism* (Cambridge, MA: Harvard University Press, 2003), 3.

5. Paul Gilroy, *The Black Atlantic: Modernity and Double-Consciousness* (Cambridge, MA: Harvard University Press, 1995).

6. On *Harlem Shadows* inspiring the Harlem Renaissance, see Michael North, *The Dialect of Modernism: Race, Language, and Twentieth-Century Literature* (New York: Oxford University Press, 1994), 8, 126. For the line "most famous poet among black Americans," see the written overview to the collection of Claude McKay letters and manuscripts 1915–1952 (bulk 1937–1947) at the Manuscripts, Archives and Rare Books Division of the Schomburg Center for Research in Black Culture, http://archives.nypl.org/scm/20737#overview.

7. Gilroy, *The Black Atlantic*, 29. Excellent studies of McKay's turn to Catholicism include Cecilia Moore, "The Sources and Meaning of the Conversion of Claude McKay," *Journal of the Black Catholic Theological Symposium* 2, no. 2 (2008): 59–79; Madhuri

Deshmukh, "Claude McKay's Road to Catholicism," *Callaloo* 37, no. 1 (2014): 148–68; and Josef Sorett, *Spirit in the Dark: A Religious History of Racial Aesthetics* (Oxford: Oxford University Press, 2016), 79–114.

8. Elizabeth A. Foster, *African Catholic: Decolonization and the Transformation of the Church* (Cambridge, MA: Harvard University Press, 2019); Matthew J. Cressler, *Authentically Black and Truly Catholic: The Rise of Black Catholicism in the Great Migration* (New York: New York University Press, 2017).

9. Claude McKay, *A Long Way from Home* (Boston: Houghton Mifflin, 1970), 10. All following citations to *A Long Way from Home* are from this edition, except when otherwise noted.

10. Eddie Doherty, "Poet's Progress," *Extension* (1946): 46.

11. Claude McKay, "Claude McKay Describes His Own Life," *Pearson's Magazine* 39, no. 5 (1918), 275–76.

12. Lara Putnam, *Radical Moves: Caribbean Migrants and the Politics of Race in the Jazz Age* (Chapel Hill: University of North Carolina Press, 2013), 49.

13. See Wayne Cooper's excellent biography, *Claude McKay, Rebel Sojourner in the Harlem Renaissance* (Baton Rouge: Louisiana State University Press, 1996).

14. McKay, *A Long Way from Home*, 200.

15. McKay, *A Long Way from Home*, 15.

16. Claude McKay, *My Green Hills of Jamaica: And Five Jamaican Short Stories* (Washington, DC: Howard University Press, 1975), 44.

17. McKay, *A Long Way from Home*, 118.

18. Claude McKay, "The Strange Burial of Sue," in *The Passion of Claude McKay*, ed. Wayne F. Cooper (Ann Arbor: University of Michigan Press, 1973), 186.

19. McKay, *My Green Hills of Jamaica*, 4.

20. Mary Gordon, "'I Can't Stand Your Books': A Writer Goes Home," in *Good Boys and Dead Girls and Other Essays* (New York: One Road Media, 2013), 55.

21. Claude McKay, "Boyhood in Jamaica," *Phylon* 14, no. 2 (1953): 134–45. Eventually, a revised version of this essay ended up in McKay, *My Green Hills of Jamaica*.

22. Walter Jekyll, preface to Claude McKay, *Songs of Jamaica* (Miami: Mnemosyne Publications, 1969), 9.

23. Conversation between Carl Cowl and McKay recorded in Barbara L. J. Griffin, Carl Cowl, and Wayne Cooper, "A Candid Conversation with Carl Cowl: Claude McKay's Last Literary Agent," *CLA Journal* 56, no. 3 (2013): 209–23.

24. Avery F. Gordon, *The Hawthorn Archive: Letters from the Utopian Margins* (New York: Fordham University Press, 2017), 55.

25. Gary Edward Holcomb, *Claude McKay, Code Name Sasha: Queer Black Marxism and the Harlem Renaissance* (Gainesville: University Press of Florida, 2009), 32.

26. McKay, *A Long Way from Home*, 228–29.

27. Carl Pedersen, "The Caribbean Voices of Claude McKay and Eric Walrond," in *The Cambridge Companion to the Harlem Renaissance*, ed. George Hutchinson (New York: Cambridge University Press, 2007), 187.

28. McKay, "Claude McKay Describes His Own Life," 275.

29. McKay, "Claude McKay Describes His Own Life," 276.

30. McKay, *A Long Way from Home*, 44.

31. McKay, *A Long Way from Home*, 44.

32. Elizabeth Muther, "'Great, Unappeasable Ghost': Claude McKay and the Theatre Guild Incident," *Modern Language Studies* 30, no. 2 (2000): 133–57.

33. McKay, *A Long Way from Home*, 117.

34. Claude McKay, "The Cycle," *Complete Poems*, ed. William J. Maxwell (Champaign: University of Illinois Press, 2004), 243.

35. McKay, *A Long Way from Home*, 44.

36. McKay, *A Long Way from Home*, 44.

37. St. Clair Drake and Horace R. Cayton, *Black Metropolis: A Study of Negro Life in a Northern City* (Chicago: University of Chicago Press, 2015).

38. Cameron McWhirter, *Red Summer: The Summer of 1919 and the Awakening of Black America* (New York: St. Martin's Press, 2011), 191.

39. McWhirter, *Red Summer*, 191.

40. McWhirter, *Red Summer*.

41. McKay, "If We Must Die," in *Complete Poems*, 177.

42. McKay, *A Long Way from Home*, 30.

43. Archival introduction to the collection of Claude McKay letters and manuscripts 1915–1952 (bulk 1937–1947) at the Manuscripts, Archives and Rare Books Division of the Schomburg Center for Research in Black Culture, http://archives.nypl.org/scm/20737.

44. McKay, *A Long Way from Home*, 47.

45. Svetlana Boym, *The Off-Modern* (New York: Bloomsbury, 2017).

46. Deshmukh, "McKay's Road to Catholicism"; Sorett, *Spirit in the Dark*, 79–114. Several Catholic authors took interest in McKay's conversion; see Mary Jerdo Keating, "Claude McKay," *Catholic Interracialist*, September 1951; Moore, "The Conversion of Claude McKay."

47. James Smethurst, "The Red Is East: Claude McKay and the New Black Radicalism of the Twentieth Century," *American Literary History* 21 (2009): 355–67.

48. Jean Wagner, "Claude McKay," in *Black Poets of the United States: From Paul Laurence to Langston Hughes*, trans. Kenneth Douglas (Urbana: University of Illinois Press, 1973), 197–258. For another good essay on McKay's conversion, see Griffin Oleynick, "The Prophet of Harlem," *Commonweal*, July 7, 2017.

49. McKay, "Claude McKay Describes His Own Life," 275.

50. Claude McKay, "Exhortation, Summer 1919," in *Complete Poems*, 330.

51. Claude McKay's sonnet "The Lynching," first published in C. K. Ogden's *Cambridge Magazine* (a British journal) in 1920.

52. Abbigail N. Rosewood, *If I Had Two Lives* (New York: Europa Editions, 2019), 5.

53. Judith Weisenfeld, *New World A-Coming: Black Religion and Racial Identity during the Great Migration* (New York: New York University Press, 2019).

54. McKay, *A Long Way from Home*, 109.

55. Quote from Alain Locke in Cooper, *Claude McKay, Rebel Sojourner*, 319.

56. Saidiya Hartman, *Wayward Lives, Beautiful Experiments: Intimate Histories of Social Upheaval* (New York: W. W. Norton, 2019), 304.

57. Hartman, *Wayward Lives, Beautiful Experiments*, 221.

58. Hartman, *Wayward Lives, Beautiful Experiments*, 227. Emphasis added.

59. Leonard Harris and Charles Molesworth, *Alain L. Locke: The Biography of a Philosopher* (Chicago: University of Chicago Press, 2008), 203.

60. Claude McKay, "Courage," in *Complete Poems*, 184.

61. Letter from Claude McKay to Walter White, September 2, 1924, Claude McKay Letters and Manuscripts, Schomburg Center for Research in Black Culture, Manuscripts, Archives and Rare Books Division. A special episode of the New York Public Library podcast, "Live from the Reading Room: Claude McKay to Walter White," provides a reading of this letter in full, April 11, 2016, https://www.nypl.org/blog/2016/04/11/live-reading-room-claude-mckay-walter-white.

62. James Baldwin, "The New Lost Generation," *Price of the Ticket: Collected Nonfiction, 1948–1985* (New York: St. Martin's Press, 1985), 309.

63. Claude McKay, "What Is and What Isn't," *The Crisis* 27, no. 6 (1924): 260.

64. Quoted in Michel Fabre, *From Harlem to Paris: Black American Writers in France, 1840–1980* (Urbana: University of Illinois Press, 1993), 69.

65. Margaret Vendryes, *Barthé: A Life in Sculpture* (Jackson: University Press of Mississippi, 2008), 14–22.

66. Jennifer Anne Boittin, *Colonial Metropolis: The Urban Grounds of Anti-Imperialism and Feminism in Interwar Paris* (Lincoln: University of Nebraska Press, 2010), 99; Edwards, *The Practice of Diaspora*, 187–234; Philippe Dewitte, *Les mouvements nègres en France, 1919–1939* (Paris: Éditions L'Harmattan, 1985); Iheanachor Egonu, "'Les Continents' and the Francophone Pan-Negro Movement," *Phylon* 42, no. 3 (1981): 245–54; Eslanda Goode Robeson, "Black Paris," *Challenge: A Literary Quarterly* (January 1936): 18.

67. Tracy Fessenden, *Religion around Billie Holiday* (University Park: Penn State University Press, 2018), 11.

68. Paulette Nardal and Philippe Grollemund, *Fiertés de femme noire: Entretiens / Mémoires de Paulette Nardal* (Paris: Éditions L'Harmattan, 2019), 22.

69. Edwards, *The Practice of Diaspora*, 16.

70. Nardal and Grollemund, *Fiertés de femme noire*, 30.

71. Edwards, *The Practice of Diaspora*, 155.

72. Paulette and Andrée Nardal, "Ce Que Nous Voulons Faire," *Revue du monde noir* 1 (1931): 1.

73. Claude McKay, "To America," *Revue du monde noir* 1 (1931): 38; Claude McKay, *Spring in New Hampshire and Other Poems* (London: Grant Richards, 1920).

74. Emily Musil Church, "In Search of Seven Sisters: A Biography of the Nardal Sisters of Martinique," *Callaloo* 36, no. 2 (2013): 375–90.

75. Nardal and Grollemund, *Fiertés de femme noire*, 26.

76. Nardal and Grollemund, *Fiertés de femme noire*, 75.

77. Nardal and Grollemund, *Fiertés de femme noire*, 76.

78. Melvyn Stokes, "Kojo Touvalou Houénou: An Assessment," *Transatlantica* 1 (2009), https://journals.openedition.org/transatlantica/4271.

79. Charles Coulston Gillispie, *Science and Polity in France: The Revolutionary and Napoleonic Years* (Princeton, NJ: Princeton University Press, 2004), 150.

80. McKay, "What Is and What Isn't," 260.

81. Claude McKay, "Author's Word," *Harlem Shadows* (New York: Harcourt, 1922), xxi.

82. Michel Fabre, *From Harlem to Paris: Black American Writers in France, 1840–1980* (Urbana: University of Illinois Press, 1993). See also Christopher L. Miller, *Nationalists and Nomads: Essays on Francophone African Literature and Culture* (Chicago: University of Chicago Press, 1998).

83. Fabre, *From Harlem to Paris*, 153.

84. Quoted in Fabre, *From Harlem to Paris*, 96. Also printed in McKay, *Complete Poems*, 231.

85. James Baldwin, "The New Lost Generation," in *The Price of the Ticket: Collected Nonfiction, 1948–1985* (New York: St. Martin's Press, 1985).

86. Claude McKay, *Banjo* (Boston: Mariner Books, 1970), 50.

87. McKay, *Banjo*, 50.

88. McKay, *Banjo*, 33.

89. McKay, *Banjo*, 35.

90. McKay, *Banjo*, 57–58.

91. McKay, *Banjo*, 250.

92. Dominic Thomas, *Black France: Colonialism, Immigration, and Transnationalism* (Bloomington: Indiana University Press, 2006).

93. Léopold Sédar Senghor, *Liberté: Négritude et civilisation de l'universel* (Paris: Éditions du Seuil, 1977), 22.

94. In 1942, Louis Thomas Achille (a Martinique cousin of the Nardal sisters who also lived in Paris) helps us see the Catholic dimensions of the *négritude* movement that McKay's work may have connected with. Louis T. Achille, "The Catholic Approach to Interracialism in France," *American Catholic Sociological Review* 3, no. 1 (1942): 22–27.

95. Nardal and Grollemund, *Fiertés de femme noire*, 26.

96. McKay, *Banjo*, 66.

97. Léa Mormin-Chauvac, "Paulette Nardal, théoricienne oubliée de la négritude," *Libération*, February 26, 2019, https://www.liberation.fr/debats/2019/02/26/paulette-nardal -theoricienne-oubliee-de-la-negritude_1711727.

98. In a September 14, 1947, letter from Betty Britton to Claude McKay, she references conversations in which McKay told her about Black religious statuary he saw in Spain. Box 1, folder 20–22, Claude McKay Collection, Yale Collection of American Literature, Beinecke Rare Book and Manuscript Library, New Haven, CT.

99. Letter from Claude McKay to James Weldon Johnson, undated, box 13, folder 38, Claude McKay Collection, Yale Collection of American Literature, Beinecke Rare Book and Manuscript Library, New Haven, CT.

100. Claude McKay, "On Becoming a Roman Catholic," *Epistle* 2 (Spring 1945): 43–45.

101. Dorothy West, *Where the Wild Grape Grows: Selected Writings, 1930–1950* (Amherst: University of Massachusetts Press, 2004).

102. Letter from Dorothy West to Claude McKay, September 13, 1935, in West, *Where the Wild Grape Grows*, 205.

103. Quoted in T. Denean Sharpley-Whiting, *Bricktop's Paris: African American Women in Paris between the Two Wars* (Albany: State University of New York Press, 2015), 119.

104. Ellen Tarry, foreword to *Saint Katharine Drexel: Friend of the Oppressed* (Boston: Pau-

line Books & Media, 2000), 9; Ellen Tarry, author's note to *Saint Katharine Drexel: Friend of the Oppressed* (San Francisco: Ignatius Press, 2002), 155.

105. Tarry, author's note to *Saint Katharine Drexel* (Ignatius Press), 155.

106. Tarry, *The Third Door*, 22.

107. Hartman, *Wayward Lives, Beautiful Experiments*, 8.

108. Tarry, *The Third Door*, 129.

109. Ellen Tarry gives a short history of the project in Ellen Tarry, "How the History Was Assembled: One Writer's Memories," in *The Negro in New York: An Informal Social History, 1626–1940*, ed. Roi Ottley and William J. Weatherby (New York: Praeger, 1967), x–xii.

110. Kennetta Hammond Perry and Kira Thurman, "Black Europe: A Useful Category of Historical Analysis," *Black Perspectives*, December 20, 2016, https://www.aaihs.org /black-europe-a-useful-category-of-historical-analysis/.

111. Claude McKay, *Harlem: Negro Metropolis* (San Diego: Harcourt, 1968), 73–76.

112. McKay, *Harlem: Negro Metropolis*, 49.

113. McKay, *Harlem: Negro Metropolis*, 206.

114. Kathryn Lofton, "The Perpetual Primitive in African American Religious Historiography," in *The New Black Gods: Arthur Huff Fauset and the Study of African American Religions*, ed. Edward E. Curtis IV and Danielle Brune Singler (Bloomington: Indiana University Press, 2009), 171–91.

115. Claude McKay, *Amiable with Big Teeth: A Novel of the Love Affair between the Communists and the Poor Black Sheep of Harlem* (New York: Penguin, 2017), 107.

116. McKay, *Amiable with Big Teeth*, 3.

117. Imaobong D. Umoren, *Race Women Internationalists: Activist-Intellectuals and Global Freedom Struggles* (Oakland: University of California Press, 2018), 43–45.

118. Tarry, *The Third Door*, 140.

119. Tarry, *The Third Door*, 140.

120. Tarry, *The Third Door*, 142.

121. Cecilia Moore notes, "Catholics schools in Harlem were crucial to development of a vital black Catholic community. It was in these schools and under the tutelage of Catholic women religious that many African American Harlemites learned about Catholicism and eventually joined the Roman Catholic church." Cecilia Moore, "Keeping Harlem Catholic: African-American Catholics and Harlem, 1920–1960," *American Catholic Studies* 114, no. 3 (2003): 6.

122. Sorett, *Spirit in the Dark*, 83. For an excellent overview, see also Matthew J. Cressler, "The History of Black Catholics in America," *Smithsonian Magazine*, June 7, 2018.

123. Albert Raboteau, *African American Religion* (Oxford: Oxford University Press, 1999), 125.

124. More thorough studies of the Friendship House are needed, particularly of the New York chapter and the afterlives of its volunteers, but some excellent studies include Karen J. Johnson's work focused on the Chicago Friendship House chapter, *One in Christ: Chicago Catholics and the Quest for Interracial Justice* (Oxford: Oxford University Press, 2018), and the unpublished, very thorough dissertation by Elizbeth Louise Sharum, "A Strange Fire Burning: A History of the Friendship House Movement" (PhD diss., Texas Tech University, 1977). See also Albert Schorsch III, "Uncommon Women

and Others: Memoirs and Lessons from Radical Catholics at Friendship House," *U.S. Catholic Historian* 9, no. 4 (Fall 1990): 371–86. A bounty of archival records can be found in the collection of Friendship House (Chicago, Ill.) records, 1937–2000 at the Chicago History Museum and in the collection of Ann Harrigan Makletzoff Papers at the University of Notre Dame Archives, Notre Dame, IN.

125. Catherine de Hueck, *Friendship House* (New York: Sheed and Ward, 1946), 1, 59–60.

126. Friendship House pamphlet, in box 1, folder 28, Ellen Tarry, letters and papers from the Friendship House, Ellen Tarry Papers, Schomburg Center for Research in Black Culture.

127. Letter from Ellen Tarry to Bishop Sheil resigning as codirector of the Chicago Friendship House, December 17, 1942. She gave advice to the Bishop for her replacement: "In all instances a 'fairy godmother' attitude must be avoided. . . . Negroes want equal opportunity to earn their own keep. . . . No white person can come into a Negro community and work FOR negroes he has to work WITH them." Box 1, folder 28, Ellen Tarry, letters and papers from the Friendship House, Ellen Tarry Papers, Schomburg Center for Research in Black Culture

128. Sharum, "A Strange Fire Burning," 137.

129. Sharum, "A Strange Fire Burning," 346.

130. Betty Schneider, reflections on Friendship House, *Community* 37, no. 3 (1978), special 40th anniversary issue of the Friendship House, box 1, folder 28, Ellen Tarry Papers, Schomburg Center for Research in Black Culture.

131. Schneider, reflections on Friendship House.

132. Johnson, *One in Christ*, 98.

133. Martin Zieliński, "Working for Interracial Justice: The Catholic Interracial Council of New York, 1934–1964," special issue, The Black Catholic Community, 1880–1987, *U.S. Catholic Historian* 7, no. 2–3 (1988): 233–62.

134. In addition to Harrigan's memoirs quoted below, see also Mary K. Jerdo's description of her start at Friendship House in Harlem, "Novice in Harlem," *The Torch*, February 1942. Box 1 and 2, Friendship House (Chicago, Ill.) records, 1937–2000, Chicago History Museum, Chicago, IL.

135. Ann Harrigan Makletzoff, Unpublished Memoirs, box 3, Ann Harrigan Makletzoff Papers (MAK), University of Notre Dame Archives, Notre Dame, IN.

136. See, for example, a letter published in a local Chicago newspaper by African American physician and local leader Kermit T. Mehlinger: "These 'let's take a peep' visitations by white suburbanites into the homes of Negro urbanites are at times farcical and ridiculous." Clipping from unknown newspaper in box 3, Friendship House (Chicago, Ill.) records, 1937–2000, Chicago History Museum, Chicago, IL. But the legacy is complex; in Chicago at least, the Friendship House seemed to evolve from these rather naive beginnings to, by the 1970s, working on prison reform advocacy and employment for previously incarcerated individuals. FH Newsletters, Friendship House (Chicago, Ill.) records, 1937–2000, Chicago History Museum.

137. Jack Kerouac, *On the Road* (New York: Penguin, 2011), 45.

138. Letter from Ellen Tarry to Betty Schneider, 1988, box 1, folder 28, Ellen Tarry Papers, Schomburg Center for Research in Black Culture.

139. Quoted in *The Passion of Claude McKay*, 301.

140. Letter from Claude McKay to Daniel Cantwell, November 14, 1944, box 2, Friendship House (Chicago, Ill.) records, 1937–2000, Chicago History Museum, Chicago, IL.

141. McKay, *A Long Way From Home*, 107.

142. "Friendship House," *Interracial Review*, 1940.

143. Edward T. Chambers, *Roots for Radicals: Organizing for Power, Action, and Justice* (New York: Bloomsbury, 2010), 90.

144. Ann Harrigan Makletzoff, Unpublished Memoirs, box 3, Ann Harrigan Makletzoff Papers (MAK), University of Notre Dame Archives, Notre Dame, IN.

145. Schorsch, "Uncommon Women and Others," 379.

146. Friendship House Pamphlet, box 4, file 3, Ann Harrigan Makletzoff, Unpublished Memoirs, Ann Harrigan Makletzoff Papers (MAK), University of Notre Dame Archives, Notre Dame, IN.

147. Ann Harrigan Makletzoff, Unpublished Memoirs, box 3, Ann Harrigan Makletzoff Papers (MAK), University of Notre Dame Archives, Notre Dame, IN.

148. Quoted in Wayne F. Cooper, *Claude McKay, Rebel Sojourner in the Harlem Renaissance: A Biography* (Baton Rouge: Louisiana State University Press, 1987), 361.

149. De Hueck, *Friendship House*, 11.

150. Ellen Tarry, "Native Daughter: An Indictment of White America by a Colored Woman," *Commonweal*, April 12, 1940.

151. Letter from Claude McKay to Langston Hughes, quoted in Tatiana Tagirova-Daley, "'A Vagabond with a Purpose': Claude McKay and His International Aspirations," *Forum for Inter-American Research* 7, no. 2 (2014): 55–71.

152. Tarry, *The Third Door*, 165.

153. Claude McKay, "Right Turn to Catholicism," box 9, folder 298, Claude McKay Collection, Yale Collection of American Literature, Beinecke Rare Book and Manuscript Library, New Haven, CT.

154. Louis T. Achille, "The Catholic Negro in the Confraternity," *Interracial Review*, 1940.

155. Quoted in Cecilia Moore, "Conversion Narratives: The Dual Experiences and Voices of African American Converts," *U.S. Catholic Historian* 28, no. 1 (Winter 2010): 39.

156. "About Us, Our History," St. Mark the Evangelist Catholic Church, accessed December 10, 2019, http://stmark138.com/our-history.

157. Ann Harrigan Makletzoff, Unpublished Memoirs, box 3, Ann Harrigan Makletzoff Papers (MAK), University of Notre Dame Archives, Notre Dame, IN.

158. Claude McKay, "Why I Became a Catholic," 32, box 1, folder 6, Claude McKay Letters and Manuscripts, Schomburg Center for Research in Black Culture, Manuscripts, Archives and Rare Books Division.

159. Betty Britton was editing McKay's texts and advising him. Letter from Betty Britton to Claude McKay, March 21, 1947, box 1, folder 22, Claude McKay Collection, Yale Collection of American Literature, Beinecke Rare Book and Manuscript Library, New Haven, CT.

160. Ann Harrigan Makletzoff, diary entry, September 12, 1942, transcribed in Unpublished Memoirs, box 3, Ann Harrigan Makletzoff Papers (MAK), University of Notre Dame Archives, Notre Dame, IN.

161. Tarry, *The Third Door*, 251.

162. Quoted in Cooper, *Claude McKay, Rebel Sojourner*, 304.

163. McKay, *A Long Way from Home* (Rutgers University Press), 88.

164. Tarry, *The Third Door*, 187.

165. Claude McKay, "The Cycle," in *Complete Poems*, 383.

166. McKay, "Right Turn to Catholicism," 13.

167. Dorothy Day to Claude McKay correspondence, Claude McKay Collection, Yale Collection of American Literature, Beinecke Rare Book and Manuscript Library, New Haven, CT.

168. Tarry, *The Third Door*, 250.

169. Letter from Ellen Tarry to Claude McKay, April 18, 1948, box 1, folder 28, McKay Correspondence, Tarry Papers, Schomburg Center for Research in Black Culture.

170. McKay, "Right Turn to Catholicism."

171. McKay, "On Becoming a Roman Catholic," 43.

172. Eddie Doherty, "Poet's Progress," *Extension* (1946): 46.

173. For an interesting history on the ambivalence of Marciniak on race, see Charles Shanabruch, "Imperatives and Political Realities: Edward Marciniak and the Fight to End Chicago's Dual Housing Market," *Journal of the Illinois State Historical Society* 109, no. 1 (2016): 71–101.

174. Letter from Claude McKay to Edward Marciniak, March 5, 1945, box 5, folder 146, McKay Correspondence, Beinecke Rare Book and Manuscript Library, New Haven, CT.

175. Quoted in Johnson, *One in Christ*, 124.

176. Eddie Doherty describes McKay's Chicago apartment in "Poet's Progress."

177. Ammon Hennacy, *Autobiography of a Catholic Anarchist* (New York: Catholic Worker Books, 1954), 79.

178. McKay, "Why I Became a Catholic," 32.

179. Letter from Max Eastman to McKay, September 9, 1946, box 3, folder 70, Claude McKay Collection, Yale Collection of American Literature, Beinecke Rare Book and Manuscript Library, New Haven, CT.

180. See, for example, an undated letter from Betty Britton (in Chicago, sometime in 1944) and a letter from J. Beirne to Claude McKay, November 15, 1944. Box 1, folder 28, Claude McKay Collection, Yale Collection of American Literature, Beinecke Rare Book and Manuscript Library, New Haven, CT.

181. McKay's description of Roy, who was modeled loosely on himself, in *Banjo*, 136.

182. Hennacy, *Autobiography of a Catholic Anarchist*, 78.

183. Letter from McKay to Ellen Tarry, undated, box 6, folder 204, Claude McKay Collection, Yale Collection of American Literature, Beinecke Rare Book and Manuscript Library, New Haven, CT.

184. Claude McKay, "The Cycle," partially reprinted in Barbara Jackson Griffin, "The Last Word: Claude McKay's Unpublished 'Cycle Manuscript,'" *Melus* 21, no. 1 (Spring 1996): 48.

185. Claude McKay, "The whites admit the Negroes have religion," in *Complete Poems*, 275.

186. Hennacy, *Autobiography of a Catholic Anarchist*, 88–89.

187. McKay, *A Long Way From Home*, 21.

188. Claude McKay, unpublished edition of *My Green Hills of Jamaica*, notebook, box 6, file 22, Claude McKay Letters and Manuscripts, Schomburg Center for Research in Black Culture, Manuscripts, Archives and Rare Books Division.

189. Bishop Sheil, introduction to unpublished *My Green Hills of Jamaica*, Microfilm Sc Rare B, Claude McKay Letters and Manuscripts, Schomburg Center for Research in Black Culture, Manuscripts, Archives and Rare Books Division.

190. McKay, "Why I Became a Catholic," 32.

191. Letter from Claude McKay to Carl Cowl, February 13, 1948, box 2, folder 50, Claude McKay Collection, Yale Collection of American Literature, Beinecke Rare Book and Manuscript Library, New Haven, CT.

192. Letter from Ellen Tarry to Claude McKay, March 4, 1947, box 2, folder 18, Ellen Tarry Papers, Schomburg Center for Research in Black Culture.

193. Tarry to McKay, March 4, 1947, box 2, folder 18, Ellen Tarry Papers, Schomburg Center for Research in Black Culture.

194. Tarry, *The Third Door*, 131.

195. Claude McKay, "Middle Ages," *Catholic Worker*, May 1946, 5.

196. "Claude McKay Is Dead," box 15, folder 457, Claude McKay Collection, Yale Collection of American Literature, Beinecke Rare Book and Manuscript Library, New Haven, CT. The archival folder labels this obituary clipping from the June 1948 issue of the *Catholic Worker*, but the digitized *Catholic Worker* archives do not show it, so it could mislabeled and from a different Catholic periodical.

197. Roxane Gay, *Bad Feminist* (New York: Harper Collins, 2014), 210–12.

198. Letter from McKay to Cowl, March 1, 1947, box 2, folder 50, Claude McKay Collection, Yale Collection of American Literature, Beinecke Rare Book and Manuscript Library, New Haven, CT.

199. Letters from McKay to Cowl, August 28, 1947, and October 17, 1947, box 2, folder 50, Claude McKay Collection, Yale Collection of American Literature, Beinecke Rare Book and Manuscript Library, New Haven, CT.

200. Frank Miller, "For Claude McKay," box 15, folder 457, Claude McKay Collection, Yale Collection of American Literature, Beinecke Rare Book and Manuscript Library, New Haven, CT. The archival folder labels this obituary clipping from the June 1948 issue of the *Catholic Worker*, but the digitized *Catholic Worker* archives do not show it, so it could mislabeled and from a different Catholic periodical.

201. Paulette Nardal, *Beyond Negritude: Essays from Women in the City*, trans. with an introduction by T. Denean Sharpley-Whiting (Albany, NY: State University of New York Press, 2009), 80.

202. James C. Hall, *Mercy, Mercy Me: African-American Culture and the American Sixties* (New York: Oxford University Press, 2001).

203. Hall, *Mercy, Mercy Me*, 16.

204. Gilroy, *The Black Atlantic*, 57.

205. Wallace D. Best, *Langston's Salvation: American Religion and the Bard of Harlem* (New York: New York University Press, 2017), 239.

EPILOGUE

1. The catalog is printed as Armelle Dutruc, *Marie-Magdeleine Davy (1903–1998) ou l'Orient intérieur: Répertoire numérique détaillé des archives de Marie-Magdeleine Davy* (Niort: Archives Départementales des Deux-Sèvres, 2012).

2. Zadie Smith, "Crazy They Call Me," *New Yorker*, February 26, 2017.

3. Tracey Fessenden, *Religion around Billie Holiday* (University Park: Penn State University Press, 2018).

4. Ann Harrigan, diary entry, June 12, 1942, box 3, Ann Harrigan Makletzoff Papers (MAK), University of Notre Dame Archives, Notre Dame, IN.

5. Natalie Zemon Davis quoted in Joan Wallach Scott, "Natalie Zemon Davis, Historian of Hope," *H-France Salon* 11, 15, no. 3 (2019): 4–5.

6. Samuel Moyn, *Christian Human Rights* (Philadelphia: University of Pennsylvania Press, 2015); James Chappel, *Catholic Modern: The Challenge of Totalitarianism and the Remaking of the Church* (Cambridge, MA: Harvard University Press, 2018); Edward Baring, *Converts to the Real: Catholicism and the Making of Continental Philosophy* (Cambridge, MA: Harvard University Press, 2019).

7. Elizabeth A. Foster's book *African Catholic* is a great example of research that explores these webbed networks, in her case between France and Africa, evoking a "Franco-African world" that includes African Catholic students in Paris, missionary priests in Africa and bishops in Paris, and activists in Africa educated in French missionary schools. Elizabeth A. Foster, *African Catholic: Decolonization and the Transformation of the Church* (Cambridge, MA: Harvard University Press, 2019). Edward Baring's *Converts to the Real* also lays groundwork in a similar direction and argues that the philosophical field of phenomenology spread around the world with remarkable speed by using Catholic networks throughout Europe and eventually the New World: "The geography of phenomenology is best described, not by the contours of mainland Europe, but by the reach of the 'universal Church.'" Baring, *Converts to the Real*, 11. For an excellent analysis of Christian activism between France and Algeria in ecumenical circles, see Darcie Fontaine, *Decolonizing Christianity: Religion and the End of Empire in France and Algeria* (Cambridge: Cambridge University Press, 2016). Finally, Julie Byrne's *The Other Catholics* is primarily an American Catholic story, but she situates the independent Catholic movement in a thoroughly transnational setting, discussing US Catholics who understand their faith "outside of Rome" and trace their lineage to two French-born bishops in the early modern period, who traveled and built relationships with independent-minded Catholics around the world: Julie Byrne, *The Other Catholics: Remaking America's Largest Religion* (New York: Columbia University Press, 2016), 297.

8. Natalia M. Imperatori-Lee, *Cuéntame: Narrative in the Ecclesial Present* (Ossining, NY: Orbis, 2018), 89.

9. See, for example, Denis Pelletier and Jean-Louis Schlegel, *À la gauche du Christ: Les chrétiens de gauche en France de 1945 à nos jours* (Paris: Éditions du Seuil, 2012).

10. Edward W. Said, "Reflections on Exile," in *Reflections on Exile and Other Essays* (Cambridge, MA: Harvard University Press, 2000), 173–86.

11. Letter from Claude McKay to Walter White, September 2, 1924, Claude McKay Letters and Manuscripts, Schomburg Center for Research in Black Culture, Manuscripts, Archives and Rare Books Division. A special episode of the New York Public Library podcast, "Live from the Reading Room: Claude McKay to Walter White," provides a reading of this letter in full, April 11, 2016, https://www.nypl.org/blog/2016/04/11/live-reading-room-claude-mckay-walter-white.

12. Paul Mendes-Flohr, *Martin Buber: A Life of Faith and Dissent* (New Haven, CT: Yale University Press, 2019), 43.

13. Byrne, *The Other Catholics*, 5.

14. Mistral's speech is quoted in Karen Peña, *Poetry and the Realm of the Public Intellectual: The Alternative Destinies of Gabriela Mistral, Cecília Meireles, and Rosario Castellanos* (Leeds: Legenda, 2007).

15. The late James Cone's new autobiography shows how this back-and-forth between art and theology can work and how Cone's imagination and soul was moved, stirred, and transformed by the prose of James Baldwin, the sounds of Billie Holiday, and speeches of Malcolm X. Cone took their art and prose into a new Christian theology that contended with the beauty and tragedy of Black experience. James Cone, *Said I Wasn't Gonna Tell Nobody: The Making of a Black Theologian* (Ossining, NY: Orbis, 2019).

16. On Lyon as an epicenter of resistance, see Gruber Monique, "La résistance spirituelle, fondement et soutien de la Résistance active: L'exemple des *Cahiers clandestins du Témoignage chrétien (1941–1944)*," *Revue des sciences religieuses* 78, no. 4 (2000): 463–87. See also Bernard Comte, *Initiatives de théologiens face à la persécution antisémite à Lyon en 1941–42* (Lyon: Institut Catholique, 1993), 15–16.

17. This lecture was published as Henri de Lubac, "Le fondement théologique des missions," *Bibliothèque de l'Union mission du clerge de France* (1941): 3–29, and partially reproduced and translated by Anne Englund in Henri de Lubac, *Theology in History* (San Francisco: Ignatius Press, 1996), 367–427.

18. Henri de Lubac, "Christian Resistance to Nazism and Anti-Semitism," in de Lubac, *Theology in History*, 487.

19. Henri de Lubac, "Internal Causes of the Weakening and Disappearance of the Sense of the Sacred," in de Lubac, *Theology in History*, 224.

20. De Lubac, "Internal Causes," 225.

21. Catherine Osborne, "Response to Stephen Schloesser," in the Syndicate Symposium on Osborne's *American Catholics and the Church of Tomorrow* (Chicago: University of Chicago Press, 2018). Thanks especially to Stephen Schloesser's essay that helped highlight these larger theological issues in Osborne's excellent book, Stephen Schloesser, "Spatial Crises: Nature-Grace, Vatican II, Immanent Frame," *Syndicate*, September 12, 2019.

22. Robert Orsi, *History and Presence* (Cambridge, MA: Harvard University Press, 2018).

23. Claude McKay, "Middle Ages," *Catholic Worker*, May 1946, 5.

24. Louis Massignon, "The *Notion* of 'Real *Elite*' in Sociology and in *History*," in *History*

of Religions: Essays in Methodology, ed. Mircea Eliade and Joseph Kitagawa (Chicago: University of Chicago Press, 1959), 114.

25. Paul Gilroy, *The Black Atlantic: Modernity and Double Consciousness* (New York: Verso, 1993).

26. Brent Hayes Edwards, *The Practice of Diaspora: Literature, Translation, and the Rise of Black Internationalism* (Cambridge, MA: Harvard University Press, 2003).

27. María Laura Picón, "J. Maritain y Esther de Cáceres: Una amistad spiritual," *Notes et Documents* 24 (September–December 2012): 54–63.

28. Joseph Anthony Amato, *Mounier and Maritain: A French Catholic Understanding of the Modern World* (Tuscaloosa: University of Alabama Press, 1975), 140.

29. Carroll Smith-Rosenberg, "The Female World of Love and Ritual: Relations between Women in Nineteenth-Century America," *Signs* 1, no. 1 (1975): 1–29. Many thanks to Jim Fisher for this resource.

30. Mary Douglas, *Purity and Danger* (New York: Routledge, 1984), 3, 101.

31. Georges Bernanos, "Dans l'amitié de Léon Bloy," appendix to *Présence de Bernanos* (Paris: Plon, 1947), 1232.

32. Mark Jordan, *Telling Truths in Church: Scandal, Flesh, and Christian Speech* (Boston: Beacon Press, 2003), 13.

33. See the chilling analysis Robert Orsi offers in "The Study of Religion on the Other Side of Disgust," *HDS Bulletin,* Spring/Summer 2019. For a full biography on Catholic sexual abuse, see Catherine Osborne, "An Updated Catholic Abuse Crisis Syllabus," *Daily Theology,* January 17, 2019, https://dailytheology.org/2019/01/17/an-updated-catholic -abuse-crisis-syllabus/.

34. Raïssa Maritain, *Les grandes amitiés* (Paris: Éditions de la Maison Française, 1941), and translated into English by Julie Kernan as *We Have Been Friends Together* (New York: Longmans, Green, 1942). The second volume was issued separately in an English translation by Julie Kernan as *Adventures in Grace (Sequel to We Have Been Friends Together)* (New York: Longmans, Green, 1945). Both volumes are currently reprinted in Raïssa Maritain, "Les grandes amitiés," in *Oeuvres complètes Jacques et Raïssa Maritain,* ed. Jacques Maritain and Raïssa Maritain, vol. 14 (Paris: Éditions Universitaires, 1982– 2000).

35. For more on the tensions and evolution around intimacy in the modern Catholic priesthood, see John C. Seitz, "A Vocation of Contested Intimacies: Catholic Priesthood in the Mid-Twentieth Century," in *Religious Intimacies: Intersubjectivity in the Modern Christian West,* ed. Mary Dunn and Brenna Moore (Bloomington: Indiana University Press, 2020), 170–95.

36. Brent Hayes Edwards, "The Taste of the Archive," *Callaloo* 35, no. 4 (Fall 2012): 972.

37. See Linell E. Cady and Tracy Fessenden, "Gendering the Divide: Religion, the Secular, and the Politics of Sexual Difference," in *Religion, the Secular, and the Politics of Sexual Difference,* ed. Linell E. Cady and Tracy Fessenden (New York: Columbia University Press, 2015).

38. Janet Jakobsen and Ann Pellegrini, introduction to *Secularisms,* ed. Janet Jakobsen and Ann Pellegrini (Durham, NC: Duke University Press, 2008).

39. See the audio footage of Dana and Mistral in the documentary film *Locas Mujeres* (Madwomen), directed by María Elena Wood (2011), and Velma García-Gorena, ed., *Gabriela Mistral's Letters to Doris Dana* (Albuquerque: University of New Mexico Press, 2018).

40. Telegram from Jacques and Raïssa Maritain to Doris Dana, January 7, 1957, Archivo Gabriela Mistral, Biblioteca Nacional de Chile, Archivo Gabriela Mistral.

41. Pope John Paul II, *Fides et Ratio*, para. 74.

42. Brooke Williams Deely, general introduction to *Pope John Paul Speaks on Women* (Washington, DC: Catholic University of America Press, 2014), 10. John Hellman, "The Humanism of Jacques Maritain," in *Understanding Maritain: Philosopher and Friend*, ed. Deal W. Hudson and Matthew J. Mancini (Macon, GA: Mercer University Press), 131; Deely, *Pope John Paul*, 10; emphasis added.

43. Several other scholars draw a direct connection between John Paul II's thoughts on sexuality and Jacques Maritain. See Prudence Allen, "A Life Shared: The Complementarity of Jacques and Raïssa Maritain," in *The Wisdom of Youth: Essays Inspired by the Early Work of Jacques and Raïssa Maritain*, ed. Travis Drumsday (Washington, DC: Catholic University of America Press, 2016), 23–48. See also the essays in *The Vocation of the Catholic Philosopher: From Maritain to John Paul II*, ed. John P. Hittinger (Washington, DC: Catholic University of America Press, 2010).

44. Camille Robcis, "Catholics, the 'Theory of Gender,' and the Turn to the Human in France: A New Dreyfus Affair?," *Journal of Modern History* 87, no. 4 (December 2015): 922.

45. Kathryn Lofton, *Consuming Religion* (Chicago: University of Chicago Press, 2017), 162.

46. Lofton, *Consuming Religion*, 288.

47. François Bernheim, "Marseille, la ville à abattre," *Mediapart*, April 7, 2016.

48. Margaret J. Bates, "Gabriela Mistral," *The Americas* 3, no. 2 (October 1946): 169.

49. Katharine Capshaw, "From Bank Street to Harlem: A Conversation with Ellen Tarry," *The Lion and the Unicorn* 23, no. 2 (April 1999): 283.

50. Gabriela Mistral, "El Reparto" (Distribution), in *Selected Poems of Gabriela Mistral*, trans. and ed. Doris Dana (Baltimore: Johns Hopkins University Press, 1961).

51. This incredible story is outlined in Licia Fiol-Matta, *A Queer Mother for the Nation: The State and Gabriela Mistral* (Minneapolis: University of Minnesota Press, 2002).

52. Examples abound, but see, for instance, Claude McKay's March 23, 1942, letter from Chicago to his New York landlord, apologizing that he will be unable to retrieve his belongings from his old apartment. Claude McKay to Mr. Kohn, March 23, 1942, "Correspondences" file, Claude McKay Letters and Manuscripts, Schomburg Center for Research in Black Culture, Manuscripts, Archives and Rare Books Division.

53. Dominique Avon, *Les Frères prêcheurs en Orient: Les dominicains du Caire (années 1910–années 1960)* (Paris: Éditions du Cerf, 2005), 129.

54. Ibrahim Madkour, tribute given at the Arab Academy of Cairo on December 20, 1962. Manoël Pénicaud cites a transcription of this tribute found in the personal papers of Louis Massignon that his family allowed him to access. Manoël Pénicaud, "L'hétérotopie des Sept Dormants en Bretagne," *Archives de sciences sociales des religions* 155 (2011): 133.

55. Cited in Émile Poulat, *L'université devant la mystique. Expérience du Dieu sans mode. Transcendence du Dieu d'Amour* (Paris: Éditions Salvator, 1999), 124.

56. Gershom Scholem in an interview published in Gershom Scholem, *On Jews and Judaism in Crisis: Selected Essays*, ed. Werner J. Dannhauser (New York: Schocken Books, 1976), 48.

57. Amos Oz and Fania Oz-Salzberger, *Jews and Words* (New Haven, CT: Yale University Press, 2014), 11.

58. Carolyn Forché, *What You Have Heard Is True: A Memoir of Witness and Resistance* (New York: Penguin, 2019), 27.

59. Daniel Delas, *Aimé Césaire* (Paris: Hachette Supérieur, 1991), 14.

60. Denis Pelletier, Jean-Louis Schlegel, eds., *À la gauche du Christ: Les chrétiens de gauche en France de 1945 à nos jours* (Paris: Éditions du Seuil, 2012).

61. Tanella Boni, "Femmes en Négritude: Paulette Nardal et Suzanne Césaire," *Rue Descartes* 83, no. 4 (2014): 75.

62. Dipesh Chakrabarty, *Habitations of Modernity: Essays in the Wake of Subaltern Studies* (Chicago: University of Chicago Press, 2002), 37.

63. Jackson Lears has been incredibly helpful in my thinking of this culture, but the community in this book suggests a third alternative to his interpretation of the neo-medieval, mystically inclined Protestant artists who laid the groundwork for the therapeutic and the conservative and fascist Catholic neo-medievalists. See Jackson Lears, *No Place of Grace: Anti-modernism and the Transformation of American Culture 1880–1920* (Chicago: University of Chicago Press, 1994).

64. Edward T. Chambers, *Roots for Radicals: Organizing for Power, Action, and Justice* (New York: Bloomsbury, 2010), 90.

65. Edward T. Chambers, *The Power of Relational Action* (ACTA Publications, 2016), 18.

66. Chambers, *Power of Relational Action*. Étienne Fouilloux, *Une église en quête de liberté: La pensée catholique française entre modernisme et Vatican II (1914–1962)* (Paris: Desclée de Brouwer, 1998).

67. David Tracy in an interview with Kenneth Woodward, "In Praise of Fragments," *Commonweal*, September 25, 2019. David Tracy, *Fragments: The Existential Situation of Our Times* (Chicago: University of Chicago Press, 2020).

68. For a similiar argument, see Judith Halberstam, *The Queer Art of Failure* (Durham, NC: Duke University Press, 2011).

69. Tracy, *Fragments*, 31.

70. My thinking here is indebted to Rebecca Solnit, "The Ideology of Isolation," *Harper's Magazine*, July 2016.

INDEX

Abd-el-Jalil, Jean Mohammed, 22, 87–91

Achille, Louis Thomas, 27, 213, 301n94

âge nouveau, L', 134, 154

Al-Badaliya, 103–4, 105–6, 109, 110

Algeria, 7, 106–7, 110–11, 265n54

al-Hallāj, Husayn Ibn Mansur, 3, 76, 78–82, 87, 89, 279n25

Alinsky, Saul, 64, 65, 249

al-Mas'adi, Mahmud, 109

Als, Hilton, 32

Amato, Joseph, 235

Anawati, Georges, 84–85, 105, 109, 111, 112

Ancelet-Hustache, Jeanne, 14, 126, 148–49, 151, 152

anti-Semitism, 132, 275n114. *See also* Judaism

Aquinas, Thomas, 129

archives, 24, 225

Arendt, Hannah, 23–24

Argentina, 8, 274n90, 275n114

Asociación de Amigos de Léon Bloy, 4

Avicenna, 150

Avon, Dominique, 74, 90–91, 104

Baldwin, James, 10, 190

Barakat, Hidaya Afifi, 92–93

Baring, Edward, 307n7

Barthé, Richmond, 190

Barthes, Roland, 17

Baruzi, Jean, 245

Bayard, Louis, 19–20

Belloc, Hilaire, 128

Benjamin, Walter, 252

Bennett, Jane, 73

Berdyaev, Nicholas, 134, 139–41, 166, 167, 292n15

Bernanos, Georges, 50, 51, 58, 132, 164

Best, Wallace, 224

Blackness: and Catholicism, 3, 6, 27, 190–91, 194, 205–6, 212, 222, 223, 224; and communism, 211–12; and Cone, 308n15; diaspora, 234; and Europe, 27, 77, 81, 83, 172, 229–30; and France, 10–11; and friendship, 175; and intellectual history, 26–27; and McKay, 20, 27, 172–73, 174–75, 179, 184, 194, 195, 203–4, 222–23, 224; *négritude*, 198, 247, 301n94; in Paris, 10–11, 190–91, 194; and religion, 203–4; and sexuality, 20; and Tarry, 205; and transnationalism, 172–73; and victimhood, 32; and white fantasies, 209, 210, 223

Bloy, Jeanne, 51

Bloy, Léon, 4–5, 16, 22, 44, 48, 49–52

Boittin, Jennifer, 191

Boni, Tanella, 247

Bourdet, Claude, 129

Boym, Svetlana, 185

Bray, Alan, 49

Brown, Peter, 2, 146, 156

Buber, Martin, 230, 236

Byrne, Julie, 231, 307n7

Cáceres, Esther de, 4, 44, 55–56, 57, 70–71, 235

Cahiers de la nouvelle époque (journal), 134,

Caillois, Roger, 67

Carver, Washington, 64

Catholicism: and Abd-el-Jalil, 88; and banality, 281n59; Black, 3, 6, 27, 190–91, 205–6, 211–12, 222, 223, 224; and colonialism, 6–9, 220–21; and conformism, 22–23; and conservatism, 247; and corporatism, 240–41; and Davy, 116–17, 143–44, 162–63; and diaspora, 234–35; and family, 13, 46; and fluidity, 245; and Franco, 53; and friendship, 3, 4, 13–14, 22–23, 71, 193, 214, 237–38; gender ideology of, 241; and Harlem, 302n121; and human rights, 13–14, 265n51; insider-outsider relationship with, 245; and intellectual history, 24–25, 26, 31, 229; and Judaism, 30, 245; and law, 46; literati, nonacademic, 230–31; margins of, 30; and Jacques Maritain, 44, 49, 57, 71; and Raïssa Maritain, 22, 44, 49, 245; and Massignon, 80, 87, 279n25; and McKay, 4, 27–29, 172, 173–74, 175, 185–86, 193, 194, 199, 211, 214, 215, 216–21, 222, 223, 224, 245; and medievalism, 13, 15; and Mistral, 3, 37, 41, 42, 44, 48, 59–60; and modernity, 13, 15, 34, 46; and nationalism, 12–13; nonorthodoxy, 246; and Paris, 25, 193–94; and politics, 13–14; and race, 173–74, 205–12; and refugees, 30; and sexuality, 13, 17–18, 87, 238; and *Sur*, 55; and Tarry, 205; and violence, 33–34; white, 31–32; and women, 24–26; and working class, 159–60

Cavallini, Giuliana, 213

Cayton, Horace R., 183

celibacy, 101, 214–15, 272n46. *See also* marriage; sexuality

Certeau, Michel de, 3, 73

Chagall, Marc, 58

Chaillet, Pierre, 131

Chakrabarty, Dipesh, 100, 247

Chambers, Ed, 249–50

Chappel, James, 13, 46

Chenu, Marie-Dominique, 27, 84, 122, 124–25, 160, 289n44

Chesterton, G. K., 83–84, 129

Chicago, 207–8, 217–18, 221–24

children, 21–22. *See also* family; marriage

Chile, 7–8, 35–36, 38, 60, 69

Christian, William, 1, 147

Christianity: and Bloy, 50–51; and d'Alverny, 150–51; and Davy, 163; and division, 33, 34, 83; Eastern, 134; and Europe, 83; and Islam, 82, 83–84, 90–91, 93, 97–98, 105, 106–9, 110, 150–51; and Jamaica, 176; and Judaism, 131–32; and Kahil, 97–98; and love, 19; and Massignon, 82, 97–98, 110; and McKay, 186–88, 219–20; and Mistral, 41; Old Testament, 131; and orientalism, 136; and social justice, 41; and violence, 163; and Weil, 162–63; and women, 150

Cocteau, Jean, 41, 70, 72

colonialism: Africa, 193–94; Arabic world, 7; Catholicism and, 6–9, 220–21; Chile, 7–8; culture, European, 8, 77; French, 7, 106–8, 193–94, 227–28, 274n82; and friendship, 8–9, 180, 193–94; and Islam, 77, 90, 103, 106–9; Jamaica, 8, 178, 179; and Kahil, 103; and Massignon, 103, 106, 110; and McKay, 178, 179, 194, 220–21

communism, 203, 204, 211

Compagnon, Olivier, 275n114

comparative religion, 135, 142–44, 231

Congar, Yves, 27, 125

Connelly, John, 30, 116

Constable, Giles, 150

conversion, 22, 47, 71, 88, 91, 135, 223–24

Corbin, Henry, 142–43

Cressler, Matthew, 174, 212

d'Alverny, Marie-Thérèse, 149–51, 152

Dana, Doris, 35, 43, 67, 69–70, 240, 251

Danay, Gertrude, 207

Daniel, Yves, 159–60

Daniélou, Jean, 124, 135, 139

Dantzic, Jerry, 225

Dar-el-Salam, 104–5

Davidson, Naomi, 85

Davis, Natalie Zemon, 228

Davy, Marie-Magdeleine: and *L'âge nouveau*, 134, 154–55; *Aimer toutes les mains*, 161; and Ancelet-Hustache, 126, 148–49, 151,

152; archives of, 24, 225; and Berdyaev, 134, 139–41, 166, 167, 292n15; and Bernard of Clairvaux, 119–20, 121–22, 130, 132–33, 138, 161–62; and Bibliothèque des étudiants catholiques, 127; and Biès, 168; and Catholicism, 116–17, 143–44, 162–63; and Centre national de la recherche scientifique, 138; and Chenu, 122; and Christianity, 163; Cistercian spiritual reading, 121; and Coltel, 126; and comparative religion, 135, 142–44, 231; and Corbin, 142; and d'Alverny, 149–51, 152; and Daniélou, 123, 124, 139; and de Blois, 121; and Deleuze, 139; and de Lubac, 122; and Descamps, 168–69; and *Dieu vivant*, 135–36; *Les dominicaines*, 122; and dreams, 167; early life of, 22, 117–18; and Eckhart, 130; and Eliade, 142; and experience, 158–59; and Fessard, 130–31, 139; and Fortelle, 127; and friendship, 117, 120–22, 124, 125, 131–32, 139–42, 145–46, 147–48, 167–69, 237; and Gilson, 118–19, 120, 123, 124; and God, 137, 154–55; and Guillaume de Saint-Thierry, 120, 121–22, 137; and Hinduism, 169; and history, 152; and impersonalism, 158, 160–61, 168; and inner religion, 136–37; and Institut Catholique, 123–26; and Journet, 145; and Judaism, 131–32; and Latin, 115, 120; and love, 130, 161–62; and Maison Simone Weil, 4, 164–66; and Jacques Maritain, 118; and Raïssa Maritain, 118; and Maspero, 135; and Massignon, 75, 86, 120, 135, 141; and medievalism, 15, 116, 127–28, 129–30, 133–35, 137–38, 144; and men, 145–46, 152; and monasticism, 116, 119–20, 121, 124, 130; and Moré, 139, 145, 158; and mysticism, 26, 115, 116, 124, 130, 135, 136–37, 144, 153, 160; and Nazism, 161; and *l'Orient*, 134; and Orthodoxy, 245, 292n105; and Perrin, 157–58; and politics, 158–62; and resistance, 115, 126–27, 130–31, 143, 165; and *ressourcement*, 122–23, 124–25, 144; and retribution, 161; and Saint-Clementine, 164–65; and sainthood, 166–67; and *la sève*, 136; and solitude, 166–

71; and Sorbonne, 118; and Stapert, 164; and totalitarianism, 163; translations of, 122–23; and USJJ, 142; and violence, 163; and Weil, 4, 146–48, 152–54, 155–64, 165–66, 169–71; and winged beings, 167–68; as woman, 151–52, 169–70

Day, Dorothy, 21, 22, 73, 208, 212, 215, 216, 218
Debevec, Liza, 9
de Blois, Pierre, 121
Deely, Brooke Williams, 241
de Hueck Doherty, Catherine, 5–6, 206, 208, 209, 211, 212, 215
de Lubac, Henri, 122, 131, 135, 232
de Porres, Martín, 213
Derrida, Jacques, 155
Deshmukh, Madhuri, 185
Dieu vivant (journal), 135–36
Dominicanism, 84, 193, 281n53
Douglas, Mary, 237
Doyle, John, 248–49
Drake, Jim, 248, 249
Drake, St. Clair, 183
Drexel, Katharine, 200–201
Duchen, Claire, 148
Dutruc, Armelle, 225

École normale supérieure, 128–29
Edwards, Brent Hayes, 11, 172–73, 191, 234, 239
Egyptian Feminist Union (EFU), 92
Eliade, Mircea, 142–43
Elie, Paul, 3
Esprit (journal), 129
Ethiopia, 204–5
Europe: and Blackness, 27, 77, 81, 83, 172, 229–30; and Christianity, 83; and colonialism, 8, 77; and Islam, 77, 81, 85, 109; and McKay, 172–73, 188, 199, 202

Fabre, Michel, 194
family, 13, 21–22, 46, 148, 151, 241–42, 262n9. *See also* celibacy; marriage
Far Right, 2, 12, 13, 60, 127–28, 129, 132
fascism: and Eliade, 143; and Judaism, 58, 132; and the Left, 247; and Jacques Maritain,

fascism (*continued*)
  53, 54; and McKay, 28–29; and medieval-
  ism, 13, 127–28, 129; and Mistral, 11, 36–37,
  43, 53–54, 58; and modernity, 13, 128; and
  orientalism, 83; and romanticism, 247–48;
  and Weil, 160. *See also* Nazism
Fernando, Mayanthi, 85
Fessard, Gaston, 130–31, 139
Fessenden, Tracy, 4, 191, 201, 227
Flying Inn, The (Chesterton), 83–84
Forché, Carolyn, 9, 246
Foster, Elizabeth, 174, 307n7
Foucauld, Charles de, 7, 71, 76, 78, 79, 87, 89
Foucault, Michel, 151
Fragments (Tracy), 252
France: and African Americans, 10–11; and
  colonialism, 7, 106–8, 193–94, 227–28,
  274n82; and exiles, 9–11; and friendship,
  14; and Islam, 10, 85, 106–8; and Raïssa
  Maritain, 11–12; and Massignon, 10; and
  Mistral, 7–8, 11, 42, 52–53; and national-
  ism, 12–13; and secularism, 85, 106; and
  Spanish speakers, 9–10, 52–53; and spiritu-
  ality, 228; and women, 148
Francis, Saint, 39–40, 42, 66, 67, 89, 93–94
Franciscanism, 15, 89, 104
Frank, Waldo, 53, 68–69, 72, 73
Frei Montalva, Eduardo, 56–57, 72
friendship: and Aelred of Rievaulx, 49; and
  Algeria, 265n54; and al-Hallāj, 80, 82;
  amitié spirituelle, 49; in archives, 24;
  Black, 175; and Bloy, 49–51, 52; and
  Catholicism, 3, 4, 13–14, 22–23, 71, 214,
  237; and Catholic Left, 12; and Chenu,
  125–26; and colonialism, 8–9, 180, 193–94;
  and Congar, 125–26; and corporatism, 241;
  as a cross, 112; and Davy, 117, 120–22, 124,
  125, 131–32, 139–42, 145–46, 167–69, 237;
  and de Blois, 121; and exile, 11, 230; failures
  of, 235–36; and family, 22, 235–36, 237–38;
  and fragments, 252–53; and France, 14;
  and Gugelot, 262n9; and Judaism, 131–32;
  and Kahil, 6–7, 95–98, 100–102, 112, 113;
  and love, 5, 16–17, 228–29; and Jacques
  Maritain, 2, 17, 18, 24, 47–49, 52, 56, 59,

  168; and Raïssa Maritain, 2, 11–12, 24,
  47–49, 52, 59, 168; and Massignon, 3–4,
  6–7, 75, 79, 80, 82, 87–88, 90, 95–98, 100–
  102, 112–13, 236; and materiality, 267n84,
  273n56; and McKay, 5, 174–76, 177, 181–83,
  185, 192–93, 195–97, 200, 210, 214, 215;
  medieval, 49; and Mistral, 11, 36, 37, 42–43,
  65–67, 68–69, 71–72; and modernity, 4, 34;
  and monasticism, 16, 117, 120, 121, 124; and
  mysticism, 124; and politics, 2, 13–14, 32–
  33; and power, 141–42, 248–50; and Protestantism, 15; and race, 5–6, 173–74, 181–83,
  208, 210; and relationships, 248–50; and
  sexuality, 16–20, 23, 80, 100–101, 214, 238–
  40; spiritual, 2, 3–4, 6, 16, 17–18, 22–23,
  49, 80, 235, 236; trains, and war recovery,
  14–15; utopian, 4, 5; and whiteness, 181–83;
  and women, 236–37; and writers, 228–29
Friendship House, 4, 206–12, 214, 249
Furey, Constance, 33, 100

Gandhi, Leela, 33
Garvey, Marcus, 27
gender, 147, 152, 241. *See also* sexuality; women
Gilroy, Paul, 173, 234
Gilson, Étienne, 116, 118–19, 120, 123, 124, 129,
  132, 149–50
Glasberg, Alexandre, 14, 131
God: and *L'âge nouveau*, 154; and authoritari-
  anism, 137; and Davy, 137, 154–55; and love,
  101; and Massignon, 86, 96, 97, 100, 101;
  and mysticism, 137; and sexuality, 101;
  and Teresa of Ávila, 284n124; and Weil,
  155–56
Godin, Henri, 159–60
Gopnik, Adam, 83
Gordon, Avery, 181
Gordon, Mary, 179
grassroots organizing, 248–50
Greater Boston Interfaith Organization
  (GBIO), 248, 249
Green, Julien, 16, 47, 51, 70
Gremillion, Joseph, 210–11
Griffin, John Howard, 70, 72
Gude, Mary Louise, 75

Hall, James, 224

Harlem, 5, 173, 188, 189, 200–217, 249, 302n121

Harrigan, Ann, 5–6, 22–23, 208, 210, 212, 213, 214, 228

Harrison, Hubert, 188–89

Hartfield, John, 183–84

Hartman, Saidiya, 20, 189, 201

Hellman, John, 241

Hennessy, Kate, 22

Herbert, Jean, 156–57

Heschel, Susannah, 77

Hinduism, 156–57, 169

history, intellectual, 24–25, 26, 32, 34, 143, 152, 226–27, 229, 231

Holcomb, Gary, 180

Holiday, Billie, 201, 225–26, 227

Hollywood, Amy, 18–19, 32, 122

Holocaust, 63–64

homosexuality, 17–18, 87, 99, 180, 189, 215, 238–39. *See also* family; marriage; sexuality

Horan, Elizabeth, 40, 52, 251, 270n9

Houénou, Kojo Tovalou, 193, 194

Hughes, Langston, 9, 224

humanism, 246

immanence, 232–33

immigration, 9, 83

Imperatori-Lee, Natalia, 229–30

Industrial Areas Foundation (IAF), 248, 249

intellectual history. *See* history, intellectual

internationalisme noir, l', 191, 195, 196

Interracial Review (journal), 212–13

Islam: and Abd-el-Jalil, 22; and al-Hallāj, 81; and Anawati, 84–85; and banality, 281n59; and Christianity, 82, 83–84, 90–91, 93, 97–98, 105, 106–9, 150–51; and colonialism, 77, 103, 106–8; and d'Alverny, 150–51; and Europe, 77, 81, 85, 109; and France, 10, 85, 106–8; and Franciscanism, 104; and Holy Spirit, 82; and Kahil, 92–94, 103–5; and love, 283n109; and Massignon, 7, 10, 74–75, 76–77, 78, 80–83, 84–86, 90–91, 93–94, 103–6, 109–10, 278n5; and mysticism, 80–82, 84; and *ressourcement*, 84–85;

and Said, 77; and violence, 107–8. *See also* Massignon, Louis; Sufism

Jakobsen, Janet, 240

Jamaica, 8, 172, 176–81, 220

James, William, 155–56

Jesuits, 131

John Paul II (pope), 240, 310n43

Johnson, Karen, 208

Jordan, Mark, 23, 238

Journet, Charles, 12, 59, 115, 145

Judaism: and Catholicism, 30, 245; and Chesterton, 129; and Christianity, 131–32; conversion from, 22; and fascism, 58, 132; and Holocaust, 63–64; and Raïssa Maritain, 9, 29, 44, 58, 63, 64, 275n114; and Middle Ages, 132; and Mistral, 44, 267n9, 271n40; non-orthodoxy, 246; in Paris, 9; and Weil, 163

Judt, Tony, 83, 162

Just Kids (Smith), 251

Kahil, Mary, 3–4, 6–7, 16, 32, 76, 77, 91–113, 278n13

Kearns, John Chrysostom, 213

Keating, Mary Jerdo, 29

Kerouac, Jack, 209

Keryell, Jacques, 94–95, 102

King, John, 55

Kripal, Jeffrey, 99

laity, 22, 23, 24, 39, 193, 295n40

Lears, Jackson, 311n63

Le Bras, Gabriel, 160

Leclercq, Jean, 121

Lettres à ses filleuls (L. Bloy), 51

Lincoln, Abraham, 19–20

Locke, Alain, 189, 190

Lofton, Kathryn, 240

love: and Bernard of Clairvaux, 130, 161–62; and Christianity, 19; and Davy, 161–62; and desire, 100–101; and friendship, 5, 16–17, 228–29; and gender, 241; and God, 101; and Islam, 283n109; and Journet, 59; and Kahil, 96–98, 102; and Jacques Maritain,

love (*continued*)
59; and Raïssa Maritain, 59; and Massignon, 96–98; nonconformist, 21; and
sexuality, 19, 101, 240; and women,
236–37
lynching, 183–84, 187

Mabarrat Muhammad 'Ali, 92–93
Madkour, Ibrahim, 104
Maison Simone Weil, 164–66
Malewicz, Malgorzata H., 150
Mandair, Arvind-Pal, 6
Mapplethorpe, Robert, 251
Marcel, Gabriel, 4
Maréchal, Joseph, 84
Maritain, Jacques: and Abd-el-Jalil, 88; and
Alinsky, 64, 65; and Argentina, 275n114;
Art and Scholasticism, 45; and Bloy, 16,
44, 48, 49, 51–52; and Cáceres, 55, 70–71;
and Carver, 64; and Catholicism, 44, 49,
57, 71; and Chile, 69; and Cocteau, 70, 72;
and Dana, 69–70; and Davy, 118; and faith,
63–64; and fascism, 53, 54; and Foucauld,
71; and Frei Montalva, 56–57, 69; and
friendship, 2, 17, 18, 24, 47–49, 52, 56, 71,
168; and Green, 16, 70; and Griffin, 72; and
Holocaust, 63–64; homosexuality, 17, 18;
household of, 46; *Integral Humanism*, 53,
54, 69; and John Paul II, 241, 310n43; and
Journet, 59; and Latin America, 54, 55, 57;
letters of, 251; and Luther, 45–46; marriage
of, 45–47, 272n46; and Massignon, 75,
113; and McKay, 27–28; Meudon (salon),
45, 46–48, 53, 55, 64–65; and Mistral, 18,
26, 35, 36, 37, 38, 44, 45, 48–49, 54, 60, 62,
63, 68, 69, 71; oblate, 15; and Ocampo, 54;
The Peasant of the Garonne, 70, 277n144;
and Peréz, 60; and politics, 2, 54, 64, 65;
and Protestantism, 45–46; and Raïssa,
18, 70–71, 239, 272n46, 277n144; and
realism, 63, 65; and Spanish Civil War, 53;
and *Sur*, 54–55; and Walcheren, 4–5; and
Whitman, 64
Maritain, Raïssa: and Bloy, 16, 44, 49, 51–52;
and Cáceres, 55, 57, 70–71; and Catholi-

cism, 22, 44, 49, 245; "Chagall," 58; and
Davy, 118; death of, 70; exile of, 11–12;
and France, 11–12; and Frei Montalva, 56;
and friendship, 2, 24, 47–49, 52, 59, 168;
household of, 46; and Jacques, 18, 70–71,
239, 272n46, 277n144; and Judaism, 9, 29,
44, 58, 64, 275n114; and Latin America,
54; marriage of, 45–47, 272n46; Meudon
(salon), 45, 47–48, 64–65; and Mistral,
26, 36, 37, 45, 63, 68; oblate, 15; poetry of,
45, 59; and politics, 2; and Protestantism,
45–46; and Sachs, 47; and Walcheren,
4–5
marriage, 45–47, 87, 89–90, 102, 177–78, 238,
272n46. *See also* celibacy; family; homosexuality; sexuality
Martel, Frédéric, 17–18, 238–39
Maspero, Henri, 77–78, 135
Massignon, Louis: and Abd-el-Jalil, 22, 87–91;
activism of, 95, 103–11; and Al-Badaliya,
103–4, 105–6, 109, 110; and Algeria, 106–7,
110–11; and al-Hallāj, 76, 78–82, 87, 89,
279n25; and al-Mas'adi, 109; and Anawati,
84–85, 105, 109; and Catholicism, 80, 87,
279n25; charisma of, 86; and Christianity,
82, 110; and colonialism, 103, 106–7, 110;
conversion of, 135; and Davy, 75, 86, 120,
135, 141; and desire, 100–101; and *Dieu
vivant*, 135–36; and Dominicans, 281n53;
early life of, 77–79; *Essai sur les origines
du lexique technique de la mystique musulmane*, 80–81; and experiential reality,
75–76; family of, 21; and Foucauld, 76,
78, 79, 87, 89; Franciscanism, 89, 104; and
friendship, 3–4, 6–7, 75, 79, 80, 82, 87–88,
90, 95–98, 100–102, 112–13, 236; and
Gandhi, 95; and God, 86, 96, 97, 100, 101;
and homosexuality, 18, 87, 99; imprison-
ment in Iraq, 79; and Islam, 7, 10, 74–75,
76–77, 78, 80–83, 84–86, 90–91, 93–94,
103–6, 109–10, 278n5; and Kahil, 6–7, 16,
76, 77, 91–113, 278n13; and Kripal, 99; and
Lacouture, 86; letters to Kahil, 94–95,
98–99; and love, 96–98, 101; and Jacques
Maritain, 75, 113; marriage of, 87, 89–90,

102; and Maspero, 77–78; and Melkite Catholicism, 245; and mystical substitution, 79; and mysticism, 80–81, 101; and orientalism, 75, 77, 78, 86; and politics, 95, 107; and Said, 75, 77; and sexuality, 87, 99–102; and Shariati, 17, 109–10, 236; and spiritual solidarities, 76; and suffering, 284n129; and Sufism, 76, 78–79, 81–82, 98, 280n34; and vow with Kahil, 93–94, 98–99; and Waardenburg, 75

Massis, Henri, 83, 128–29

Maurin, Peter, 73

McGinn, Bernard, 101

McKay, Claude: and Achille, 213, 301n94; and African diaspora, 190–91, 194; *Amiable with Big Teeth*, 204–5; *Banjo*, 195–98, 219, 242; baptism of, 216, 217, 223; Baptist, 176–77; and Black Madonnas, 199, 214; and Blackness, 20, 27, 172–73, 175, 179, 184, 194, 195, 203–4, 222–23, 224; and Britton, 214; and Burke, 200; and Cantwell, 217; and Catholicism, 4, 27–29, 172, 173–74, 175, 185–86, 194, 199, 211, 214, 215, 216–21, 222, 223, 224, 245; and *Catholic Worker*, 222; and Catholic Youth Organization (CYO), 217; and Césaire, 198; and Chambers, 210; and Chicago, 217–18, 221–24; and Christ, 216; and Christianity, 186–88, 219–20; "Cities," 194–95; and colonialism, 178, 179, 194, 220–21; and communism, 203, 204, 211; conversion of, 172, 175, 188, 199, 216, 218, 223; "Courage," 189; "The Cycle," 216; and Day, 212, 215, 216, 218; death of, 222; and de Sales, 218; early life of, 176–80; and Eastman, 182, 200, 209–10, 215, 218, 297n1; and Ethiopia, 204; and Europe, 172–73, 188, 199, 202; "Exhortation, Summer of 1919," 186–87; exile of, 230; and fascism, 28–29; and Father Divine, 203; and Federal Writers' Project, 201, 202; and friendship, 5, 174–76, 177, 181–83, 185, 192–93, 195–97, 200, 210, 214, 215; and Friendship House, 4, 209, 211, 212, 214, 220; and Garcia, 219; and Garvey, 217, 220; and Hamid, 203; and

Harlem, 173, 188, 200–217; and Harrigan, 210; and Harrison, 188–89; and Hennacy, 218–19, 220; and Houénou, 193, 194; "If We Must Die," 184; and intellectual history, 28–29; and Jamaica, 8, 172, 176–81, 220; and Jekyll, 178–80; and Johnson, 199, 222; and Keating, 210, 215, 217; and Locke, 189; *A Long Way from Home*, 181–83, 185, 210, 215, 220; "The Lynching," 187; and Marciniak, 217; and Jacques Maritain, 27–28; and marriage, 177–78; and Marseilles, 195–96; and Hope McKay, 22, 188; and medievalism, 16; and men, 217, 224; and Michael, 182–83; and modernity, 174; *My Green Hills of Jamaica*, 179, 220, 221; and mystical body of Christ, 211; and mystic chapels, 203; and mysticism, 196–97; and Nardals, 191, 192, 193, 198, 205, 223; and New Mexico, 218–19, 220; and Paris, 10, 11, 190–91, 193–95, 198; poetry of, 178–79, 184–85, 186–87, 188, 216; and Protestantism, 174, 177–78, 180; and racism, 173–74, 181–83, 185, 187, 212; and radicalism, 185–86; and religion, 174, 175, 186, 188, 196–98, 202–4, 213–14, 218, 231–32; and resistance, 186–87, 189; and Schomburg, 202; and Senghor, 194; and sexuality, 20, 177–78, 180, 215, 239; and Sheil, 217, 218, 221; and Socé, 198; *Songs of Jamaica*, 179–80; and Spain, 198–99, 220; and spirituality, 186; "The Strange Burial of Sue," 178; and suffering, 32; and Tarry, 172, 175, 200, 201–2, 203, 205, 209, 212, 215–16, 217, 221–22; unemployment of, 28; and United States, 172–73, 181, 185; and West, 200; and whiteness, 179, 181–83

McLoughlin, Sally, 248–49

medievalism: and Ancelet-Hustache, 148–49; and Catholicism, 13, 15; and d'Alverny, 150–51; and Davy, 15, 116, 127–28, 129–30, 133–35, 137–38, 144; and fascism, 13, 127–28, 129; and friendship, 49; and Gilson, 118–19; and Italy, 265n48; and Judaism, 132; and McKay, 15–16; and monasticism, 16, 116; and nationalism, 265n46, 289n57;

medievalism (*continued*)
  and *l'Orient*, 134; and piety, 15–16; and
    realism, 133; and women, 148–51, 289n46;
    and xenophobia, 129
Mehlinge, Kermit T., 303n136
memory, 251
Mendes-Flohr, Paul, 230
Merton, Thomas, 51
Meudon, 45, 46–48, 53, 55, 64–65
Michel, Florian, 119
Mission de France, 159–60
Mistral, Gabriela: awards of, 67–68; and Bar-
    rios, 39–40; biographies of, 270n8; and
    Brazil, 59–60; and Cáceres, 44, 55, 56;
    and Caillois, 67; and *campesinos*, 40, 41,
    68; and Catholicism, 3, 37, 41, 42, 44, 48,
    59–60; and Catholic Left, 69; and Chile,
    7–8, 35–36, 38, 244; and Christianity, 41;
    and Dana, 35, 43, 67, 69–70, 240, 251; and
    Darío, 39; death of, 35, 69; "Distribution,"
    243–44; early life of, 38–39; "Emigrada
    judía," 58; "The Fall of Europe," 67; and
    fascism, 11, 36–37, 43, 53–54, 58; and
    France, 7–8, 11, 42, 52–53; and Francis-
    canism, 42–43; and Frank, 68–69, 72,
    73; and Frei Montalva, 56–57, 69, 71, 72;
    and friendship, 11, 36, 37, 42–43, 65–67,
    68–69, 71–72; and Guillén, 40–41, 46, 58;
    hagiographies of, 41; "La Hella," 30–31;
    and Institute for International Intellectual
    Cooperation, 10, 42, 54; and Judaism, 44,
    267n9, 271n40; "Lámpara de catedral,"
    62–63; and Jacques Maritain, 18, 26, 35, 36,
    37, 38, 44, 45, 48–49, 54, 60, 62, 63, 68, 69,
    71; and Raïssa Maritain, 36, 37, 44, 45, 59–
    60, 63, 68; and Meudon, 45, 46–47, 53, 55,
    64–65; and Mexico, 40–41; and mysticism,
    63; and neo-medievalism, 15; and Neruda,
    28; and Nervo, 40; and Ocampo, 17, 48–
    49, 54, 57; "La palabra maldita," 66; and
    peace, 66; and Pérez, 60; and Pinochet,
    244; and Pius XII, 68; poetry of, 38–39,
    40, 59, 61–63, 67; and politics, 39–40, 63;
    and poverty, 231; and social justice, 41–42;
    and Sor Juana, 40; and Spanish Civil War,
    53, 54; and *Sur*, 54–55; and teaching, 39,
    42; and Teresa of Ávila, 42; and Tomic,
    69; and World Alliance for International
    Friendship, 62; and Yin-Yin, 22, 46, 58, 61;
    and Zweig, 60–61
modernity: and Catholicism, 13, 15, 34, 46;
    and family, 46; and fascism, 13, 128; and
    friendship, 4, 34; and McKay, 174; and
    mysticism, 137; and racism, 174
Molina, J. Michelle, 267n84, 273n56
monasticism, 15, 16, 116, 119–20, 121, 124
Moore, Cecilia, 206
Moré, Marcel, 139, 145, 158
Mulvoy, Michael, 205–6, 213
mystical body of Christ, 211
mysticism: and authoritarianism, 137; and
    comparative religion, 135; and Davy, 26,
    115, 116, 124, 135, 136–37, 144, 153, 160; and
    enchantment, 73; and friendship, 124; and
    God, 137; and Kahil, 101; and Massignon,
    80–82, 84, 101; and McKay, 196–97; and
    Mistral, 63; and modernity, 137; and
    monasticism, 116; and politics, 63, 131;
    and sexuality, 101; and Weil, 153–54, 160;
    and women, 149

Nardal, Jane, 191–92, 195
Nardal, Paulette, 3, 20, 27, 28, 32, 191–93, 195,
    198, 205, 223, 246
Nazism, 129, 131, 160, 161, 248
négritude. See under Blackness
"Negro History of New York" (Federal Writers'
    Project), 201–2
Nelson, Maggie, 21, 100
neo-scholasticism, 232
nouvelles familles spirituelles, 4

Oblate Sisters of Providence, 227
Ocampo, Victoria, 8, 17
O'Connell, Maureen, 32
Oliphant, Elayne, 281n59
O'Mahony, Anthony, 74
orientalism, 75, 77, 78, 82, 83, 86, 136
Orsi, Robert, 233, 269n106
Osborne, Catherine, 232

Palacios, Miguel Asín, 81
Paris, 9–11, 25, 52, 190–93, 274n82
Pearson, Drew, 14–15
Pellegrini, Ann, 240
Pelletier, Denis, 52, 247
Pérez, Luis Arturo, 60
Perrin, Joseph-Marie, 157
Perry, Kennetta Hammond, 202
Petro, Anthony, 100–101
Picón, María Laura, 36, 55–56
Pinn, Anthony, 19
Pius XII (pope), 68, 94, 103
politics: and Alinsky, 65; and Catholicism,
    13–14; and Davy, 158–62; and friendship,
    2, 13–14, 32–33; and Jacques Maritain, 2,
    54, 64, 65; and Raïssa Maritain, 2; and
    Massignon, 95, 107; and Mistral, 39–40,
    63; and mysticism, 63, 131; and Weil,
    158–62
Poulat, Émile, 119, 154, 294n32
Power of Relational Action, The (Chambers),
    250

race riots, 183–84
racism, 11, 173–74, 181–85, 187, 205–12
religion: and Blackness, 203–4; comparative,
    135, 142–44, 231; inner, 136–37; and McKay,
    174, 175, 186, 188, 196–98, 202–4, 213–14,
    218, 231–32; and mysticism, 135; and Orsi,
    269n106; and violence, 136, 163
ressourcement, 26, 84, 115–16, 122–23, 124–25,
    144, 150, 289n44
Revue du monde noir (journal), 192
Robcis, Camille, 241
Robert, Dana, 15
Roth, Joseph, 12
Rothberg, Michael, 30
Russia, 53, 139–40, 192
Ryad, Umar, 77

Sachs, Maurice, 72
Safi, Omar, 81
Said, Edward, 75, 77, 230
saints, 146–47, 155–57, 166–67, 295n40
Sanos, Sandrine, 128–29

Saraswati, Swami Sivananda, 156–57
Sartre, Jean-Paul, 129
Schielke, Samuli, 9
Schlegel, Jean-Louis, 52, 247
Schneider, Betty, 207, 209
Scholem, Gershom, 132
Schomburg, Arturo, 202
secularism, 240, 246. *See also* modernity
Seelisberg (Switzerland), 132
segregation, 181, 183
sève, la (the sap), 136, 232–33
sexuality, 16–20, 23, 87, 99–102, 177–78, 189,
    214, 238–40, 241, 310n43. *See also* celibacy;
    family; homosexuality; marriage
Shariati, Ali, 17, 109–10, 244
Sheil, Bishop, 217, 218, 221, 303n127
Shore, Marci, 34
Smith, Bonnie, 152
Smith, Patti, 251
Smith, Rachel, 121
Smith, Zadie, 225–26
Smith-Rosenberg, Carroll, 236–37
Snyder, Timothy, 126
Sorett, Josef, 185, 260
Sor Juana Inés de la Cruz, 40
South America, 54, 55
Spain: Black Madonnas, 199, 214; Civil War,
    53; and Jamaica, 220; and McKay, 198–99,
    220; refugees in Paris, 9–10, 52–53
Stevens, Harold A., 207, 208, 212–13
Stewart, Jeffrey C., 190
Sufism, 76, 78–79, 81–82, 98. *See also* Islam
Sur (journal), 54–55

Tarry, Ellen, 3, 6, 172, 175, 200–202, 203, 205–6,
    208, 209, 211, 212, 213, 215–16, 217, 221–22,
    226, 243, 303n127
Témoignage chrétien (journal), 131
Teresa of Ávila, 284n124
Thérèse of Lisieux, 147
Thomism, 118–19
Thurman, Kira, 202
Timothy, Sister, 213
Tracy, David, 72, 252
transcendence, 233

Turner, Victor, 73
twentieth century, 9

underworld, 23
Université Saint-Jean de Jérusalem (USJJ), 142
utopianism, 4, 5

Vajda, Georges, 132, 135
Vatican II, 25–26
violence, religious, 136, 163

Waardenburg, Jean Jacques, 75
Wagner, Jean, 186
Walcheren, Pierre van der Meer de, 4–5, 50–51
Wall, Bernard, 13, 128
Wasserstrom, Steven, 142
Weil, Simone: *Attente de Dieu*, 157, 158; and
    Christianity, 162–63; and Davy, 146–48,
    152–54, 155–64, 165–66, 169–71; and expe-
    rience, 158–59; and family, 22; and fascism,
    160; and fragments, 252; and God, 155–56;
    and impersonalism, 158, 160–61; and
    institutions, 163–64; and Judaism, 163; and
    Moré, 158; and mysticism, 153–54, 160; and
    Ozouf, 170; and Perrin, 157–58; and poli-
    tics, 158–62; and saints, 156–57; as woman,
    147–48, 169–70; and workers' rights, 158–
    59, 160. *See also* Maison Simone Weil

Weisenfeld, Judith, 188
West, Dorothy, 11
whiteness, 5–6, 26–27, 31–32, 179, 181–85, 209,
    210, 211–12, 223
Whitman, Walt, 64
Wilkins, Agnes, 75
Wolfson, Elliot, 100
women: and Catholicism, 24–26; and Chris-
    tianity, 150; Davy, 4, 151–52, 169–70; and
    France, 148; and friendship, 236–37;
    and history, 152; intellectuals, 25–26;
    and medievalism, 148–51; and religious
    history, 25–26; and retribution for Nazi
    collaboration, 161; scholars, 148–52; Weil,
    147–48, 169–70
working priests, 159–60, 294n32
World Alliance for International Friendship
    through the Churches, 62

xenophobia, 12, 43, 44, 54–55, 83, 86, 128, 129,
    135

Yanes, Kathleen, 207

Zade, Paul Mulla, 88
Zanca, José, 274n90
Zweig, Stefan, 60–61